TALKING TO ADULTS

The Contribution of Multiparty Discourse to Language Acquisition

Edited by

Shoshana Blum-Kulka
Hebrew University, Jerusalem

Catherine E. Snow
Harvard University

2002

LAWRENCE ERLBAUM ASSOCIATES, PUBLISHERS
Mahwah, New Jersey   London

Lawrence Erlbaum Associates, Inc., Publishers
10 Industrial Avenue
Mahwah, New Jersey 07430

Cover design by Kathryn Houghtaling Lacey

Library of Congress Cataloging-in-Publication Data

Talking to adults : the contribution of Multiparty Discourse to Language Acquisition / edited by Shoshana Blum-Kulka, Catherine E. Snow.
    p. cm.
Includes bibliographical references and indexes.
ISBN 0-8058-3660-8 (cloth : alk. paper) – ISBN 0-8058-3661-6 (pbk. : alk. paper)
    1.   Language acquisition—Parent participation. 2. Discourse analysis. 3. Parent and Child. 4. Pragmatics. I. Blum-Kulka, Shoshana. II. Snow, Catherine E.

P118.5 .T35 2002
401".93—dc21

                                                    2001051294

Books published by Lawrence Erlbaum Associates are printed on acid-free paper, and their bindings are chosen for strength and durability.

Printed in the United States of America
10   9   8   7   6   5   4   3   2   1

Contents

Editors' Introduction

THE PRESENT VOLUME

History

The question of how adults' speech to children affects the process of language acquisition has attracted researchers' attention since the late 1960s, when the first studies characterizing the nature of input to young language learners were undertaken. An edited volume entitled *Talking to Children*, published in 1977, brought together much of that early work, including a number of chapters devoted to the topic of baby talk, anthropological linguists' descriptions of the special lexical and grammatical forms used with young children. Thus, *Talking to Children* (edited by Snow & Ferguson, 1977) in a sense constituted a bridge between an old tradition of research into "sociolinguistic registers" including baby talk and new work that analyzed similar data in new ways. The newer work was carried out within a theoretical context defined by freshly formulated questions about language acquisition that drew attention to the nature of linguistic input to language learners as one factor influencing language development.

The body of research on input to young children, and on related topics such as input to second language learners, teacher talk in preschool classroom settings, adjustments in talk to children with various disabilities, and social and cultural differences in the nature of talk addressed to children,

1

expanded quickly. By the early 1990s, a second edited volume was published, entitled *Input and Interaction in Language Acquisition* (edited by
Gallaway & Richards, 1994) devoted to providing an overview of the full
array of research findings concerning input. In contrast to *Talking to
Children,* which was a collection of original research reports, *Input and Interaction* consisted of extensive reviews of literature, reflecting the enor-
mous growth of interest in these topics. The forward to *Input and Interaction* describes it explicitly as follows:

> [It's] an up-to-date statement of the facts and controversies surrounding
> "Baby Talk," its nature and likely effects. With contributions from leading
> linguists and psychologists, it explores language acquisition in different cul-
> tures and family contexts, in typical and atypical learners, and in second and
> foreign language learners. It is designed as a sequel to the now famous
> *Talking to children.*

Input and Interaction contained 10 chapters summarizing and analyzing
the work that had been carried out in the period since *Talking to Children,*
and included references to well over 500 original research papers. It is
clear from reading the chapters in *Input and Interaction in Language Acquisition* that the notion of input had been redefined and enriched, whereas
much of the work reviewed and reported in the 1977 book was purely descriptive. The papers in the 1977 book operated from the presumption
that characteristics such as phonological clarity, grammatical simplicity,
and redundancy were the crucial defining features of "baby talk." By 1994
input was seen as conversational, interactive, transactional. The papers in
Gallaway and Richards provide richer descriptions and more problem-
focused analyses of the interactions in which children and other language
learners engage, with a primary emphasis always on the question of how
these interactions simplify the problem of language acquisition for the
learner.

Though enormously informative, the work reported in Gallaway and
Richards (1994) is limited in a number of ways. First, the data being analyzed were almost all derived from two-party interactions—a child alone
with a parent or a learner–teacher dyad isolated from a classroom context.
Many of the studies analyzed interaction during fairly structured tasks, but
even those that adopted naturalistic observational methods, for example,
recording conversations at home during the normal course of daily life,
typically limited the focus of their analysis to dyadic relations. Similarly,
even the studies that went beyond the mother–child dyad to consider the
role of siblings and fathers in language acquisition (such as those reviewed
by Barton & Tomasello, 1994) mostly used the dyadic setting with these alternate conversational partners. Dyadic interactions probably do not dominate the experience of most children, so the degree to which the situa-

tions typically analyzed inform us fully about the nature of input to language learners can be questioned.

The work in Gallaway and Richards (1994) could be said to reflect the dominant paradigm within research on input to language learners—an approach influenced by the procedures and preferences of laboratory psychologists. The very important question this research addresses is what sort of information about the nature of the adult language system is available to the learner—are there aspects of input that can be related to relatively rapid and trouble-free acquisition? This question has dictated an analytic approach, an approach that characterizes the child as someone acquiring skills through exposure to certain language structures.

An alternative conception of the child language learner can be encountered in the work of researchers who have taken a more anthropological approach to collecting data about interaction with young children. This approach is exemplified in the work of researchers such as Heath (1983), Scheiffelin (1990), and Ochs (1988), who have collected ethnographic data in naturalistic settings, focusing as much on the participation structures into which children can enter as on the exact nature of the language used by them. Researchers within the more anthropological paradigm see language as a cultural practice, and thus describe language acquisition as a socializing process—a process played out through language of acquiring the language use skills, rights, and values that constitute membership in a group. For such researchers, issues such as who may talk to whom, what language performances are highly valued, what cultural norms link language to social context, and what parents believe about how children learn to talk are very important. The descriptions they provide include rich evidence about the opportunities children have to learn certain sorts of social practices, but typically less documentation concerning what learning has actually occurred for a particular child as a result of a particular experience. Nor does this research normally provide a basis for estimating the frequency of various sorts of opportunities to learn about the social practices of interest, thus excluding the possibility of relating quantity or quality of exposure to speed of acquisition.

Research within the anthropological paradigm has documented the importance of one of the basic premises of the volume we present here—the premise that children are offered unique opportunities to learn from participation in multiparty interactions, because the demands and the displays inherent in multiparty interactions are different from, and more challenging than, those inherent in dyadic interactions. The anthropological approach to studying input is distinct from the psychological approach in eschewing structured or non-natural contexts for observation and in viewing the child's task of learning language more holistically, as one of achieving cultural membership rather than accomplishing particular skills. The psychological approach, on the other hand, has documented the importance of understanding differences in different children's experiences of interaction, showing that those differences have consequences for children's learning.

Why This Book?

The goal of the volume presented here is to focus on children learning language in naturalistic contexts. We take *naturalistic* to imply contexts that are often multiparty, that involve both multigenerational and peer interaction (or at least interactions in which the child's relationship to more than one adult or one child is simultaneously relevant). Most of the work presented in this volume focuses on multiparty and multigenerational contexts, but we see the ideas suggested as equally relevant to multiparty peer interactions. We see this work as different from most of that in Gallaway and Richards (1994) precisely in that we focus on the value of such multiparty interaction, but also as different from previous work in the anthropological tradition in that our interest in describing input derives from an interest in what and how children learn and how that relates to their opportunities to learn. In other words, we view input from the perspective of both the adults and the children involved in the interaction. Thus, we hope to merge the strengths of the more cognitivist, psychological approach (its interest in the process of learning, its analysis of the learning task, its demand for evidence about what the child has learned, its focus on individual differences among children) with those of the more descriptive, anthropological approach (attention to the full array of opportunities to learn, recognition of the interconnectedness of being socialized into appropriate language use and achieving membership in a culture, consideration of alternate routes to any learning outcome).

THE ADVANTAGES OF BEING MORE THAN TWO

We argue, then, that there are important things about language and about cultural membership that children would not have the chance to learn if they had access to only dyadic interactions. Some of these things have to do with quantity of input—that one simply hears more language if one is hearing it from many interlocutors. Others have to do with quality—that certain complexities of role, of dealing with subsets of interlocutors as addressees, of having various relationships displayed within a particular interaction are possible only if more than two people are involved. Others have to do with the code—that the need to incorporate different varieties, dialects, or languages is much more likely to be present with several interlocutors. Thus, we argue, becoming a full-fledged member of society, in which participating in groups, engaging a variety of interlocutors, and taking on a wide range of roles are prerequisites, requires participating as a child in multiparty interactions. It is the goal of the chapters in this volume to describe, for a number of specific cases and across a variety of cultures, what participation in multiparty interactions looks like, and what we can conclude children learn from it. Here we briefly preview some of the issues that emerge:

Quantity of Input. Hart and Risley (1995) documented the amount of input available to children in different families varying in social class. Though it is difficult from their report to determine the occurrence of dyadic versus multiparty interactions, it is clear that the sparsest input was provided to children in single-parent, socially isolated, welfare-dependent families. The amount of language such children heard, and the size of the vocabularies they achieved, were strikingly smaller than in two-parent families or in families with many visitors. Similar findings emerged from analyses of dinner table conversations collected as part of the Home-School Study (Dickinson & Tabors, 2001; Snow, 1991). Mealtimes at which at least two adults were present were longer, contained more language per unit time, and were more likely to include stories, explanations, and other discourse contexts that offered opportunities to hear challenging vocabulary and grammar, than mealtimes in single-parent families with no visitors. Thus, on the assumption that children who hear more talk learn to talk faster and better, there are advantages to having more adult sources of input and to having exposure to contexts in which more than one adult is present at any given time.

Social Relationships. The mother–child relationship is the only one that needs to be played out in dyadic interactions. The mother is more knowledgeable, a source of nurturance and of limits, the responsible party. The child is the learner, a seeker of nurturance and a tester of limits, with greater resources of playfulness and irresponsibility. This simple complementarity can be greatly complicated if a sibling enters the interaction—then the mother may need to differentiate her level of nurturance or style of discipline, and the siblings have their own issues of dominance, competitiveness in access to the mother, potential for collaboration, possibly domains in which their shared competence is greater than the mother's. If at this point Dad comes home, then Mom's role as supreme arbiter and ultimate source of knowledge may (or may not) be threatened, and opportunities arise for exploitation of parental authority precisely because it is distributed ('but Daddy said I could'). Children have opportunities to learn something about the role of mother or father from dyadic interactions, but they have opportunities to learn about the roles of wife, husband, friends, siblings, and parent to another only from multiparty interactions.

Varieties of Language.   Closely associated with the potential for enrichment of learning about social roles from multiparty interactions is the opportunity to learn about language varieties. Different members of a family always speak slightly different varieties: childhood slang is different from adult slang; persons in authority speak differently from those without power. Thus, French children may *tutoyer* each other but *vousvoyer* their parents, who however can *tutoyer* them back. In some families, the parents speak different dialects, or one parent is a second language speaker of the familial language and thus has a characteristic accent or set of errors. It is interesting to speculate how children in these families learn which is the higher status dialect or more correct variety, and the role played by multiparty interactions in these discoveries. In many families, the two parents preferentially speak two different languages—thus bilingualism might become an option for the child through dyadic interactions with the two parents separately, but learning about code switching and code mixing requires multiparty interactions.

Irony, Humor, Indirectness, and Other Nonliteral Language Uses.   The train station in Cambridge, England, has two platforms. In response to a confirmation check by one of us whether the platform she was standing on was the right one for the train to London, a young teenage girl responded "hopefully," confirming yet again the British aptitude for humor and understatement. How are such cultural notions of indirect uses of language acquired? How do children learn the culturally appropriate levels of (in)directness for directive and expressive speech acts? How do they learn to interpret indirectness? No doubt aspects of these varied phenomena can surface in dyadic interactions between primary caretakers and young children, as shown for example by Patricia Clancy (1986) for Japanese mother–child interactions (though the Japanese mothers took advantage of the presence of a visitor in the household to point out to children that people do not always mean what they say). We would argue that participation in multiparty and multigenerational talk enriches this process in several ways. For the child, being with adults who talk to each other as well as to the children presents occasions for overhearing forms of adult irony presumably not available to children in peer interactions; in some cultures, it might mean being teased simultaneously by several adults and learning to respond with the expected assertiveness and wit; and it always means participating in rich and multifaceted forms of discourse expressing the culture's notions of politeness and preference for various forms of reasoning.

Participation Roles.   Dyadic interactions allow for only a limited range of interchange of speaker and listener roles: Though speaker roles assumed may vary—one may speak as the "author" responsible for his or her own words or as the animator of the words of others through quotes, for example—listener roles are quite limited. Conversational engagement by default defines the "listener" as the ratified addressee of the talk, and the only way to step out of this role is to break the conversational engagement. The addition of just one more person to an interaction changes the picture completely. Any one of the individuals present may be treated alternatively as an addressee or as a ratified side participant, whereas speakers have also the resources to frame others present as unratified overhearers or even worse, as "illegal" eavesdroppers. Our analyses of middle-class dinner table conversations in the United States and Israel (Blum-Kulka, 1997) show that in such intergenerational, multiparty contexts, children gain experience in a wide range of participation roles. They act as coauthors to stories about their own experience, as animators of the words of others, as addressees in direct conversational engagement with adults and siblings, as side participants for all family talk acknowledging their presence as ratified participants, and occasionally also have the less pleasant experience of being positioned by the adults as overhearers or eavesdroppers (e.g., *"Johnny didn't take his nap so he is feeling grouchy tonight"*). Thus the multiparty scene of diversity and shift of participation roles offers rich apprenticeship opportunities for children learning to engage conversationally with others.

Raised Accountability Demands. When several people are engaged in a conversation, there are also several sources of challenge to the authority of any speaker. The mothers of young children are likely to be fairly indulgent in ratifying their versions of events. Such children encounter new problems of negotiation when other adults or children (siblings, cousins, friends) are present who are likely to question or contest a particular presentation of reality. The child may well need to present arguments for his version of events, or summon support for her interpretation. The presence of more parties automatically increases the number of competing proposals, and raises the stakes in defense of any particular proposal.

Decontextualized Language, Reasoning, and Argumentation. Related to the increased demands on children to discharge accountability for their statements in multiparty settings, children in such settings are more likely to be exposed to and to be asked to produce decontextualized language. In dyadic interactions, particularly dyadic interactions between intimates, it is relatively easy to accommodate fully to the background knowledge one shares with one's interlocutor. In multiparty interactions, the level of shared background knowledge may differ for each pair of interlocutors; thus telling a successful story or giving a successful explanation may well require filling in lots of detail for some listeners while avoiding redundancy for others. Addressing a discourse to a subset of individuals in a multiparty setting requires adapting to varying listener needs, and thus imposes additional demands to justify aspects of the telling, support an argument, or else to respond to complaints and/or demands for repair. Thus children in multiparty settings have enhanced opportunities to learn about adapting to the absence of shared knowledge and about linguistic devices for ensuring comprehension of complex messages.

Raised Online Planning Demands. One of the striking differences between young children and adolescents in their language accomplishments is that adolescents have achieved adult levels of fluency—speed of production of syllables, and capacity for online sentence planning. Such fluency is crucial in competitive conversational interactions—participants who cannot start speaking quickly when a pause occurs, and who cannot keep speaking so as to hold the floor, get much less chance to participate than do their more fluent peers. In dyadic interactions, particularly dyadic interactions between a young child and a nurturant adult, the child suffers rather little from dysfluency. The adult supports the child's participation, avoids interruptions, and scaffolds contributions. In intergenerational multiparty interactions, young children may have more need to fight to get and keep the floor, but there too they may be aided by adult efforts to protect their turns from encroachments. In peer multiparty interactions, young children need to "work hard" conversationally to ensure their speaking roles. In both types of multiparty interactions, young children have experiences that can motivate their accomplishment of greater fluency and help them develop skills of turn monitoring to ensure their own conversational rights.

Genre Shifting. We view genres as relatively stable types of interactive discourse, as socially and culturally established discursive ways of achieving different ends by using language. The wide range of both narrative and expository genres in oral and literate forms with which children eventually need to familiarize themselves can find only limited expression in dyadic interactions. On the other hand, the study of mealtime talk in middle-class families (Blum-Kulka, 1997) shows a rich array of genres in dinner talk. Participants shift genres with thematic frames of talk. Thus the business of having dinner is dealt with through the instrumental language of directives and compliments; talk about family members' news of the day enhances narratives, whereas talk about topics of nonimmediate concern may require a variety of genres, including explanatory and argumentative talk. Our recent observations in Israeli preschools reveal not only an extremely rich array of genres in young children's peer interactions (including narrative, argumentation, and explanations) but also a complex and subtle repertoire of framing devices (*"let's pretend"*) through which children manage to sustain and build (in-frame) coherence and to shift between frames. Yet except for the study of narratives, studies of language and pragmatic acquisition only rarely address the issue of development from a genre perspective. We would like to suggest that such a perspective—studyable in contexts where a multiplicity of genres is to be expected, such as social gatherings involving children—is important for understanding the way children learn the conversational and literate genres they need, as well as when and how to shift between them.

Multiple Perspectives on Truth, Tellability, and the Social Construction of Knowledge. A woman musician complains about the choir she is conducting; her husband contests her interpretation of her relations with the choir and tries to persuade her to step down. In Western cultures, such conversations often take place at dinner with the children, allowing them to infer underlying cultural orientations to truth and tellability. Ochs, Taylor, Rudolph, and Smith (1992) suggested that such multiple perspectives offered at storytelling in families enhance theory building, promoting the types of critical thinking necessary in the modern world. Simultaneously, family storytelling allows for the negotiation of cultural notions of tellability: Certain topics may be censored, others encouraged, and the factuality of the tale may or may not become an issue, depending on culture. The social construction of knowledge at family gatherings may also take the form of teaching sequences, where one knowledgeable party is self-appointed or called upon to provide explanations of social and natural phenomena (Keppler & Luckman, 1991). The multiplicity of perspectives offered for any given topic or issue in multigenerational talk does not necessarily need to be adult generated or represent only adult points of view; during storytelling at dinner, children can and do collaborate with adults in the negotiation of the point of the story. The possibility for a balanced adult–child reciprocity of perspectives is striking in certain instances of families watching television together. For instance, Cohen (2000) showed how, when Israeli families are watching "The Simpsons" together, it is the children who are often called upon to explain to the adults bits of humor that presuppose familiarity with American youth culture. In dyadic interactions between children and adults, the adult is the knowledgeable and authoritative party, and by necessity his or her perspective will tend to dominate. To develop critical thinking and learn to participate in the social construction of knowledge, children need to experience multiple perspectives, such as those available in multiparty, multigenerational and peer talk.

THE BOOK AT HAND

Just as *Talking to Children* (Snow & Ferguson, 1977) focused on description more than analysis, this first step into the domain of understanding multiparty discourse includes much that is purely descriptive. The chapters that make up this volume provide descriptions of the characteristics of conversations in which young children participate in Greece, Norway, Israel, North America, Sweden, Italy, and Mayan Mexico. Many of the conversations analyzed were recorded during meals—a context that in many cultures has multiple participants by default, and where considerable opportunities for language socialization present themselves.

The first part of the book focuses on opportunities to learn how to produce extended discourse, in family and peer settings. Beals and Snow examine some relations between the stories children engage in telling and hearing at dinner, and their capacity to respond more autonomously when asked to "perform" a narrative. Georgakopoulou explores children's rights and responsibilities as storytellers at Greek dinner tables, and the functions of dinner table narratives in making particular points, creating alliances, socializing children into culturally unique adult notions of tellability, enhancing children's narrative skills, and reinforcing familial roles. Aukrust's chapter contrasts the social, egalitarian rule orientation of Norwegian dinner table stories and explanations with the more individualistic focus of North American discourse, displaying how participation in these different discourse modes creates different skills and personas for children growing up in the two cultures. Blum-Kulka focuses on explanations in Israeli dinner table talk, considering how explanatory talk provides children with exposure to a particular way of thinking, represents an elaborated orientation to meaning, and provides practice in juggling perspectives on truth, all potential contributions to children's school success. Nicolopoulou assesses the impact on low-income children's talk of opportunities to participate in a particular kind of multiparty storytelling—dictating stories to be acted out by one's classmates. She documents the value of having to "take stories public" for children's understanding of the need for explicit and elaborated talk.

The second part of the book focuses on affective and nonliteral aspects of language use. Herot considers how affect is conveyed in the context of talk, by tone of voice, and what the effect is of multiparty versus dyadic interactions. Nevat-Gal displays the value of humor at the dinner table in promoting cognitive sophistication. Fasulo, Liberati, and Pontecorvo analyze the poetics of children's talk, emerging from language games with adults. The authors argue for the centrality of the genre of speech play and verbal games in helping young children attain speaker's position and in generally easing their way into multiparty conversations.

The third part includes chapters that emphasize cultural differences in pragmatic development. The Tzeltal speakers studied by Brown use challenges and threats in interacting with young children, thus providing opportunities for the children to come to understand when adults are lying. Aronsson and Thorell analyze children's peer play to reveal how much children know about multivoicedness and a multiplicity of roles. Finally, Kasuya explores the nature of interaction in bilingual families, to show how the achievement of bilingualism for young children relies on the effective manipulation of multiparty contexts for language learning.

In a concluding chapter, we consider briefly a number of domains that would ideally all have been subjects of chapters in this book, but that had to be excluded because no one has yet undertaken systematic research on them from a multiadic perspective. Perhaps another volume, 30 years hence, will include them all.

The chapters collected in this volume all reflect the changes over the last 35 years concerning our views of language acquisition. While coming to understand how much more than just grammar children need to learn, we have also come to understand the many, rich, and varied opportunities to learn afforded by participation in family and peer groups. These chapters include considerations of individual differences among children in what they might be learning, and recognize as well the importance of quantity as well as quality of learning experiences. We hope these chapters invite researchers interested in language development to broaden their perspectives on the contexts for language learning and on the nature of what children must learn.

REFERENCES

Barton, M. E., & Tomasello, M. (1994). Phonetic and prosodic aspects of Baby Talk. In C. Gallaway & B. Richards (Eds.), *Input and interaction in language acquisition* (pp. 109–134). Cambridge, England: Cambridge University Press.

Blum-Kulka, S. (1997). *Dinner talk*. Mahwah, NJ: Lawrence Erlbaum Associates.

Clancy, P. (1986). The acquisition of communicative style in Japanese. In B. Shieffelin & E. Ochs (Eds.), *Language socialization across cultures* (pp. 213–250). Cambridge, England: Cambridge University Press.

Cohen, A. (2000). Prime time television "fable families": Political and social satire for segmented audiences. *Emergencies, 10*(1), 105–118.

Dickinson, D., & Tabors, P. (Eds.). (2001). *Building literacy through language: Home and school.* Baltimore: Brookes.

Gallaway, C., & Richards, B. (Eds.). (1994). *Input and interaction in language acquisition.* Cambridge, England: Cambridge University Press.

Hart, B., & Risley, T. (1995). *Meaningful differences in the everyday lives of young American children.* Baltimore: Brookes.

Heath, S. B. (1983). *Ways with words: Language, life and work in communities and classrooms.* Cambridge, England: Cambridge University Press.

Keppler, A., & Luckman, T. (1991). "Teaching": Conversational transmission of knowledge. In I. Markova & K. Foppa (Eds.), *Asymmetries in dialogue* (pp. 143–166). Savage, MD: Barnes & Noble.

Ochs, E. (1988). *Culture and language development: Language acquisition and language socialization in a Samoan village.* Cambridge, England: Cambridge University Press.

Ochs, E., Taylor, C., Rudolph, D., & Smith, R. (1992). Storytelling as a theory-building activity. *Discourse Processes, 15,* 37–72.

Schieffelin, B. (1990). *The give and take of everyday life: Language socialization of Kaluli children.* Cambridge, England: Cambridge University Press.

Snow, C. E. (1991). The theoretical basis for relationships between language and literacy development. *Journal of Research in Childhood Education, 6,* 5–10.

Snow, C., & Ferguson, C. (Eds.). (1977). *Talking to children: Language input and acquisition.* Cambridge, England: Cambridge University Press.

Part I

ISSUES IN THE DEVELOPMENT OF EXTENDED DISCOURSE: NARRATIVES AND EXPLANATIONS

Deciding What to Tell: Selecting and Elaborating Narrative Topics in Family Interaction and Children's Elicited Personal Experience Stories

Diane E. Beals
University of Tulsa

Catherine E. Snow
Harvard University

Children's storytelling has most often been studied as a skill, from the perspective of questions about how the characteristics of mature narrative emerge. Accordingly, the bulk of data available about narrative development comes from elicited or prompted stories. McCabe's foundational work (Peterson & McCabe, 1983), for example, analyzed a collection of stories prompted by the narrator in the course of casual conversation, during which the adult told stories and solicited in response stories about similar topics. Berman and Slobin (1994) analyzed stories that were elicited in response to a wordless narrative picture book, thus even more constrained in topic. These two lines of work have been very productive and enlightening, but do not help us to understand the conditions under which children naturally tell stories.

Those conditions are, we argue, likely to arise in the context of varying settings and participation structures, many of which involve more than a single adult. Children tell spontaneous stories in the course of peer play and family talk, and their stories are elicited in classroom settings as well as during dinnertime. In this chapter, we concentrate on the stories told by a group of children observed in two settings—the dinner table, where stories are told to (and in competition with) other family members, and a three-way conversation with the mother and an unfamiliar adult. In this last situation, the child's mother was free to provide support, but the social expectation was that the child would be the primary narrator.

The differences between these settings and participation structures are many, and no doubt worthy of deeper study. But in this chapter we concentrate on considering relations between them. One simple hypothesis is that good child narrators will shine in both settings, displaying control over the capacities to select a tellable topic, to produce a coherent narrative, and to engage the audience in ways that should be effective no matter what the audience. Another slightly more complex model sees the mealtime conversation as the training ground for more autonomous narratives; because single-party "performed" narratives are often invited from children at the dinner table, children may have opportunities there to hone skills that will come in handy when performing in contexts that demand more autonomy, such as "sharing time" in classrooms or the elicited narrative task we set for the children we studied. Yet another model would distinguish the skills needed to be a good narrator in a multiparty conversation like those at mealtime from the skills of autonomous performance. Conversationally embedded narratives require strategies for capturing the floor, for engaging immediate interest from the audience, for soliciting support when it is needed, for constructing narrative utterances online, and for responding to audience feedback. Autonomous performance narratives, on the other hand, occur in protected interactive spaces, but are subject to somewhat higher demands for tellability, cohesion, and drama. In this chapter, we explore 620 conversationally embedded narratives and 40 elicited narratives produced by the same group of 3-, 4-, and 5-year-old children. In particular, we focus on questions about what topics are tellable in the two contexts, and how responsibility for telling is shared between the 5-year-old and the other participants.

PROCEDURES

The data for this study are drawn from the Home-School Study of Language and Literacy Development (Dickinson & Tabors, 2001; Snow, 1991). The study followed 83 children from their preschool years through the early elementary grades. With the focus on identifying oral language situations and environments that were predictive of later language and literacy skill, the study collected a number of types of conversation at home between mothers and target children at ages 3, 4, and 5. At the end of the visit, the researcher left a blank audiotape and recorder and asked the mother to record a typical family mealtime. Each year, a subset of the families failed to follow through on recording a mealtime; however, we were able to collect 64 tapes when the children were 3 years old, 45 at age 4, and 51 at age 5, from a total of 68 different families. Elicited narratives were gathered at the age 5 home visit. The home visitor told a "scary" personal story to the child, and asked the child if she or he could tell about a similar experience, while the mother stood by, available to support the child.

Subjects. The subjects in the study were from low-income families in the greater Boston area. Of these families, about one third were African-American or Hispanic. Whereas elicited reports required the child to tell a story independently or with the mother's support, mealtime narrative talk usually involved more than just the mother and target child; some families had siblings or other children present. Fathers were present in 52 of the 160 mealtimes. Some families included other adults; for example, two families consisted of the mother, child, and grandparents.

Data Analysis. Each recorded mealtime and elicited report conversation was transcribed according to Codes for Human Analysis of Transcripts (CHAT) conventions laid out by the Child Language Data Exchange System (CHILDES) (MacWhinney, 1995; MacWhinney & Snow, 1990).

Coding Scheme: Mealtime Narratives. First, each instance of narrative talk was identified within the transcripts; there were 620 narratives in the 160 transcripts, across the 3 years. Each narrative was coded for who initiated the topic of the story (adult, target child, or other child in family), and who told the story (adult, target child, another child, jointly told with target child contributing, jointly told by others, without target child contributing). In addition, each narrative was coded as to whether it was a dramatic or emotional (e.g., exciting, funny, frightening) topic as demonstrated in the telling and the audience response, or whether it was a more mundane topic about immediate past or future events, without the affect that appeared in the dramatic retellings. Dramatic topics were also coded as displaying either positive affect around a personal story (such as amusing, fun, or exciting topics), negative affect around a personal narrative (such as scary or vexing topics), or a retelling of an exciting, fun, or scary story from a book, movie, or other people's narratives. The mundane topics were further coded for their reference to either an immediate past event or immediate future plans. Examples of mealtime narratives demonstrate the difference between dramatic and mundane narratives:

Example 1: Dramatic topic (Bradley, age 3)

Child: One day I was sleeping in my bed for [/] for a long long time and thunder and lightning came from outside and I was trying to . . . [sneezes]

Child: And I was trying to find something that was yellow outside in the dark all by itself!

Child: And it came out.

Child: And it was thunder and lightning and I hided from it!

Grandma: Hmm.

Mother: Hmm.

Grandpa: And you hided from it?

Child: Yeah.

Grandpa: Where did you hide?

Grandpa: Under your blankets?

Child: No under my covers.

Example 2: Mundane topic (Diane, age 4)

Mother: So what are you going to do at your party?

Mother: Huh?

Child: (grunting).

Mother: What are you going to do?

Mother: Are you going to dance?

Child: And I'm going to hop.

Child: I'm gonna hop.

Mother: You're gonna hop?

Mother: Oh boy.

Coding Scheme: Elicited Reports. Whereas young children at mealtimes sometimes were asked to report on recent events, rarely was the pressure on them to perform narratives terribly strong, and there was often competition for the floor and the telling rights during narration. In the elicited narrative setting, on the other hand, there was considerable moral pressure on the child to perform the task autonomously, and on the mother to support those autonomous performances. The tasks that had to be accomplished by mother and child included selecting an appropriate (i.e., topic-relevant) and tellable narrative, then producing a sufficiently informative narration. In analyzing approaches to this task, we have categorized the maternal and child contribution into the same domains as used in the mealtime narratives: selecting a topic, and actually telling the story.

Three separate dimensions of each scary story were coded, on a 5-point scale, to indicate how responsibility for that dimension was shared between mother (or other adult) and child. In each case, a score of 1 was applied if the child took responsibility alone, 2 if the child was primarily responsible but received a bit of help, 3 if child and mother shared responsibility evenly, 4 if mother basically did the work but the child participated, and 5 if the mother did it alone. The dimensions coded were: (a) taking responsibility for selecting the topic, (b) taking responsibility for telling the events of the incident, (c) taking responsibility for evaluating the story, indicating personal experiences, and (d) clarifying the high point of the story (Peterson & McCabe, 1983). Each story was also given a more global rating on the quality of the narrative overall, from 1, a rating assigned to complete narratives with high point and resolution, to 3, a rating of a primitive narrative characterized by a loosely organized list of some events.

MEALTIME NARRATIVE RESULTS

A total of 620 narratives were found in the 160 mealtime conversations when the target children were 3, 4, and 5 years old. Table 1.1 presents the frequency of narratives across the three mealtimes.

Who initiated and told the narratives? Table 1.2 indicates that the adults present at the mealtimes took the largest responsibility for selecting topics and telling narratives. Many topics (374 of 620, 60%) were initiated by adults, whereas the target children initiated 169 narratives (27%). In most of the narratives (388), target children were involved in the telling

TABLE 1.1
Frequency of Mealtime Narratives

Age	# of Tapes	# of Narratives
3	64	236
4	45	176
5	51	208
Total	160	620

TABLE 1.2
Frequency of Mealtime Narratives by Teller and Initiator

	Initiated By			
Told By	Adult	TC	OC	Total
Adult	105	11	1	117
Adult + TC	204	112	26	342
TC alone	5	40	1	46
OC alone	60	6	49	115
Total	374	169	77	620

Note. TC = target child. OC = other child.

(although only 46 were produced by the target child alone), whereas 117 were told by adults alone. About one third of all the stories (215) have no direct involvement of target child, either as initiator or teller (see Table 1.2). Siblings and other children present at the mealtimes initiated topics 115 times, but told only 77 stories.

Of the 620 narratives identified in the three corpora of mealtime transcripts, only 40 were narratives in which the target child (who was 3, 4, or 5 years old) both selected the topic and bore the primary responsibility for telling the story. The topics of these stories varied widely from dreams to exciting events observed at school to retellings of fairy tales (see Table 1.3).

What kinds of topics were initiated? In general, the target children initiated reports about "what happened today" 62 times, 36% of all their initiations, whereas parents did so 166 times (44%). The "telling my day"

TABLE 1.3
Topics of Narratives Selected and Told
by Target Children During Mealtimes

Immediate Past or Future Topics	Dramatic (Negative, Retelling, and Positive) Topics
catch and eat	Freddy Krueger
coloring	ghosts in the bed
dropped fork	scallops and lobsters
friend's name	threw up at school
licking ketchup	
made up story	Cookie Monster
McDonald's balloons	Ninja Turtles
phone message	Red Riding Hood
pool party	Bambi
retelling dream	
stay up late	
go to bed hungry	falling down stairs
cap gun	got lost
chair	hot splash
chopping food	pretend gun
Christmas album	pretend tiger
go in car	pretend news story
say excuse me	
school	
smack her	
spray open car windows	
lots of spaghetti	
tape recorder	
chicken crossing the road	
comic books	
unclear	

story has been noted as a common phenomenon in U.S. dinner table conversations (Blum-Kulka, 1997). Example 3 shows a common approach to these in the mealtime narratives; the mother asks something about the day, and the child replies in short, rather unenthusiastic utterances. Example 4, on the other hand, presents a mundane topic initiated by the child at age 5 and discussed in greater depth with explanations of people's actions in the narrative.

Example 3 (Brittany, age 3)

Mother: Did you have fun at Auntie Vi's house today?
Child: Mmhm.
Mother: What did you do?
Child: [unintelligible word].
Mother: Did you?
Child: [unintelligible word].
Mother: And who?
Child: [unintelligible word].
Mother: Who?
Child: Theodore!
Mother: Oh Theodore.
Mother: He came over again?
Child: Yep!
Mother: Oh.
Child: No.
Child: Jason.
Child: Jason.

Example 4 (James, age 5)

Child: I—I went to call you from my Mama's when Grandma wasn't home.
Father: That's your Uncle Richard's fault.
Father: We're going to find him.
Father: And take care of him for that.
Child: No.
Child: My Gram's her fault.
Child: She wasn't home.
Child: It was her fault.
Father: She wasn't home because she went with . . .
Child: He—she—she didn't went with Richard.

Child: He took Richard's car!
Father: Yeah.
Father: To go pick up Richard's other car.
Mother: His new car.

Overall, in these conversations 458 of the 620 stories dealt with reporting of immediate past or planning of immediate future activity (see Table 1.4), and most of these (294, or 64%) were initiated by the adults. The target children initiated 111 (24%) of these more mundane topics.

Interestingly, dramatic topics were introduced 54 times by adults, whereas children introduced them 39 times. For adults, dramatic topics represent only 14% of their overall initiations, whereas for the children they represented 23% of their topic selections. Children were more likely to initiate dramatic topic narratives than were mothers and fathers. They seemed to bring up topics that were of particular interest to them, whereas apparently parents often raised topics just to get the children talking more.

Table 1.5 indicates that, on average, mothers initiated 2.3 topics per mealtime narratives, whereas the target children selected one topic for a narrative; overall, narrative initiations were relatively infrequent events. The adults present at the mealtimes initiated an average of almost two mundane narratives per mealtime, and about one third of a dramatic topic for each mealtime (one dramatic narrative initiated for every three mealtimes). On average, target children selected slightly more than one immediate or mundane topic over two mealtimes, with a slight increase as the children got older (from a mean of .55 topics per mealtime at age 3, to .67 at 4, and .75 at 5). This upward trend was accompanied by a corresponding slight downward trend in selecting dramatic topics, from an average of 0.34 per mealtime at age 3, to 0.20 at age 4, and 0.16 at age 5.

TABLE 1.4
Frequencies of Types of Topics by Initiator During Mealtimes

| | Initiated By | | | |
	Adult	TC	OC	Total
Immediate Past	166	62	35	263
Immediate Plan	128	50	17	195
Dramatic - pos. affect	25	15	4	44
Dramatic - neg. affect	19	16	12	47
Dramatic - retelling	10	8	2	20
Other	26	18	7	51
Total	374	169	77	620

Note. TC = target child. OC = other child.

TABLE 1.5
Frequency of Types of Topics (and Means Per Transcript)
Over Time During Mealtimes

Age	N	Adult Imm.	Adult Dram.	Adult Total[a]	TC Imm.	TC Dram.	TC Total[a]
3	64	123	25	154	35	22	63
		(1.92)	(0.39)	(2.41)	(0.55)	(0.34)	(0.98)
4	45	86	13	106	30	9	43
		(1.91)	(0.29)	(2.36)	(0.67)	(0.20)	(0.96)
5	51	85	16	114	47	8	63
		(1.67)	(0.31)	(2.23)	(0.73)	(0.16)	(1.24)
Total	160	296	54	374	112	39	169
		(1.85)	(0.34)	(2.34)	(0.70)	(0.24)	(1.06)

Note. TC = target child.
[a]Includes Immediate, Dramatic, and Other categories.

In Table 1.6, we present an analysis of the mean length of turn in the mealtime settings. Turns were longer in narrative talk than they were in the transcripts overall. On average, target children used 5 words per turn in the full transcripts compared to an average of 6 words per turn in narratives, whereas mothers, on average, used 7.5 words per turn overall, and 9.4 words per turn in narrative talk. But a striking contrast in mean length of turn appears among varying topic initiator–narrator combinations. When target children initiated a topic and adults narrated, children had a very low average of 4 words per turn, whereas mothers approached 12. The mother took on the responsibility of telling the narrative and, thus, took longer turns to get the story across. When the adult initiated the narrative and the child told the story, children averaged 7.3 words per turn and the average

TABLE 1.6
Mean Length of Turns (in Number of Words)
for Both Mealtimes and Elicited Scary Stories

	Mother	Father	Target Child	Experimenter
Mealtimes				
Overall transcripts	7.59	6.32	4.95	NA
Narratives only	9.35	7.39	6.02	NA
TCAD	11.88	7.33	3.89	NA
ADTC	10.00	0.00	7.25	NA
TCTC: dramatic	4.48	3.00	12.84	NA
Elicited scary stories				
Overall transcripts	8.72	4.00	6.82	18.47

Note. TCAD = target child initiated, adult told story; ADTC = adult initiated, target child told story; TCTC = target child initiated and told story.

maternal turn was 10 words long. When the target child initiated and told a story about a dramatic topic, they averaged an impressive 12.8 words per turn, whereas mothers averaged only 4.5 words per turn. Examples 1 and 2 demonstrate how this trend plays out in such conversations.

Using contingency tables to analyze the categorical variables of mealtime narratives, we found that there is a 17.8 times greater chance that an adult tells a story after initiating a topic than does a target child. Also, target children are 4.7 times more likely to be involved in a joint storytelling when they initiate the topic, than when adults initiate. Adult-initiated stories are much more likely to be self-told than are children's topics; child-initiated narratives appear to draw in parents and other family members at the mealtimes.

ELICITED REPORT NARRATIVES

Although 69 children were asked to participate in the scary story task, in many cases no narrative discourse of any type actually took place. In 40 cases, stories did get told, of which 19 were initiated and told independently by the child (see Table 1.7). Eight more target children initiated independently but got some help in telling. Three children neither initiated nor told a story, leaving their mothers to do all the work. Thirteen children got help in topic selection (sometimes a lot), and 18 children needed help in telling (sometimes, in fact, they contributed almost nothing themselves to the telling). Eight children overall needed a great deal of help in both selecting a topic and narrating.

The elicitation for the scary story is itself a scary story, about a near-miss auto accident or a threatening dog, told by the adult interviewer. One

TABLE 1.7
How Independently Do Children Select
Topics and Tell Elicited Reports?

| Told By | Rating | Topic Selected By | | | | | |
| | | TC | TC + Mother | | Mother or No One | | Total |
		1	2	3	4	5	
TC	1	19	0	1	0	2	22
TC + mother	2	4	0	0	0	0	4
	3	4	0	0	0	1	5
	4	0	1	0	0	5	6
Mother or no one	5	0	0	0	0	3	3
Total		27	1	1	0	11	40

Note.   TC = target child.

problem that children faced when asked to respond with a story of their own was that they often defined the task of responding appropriately rather narrowly—as if they were being asked for narratives about the specific topic of auto accidents or dogs—instead of the broader topic of "something that scared me." Thus it is perhaps not surprising that among the more successful narratives were ones produced by children who actually could relate accident or dog stories, like the following:

Example 5 (James)

Experimenter:	Have you ever had something scary like that happen to you?
Child:	Hunhunh.
Child:	But if I were you I would stop.
Child:	And if—and stand still, like this. [crossing arms over chest]
Experimenter:	Oh that's a good idea.
Child:	And if he knocks you over, he'll think you're a log.
Experimenter:	Oh that's a good idea.
Experimenter:	Can you tell me something scary like that that's happened to you?
Child:	[laughs].
Experimenter:	Such as something scary that happened to you?
Child:	Uh, I saw a dog.
Child:	He was—my dad came home.
Child:	My grandpa dropped him off.
Child:	And the dog tried to get in the locked door downstairs.
Child:	But my dad said 'hunhunh, you can't come up.'
Experimenter:	Wow. That's scary.
Child:	Mmm.
Child:	Wasn't even scared.
Experimenter:	Oh really?
Mother:	It was a big dog.
Child:	Wasn't scared.
Mother:	Yeah.
Experimenter:	Okay thanks.

In the following example, Bradley did ultimately produce a scary incident related to a car, but his initially selected narrative topic related to cars with a humorous rather than frightening event:

Example 6 (Bradley)

Experimenter:	Has anything ever happened, anything like that ever happened to you? Or you and your mom?
Child:	I saw something funny one d .. yesterday when we were coming home?
Child:	A truck with a board on the back? Carrying a tow truck? And a tow truck carrying a car.
Mother:	A tow truck, carrying a tow truck, carrying a car. And we thought that was really funny!
Child:	[laughs].
Mother:	[laughs] Huh?
Mother:	Because you usually just see a tow truck on a car.
Experimenter:	Mmm. So can you and your mom tell me anything that hap .. like that that h .. has happened that is uh scary? Something scary that happened to you?
Child:	Uh . . . yes!
Mother:	What was scary that happened?
Child:	Um, when we went in the big puddle and you thought your car, and you told me it would it would die? Last year?
Mother:	Oh when we drove through the giant puddles down at um the lights? Down there?
Mother:	And Mama was, Mama was afraid that her car wasn't gonna make it through because her car died one time. And I think I got Bradley a little nervous! [laughs].

If children did not have such topic-appropriate tales available to them, how did they approach telling stories? Genuinely scary stories not directly related to these topics were offered by some children, such as Donnie in the following example:

Example 7 (Donnie)

Experimenter:	Can—can you tell me a story of something like that?
Child:	Yeah.
Experimenter:	What?
Child:	One time um Mother woke up.
Child:	She thought there was a guy downstairs who broke in our cellar window.
Experimenter:	Uh-huh.

Child:	And it wasn't.
Experimenter:	Uh-huh.
Child:	It was just ice.
Experimenter:	Oh.
Child:	And then she woke all of us up.
Experimenter:	Because she thought it was a robber in the house.
Child:	Yeah.
Experimenter:	Hmm, that happened to me once too.
Experimenter:	It was at night.
Child:	And if my brother was here my brother would go downstairs.
Experimenter:	Oh-: but it was only ice?
Child:	[nods].
Experimenter:	That was lucky.

Twenty-seven children managed to come up with more or less appropriate topics on their own; these included such topics as scary movies and dreams, physical attacks from siblings, falls from swings, and so on. Another four readily accepted maternal suggestions for topics, which included dog bites and scary dreams. One of these children acknowledged her mother's proffered scary topic, but failed to develop a narrative about that topic, instead telling her own related story, one that included a number of sophisticated narrative features but did not fit into the genre of "scary story":

Example 8 (Maria)

Experimenter:	Has anything scary like that ever happened to you?
Child:	[shakes head]
Mother:	Have you been scared?
Child:	Mmhm.
Mother:	By whom?
Child:	By Matthew's dog.
Mother:	Oh Matthew [laughs] yeah yeah.
Mother:	Little dog but small dog but she didn't really knew the dog. So yeah . . .
Child:	But I wasn't scared of the white dog.
Child:	That died.
Mother:	Yeah.
Mother:	Yeah the other one.

Child:	Matthew had another dog and he was white.
Child:	And he died.
Experimenter:	Oh.
Mother:	Yeah.
Mother:	But then uh, they bought another one.
Mother:	That's the family wh . . where I used to work.
Child:	And now he's black.
Mother:	The dog? Yeah.
Mother:	The little dog.
Mother:	Because they had a . . a white one.
Mother:	He died, but then, she wa . . she grew up with that dog.
Experimenter:	Oh.
Mother:	And then uh [///] I mean not grew up but she was used to.
Mother:	But I used to work for them.
Child:	You know.
Child:	One day uh Matthew told me 'Maria that's so big you're six' and I said 'no I'm five!'
Child:	Then um then Matthew goes my um Mom, 'she's six?'
Child:	She said 'no Matthew she's still five.'
Mother:	Yeah, um, he's retarded.

But eight children never managed to agree on a topic, and thus did not produce or participate in any talk that approached narrative discourse.

Responsibility of actually telling the story was similarly distributed. Some children managed with no parental support, and others contributed nothing beyond brief answers to highly structuring maternal questions. We have seen in earlier examples relatively autonomous child narratives. Jenny, in contrast, receives a lot of support, both from her mother and from her grandfather, in formulating the narrative that actually gets told:

Example 9 (Jenny)

Experimenter:	But can you tell me something scary that's happened to you?
Child:	No!
Experimenter:	No?
Child:	Nothing.
Grandpa:	Well no how about not getting off the bus.
Mother:	Yeah why don't you tell her about that?

Grandpa:	Yeah why don't you say tal . . talk about that?
Grandpa:	When Grandfather was uh, a little late coming around the corner with uh, with the baby.
Mother:	She panicked and she started getting scared and tried to . . she wouldn't get off the bus . . school bus.
Grandpa:	She wouldn't get off the bus.
Child:	I can't.
Child:	I can't.
Grandpa:	Why can't you?
Child:	Because I need the um.
Mother:	She needs a note.
Child:	A note.
Grandpa:	Oh you need a note, to get off the bus.
Child:	Yeah.
Child:	Yeah.
Grandpa:	The school bus . . school bus driver knows now that if I uh if I'm late getting around the corner because of the baby . . .
Child:	Where do you take him?
Grandpa:	Huh?
Child:	Take him.
Mother:	[laughs]
Experimenter:	Wow that is scary.
Experimenter:	But you got that all worked out now?
Mother:	Well school's over.
Grandpa:	Yeah the school bus driver the girl says to me.
Grandpa:	She says
Grandpa:	'Well she screams you know if you're not there.'
Mother:	Hannah.
Child:	I don't scream she lies.
Mother:	Oh [laughs].
Grandpa:	That's why she had to go around the block?
Child:	Yeah I dropped my satchel.
Grandpa:	By the time we got there.
Mother:	I know.
Child:	I dropped my satchel.
Experimenter:	Sounds like he's always there though huh?

Experimenter: He might be a little bit late with the baby but he always gets there.
Mother: Mmhm.
Experimenter: Yeah.
Grandpa: Why yes.
Mother: He wouldn't leave his granddaughter behind for anything huh Jenny.
Experimenter: That's right.
Child: Yeah!
Mother: Yeah [laughs]?

In scary stories like the previous examples, target children who initiate the topic with little or no help are 28.5 times more likely to tell the story with little or no help than those who have difficulty initiating their own topic.

RELATIONS BETWEEN MEALTIMES AND ELICITED REPORTS

As the questions articulated in the introduction suggest, we were interested in the possibility that children who had considerable practice at the dinner table turned out to be better autonomous narrators in the elicitation settings. Such was not the case. No correlations were found between rate of initiation of topics by target children at mealtimes and the elicitation setting. Nor were any correlations found between target children's frequency of telling stories and their level of involvement in telling the scary story. Nor did strong relationships emerge between the maternal roles at mealtimes and the elicitation setting for either choosing a topic or narrating a story.

On reflection, it is, however, not so surprising that features of the stories at meals and during elicitation sessions were not related. The demand characteristics and participation structures in these two settings were very different. Stories at the dinner table are more successful if collaborative, with the involvement of multiple family members, whereas in the elicitation session the implicit definition of success was for the child to tell a story autonomously. Furthermore, children at the dinner table have the right to initiate topics of particular interest to them, and to do so at a time when they are interested in telling them. Thus we perhaps should have expected that the dinner table stories provide a better estimate of children's narrative competence.

Both mealtime narratives and elicited scary narratives are multiparty conversations, one natural and generally private, and the other more experimental and public. The latter shares with classroom practice the social expectation to display one's ability in a performance setting, although in this study there is also appreciable pressure on the mother to aid the child in selecting a topic and telling an important narrative. The former task, initiating and telling stories in everyday, natural mealtime conversation, however, allows children to participate in more free-flowing conversational narratives that provide experience and practice in the various formal and informal skills involved in narrating, such as choosing a tellable topic, narrating it with varying levels of support from the family members present at the table, and monitoring the audience for comprehension and response. Informal conversational settings such as mealtimes provide the training ground for telling stories, whereas elicited narratives allow us to evaluate a child's independent storytelling skills.

These results demonstrate clearly the importance of assessing a variety of contexts in order to reflect children's narrative competence fully. In addition, stories like Jenny's suggest the importance of providing for a variety of topics. Both at the dinner table and in the elicitation sessions, being a successful narrator, though, required bringing to bear a variety of interactive and linguistic skills, some related to the presentation of content, and some related to the management of the interaction. The lack of direct relationships between the performance of children in the two settings we examined may well reflect the differing exploitation of subsets of these skills in the two contexts. Thus these results suggest the value of thinking about narrative competence as a mosaic of skills, within which each tile is acquired through its own interactive history and/or cognitive breakthrough. Because storytelling in different settings, at least for young children, may rely on only a portion of the available tiles, it is difficult to trace the impact of core narrative skills across different settings.

The question with which we began this study was "Do children learn something at the dinner table about appropriate and tellable topics?" The findings suggest compellingly that, at least by the age of 5 (but often as early as age 3), children already know a great deal about engaging narrative topics—and when able to pursue those topics, also about how to tell competent narratives. Their parents, in fact, are more limited in their selection of narrative topics, concentrating on the mundane and on attempts to elicit narratives in ways that are rarely effective, such as, "so what happened at school today?" Parents were also seen to vary enormously in their capacity, when asked to help their children tell scary stories, to select successful candidate topics, and to structure the interaction so that the child became the prime narrator. In other words, narrative success in these interactions, and perhaps more generally in social settings, often depends on interactants' capacities to support each other's topic selection and storytelling as much as it does on any individual's narrative competence.

REFERENCES

Berman, R., & Slobin, D. (1994). *Relating events in narrative: A crosslinguistic developmental study.* Hillsdale, NJ: Lawrence Erlbaum Associates.

Blum-Kulka, S. (1997). *Dinner talk: Cultural patterns of sociability and socialization in family interaction.* Hillsdale, NJ: Lawrence Erlbaum Associates.

Dickinson, D., & Tabors, P. (2001). *Building literacy with language: Young children learning at home and in school.* Baltimore: Brookes.

MacWhinney, B. (1995). *The CHILDES project: Tools for analyzing talk* (2nd ed.). Hillsdale, NJ: Lawrence Erlbaum Associates.

MacWhinney, B., & Snow, C. E. (1990). The Child Language Data Exchange System: An update. *Journal of Child Language, 17,* 457–473.

Peterson, C., & McCabe, A. (1983). *Developmental psycholinguistics: Three ways of looking at a child's narrative.* New York: Plenum.

Snow, C. (1991). The theoretical basis for relationships between language and literacy in development. *Journal of Research in Childhood Education, 6,* 5–10.

Chapter 2

Greek Children and Familiar Narratives in Family Contexts: En Route to Cultural Performances

Alexandra Georgakopoulou
King's College, London

Narrative is widely held as a fundamental mode of discourse, unquestionably primary in everyday social lives, and central to the organization and sense making of personal and sociocultural experience (Bruner, 1990; also see Georgakopoulou & Goutsos, 1997). It is thus not surprising that pragmatic studies of socialization have consistently privileged the development of narrative mode. Recent work has focused on children's participation in narrative events occurring within family life, as an ideal point of entry into the interactive, jointly achieved aspects of the socialization process. Work with this emphasis has documented the culture-specificity of family narrative activities; in addition, it has provided valuable methodological tools for establishing links between the microanalysis of storytelling practices and macrolevel, sociocultural stances and norms bearing on children's socialization (e.g., Blum-Kulka, 1993, 1997; Blum-Kulka & Snow, 1992; Erickson, 1982; Ochs & Taylor, 1992).

Drawing on such studies, this chapter's framework eclectically combines narrative microanalysis with ethnographic and social constructionist approaches to discourse in order to elucidate family narrative practices in Greece that involve children as (co-)tellers, characters in tales, and addressees. In brief, the point of departure for this study is that narrative is a mode of sociocultural, symbolic action that is performed interactively and *in situ*. In a similar vein, its socialization is a joint, discursive achievement, that is, on one hand, locally occasioned and, on the other hand, enmeshed in larger (cultural) structures of meaning. In view of the aforementioned,

the present discussion is centered on the main participation roles and social relations that Greek children enact and gain experience in through
multiparty family interaction. The aim of this microanalysis is to uncover
how the local production of meaning invokes but also comprises global
norms such as cultural concepts of narrative tellability (cf. Aukrust, chap.
3, this volume) and self-presentation.

Storytelling in Greece has been well documented as a major communication mode in everyday interactional contexts (Georgakopoulou, 1997),
thus deeming the society worthy of characterization as narrative oriented
or narrative biased (Georgakopoulou & Goutsos, 2000). In such contexts,
stories have been found to exhibit a systematic use of a constellation of devices that key them as performances (Georgakopoulou, 1997), that is, as
dramatized deliveries during which the tellers assume responsibility to
display to their audiences verbal artistry and communicative skill (Bauman, 1993). These performance devices include the sustained use of narrative present, the animation of characters' speech and thoughts, the
proximal deictics *now* and *here* instead of *then* and *there*, various repetition
forms, and rhythmic intonational and thematic segments that are evenly
balanced across the texts as a whole and are mostly organized around tripartite patterns (Georgakopoulou, 1998a). Despite these findings, the
cultural functions of Greek storytelling and its uses for pragmatic socialization have been hitherto neglected. This chapter thus attempts to redress
this balance by focusing on family narrative events, in particular on the telling of familiar or shared stories, which, through participant observations
and recordings, proved to be salient in family conversations. Familiar stories can be subdivided into *family stories* and *child stories*. The former are
known to all members of the family (cf. family fables, Blum-Kulka, 1997),
and can be assumed to be retold stories (Norrick, 1997), whereas the latter
involve the target child (normally the story's protagonist) and are known to
the child, one adult (normally the mother), and/or the siblings.

Familiar stories have been shown to constitute a vital component of all
conversational contexts, in particular those involving intimates. In such
contexts, they have been found to fulfill some of the pivotal functions of storytelling, such as the enhancement of group rapport and the ratification of
group membership (Norrick, 1997). As is shown in the data at hand, their
telling reveals a cultural emphasis on the socialization of the delivery of narratives as performances; at the same time, it is strategically and methodi-
cally linked by participants to current interactional concerns, that is, contextualized. Though it is fair to say that in some cases the stories' functions
in local contexts cannot be disassociated from the presence of a participant
observer as a "familiar guest," the discussion illustrates their immense potential for reformulation. It also argues for their significance as indexes of
culturally bound familial identities and expectations of children.

DATA

My systematic study of Greek conversational storytelling in informal communication between intimates has suggested that in cases of adult–child
storytelling within multiparty interactions of family with nonfamily members (e.g., dinner parties with guests), children are to be seen but not
heard; in fact, they are encouraged to socialize among themselves and let
grown-ups get on with their "grown-up" conversations (Georgakopoulou,
1997). In the few cases in which stories are primarily addressed to them,
the children, as a rule, assume the role of passive listeners. In those environments, however, I came across two modes of children's participation in
adult socializing that struck me as worthy of closer study within family contexts. The first was the child functioning as story elicitor. Children frequently prompted their parents to relate family stories, mostly humorous,
involving either events experienced by the family or anecdotes from the
parents' childhood, student life, and so on. Second, the most daring children, once they managed to secure storytelling rounds on familiar tales,
ended up telling a familiar story themselves, typically in a performed way.
As is shown later, both these modes of child participation in narrative are
salient in the present data as well.

   This chapter is based on 100 familiar or shared narratives that were extracted from conversations in five middle-class families in Greece. The
larger ongoing project involves 10 families, all with professional parents
and at least two school-age children (between 7 and 11 years old). These
have been taped in their homes from about 5 PM until the end of their dinner in the presence of myself acting as a participant-observer. I was introduced to the families through my contacts with schoolteachers. Reminiscent of Blum-Kulka's (1997) observations of Israeli families, these Greek
families accepted me from the outset as a familiar guest. Questions about
my personal life were asked without any inhibition, but equally, I was regu-
larly invited by the families to provide my opinion on family matters. In
addition, I was frequently the primary recipient—and adjudicator—of stories involving children (cf. Blum-Kulka, 1997; Ochs & Taylor, 1992).

   The family mealtime has been argued to be an important time slot for
conversations and narrative events. A caveat has been introduced, however, with regard to the cross-cultural applicability of its rules and expectations (Blum-Kulka & Snow, 1992). Indeed, during data collection, it became evident that the families did not focus on narrative so much at the
dinner table, as the dinner activity itself was somewhat unstructured: Fathers were rarely there and times fluctuated depending on the children's
afternoon extracurricular schedule (e.g., tuition in foreign languages, mu-
sic, sports, etc., as a rule provided outside day schools in Greece). A fair
amount of conversation and storytelling occurred during the Greek con-

cept of afternoon (5 PM–7 PM) when parents would have a coffee and children would be treated to pudding, ice cream, or fruit (a rough equivalent of "teatime").

PARTICIPATION MODES IN FAMILIAR STORYTELLING

Story Ownership and Entitlement

Narrative space in the data is, unsurprisingly, occupied mostly by adults (63% of the total number of narratives vs. 37% by children), in particular mothers, who were found to relate almost twice as many stories as fathers. Shared or familiar stories amount to more than half of the total number of stories. Thematically, *family stories* involve events from the family's (recent or nonrecent) past and *child stories* relate recent events from the target child's life (e.g., achievements, mishaps, various incidents at school); these are typically initiated by mothers and primarily addressed to the father or the participant-observer (for comparable family narrative events, see Miller, Potts, Fung, Hoogstra, & Mintz, 1990; Ochs & Taylor, 1992).

Within child stories, an important distinction proved to be that between events that are known and events that are experienced or eyewitnessed. Different ownership and entitlement issues, that is, who can tell whose stories (Shuman, 1986), pertain to each case. Specifically, when siblings happen to know of the events of a child story without having experienced or eyewitnessed them, they are not allowed to tell the story in question. A child story can be narrativized only by the child who experienced its events; in other words, the rule of thumb seems to be "don't tell your brother's or sister's story unless you were there when it happened." Consider the example in Table 2.1: The parents comment on the fact that their eldest son's (George's) "misdemeanors" are attributable to bad influences; Nikos, the younger brother, chips in and attempts to offer a story that will substantiate the parents' views.[1]

Nikos' first contribution (look, when George . . . he goes) is construed by the mother as a reference to a specific event rather than as a generalized observation. Her query puts forth an entitlement rule, by which Nikos is entitled to tell his brother's story only if he has eyewitnessed the events.

---

[1]The transcription symbols used in Tables 2.1 through 2.7 are adapted from the standardized system developed within conversation analysis and are as follows: // overlapping utterances; = continuous utterances; : extension or prolongation of a sound; :: longer extension; ? rising intonation; ! animated tone; > < delivery at a quicker pace than the surrounding talk; (( )) editorial comments; , end of intonation unit, continuing intonation; . stopping fall in intonation; . . a pause of less than 0.5 seconds; . . . a pause greater than 0.5 seconds; CAPITALS denote louder talk than the surrounding one.

TABLE 2.1
Whose Story is This Anyway?—Mother, Father, Nikos
(7-Year-Old Boy), George (10-Year-Old Boy)

Conversation in Greek	Translation
FAT: *To Joryo tom barasirun para-poli*	George is easily influenced
MOT: *o Vasilis o Kostopulos pi çi*	By Vassilis Kostopoulos for instance
GEO: *o Vasilis oçi, o Panajotis, o Pandelis*	Not by Vassilis, but by Panajotis, Pandelis
NIK: *cita ama kaθete o Joryos ce citai sto binaka pai//*	Look, when George sits like this and looks at the board, he goes//
MOT: *esi pu isuna? pu ta kseris afta, siɣnomi δilaδi jati δe milas ja ton eafto su*	And where were YOU? how do you know about these things, excuse me, cause you are not talking about yourself now
NIK: *oxi, mja fora sta kaliteχnika ton iχa δi*	No, I saw him once during an Arts class
MOT: *a δen gzero*	Well I don't know about that
NIK: *pu o Jorgos citaze tom binaka, c'o Pandelis itan apo piso tu, e apo piso leo, apo δipla tu, ce vareθice o Pandelis liyo . . na citazi stom binaka, ce tom birazi . . . ((continuation))*	When George was concentrating on the board, and Pandelis was behind him, sorry what am I saying? Next to him, and Pandelis got bored of concentrating, and he starts winding him up . . . ((continuation))

Note. MOT = mother; FAT = father; NIK = Nikos; GEO = George.

Nikos in turn resists the deprivation of storytelling rights by claiming eyewitness access to the events. Entitlement is no longer an issue and he goes on to tell the story. The aforementioned entitlement restriction does not apply to parents. Instead, child stories of known but not coexperienced events are systematically co-owned. This pattern arguably reveals culturally defined rules for entitlement and ownership of experience, according to which children are socialized to accept that their life's tales are co-owned with their parents.

The entitlement restrictions applying to siblings' stories are lifted in the case of co-experienced or eyewitnessed events: These are co-owned by all members of the family, be they children or parents. Entitlement to familiar tales is not exclusively regulated by co-ownership. Culturally defined notions of competent narrative performances also come into play; this is evidenced by the fact that a fair portion (17%) of familiar narratives in the data are child prompted or elicited. Prompting normally consists of an explicit ratification of one of the two parents as the teller of the elicited story followed by the abstract of the story: for example, *mama, pes ti içe jini me to farmako, pu to χa pji olo?* (Mummy, tell about what happened with the medicine, when I had it all?). This pattern of elicitation is arguably linked with cultural attitudes and values placed on the delivery of narratives as performances in a community that stresses the performative. By granting the floor to one of the parents, children implicitly accept the view of storytelling as an arena for display of communicative skill and competence; they also seem to subscribe to the value system that accords a special conversational status to the competent performer. As is shown later, this performer is throughout the story's telling respected as the main teller with strong floor-holding rights.

Contextualization

Entitlement issues are only part of the regulatory forces operating in the telling of familiar stories. Of equal—if not greater—importance are the ways by which the actual telling, once it is embarked on, is contextualized and made relevant to the ongoing interaction. Far from being the teller's prerogative, this process is the outcome of a moment-by-moment collusion on or negotiation of the story's point jointly achieved by the participants, parents and children included. To begin with child stories, the contextualization of their telling is as a rule orchestrated by the mothers, who tend to become informed of the stories' events before the fathers (cf. Ochs & Taylor, 1992). As a result, it is mostly mothers who initiate and tell child stories. The children are often allocated the role of side or non-ratified participants (cf. Blum-Kulka, 1997), whereas the primary recipient is the father or, less commonly, the participant-observer. In the Table 2.2, the mother at first attempts to elicit the account from the child but, when this fails, she addresses it to the father.

In Ochs' and Taylor's data (1992), stories involving children were argued to be instantiations of the family hierarchy and to serve as forms of parental—primarily paternal—control or adjudication (in Foucault's terms, *panopticon*) of the children's behavior. Similarly, the contextualization of child stories in the data suggests their significance in (re)affirming codes of morality and social order by underscoring their breach by children or, equally, by celebrating, that is, praising and rewarding, the children's conformity to them. In both cases, child stories develop and promote to the children a specific sense of self with cultural norms regulating what is right and what is wrong. One of those cultural norms involves the parental pride expressed in the children being assertive, even naughty and unruly, if this entails a certain amount of wit (cf. Miller et al., 1990). Specifically, in Table 2.2, the "naughty" incident with the cat, though initiated to contradict Nikos' complaint (Turn 1), is subsequently framed by the mother as humorous and entertaining rather than as a serious violation of moral rules: The entire episode (Turns 4 and 6) is delivered in an animated tone, and one of the children is affectionately referred to as "this gentleman over

TABLE 2.2
Mother, Father, and Nikos

Conversation in Greek	Translation
1 NIK: *proχθes me γradzunise eδo*	((Referring to the family's cat)) two days ago she scratched me here
2 MOT: *ti ekanes omos esi prota?*	Yes, but what had you done to her beforehand?
3 NIK: *ce meta tis kovo mja //bunja*	and then I //punch her
4 MOT: *pirane ena lastiχo, ap'afta pu ta δenune etsi, ce m'afto ton girjo apo δo, ci tris to δesane stin ura tis ftoças, c'arçise na treçi*	((turning to the father smilingly)) they took one of those rubber things, with this gentleman over here, ((referring to her other son)) and they tied it to the poor cat's tail, and she started running
5 FAT: *pote to kanane afto?*	When did they do that?
6 MOT: *χtes to vraδi, pos δe do gremisane, afto na treçi edo! Evlepe to topi pu to cinijuse apo piso, ce trelaθice, su lei ti ejine?*	Last night, I thought they were going to pull the house down, this one ((pointing to the cat)) running like mad, seeing the string with the ball in its end following her, and she went crazy she says ((to herself)) what's going on here?
7 NIK: *c'anakalivame //ta iχni tis*	And we were recovering //her traces
8 FAT: *anakaliptame*	Uncovering
9 MOT: *θa mas klinis kanena rima tora?*	Will you conjugate any verbs for us now?

Note. MOT = mother; FAT = father; NIK = Nikos.

here." As a result, Nikos feels free to chip in (Turn 7). His contribution leads to a parental grammar lesson on verb conjugations that signals the end of the story: This provides more evidence for the fact that both parents do not see any serious breach of codes in the reported "naughty" incident and are thus not intent on extracting from the story a moral lesson for Nikos.

In addition to naughty but enterprising behavior, other attributes that prove to rank highly in parents' expectations of children are those of openness, sociability, and popularity in the peer group, in particular among members of the opposite sex. In cases of stories foregrounding the children's behavior, the children are willing to act as the main tellers, whereas they are less inclined to do so when their stories are put on display for parental adjudication (cf. Ochs & Taylor, 1992). On some occasions, they even counterbalance the control that can be exercised through child stories, by initiating child stories themselves with the aim of rallying support for their actions or, generally, of proving a point. In such cases, they address their story to the parent or person(s) who do not know about the events in question. This is illustrated in Table 2.3, when the child primarily addresses the incident of his haircut to me (as the familiar guest) in order to elicit my support for his view that his hair is better when it is long. When his mother chips in to defend her actions, Panagiotis brings up two examples to strengthen his point.

In a similar vein, in Table 2.4 Tassos prompts his mother to display a child story concerning the visit to his school of an author of children's books. The prompt is contextualized as an argument in favour of Tassos' complaint that his school and extracurricular commitments are too heavy. Subsequently, his exchange with his mother negotiates the point of the author's invoked reported speech.

TABLE 2.3
"I'm Blond Too"—Panagiotis (7-Year-Old Boy), Mother, Alexandra

Conversation in Greek	Translation
1 ALEX: *san gzenes ine i simaθitries su aftes, ine ksanes*	They don't look Greek those two classmates of yours, they are blond
2 PAN: *c'eγo ime ksanθos omos, ta malja mu ama su δikso . . s'oles tis fotoγrafies pu imuna mikros, ta malja mu itan syura, tora isjosan, jati mu ta kopse i mama*	I'm blond too though, my hair, if I show you pictures of mine . . as a baby, you'll see that my hair is curly too, now it's straight, cause Mom had it cut.
3 ((shows)) *Na pu iχa syura malja, ce tora mu ta kopsane. Proχθes me pije i mama, c'ego den iθela ce//*	See here? I had curly hair, and now it's cut. Two days ago Mummy took me to the hairdresser's, and I didn't want to go, and//
4 MOT: *Ne ala kseris . . . t'aγorja dem brepi na χun ce pola syura makria malja, pjo orea den ine etsi adrika?*	Yes, but you know . . . boys shouldn't have lots of curly hair, isn't it nicer like this, more masculine?
5 PAN: *ne, i Maria i Konδili omos?*	Yes, but what about Maria Kondili?
6 MOT: *Afti ine koritsi, eδo leme j'aγorja //emis*	She's a girl, we are talking about boys //here
7 PAN: *ne o Macis vazi kokalaci omos*	Yes but Makis wears his hair in a pony tail
8 MOT: *A . . eχume ena ksaderfaci, pu vazi kokalaci, enas ksaderfoz mas more ikositrio χronon, eçi makria malja, kseris tora . . .*	((turning to me)) Right, we have a cousin who has a pony tail, he's twenty-three years old, long hair, and so on, if you know what I mean . . .

Note. PAN = Panagiotis; MOT = mother; ALEX = Alexandra.

TABLE 2.4
Mother, Tassos (8-Year-Old Boy)

Conversation in Greek	Translation
TASSOS: *Pes mama ja ti Loizu ti ipe:?*	Mummy, tell about Loizu what she said
MOT: *Ti ipe i Loizu Taso?*	What did she say Tassos?
TASSOS: *Ipe na mi stelnete ta peðja musici* //*ce*	She said don't send your kids to music //and
MOT: *ðen ipe na min ta stelnete Tasu:li*	She didn't say don't send them Tassu:lis
TASSOS: *IPE::*	SHE DI::D
MOT: *Ipe na pijenun se ola, ala na pezun kjolas, oçi mono frodistirja ce djavazma, min to ðjastrevlonume tora. ESI ðilaði ti θa protimuses?*	She said they should do all those things, but have time to play too, not just tuition and homework, let's not distort things here. What would YOU prefer?
TASSOS: *Na eχo efkola aglika ce ðjavazmata, ce ton ipolipo χrono na pezo*	Easy English and not too much homework, so that I can play the rest of the time
MOT: *Esena su lipi to peχniði omos?*	But do you miss playing?
TASSOS: *oçi . . ala ektos apo mja mera=*	No . . except for one day=
MOT: =*ti Bemti*	=Thursdays
TASSOS: *oçi, tin Tetarti*	No, Wednesdays

Note. MOT = mother; TASSOS = Tassos.

The previous examples illustrate how it is not just parents who strategically employ child stories as a means of appealing to the coparticipants' control or praise of the target child's behavior. Children also fashion tales about themselves to suit local purposes, such as putting forth a view or an argument, or, generally, calling upon further dissection and analysis by the family members (also see discussion of the story of the song contest, in the section Family Positionings in Familiar Stories). Compared to child stories, the contextualization of family stories involves less negotiation of the point, in view of the stories' special place in the family's history. Constituting part of the family's collective memory does not, however, mean that family stories are not tied to local interactional concerns. In fact, as building blocks of shared interactional history, family stories are frequently retrieved and reformulated as ideal guides on current and future family situations (see discussion in the section Family Positionings in Familiar Stories).

Children as Cotellers

Collaborative family narration has been shown to socialize children into
cultural participation modes. As Berman and Slobin (1994) noted, in this
strand of research, it is important for the analyst to identify first what constitutes a culturally defined adult model of narrative competence. My previous study of Greek storytelling suggests (Georgakopoulou, 1997, 1998a)
that for full-fledged performances to be constructed, the audience's participation needs to be channeled so as to uphold one main teller, responsible for the rhythmic deployment of narrative action, while being aided by
secondary tellers in the foregrounding of salient events. Furthermore, the
audience's involvement or challenge (Blum-Kulka, 1997) is predominantly with respect to the tale rather than the telling (rights) or the teller
(e.g., their views, stances, etc.). The children's participation modes in
shared narratives are congruent with the aforementioned cultural norms
pertinent to narrative performances. Specifically, once an adult takes up a
narrative delivery, as a rule he or she remains the main teller to the end,
with significant participation from the child who is involved in the story as
a character or protagonist. The children's contributions place emphasis
on the narrativization of the events into full-fledged and competent performances rather than on the negotiation of telling rights. This means
that they evaluate the main events or, on the whole, enhance the story's
high point (climax), and supply details perceived as strategic for the plot.
Challenges to the tale commonly manifest themselves as disagreement
about details. Consider the example in Table 2.5.

    The first contribution by George (Turn 2) in the culturally favorable tri-
partite scheme (Georgakopoulou, 1997) adds to the vividness of the description of the children's room. Similarly, his contribution in Turn 10
also takes the form of a tripartite scheme of habitual action. In Turn 4,
George interrupts to bid for an upcoming story. (In their attempt to secure the floor, children typically express their intention to embark on a
story, sometimes well in advance, to ensure they have reserved their place
in the storytelling round.) The rest of the contributions in the preceding
story illustrate the children's concern with getting the details right and thus
jointly formulating the story's point with the teller. For instance, in order to
supply the appropriate details, George delegitimizes the main storyline and
momentarily assumes main-teller rights (Turns 14, 16). Similarly, when the
mother reaches the climax of her story, Nikos' contribution highlights the
climactic events. It consists of an exclamation phrase and the emphatic repetition of the evaluative coda that happens to be a characterization of him.
In this way, this familiar tale proves to be a building block in the family's
interactional history that provides a ready-made basis for the characterization of the two siblings and their personality differences.

TABLE 2.5
I Was a Rebel—George, Nikos, Mother, Father, Theodore
(10-Year-Old First Cousin Who Lives Downstairs
and Spends a Lot of Time With the Family)

Conversation in Greek	Translation
1 MOT: *Ala ecino pu mu içe kani ediposi, itan i ðjafora ton ðjo peðjon. Iχa ena ðomatjo tu peχniðju,moceta stromeno olo, peðotopos . . . stroma //kato*	But what had impressed me, was the difference between the two of them as babies. I had a room full of toys, it had a carpet, a mattress . . . and //nothing else
2 GEO: *ce treχame, ce piðajame, ce peftame pano sto stroma*	And we were running, and jumping, and falling on the mattress
3 MOT: *ena stroma pano sto patoma, tipot'alo, ja na kaθonde na ksekurazonde, mja vivlioθici jemati scilja ce peχniðja*	a mattress on the floor and nothing else, so that they'd have something to sit on, ((it also had)) bookshelves full of teddy animals
4 GEO: *A::, θa po ti iχa kani me ti vivlioθici=*	Ah:: right I'll say what I did with the bookshelves=
5 MOT: *=o Nikos apo enos etus viðose to bukali, iχa mja kolonja, i opia içe krikus meγalus, me mikra mikra . . poli //mikri epano*	Nikos aged one screwed a bottle of perfume which had a big screwy basis and //a narrow neck
6 NIK: *plastici*	((It was)) plastic
7 MOT: *plastici. Lipo:n . . o Joryos sta ðio χronja arçise na to perni akrivos, aftos ston ena χrono monos tu, mja fora tu to ðiksame, arçise ce to evaze, to pjo meγalo, to pjo mikro meta, na po oti ton içe ði to Joryo*	Yes plastic. So:: George aged two started trying to close it, but ((emphatic)) he (i.e Nikos)) at exactly one he managed to do it on his own. We opened the bottle for him once, and he worked it out, he had not seen George doing it or anyone else
8 GEO: *To baulo pu mas evazes ja na mi vγume ekso?*	Tell about that thing you were putting us in so that we couldn't go out
9 MOT: *a ne to parko*	Right yes, the playpen
10 GEO: *>skarfaloname anevename kaname<*	>we climbed went up did all sorts of things<
11 MOT: *o Jorgos o kakomiris kaθotane epeze, ekane tis ipolipes ðuljes sto parko mesa, o Joryos meγalose kanonika, etsi meχri ta ðjomisi, meta ton aniksa kanonika*	Poor George was sitting there playing, doing everything in there, he practically grew up there, he was there until he was two and a half, and then I let him out

(Continued)

TABLE 2.5

Conversation in Greek	Translation
12 GEO: δe me anikses	You did not let me out
13 MOT: elipa //ce	I was out //and
14 GEO: perimene na po, erχotan o Θoδoris pano c'o Nikos ce mas kliδoses olus eci mesa	Wait, let me say this, Theodore used to come up, and you locked us all three with Nikos inside
15 MOT: oçi to Niko!	Not Nikos!
16 GEO: oçi de vjice o Nikos, emis vjikame, protos eγo me toΘoδori, skarfalonume, eγo skarfalono protos, pefto kato, erçete c'o Θoδoris apo piso, o Nikos mesa fonaze eci pera, vγalte me c'emena, δen don vγalame afton, c'erçete i mama ce mas ksanavazi mesa, ksanavjenume emis, ce tote ton evγale	No Nikos stayed in there, but we got out first, it was me, we climbed up with Theodore, I climb up first, fall onto the other side, and then Theodore comes, and Nikos was left behind, and he was crying get me out of here, but we didn't get him out, ((turning to me)) and Mom comes and puts us back in, and then we get out again, and then she let Nikos out too
17 THEO: Pandos δe mas vγalate apo δjo χronon	Yes you didnt let us out when we were two
18 MOT: meχri δjo χronon isaste mesa ce pezate	You were playing in until you were two
19 THEO: meχri tesaron	Well until we were four
20 FAT: ((laughs)) e, isaste ja padria tote	Ready to get married then weren't you?
21 MOT: oçi tesaron Θoδori, tesaron mu fenete meγalos, telospandon. Molis evlepe o Nikos c'arxise na perpatai, to vazo ce to Niko mesa, ja na tus elenχo ce tuz δjio. Lipo:n faringitiδa, saranda pireto, epimoni:! Milame ja to kati alo. Pai afto, pernane pende meres jinete kala, ton ksanavazo mesa, pali faringitida apo to klama.	Not four Theodore, not that long. Anyway .. when Nikos started walking, I put him in too, so that I could keep an eye on both of them, next thing you know Nikos suffers from laryngitis, and a temperature of 40 Celsius degrees. We are talking persistence here. Upon recovery, five days later, I put him back in, again laryngitis, cause he had been crying nonstop.
22 NIK: Panajitsa mu!	Oh my god!
23 FAT: klizmenos δen gaθete=	He can't stand being put inside=
24 MOT: =tin epanastasi=	((he starts)) a rebellion=
25 NIK: =epanastatis	((I'm)) a rebel

Note. GEO = George; NIK = Nikos; MOT = mother; FAT = father; THEO = Theodore.

In comparison to what seems to be the norm in adult narrative co-construction, children's participation in familiar tales documents a strict requirement for adherence to factuality, as reflected in the increased preoccupation with details. This emphasis on details is a way of asserting one's co-ownership of a story and the right to contribute to the formulation of its point (cf. Norrick, 1997). At another level, it can be tentatively suggested that, developmentally, this tendency seems to represent a phase during which Greek children draw on certain strategies of involvement more than others. In Tannen's terms (1989), details constitute major involvement strategies—also common in Greek stories—in that they evoke the familiar, the particular, and a sense of concreteness. In the data, it is arguable that their prominence in the children's participation modes reveals the cultural emphasis placed on the eyewitnessed events, the lived, and the vividly remembered. If the essence of Greek performances is to convey a sense of immediacy and reliving of the evoked scenes (Georgakopoulou, 1997), then the importance of details for children, who are still in the process of developing the full range of rhetorical options for signaling involvement, becomes evident.

Children as Main Tellers-Performers

It has been argued that familiar narratives present children with opportunities for significant conarration and parity in access to adult discourse (Blum-Kulka, 1997). In the data, they also allow for the deployment of a performed telling: First, parental scaffolding is restricted during the children's telling of familiar tales; second, in a competitive arena where children need to try hard to secure turns, this is one occasion on which they are given the floor to perform. Children's displays of shared stories are normally integrated into storytelling rounds thus following upon and being triggered by adults' stories. This pattern of display constitutes an ideal point of entry into the acquisition of local norms for integrating one's narration into evolving narrative events. The story in Table 2.6, part of a storytelling round, was signaled by George as upcoming during the narration of the story earlier in Table 2.5.

The delivery in Table 2.6 attests to the emergence of a culture-specific narrative style in view of the narrative strategies that George has at his disposal. The story is organized in brief, (mainly) three-line stanzas (i.e., intonational and thematic units—Gee, 1990—displayed in the form of a poem and numbered above). As already suggested, this pattern of organization has been documented as prevalent in adult narration, too (Georgakopoulou, 1997). Transitions from one stanza to another avoid lexical markers and favor tense switches, mostly from the imperfective past that encodes background action to the narrative present that accentuates the

TABLE 2.6
The Story of the Bookshelves

Story in Greek	Translation
GEO: *(1) Tin ali fora eγo iχa ta jeneθlia mu* *ce kaθomaste eci pera* *ce pezame.*	The other time I had my birthday and we were sitting there and playing.
(2) Ce fevγune *c'erχonde eδo pera i pjo poli* *trone γliko.*	And then most kids leave and come to this room and have their cake.
(3) Irθane eδo *eγo to efaγa to γliko mu* *piγa mesa* *imuna mikros.*	So they came here I had my cake too went back in small as I was.
(4) Arçizo eγo *leo prepi na pjaso ecino to peχniδi* *to içe vali poli psila i mama.*	And I start I say to myself I've got to get to that toy Mummy had put it high up.
(5) C'aneveno eχo sti skala *skarfalono sti vivlioθici* *ja na pjaso ecino to peχnidi psila.*	And I climb up the ladder climb to the bookshelf to get to the toy up there.
(6) Pefti i vivlioθici *pefto c'ego kato* *me plakoni i vivlioθici sena rafi.*	The bookshelves fall down I fall down too the bookshelves fall on me ((I get stuck in one of the shelves))

Note. GEO = George.

turn of events. Typically, the climactic action is preceded by the device of thinking to oneself (introduced by the verb *leo,* which covers instances of both direct speech and thought). The climax itself is rendered in a typical tripartite scheme: The bookshelf and the child are presented as agents of the same parallel action and the third line, the resolution, links them up in an agent–patient type of relationship. Stories in Greek, rather than explicitly evaluating or resolving their high point, tend to be climacto-telic (i.e., ending-at-the-high-point). The high point is thus a slot where audience contribution is expected. In the story in Table 2.6, an evaluative exclamative is provided by me *(Gosh!),* whereas references to the results of the high point are supplied by the parents (MOT: *We found him in the other room, it had no books, lots of teddies, but the child was found inside a shelf in the gap;* FAT: *It was empty, and it had a cushion).*

The parents' supply of evaluative comments and description during children's tellings is also illustrated in the story in Table 2.7. In that case, Sophia, the 7-year-old teller, tends to foreground the local implications of

TABLE 2.7
A Family Holiday—Sophia (7-Year-Old Girl), Mother

Conversation in Greek	Translation
1 SOPHIA: *A na sas po, pijename eci sta votsala, c' içe kati sosivja, kitrina, c'eyo me to baba anevename eci c'eyo iχa ta poδja mu sto baba, pano ston omo tu, ce kratjomuna eci, ce katevename, ce δen iχa katsi kala eci pera, ce χtipisa tim blati mu, ce opos katevikame kato tu leo, baba baba foviθika, ce mu lei meta apo liji ora, Sofia na su po tin aliθja c'eyo foviθika*	((turning to me)) Oh let me tell you, we were going to the pebbles, and there were some lifebelts, yellow, and Dad and I were going up, and I had my legs around his neck, and I was holding on, and we were going down, and I wasn't holding tight, and I hurt my back, and when we went down, I tell him Dad Dad I was scared, and after a little while he tells me, Sofia, to tell you the truth, I was scared too
2 MOT: *eyo dem biya, foviθika*	I didn't go, I was too scared
3 SOPHIA: *itane meyali pisina, içe triandaδio skalja, ce patajes kuδuni drun drun, ce meta pijene liya cimata, ce meta meta drin drin, ola ta cimata pano*	= it was a huge swimming pool, it had thirty-two steps, and you rang a bell clank clank, and then a few waves came, and a bit later, clank clank, all the waves toward us
4 MOT: *=içe poles pisines, δilaδi itan terastjos χoros, pu θa çe mesa dekapende pisines, fandasu tora, kseris me obreles etsi poli orea, c' içe ce skales siδerenjes psiles, opos eleje i Sofia, c'epefte tsuliθres tsuliθres, ce vlepame sto vaθos mja pisina, tin ora pu bikame, ce δen gzerame ti ine*	It had lots of swimming pools, I mean it was a huge area, it must have had about fifteen swimming pools, you can imagine now, with umbrellas and the rest, lovely place, and it had stairs, iron and tall, like Sofia was saying, and from there people could slide all the way down, so we saw that pool down there when we came in, and we didn't know what it was
5 SOPHIA: *emis kserame me to baba, c'akume ena drin ce vlepume ton gozmo ce pijene sti bisina, içe cimata*	We did, with Daddy, and we hear a sound, ding dong, and we see the folks going to the pool, and it had waves
6 MOT: *Ti ejine? Afto itan to sima oti i pisina evyaze cimata*	So this was a signal that the pool would generate waves
7 SOPHIA: *>liya liya liya< cimata, ce benume mesa ce lei o babas, bravo tora θa kani cimata, ce lei orea, erχonde cimata, ce meta arçizune ta meyala cimata, ce lei oχ!*	>few few few< waves, and we get in and Dad says, excellent, now it'll make lots of waves, and he says great, and then the big waves start coming, and he says wow!
8 MOT: *milame po po::, pola cimata!*	We're talking lots and lots of waves!

Note. SOPHIA = Sophia; MOT = mother.

the narrated events as opposed to evaluating them globally; this developmental feature has been attested as typical of that age (Bamberg & Damrad-Frye, 1991). Her mother's contributions (i.e., evaluation of the high point, Turns 2, 8; description, Turns 4, 6) are thus instrumental for establishing global interconnectivity. They nonetheless neither challenge Sophia as the main teller of the events nor interrupt her during the buildup of her animated narration. The conarration is in fact constituted of a series of orchestrated moves, with zones during which the secondary teller is a recipient, and with acceptable slots for her contributions.

As can be seen in Table 2.7, Sophia's narration breaks into the perfomance mode of Greek storytelling: For example, note the narrative present throughout both for the action and for the instances of direct speech (all introduced by the verb *leo*), the tripartite patterns (e.g., three-time repetition of "few" in Turn 7, and three instances of direct speech with increasing intensity, Turn 7: *and Dad says excellent . . . and he says great . . . and he says wow!*).

FAMILY POSITIONINGS IN FAMILIAR STORIES

In the light of the previous discussion, it can be argued that the cultural implications of familiar stories for children's pragmatic socialization mainly lie in the events' preparatory roles for competence in narrative performances valued in the community. The hallmarks of such performances are animated and dramatic deliveries of the tale that build up to the high point and frequently end there. Audience participation is so channeled as to not interrupt the rhythm or hamper the skilled delivery of the teller; instead, it is aimed at enhancing the tale, in particular its high point.

In addition to acculturation into modes of delivery, the telling of familiar tales also provides opportunities for reaffirming the significance, organization, and tellability of the family's experience (Miller et al., 1990; Snow, 1991). In various degrees of directness, familiar tales propose tellable images of children's and parents' behavior and roles. These can be analytically located in the processes of positioning involved in any narrative construction, that is, in the discursive practices by means of which the tellers construct themselves as observably and intersubjectively coherent participants through jointly produced story lines. Building on Davies and Harré (1990), Bamberg (1997) located a storyteller's positioning at three levels. Level 1 involves the positioning of the characters vis-à-vis one another in the tale world; at this level, relationships between characters are drawn in a particular type of protagonist and/or antagonist relationship. At Level 2, the tellers position themselves locally and situationally, as well as with regard to an audience in the act of narrating. Level 3, an achievement of Levels 1 and 2, is the positioning of tellers vis-à-vis themselves with claims that they hold to be true and relevant above and beyond the local conversational situation. With regard to Level 1, as already seen, a common positioning pattern in the data involves the portrayal of children in a positive light, for example, as sociable and popular (see later discussion of the song contest), or, as witty and enterprising even when naughty (Tables 2.2, 2.5). Parents are typically positioned as proud of their children's achievements or as concerned, with mothers holding the monopoly of the devoted parent. For instance, in the storytelling round of familiar tales, from which the stories in Tables 2.5 and 2.6 are extracted, the mother is consistently positioned as the character who cared or was extra concerned in the first years of the children's lives. In the story "When George Was Nearly Drowned," she tells of how she saved her son's life. In the evaluation of the climactic event, she positions herself as the most concerned of the two parents as follows: *And then I took this one here to my arms, I was in such a shock, and I was crying. And John wanted to hold the child, cause as a father he was upset, and I wouldn't give it to him, and I was saying, go away go away, I hated John at that point, cause he'd said to me stop fussing over the child, cause we were thinking of the guests ((the incident involved the child choking himself with the eye of a teddy bear while he was alone in his room and the parents were entertaining guests))*.

Overall, positionings at Level 1 convey powerful messages for culturally sanctioned roles and obligations of family members. Thus, their effect on Level 2 positionings is that of a reminder—and enhancer—of the family's ingroup cohesion that at the same time provides guidelines on the family's current concerns. For instance, in the story "When George Was Nearly Drowned," the positioning of the parents, in particular the mother, as concerned for their children, both in the tale world (Level 1) and beyond (Level 3), was exploited locally (Level 2) as a reminder of this longstanding parental devotion, and, subsequently, as a plea for decent behavior on the part of the children. The story's ending tellingly led to a mild parental scolding of George for not eating his luncheon at school, the moral being: "Every time you are about to misbehave, think of what your mother went through to bring you up." In this way, rather than just serving to rewaken and enjoy shared memories, the story also acted as a guide for immediate familial concerns.

Similarly, the synergy of positionings at all three levels is nicely illustrated in the story that I have titled "A Song Contest" (not cited here for reasons of space). The story is used by the main teller, the father, as an example of Andreas' sociability and lack of shyness, personality traits that, as already suggested, are typically proposed to the children as desirable. The story involves a song contest, which Andreas, 8 years old at the time of the story's telling, and 6 at the time of the events, decided to join without any prior singing lessons or preparation. The story foregrounds Andreas' ability to handle public appearances as a result of his sociable nature. Andreas coconstructs the tale in the modes of participation discussed earlier: He highlights the peak events (e.g., he sings some lines from his entry song), he emphatically repeats the result of the contest ([I came] *Se::cond!*), and he negatively evaluates the female winner's song. Throughout the story, Andreas accepts the proposed positionings of him, that is, his attributes of sociability and public composure, both as a character in the related tale (Level 1) and as an individual above and beyond the immediate storytelling situation (Level 3). In the end, however, he proposes his own positioning vis-à-vis himself (Level 3) by way of the following moral coda: "If the contest takes place this year too, I will sing a song that I know well, something that we have been taught in class." The proposed positioning is endorsed by the father, and the two discuss possible entries for next year's competition. Thus, by means of coconstructed positionings by Andreas and his father, the story is contextualized both as a ready-made basis of characterization of Andreas and as a guide for planned future action.

"The Song Contest" narrates events that are located outside the family domain, and as such, it takes one of the two common forms in the data: It is a story of triumph of a family member as opposed to a story of threat posed to the family by the outside world. When placed in the public as opposed to the domestic sphere, familiar stories still stress the roles, expectations, rights, and obligations involved in being a family member. The family is thus positioned as a close-knit group with strong bonds and intimacy relationships. This positioning arguably points to the socialization of a relational, ingroup-oriented conception of personhood; as such, it is congruent with cultural values that have been found to be salient in Greece, such as ingroup involvement and interdependence (e.g., Triandis, Bontempo, & Villareal, 1988).

CONCLUDING DISCUSSION

This study's point of departure was that family narrative practices of socialization are highly ordered and systematic activities, routinely placed within a larger cultural framework of values and conventions. This framework bears on the ways in which participants, on one hand, attend and orient to the activity of narrating and, on the other hand, frame and situate the self and others in their accounts. These ways were uncovered here by a focus on shared or familiar stories, which were subdivided into family stories and child stories. With regard to child stories, it was argued that the distinction between known events and experienced or eyewitnessed events regulates story ownership and entitlement issues.

Close analysis of the participation modes in familiar stories suggested that their significance for socialization is intimately linked with their functions in local contexts. On one hand, the telling of family stories provides guidelines for immediate concerns as well as opportunities for reformulation of the stories' point in accordance with local purposes. On the other hand, the telling of child stories typically serves the creation of interactional alliances, either between parents, in their attempt to evaluate children's behavior, or between a parent/adult and the child teller, in the latter's attempt to make a complaint, prove a point, secure support for an action, and so on. In both cases, familiar stories systematically socialize children into culturally defined notions of narrative tellability. The fact that the telling of familiar narratives is frequently child prompted or elicited attests to the children's socialization into accepting that their—and their family's—tales are co-owned with their parents. Furthermore, it indexes cultural values placed on the delivery of narratives as performances that display communicative skill.

The children's contributions to the telling of familiar stories were also found to be congruent with a cultural style of performance that values the rights of a main teller. Specifically, children evaluated main events or, on the whole, enhanced the story's high point (climax) and (over)supplied details as strategies for signaling involvement with the tale's events. Children's own displays of shared stories were typically integrated into storytelling rounds of familiar stories following upon adults' stories. Furthermore, they were delivered in the cultural narrative style of replaying, with more or less sustained use of performance devices.

Finally, through the analysis of the stories' positioning strategies, the discussion attempted to link the aforementioned narrative practices with the socialization of messages pertaining to family roles and relationships. It was argued that children are commonly positioned as having the positive attributes of sociability and wit even when naughty. Parents are typically positioned as proud of their children's achievements or as sufferers of the consequences of the children's (minor) violations of social rules, with mothers monopolizing the role of the devoted parent. It was tentatively suggested that the conception of "self" conveyed to children through such positionings is ingroup oriented and interdependent.

The findings herein can serve as a point of departure for fine-grained developmental studies of the patterns of children's participation in family narrative events. They can also point to avenues of further contextualization of such narrative events through detailed treatments of family environment parameters, such as size, sibling relations, contacts with the extended family (still prevalent in Greece), and so on. Furthermore, the implications of the significance of familiar tales as attested here for the Greek children's passage to or development of literacy beg investigating. It has been argued that A-event stories, that is, stories the events of which are known only to the teller, constitute a better preparation for the autonomous, decontextualized language that is demanded of children in school than do tellings of shared events (Blum-Kulka & Snow, 1992). From this point of view, the frequency of familiar stories in family settings suggests a cultural preference for orality-based modes of communication that invoke shared knowledge and assumptions and place emphasis on the interpersonal relations between the interactants. That the jointly experienced is highly valued as a backdrop of shared assumptions is also evident in other contexts of narrative communication in Greece: interactions between friends, ranging from teenagers to middle-age people, thrive on the (re)tellings of or allusions to (in)group stories (Georgakopoulou, 1998b). This salience of familiar stories is also congruent with the widely held view that Greek society in its various discourses, oral and written, literary and nonliterary, is characterized by the mark of primary or secondary (residual) orality (see Tziovas, 1989) that emphasizes the shared and known. That said, even if an intimate connection between Greek orality practices and familiar stories can be easily established, the roles and values of the latter with regard to literacy cannot be that easily discarded. It is notable that the kind of oral narrative structure that enables a smooth transition from orality to literacy is culturally variable (e.g., Minami & McCabe, 1995). From this point of view, familiar stories in the data seem to be suited to literacy concerns on account of their tellability and their contextualized functions. Specifically, the tellability of familiar stories by and large hinges on the form rather than the content (Sherzer, 1982). In an educational system that opts for the rhetorics of "how" rather than "what" (Kostouli, 1992), familiar stories thus seem to have a vital preparatory role. Furthermore, though decontextualization is mentioned as the *sine qua non* of literacy, its close counterpart of recontextualization should not be omitted. The reformulation of states of affairs, processes, views, and so on, for different purposes, audiences, and situations is an integral part of literacy skills. As was shown earlier, the tellings of familiar stories are in fact (re)contextualizations, that is, not given and predetermined but locally occasioned. As such, their importance for the socialization of reformulation skills should not be underestimated.

To end, further implications of this study pertain to the great need for further research on the socialization of the narrative genres and styles privileged by different communities. To quote Bauman (1993), the agenda of such research involves "charting the culturally shaped, socially constituted and situationally emergent" (p. 195). The present study is intended as a small contribution to furthering this agenda.

REFERENCES

Bamberg, M. (1997). Positioning between structure and performance. Oral versions of personal experience: Three decades of narrative analysis. *Special Issue of the Journal of Narrative and Life History, 7,* 335–342.

Bamberg, M., & Damrad-Frye, D. (1991). On the ability to provide evaluative comments: Further explorations of children's narrative competencies. *Journal of Child Language, 14,* 253–290.

Bauman, R. (1993). Disclaimers of performance. In J. H. Hill & T. Irvine (Eds.), *Responsibility and evidence in oral discourse* (pp. 182–196). Cambridge, England: Cambridge University Press.

Berman, R., & Slobin, D. (Eds.). (1994). *Relating events in narrative: A cross-linguistic developmental study.* Hillsdale, NJ: Lawrence Erlbaum Associates.

Blum-Kulka, S. (1993). "You gotta know how to tell a story": Telling, tales and tellers in American and Israeli narrative events at dinner. *Language in Society, 22,* 361–402.

Blum-Kulka, S. (1997). *Dinner talk. Cultural patterns of sociability and socialization in family discourse.* Mahwah, NJ: Lawrence Erlbaum Associates.

Blum-Kulka, S., & Snow, C. (1992). Developing autonomy for tellers, tales, and telling in family narrative events. *Journal of Narrative and Life History, 2,* 187–217.

Bruner, J. (1990). *Acts of meaning.* Cambridge, MA: Harvard University Press.

Davies, B., & Harré, R. (1990). Position: The discursive construction of selves. *Journal of the Theory of Social Behaviour, 20,* 43–63.

Erickson, F. (1982). Money tree, lasagna bush, salt and pepper: Social construction of topical cohesion in a conversation among Italian-Americans. In D. Tannen (Ed.), *Analyzing discourse: Text and talk* (pp. 43–71). Washington, DC: Georgetown University Press.

Gee, J. P. (1990). *Social linguistics and literacies. Ideology in discourses.* Basingstoke, England: Falmer Press.

Georgakopoulou, A. (1997). *Narrative performances. A study of Modern Greek storytelling.* Amsterdam/Philadelphia: Benjamins.

Georgakopoulou, A. (1998a). Conversational stories as performances: The case of Greek. *Narrative Inquiry, 8,* 319–350.

Georgakopoulou, A. (1998b). Doing youth in and through conversational narratives. In J. Verschueren (Ed.), *Language and ideology. Selected papers from the 6th International Pragmatics Conference* (pp. 125–142). IPrA Research Center, Antwerp.

Georgakopoulou, A., & Goutsos, D. (1997). *Discourse analysis.* Edinburgh, Scotland: Edinburgh University Press.

Georgakopoulou, A., & Goutsos, D. (2000). Revisiting discourse boundaries: The narrative vs. non-narrative modes. *Text, 20,* 63–82.

Kostouli, T. (1992). On the structure of textual rhetoric: Some evidence from Greek narratives. *Text, 12,* 373–395.

Miller, P., Potts, R., Fung, H., Hoogstra, L., & Mintz, J. (1990). Narrative practices and the social construction of self in childhood. *American Ethnologist, 17,* 292–309.

Minami, M., & McCabe, A. (1995). Rice balls versus bear hunts: Japanese and Caucasian family narrative patterns. *Journal of Child Language, 22,* 423–446.

Norrick, J. (1997). Twice-told tales: Collaborative narration of familiar stories. *Language in Society, 26,* 199–220.

Ochs, E., & Taylor, C. (1992). Family narrative as political activity. *Discourse & Society, 3,* 301–340.

Sherzer, J. (1982). Tellings, retellings and tellings within tellings: The structuring and organization of narrative in Kuna Indian discourse. In R. Bauman & J. Sherzer (Eds.), *Case studies in the ethnography of speaking* (pp. 219–273). Austin, TX: Southwest Educational Development Laboratory.

Shuman, A. (1986). *Storytelling rights. The uses of oral and written texts by urban adolescents.* Cambridge, England: Cambridge University Press.

Snow, C. E. (1991). Building memories: The ontogeny of an autobiography. In D. Cicchetti & M. Beeghly (Eds.), *The self in transition: Infancy to childhood* (pp. 213–242). Chicago: University of Chicago Press.

Tannen, D. (1989). *Talking voices. Repetition, dialogue, and imagery in conversational discourse.* Cambridge, England: Cambridge University Press.

Triandis, H. C., Bontempo, R., & Villareal, M. J. (1988). Individualism and collectivism: Cross-cultural perspectives on self–ingroup relations. *Journal of Personality and Social Psychology, 54,* 1523–1538.

Tziovas, D. (1989). Residual orality and belated textuality in Greek literature and culture. *Journal of Modern Greek Studies, 7,* 321–335.

Chapter 3

"What Did You Do in School Today?" Speech Genres and Tellability in Multiparty Family Mealtime Conversations in Two Cultures

Vibeke Aukrust

Institute of Educational Research, Blindern, Norway

In this chapter, we follow a group of young Norwegian and American children into their kitchens and dining rooms to observe the conversations they have with their families during mealtimes. Like other modern children, these children grow up in a variety of family constellations, some of them living with their mothers, some with two parents. Some children have siblings, others not. However, all these families also have something in common; they all have a child around the age of 3, the family members talk together while they eat, and they have agreed to allow the talk be recorded. The purpose of this chapter is to discuss the influence of the participation structure, whether multiparty or two-party, on the opportunities these young children in two different cultures are offered for conversational participation and pragmatic learning during mealtimes.

Why Compare Dyadic and Multiparty Interaction? Former studies have documented the qualities of scaffolded (Bruner, 1983) or "fine-tuned" (Snow, 1995) dyadic interaction in which the language-learning child is interacting with a more competent other in the "zone of proximal development" (Vygotsky, 1978) or in "joint attentional processes" (Tomasello, 1988), adjusting her conversational support to the child's level of mastery. Other studies have found that through interacting with partners who are less "fine-tuned" to their linguistic level, children experience other forms of talk that may help broaden their repertoire of ways of talking (Tomasello, Conti-Ramsden, & Ewert, 1990). Cross-cultural studies of children growing up in non-Western cultures have suggested that even young children learn language primarily in multiparty interaction, and thereby challenged our understanding of optimal or necessary interactional conditions for learning to talk (Lieven, 1994; Ochs & Schieffelin, 1984; Rabin-Jamin, 1998). In this chapter, focus is placed on ways of talking in multiparty as opposed to dyadic interaction in families with young children growing up in two Western countries. The argument I develop is that to be able to discuss the impact of multiparty versus dyadic interaction on children's opportunities for conversational participation and pragmatic skills acquisition, we may have to take into account (a) the notion of speech genres, and (b) the notion of culturally specific tellability. First, speech genres are relatively stable types of discourse that may invite different sorts of participation. Some genres may be more frequently and complexly developed when more persons are present, whereas other genres may invite two-person interaction even in multiparty settings, such as the intimate secret whispered to the person sitting nearby. Second, cultures may differ with respect to what is worth talking about, for example, whether to make something known that is new to at least one participant at the dinner table or to elaborate on something already shared by the participants. With several family members present at the table, there is a greater chance of somebody not being familiar with an event, increasing a story's tellability if such tellability is commonly related to nonshared knowledge. On the other hand, if talking about something already known is culturally common, multiparty as opposed to dyadic interaction may not challenge other kinds of talk in this specific regard. I discuss the impact of genres and tellability by first examining whether the narratives and explanations developed at the meal tables in Norway and the United States differ in the extent to which they invite polyadic versus monologic or dyadic forms of talk. In the second section of this chapter, I examine a particular narrative topic, school, which has been found to be common in Norwegian mealtime conversations though infrequent in American (Aukrust & Snow, 1998). Narratives about school may be distinguished from most other narrative topics by the child being the one to know the events talked about the best, though other interlocutors normally, but not always, may have scripted knowledge of the event. School narratives are used to discuss how culturally molded tellability in dyadic as opposed to multiparty interaction has an impact on the development of specific pragmatic skills, for example, identifying different layers in communication or negotiating narrative accountability when challenged.

Why Meals?   In several recent studies, meals have been found to expose children to a wide range of speech genres—for example, narratives and explanations—and to local cultural rules regulating discourse, for example, choice of topics and genres, and turn-taking rules (Beals & Snow, 1994; Blum-Kulka, 1997; Blum-Kulka & Snow, 1992; Junefelt & Tulviste, 1997; Ochs, Taylor, Rudolph, & Smith, 1992). Meals seem to create culturally specific discourse environments in which children can both listen to adult talk and participate in collaboratively produced discourse.

Why Narratives and Explanations? Speech genres have been identified as basic devices for development and socialization (Bruner, 1996; Wertsch, 1998). Though they differ in their rules of organization, the narratives and explanations in which young children participate share some features—for example, being produced during conversational exchanges between interlocutors, in extended segments of text, and often over several turns. Narratives are organized around time, offering particular discourse rights to interlocutors who have participated in the narrated event themselves. Narratives may, from this perspective, invite less discourse cooperation in multiparty settings, but may on the other hand increase the possibility of some of the participants not possessing knowledge of the narrated event, thereby inviting discourse support and encouragement from the other participants. Explanations, establishing relationships between objects, events, or concepts, may in multiparty interaction benefit from the fact that the participants contribute different suggestions concerning why something happened or what something was like. Explanatory talk may, however, be a challenging discourse form with young children, and explanations may therefore invite scaffolded two-person interaction even in multiparty settings. There are certainly several reasonable hypotheses about how narratives and explanations as speech genres may "behave" in multiparty compared to dyadic interaction involving a young child. So far as Norwegian and American mealtimes are concerned, intercultural differences in the children's discursive experiences have been documented, particularly in the frequency and type of narratives and explanations, with Norwegian families developing more narratives and American families more explanations. Narratives and explanations seemed to serve as distinct cultural resources for Norwegian and American children during mealtimes (Aukrust & Snow, 1998).

Why Compare Norwegian and American Conversations? Children growing up in Oslo, Norway, and Cambridge, Massachusetts, share similar living conditions within many dimensions potentially relevant for the problem of how multiparty as opposed to dyadic interaction influences children's development of pragmatic skills. All the children in Oslo as well as Cambridge attended preschool for several hours every day, which gave the children daily experience of participation in complex forms of multiparty interaction involving children as well as adults who knew them less well than their parents. There is no documentation suggesting that the one culture favors either multiparty or dyadic interaction more than the other (as has been documented in comparative studies of other cultures, see, e.g., Rogoff, Mistry, Goncu, & Mosier, 1993).

On the other hand, comparative accounts of Scandinavian countries in contrast to the United States have stressed differences along some dimensions that may be potentially relevant for the study of relationships between different participant structures and children's learning of pragmatic skills. Though the study compares two relatively similar groups, the two societies afford a contrast between different forms of individualism, and related to that, a contrast between social and cultural homogeneity and heterogeneity. Considering Norway in particular, anthropologists normally agree on two variables that distinguish it from most other societies (Kiel, 1993; Klausen, 1995), namely strong emphasis on equality and belongingness to the local community. Eriksen (1993) suggested calling the democratic ideology particular to Norway "egalitarian individualism," which may be identified as different from the more competitive American individualism (Bellah, Madsen, Sullivan, Swidler, & Tipton, 1985; Lightfoot & Valsiner, 1992), though other authors have warned against the use of an overriding concept like individualism, pointing to the variation on the individual, institutional, and subcultural levels in relationships between the individual and the collective (Schwartz, 1994). Greenfield (1994) suggested replacing the traditional individualism/collectivism dimension with interdependence/independence due to its less ideological and more developmental connotations. Other comparative accounts (Löfgren, 1993) have stressed the importance of cultural homogeneity over diversity, as well as the existence of implicit and accepted rules about the qualities of good citizenship in Scandinavia, as opposed to the more explicit and foregrounded civic values in the heterogeneous United States.

However, there are no simple relationships between broad, sociological parameters of culture and the detailed parent–child interactions revealed in microanalytic studies. Many variables relevant to the study of pragmatic skills may mediate between broad cultural parameters and the actual interaction parents have with their children. Variables like social class, urbanity, mobility, and general rapidity of cultural change may influence the way parents interact with and qualify their children in pragmatic skills necessary for becoming competent members of the culture-to-be. Nevertheless, details of adult–child interaction, which generally have an invisible quality for the persons involved as well as for native observers, may become more visible through pursuing a cross-cultural approach. The cross-cultural angle of the study has been chosen to increase the visibility of practices that may be common to both cultures as well as those that are specific to each in the learning of pragmatic skills in either multiparty or dyadic interaction in Cambridge and Oslo.

METHOD

The study was designed to produce data on how family talk was embedded in cultural contexts. This was done by collecting family mealtime conversations as well as gathering information on parents' culturally based beliefs concerning how children learn to talk. The analysis of the mealtime conversations is focused on here, whereas findings from the parental belief interviews are referred to only when specifically relevant to the discussion of these conversations.

Subjects

Twenty-two Norwegian children (13 girls and 9 boys) and 22 American children (10 girls and 12 boys), with their families, participated in the study.[1] The families were recruited through the target child's preschool and were invited to take part in a comparative study of young children's participation in conversations. The children had to be between 2.9 and 4.0 years of age and speak, respectively, Norwegian and English at home. None of the families came from identified subcultures within either society; all the mothers were born in Norway and the United States respectively and the target children were monolingual.

The Norwegian children were recruited from six different public preschools offering full-day care, and located in a low- and middle-income suburb of Oslo. The first 22 families who agreed to participate were included. A majority (75%) of the Norwegian children invited agreed to participate in the study. The American children lived in and around Cambridge, Massachusetts, and attended any of several different preschools. A minority of the Cambridge families invited agreed to participate. Because the Oslo and Cambridge families responded somewhat differently to the invitation to participate, and as this element of self-selection may have generated samples that differed on key variables, a pair-wise matching procedure was adopted to ensure comparability between the two groups.

---

[1]The subject information offered here applies to the mealtime data. As interviews were conducted with only 11 of the 22 American parents participating in mealtime recordings, the cultural belief interview was, in addition, carried out with nine other American parents not otherwise participating in the study. All the 22 Norwegian families recording mealtime conversation did participate in the cultural belief interviews.

Social class as well as family constellation and size covary with ways of talking in families (Hart & Risley, 1995). A pair-wise matching procedure giving priority to maternal educational level as well as family constellation and size was adopted to ensure comparability between the two groups. Owing to differences in mean and variance of adults' educational level, as well as in family economics in Cambridge and Oslo (Hornor, 1995; Statistics Norway, 1998), the two groups of children were matched as a first priority with regard to their mothers' relative educational level within their own country. The second priority in the matching process was the number and characteristics of the participants in the taped mealtime conversations: whether one as opposed to two or more adults participated, and whether siblings participated. Four pairs were matched to just one of these participatory dimensions, the other 18 pairs were matched in both dimensions. As participatory constellation had priority in the matching procedure, the mealtime recordings were useful for an analysis of children's conversational participation in multiparty as opposed to dyadic interaction. Eight families in each sample recorded dyadic mealtime conversations, that is, between the target children and their mothers. The 14 other mealtime recordings in each sample consisted of mixed forms of multiparty interaction (see Table 3.1). Five Norwegian and seven American families recorded a meal with the target child and two or more adults participating. In four Norwegian and three American families, one to four siblings participated in addition to two or more adults. Grandparents, uncles, and aunts joined the meal in a few families, as well as on one occasion an adult friend of the family. Five Norwegian and four American target children shared their meals with one to three siblings in addition to one parent. Though the multiparty families were generally small (in Oslo varying from three to five members with an average of 3.6, in Cambridge from three to seven members with an average of 3.8), even a group of three is distinctly more complex than a dyad from the point of view of possible conversational constellations. The Cambridge data set consisted of 8,118 utterances of which 31.7% (2,575 utterances) were produced within the eight dyads, whereas the Oslo set consisted of a total of 7,914 utterances, with 32.1% (2,541 utterances) of these being produced in the family dyads. The amount of talk produced within the families of two as opposed to

TABLE 3.1
Participant Constellation During Mealtime Recordings

	Mother and Target Child	Two or More Adults and Target Child	Two or More Adults, Sibling(s), and Target Child	One Parent, Sibling(s), and Target Child
Oslo families	8	5	4	5
Cambridge families	8	7	3	4

larger families turned out to be surprisingly similar across the two samples in spite of considerable variation in amount of talk within each sample.

Mealtime Recordings

Data Collection Strategy. Each family was provided with a tape recorder and asked to record during an ordinary meal for at least 10 minutes. The fact that the meal was recorded may of course have influenced the mealtime participants. Even dyadic mealtime conversations may have represented subtle forms of multiparty interactions to the extent that the participants also implicitly addressed their talk to the nonpresent observer. However, we explained to the parents that we wanted to disrupt ordinary family conversation as little as possible, and care was also otherwise taken to make the situation of being recorded as ordinary as possible, for example, by explaining how to delete recordings they did not consider returning.

Transcription and Data Reduction. Audiotaped mealtime interaction was transcribed into computer files using the transcription conventions of the Child Language Data Exchange System (CHILDES; MacWhinney, 1991; MacWhinney & Snow, 1990). Transcripts were verified for content and were checked for adherence to transcription conventions, using the automatic checking facilities of the CHILDES system. Utterance boundaries were based primarily on intonation contour, and secondarily on pause duration.

Data Analysis. Coding and analysis focused entirely on narratives and explanations, leaving out the here-and-now anchored themes, for instance, conversations about the food and the ongoing interaction ("Could you pass the milk?"; "I need a spoon"; "It's meat loaf and this time I made it with ground turkey so it's really like a turkey loaf"; "I want you to sit down and eat a bite"), politeness and other mealtime rituals ("What do you say when you leave the table?"; "You have to say your grace now"), conversations about being observed ("now the tape recorder is working"), and giggling, laughing, and playful interaction, which occupied quite some time during the meal in several families. Some of these here-and-now anchored conversations met the criteria of explanations, like "Give me the fish. I love fish" or "Look at those mosquito bites on your back. They like you huh?" The percentage of utterances devoted to this immediate and partly instrumental talk that did not qualify as narratives or explanations was approximately equal across the Norwegian (55.4%) and American (61%) groups.

Narratives were defined as conversational segments combining at least two event elements along an explicit or implicit timeline (Ninio & Snow,

1996). Events in the past as well as the future were included. Narratives were also subcategorized in terms of space (home, preschool, "distant outside world") and time (immediate vs. more distant past and future) referred to. Conversational sequences in which the participants referred to events in the past or future—without, however, combining two or more event elements—were coded as seminarratives ("What did you have for dinner in school today? Did you have sausages? Did you have fish bolls?"). Such segments did not qualify as narratives, but including them seemed important because they clearly referred to a past or future event.

Explanations were identified by adopting a definition offered by Beals (1993):

> [An explanation is an] interactional exchange in which there is an indication by one party that there is something he or she does not understand or an assumption on the part of the speaker that she knows something the addressee needs to know; this request or assumption is followed by the speaker explicitly expressing the logical relationship between objects, intentions, events and/ or concepts. (p. 497)

The categories for identifying explanations were more specifically defined by some specific "questions of concern" drawn from Beals: "why I tell you something," "why I want or feel something," "why I am doing something," "why something happened," and "what something means/is like."

The Parental Belief Interviews

The "developmental niche" framework (Harkness & Super, 1992) has turned attention to parental cultural beliefs embedded in cultural customs and practices of childrearing. Such beliefs may influence the ways that parents organize daily routines for their children, and this was a starting point in the construction of a semistructured parental belief interview. The parents were invited to describe in as much detail as possible their conversations with the child on a particular day (the day of interview or the day before) as these were embedded in the child's everyday routines from morning until bedtime. The interviews, which lasted between 1 and 2 hours, were audiotaped and later transcribed. They are used here for the specific purpose of exploring parental cultural beliefs about narrative tellability.

RESULTS

Participant Structure in Multiparty Versus Dyadic Interaction: Does Genre Matter?

Children Participated Less in Multiparty Than in Dyadic Interaction. The observed meals in either culture had one extraordinary aspect in common with potential relevance for participant structure: The 3-year-old family member was participating in a language study and was the target person at the table. The recorded meals tell something about how families within and across the two cultures responded to this particular construction of a family meal. There was never more than one circle of conversation even in the larger families in either Oslo or Cambridge. Overlapping utterances on the tapes were in all cases part of the same conversation with two exceptions: On some few occasions, the target child was making playful noises while other mealtime participants talked, or a family member left the table to answer the phone. Though multiple conversations, demanding skills in justifying participant rights, have been found in other contexts of multiparty mealtime interaction (Blum-Kulka, 1997), the two-party and multiparty mealtime interaction observed here were not distinguished in this particular respect.

In both Oslo and Cambridge, the target child participated more in the dyads than in multiparty interaction. The Cambridge children produced on average 48.2% (range 40.6%–58.2%) of the total number of utterances in the dyads, whereas the corresponding number for Oslo children was 44.0% (range 33.8%–49.0%). The intrasample variation concerning relative frequency of child participation in dyads was generally small, suggesting that both cultures have conversational conventions protecting young children's participation. Even though the adult might have been the one to do most of the conversational work, the child was supposed to respond to adult talk by some kind of confirmation; otherwise the conversation would break down or shift to a different topic. There were no examples of clearly monologic talk by either the child or the adult in the dyads. The high level of child participation in dyadic interaction was partly an effect of the mother checking that the child followed her by waiting for the child to respond, partly an effect of the mother responding to the child's initiatives. Dyadic mealtime interaction inhabited more clearly the qualities of scaffolded interaction, characterized by the more mature partner adapting to the child's participation to ensure development of shared understanding.

The target children participated somewhat less in multiparty interaction in both cultures. The Cambridge target children offered on average 33.7% of the utterances (range 16.8%–53.9%) in multiparty interaction, whereas the Oslo children similarly had 34.9% (range 19.8%–49.7%) of the utterances in multiparty interaction. The still relatively high average level of child participation may suggest that the families paid particular attention to the target child as a result of being recorded, and may more generally reflect beliefs in the developmental importance of conversational participation. The fact that the target children who participated the least all came from families with older siblings, who tended to be more efficient negotiators of floor access, supports the last supposition. The variation between families in the target child's participation (in percentage of total utterances during the meal) was considerably larger in multiparty interaction than in dyadic interaction. Young children may in this respect be seen as more vulnerable in multiparty interaction. However, even though families varied in the extent to which they invited the young child's participation, different forms of multiparty interaction had in common that the child was offered opportunities for learning pragmatic skills not otherwise needed in dyadic interaction. Even just one circle of conversation in multiparty settings may demand skills in ratifying participant rights as addressee or side participant. Narratives and explanations not addressed to the target child, but to other interlocutors in multiparty conversations, offered the child opportunities to develop skills in interpreting such addressivity and in judging when and how to negotiate floor access as well as identifying such strategies used by others.

Narratives and Explanations "Behave" Differently in Dyadic Versus Multiparty Interaction With Young Children. Oslo families had a higher relative frequency of narrative utterances in the total sample (30.9%) than Cambridge families (16.0%), as seen in Table 3.2. Multiparty interaction resulted in more narrative talk in both cultures than did dyadic interaction. The average relative frequency of narrative utterances in the American families was 10.9% in the dyads and 19% in multiparty interaction. In the Oslo sample, the average relative frequency of narrative utterances was 25.5% in dyads and 35% in multiparty interaction respectively.

Cambridge families had a higher relative frequency of explanatory utterances in the total sample, 22% as opposed to 11.7% in the Oslo sample (see Table 3.2). Oslo families had more explanatory utterances in dyadic interaction (16.3%) than in multiparty interaction (9.1%), whereas there were no differences in Cambridge explanatory discourse when the frequency of explanatory utterances in dyadic interaction (21.6%) was compared with multiparty interaction (22.1%).

TABLE 3.2
Average Relative Frequency of Narrative and Explanatory Utterances, in Total Sample, in Dyads, and in Multiparty Interaction

	Narratives Total Sample	Narratives Dyads	Narratives Multiparty	Explanations Total Sample	Explanations Dyads	Explanations Multiparty
Oslo families	30.9	25.5	35.0	11.7	16.3	9.1
Cambridge families	16.0	10.9	19.0	22.0	21.6	22.1

In conclusion, there was more narrative talk in multiparty interaction in both cultures. The Cambridge families developed explanatory discourse as often in dyads as in multiparty interaction. Oslo families had significantly less explanatory talk than the Cambridge families, but actually tended to explain more in dyadic than in multiparty interaction. There is considerable intragroup variation, and the tendencies described are therefore clearly tentative. Nevertheless, the results do suggest that narratives and explanations may invite different forms of participation in multiparty versus dyadic settings, which is examined later.

Participant Structure in Narrative and Explanatory Talk. To describe participatory structure in narrative and explanatory exchanges, four categories were developed, with only the first two being relevant for dyadic interaction. The subcategories were distinguished on the basis of number of mealtime participants offering utterances that contributed substantially to the development of a narrative or explanation. The subcategories did not distinguish between different styles of interacting, for example, stories as conarrated, constructed through question–answer sequences, or told by a main teller with only sparse contribution from the audience. The category "one speaker" refers to narratives or explanations developed by one of the interlocutors. Also included in this category were exchanges such as simple listener confirmations offered by other interlocutors, like "yes" and "no," or an out-of-context comment ignored by the person offering the narrative or explanation. The category "two speakers" was developed to capture narratives and explanations provided by two interlocutors, offering at least one utterance each that was substantially more than a simple listener confirmation or an out-of-context comment. The category "mainly two speakers" refers to narrative or explanatory talk mainly provided by two interlocutors, but with one or several other interlocutors contributing a reduced repetition of a former utterance or a simple confirmation or encouragements like "mm" or "yes." The category "several speakers" refers to narratives or explanations clearly developed by more than two interlocutors.

The narratives in dyadic interaction were generally offered by both interlocutors (see Table 3.3). In the 30 narrative segments identified in the Oslo dyads, the target child participated in all of them, whereas in the 16 narrative segments identified in the Cambridge dyads, the child participated in all except 2. Narratives in multiparty interactions were mostly told in a way that involved more than two speakers in both Oslo and Cambridge. The category "several speakers" included more participants in both samples than the sum of participants in the categories "two speakers" or "mainly two speakers." Narratives told in multiparty interaction most commonly involved all or at least several of the participants at the table, and the target child participated in all of them in Oslo and in most of them in Cambridge.

TABLE 3.3
Participant Structure in Oslo and Cambridge
Multiparty and Dyadic Narrative Talk

		Oslo Families	Cambridge Families
Multiparty interaction	one speaker	1	1
	two speakers	11	11
	mainly two speakers	9	10
	several speakers	36	24
Dyadic interaction	one speaker	0	2
	two speakers	30	14

The participatory status of explanations was more mixed than for narratives (see Table 3.4). Explanatory segments were generally shorter than narrative segments, and a higher frequency of explanations was offered by one person in dyadic interaction compared to the number of narratives offered by one narrator in dyadic interaction. The average length of narrative segments was 27.9 utterances for the Oslo sample and 21.2 for the Cambridge sample, whereas the corresponding average length of explanatory segments was 6.3 for Oslo and 6.1 for Cambridge. If a segment is sufficiently short, less people will naturally be involved in developing it. However, a closer examination of the explanations did suggest that they also invited a different form of participation compared to narratives. Adults did more of the discursive work in explanations compared to narratives. Children, on the other hand, participated significantly less in explanatory talk than in narrative talk, or indeed in all-mealtime talk (Aukrust & Snow, 1998). When dyads developed an explanation, the adult and the child were most often both participating, though there were several examples of short explanations requested or offered by only one of them. Short explanations were also often found in multiparty interaction,

TABLE 3.4
Participant Structure in Oslo and Cambridge
Multiparty and Dyadic Explanatory Talk

		Oslo Families	Cambridge Families
Multiparty interaction	one speaker	22	43
	two speakers	50	77
	mainly two speakers	8	22
	several speakers	17	38
Dyadic interaction	one speaker	15	14
	two speakers	38	73

suggesting that participants in dyadic as well as multiparty interaction could offer or require an explanation without the interlocutors having to respond to it. In multiparty interaction, several different types of explanatory participation were identified. The most common participatory categories for explanations within multiparty interaction were "two speakers" and "mainly two speakers," reflecting the fact that the target child did not participate in every explanation. In about half of the "two speakers" explanations in multiparty interaction (34 out of 77 in the Cambridge sample, 24 out of 50 in the Oslo sample) the target child did not participate at all. Other explanations involving two speakers resulted from the target child requiring an explanation or the adult offering an explanation, commonly without other mealtime participants being involved in the explanatory exchange. In both samples, there were examples of explanations provided by several partners in the conversation, and the target child participated in most of these (with the exception of five cases in Cambridge and four in Oslo).

In multiparty interactions in both cultures, several family members would more often than not be involved in telling a narrative, whereas explanations commonly tended to be developed by just two of them. This pattern was found at the sample level as well as within specific families' development of narratives and explanations in multiparty interactions. However, variations should also be noted between families. In one Cambridge family, which included mother, father, and the target child, the father did not participate in any narrative talk although he participated in every explanation. All narratives in this family were developed by mother and child, whereas every explanation included the father.

Generally, explanations appeared as relatively short exchanges, most often initiated either by the target child or a sibling requiring an explanation, or by an adult spontaneously offering one, in all cases exchanges that would often not include other speakers. Compared to narratives, explanations appeared as a genre inviting more asymmetric interactions in both cultures. Parents seemed partly to create "pockets" of scaffolded two-person interaction within multiparty settings when trying to explain something to their young child.

Though multiparty interaction did not invite more explanatory talk, it did trigger more narratives. The families in Cambridge and Oslo developed many different forms of narratives, which were subcategorized in terms of the topic referred to, its distance in time from the present (close as well as distant past and future), and psychological space (events happening at home, family events taking place outside home as well as school events). Except for close future "distant world" narratives, a type of narrative that was slightly more frequent in the Cambridge sample, the Oslo families developed many more narratives within either narrative category.

The largest difference was related to family narratives about school, which were very common in the Oslo sample, but more rarely undertaken in Cambridge. The next section of this chapter examines pragmatic learning within such narratives about school in dyadic and multiparty interaction.

Narratives About School

Tellability and Novelty. The Oslo families developed 39 narratives about school, found in 18 of the total 22 Oslo families. Seven Cambridge families altogether related 13 narratives about school. The difference between the samples became even clearer when seminarratives about school were included. As opposed to 8 such seminarratives for Cambridge, 22 were included in the Oslo sample. The parental interviews further confirmed this tendency. Most Oslo parents reported that school was a main topic at home, whereas Cambridge parents on the contrary stated that their children never or rarely talked spontaneously about school. Furthermore, Oslo parents primarily reported talking about the everyday preschool routines of meals, play, and other daily activities as well as about who was involved in these activities. Several Oslo parents mentioned that the child would not "talk about special events, but more the everyday activities." What both or all interlocutors knew about everyday life seemed to possess tellability in the Oslo sample. Just a few Cambridge parents reported their child talking about school, as in the following interview excerpts: "He won't give you a narrative, very unusual. We would have to ask specific questions" or "She would never spontaneously talk of school. I really have to ask a thousand times." Some Cambridge parents argued that the child did not speak about school because "he thinks we know already, even if we were not there," suggesting that a school event was less tellable if the interlocutors had shared knowledge of it. School narratives therefore appeared as a useful starting point for exploring differences in tellability.

Mealtime narratives about school were generally related to an event in the near past, somewhat less frequently to the near future. Distant-time narratives about school events were rare in both samples. School narratives in Oslo as well as in Cambridge would typically deal with an event that the child had participated in recently, and of which the parents who had brought or picked up the child from school had some scripted knowledge; they were thus able to offer conversational support. In Labov and Fanshel's (1977) terminology, school narratives would most commonly refer to events that were a mixture of A-events (known only to teller) and O-events (scripted events, generally known). This distinction of focusing on to whom the narrated event is known is important for several reasons. Former studies (Blum-Kulka & Snow, 1992; Heath, 1983) have suggested that children growing up in cultural groups favoring A-event narratives are of-

TABLE 3.5
Number of Families Developing School Narratives
in Oslo and Cambridge Families, in Total Sample, in Dyads,
and in Multiparty Interaction

	Oslo Families	Cambridge Families
in total sample	18 of 22	7 of 22
in dyadic interaction	6 of 8	1 of 8
in multiparty interaction	12 of 14	6 of 14

fered a type of pragmatic socialization that qualifies them for the forms of decontextualized language they meet in school. Georgakopoulou (chap. 2, this volume) discusses the possibility of culturally specific pathways in the transition from oralilty to literacy. She suggests that the high value placed on shared, familiar stories in Greek families may constitute good preparation for acquiring literacy in an educational system with emphasis on form and the rhetoric of "how." In cultures emphasizing narrative novelty, school events may have more tellability in multiparty interaction, which is more likely to include interlocutors who do not know of the event.

Table 3.5 presents the distribution of school narratives in the 18 Norwegian and 7 American families that developed school narratives. The table shows that Cambridge preschool narratives with one exception took place in a multiparty interaction. In Oslo mealtime conversations, on the other hand, narratives about school were as frequent in dyadic as in multiparty interactions, suggesting that what was already partly known to the interlocutors possessed tellability to a larger extent than in Cambridge. However, though Oslo school narratives seemed to require less novelty to be tellable, they did not paraphrase what was completely known to everybody at the table. Rather they were characterized by a narrative style focusing on the unknown details of otherwise well-known everyday events.

Negotiating Whom They Talked About. A characteristic of the Oslo families was to elaborate on particular details that were not fully known to all interlocutors: *who* the child had been with, *what* had happened, and *where* the event had taken place. This specific narrative style is explored here in the negotiations about whom they discussed. Though generally more common in the Oslo families, this style of focusing on unknown slots within well-known routines was not exclusive to them, as the following excerpt from a Cambridge family illustrates. Negotiations concerning whom they talked about were in this case complicated by the target child's brother referring to a person at school that the mother was not able to identify. The conversation never developed into a full-fledged school narrative as the interlocutors did not reach agreement on whom they were talking about (scored as seminarrative):

Excerpt 1 (American multiparty interaction. Participants: Mother, older brother, target child Jim 3.8 years old)

(1) Jim: Mama my teacher said no.
(2) Mother: your teacher said no?
(3) Jim: <she said> [/] <sh(e)> [/] she said show and tell was [///] the bus man says Friday [!].
(4) Mother: Friday?
(5) Mother: oh.
(6) Mother: <who said that> Joe? [overlap>]
(7) Jim: <xxx [\]> [<overlap]
(8) Brother: no Bill.
(9) Mother: Bill?

The Norwegian narrative style tended toward mentioning a large number of persons at school who were most often referred to as surrounding the target child protagonist and less often as the protagonists themselves. Norwegian preschool narratives included references to 78 persons mentioned by name or position ("teacher"), not including references to mealtime interlocutors that could also be part of the preschool narrative. This narrative style was identified in both multiparty and dyadic family interaction. American school narratives on the other hand included a smaller gallery of people, 25 persons altogether. Negotiating whom they talked about was therefore more frequent in an Oslo than in a Cambridge multiparty interaction. Compared to Cambridge school stories Oslo narratives also exhibited a greater variation in who the protagonist was.

In conclusion, the differences between Oslo and Cambridge in the frequency of school narratives in dyadic versus multiparty interaction resulted from cultural notions of tellability (the value of novelty) as well as narrative style (populating school narratives). The closing discussion emphasizes the fact that multiparty interaction as opposed to dyadic interaction offered certain particular conditions for pragmatic learning in either culture. Multiparty interaction increased children's exposure to meta-levels when talking about school and increased demands on narrative accountability. This is explored in the next subsection.

Meta-Levels in School Narratives.   Teasing, irony, and pretence, often not addressed to the target child, but to other interlocutors seemed to presuppose an audience. Multiparty interaction thus offered the child opportunities for learning pragmatic skills related to identifying meta-layers in communication. Excerpt 2 is from a Norwegian multiparty narrative about school that included target child Liv, her mother, and a 2-year-older brother. The brother had formerly been in Liv's group of toddlers, but was now spending the mornings in a group of older children in a different part of the same school. The mother introduced a typical topic of conversation about who was present at preschool (Lines 1 & 3). When Liv mentioned the teacher, the brother gave the impression of not understanding to whom she referred (Lines 8, 10, & 12). The brother's voice clearly suggested an element of pretence in emphasizing that he did not understand who his former preschool teacher was and thereby maybe distancing himself from the toddler group. Liv's narrative contributions in Excerpt 2 were simple. Nevertheless, such narrative participation may have presented opportunities for learning pragmatic skills such as identifying pretence and deliberate nonunderstanding:

Excerpt 2 (Norwegian multiparty interaction. Participants: mother, brother 5 years old, target child Liv 2.10 years old)

(1)	Mother:	var Bente i barnehagen i dag da?	*(was Bente at school today?)*
(2)	Liv:	nei.	*(no.)*
(3)	Mother:	var ikke Bente der?	*(wasn't Bente there?)*
(4)	Liv:	var Kari.	*(Kari was.)*
(5)	Mother:	var det Kari?	*(Kari was there?)*
(6)	Liv:	nn.	*(nn.)*
(7)	Mother:	ja.	*(yes.)*
(8)	Brother:	Kari.	*(Kari.)*
(9)	Liv:	ja.	*(yes.)*
(10)	Brother:	Kari?	*(Kari?)*
(11)	Mother:	nn # hun *passet* deg når du var liten og.	*(nn # she looked after you when you were little as well.)*
(12)	Brother:	Kari # hva heter hun for no # Kari?	*(Kari # so what's she called again # Kari?)*
(13)	Liv:	ja.	*(yes.)*

Excerpt 3, another example of pragmatics learned in such negotiations concerning whom was talked about, includes, in addition to target child Per, a 3-year-older brother and their parents. The family had already been talking about Per's school playmates when the mother invited him to give a more extensive report and asked Per whom else he had been together with during the morning (Line 1), a typical way of building up an Oslo school narrative. The older brother as well as Per mentioned his best female friend (Lines 2 & 3). The father responded by teasing Per about this female friendship (Lines 5 & 7), whereas Per returned the father's comment by spontaneously creating a new expression "turtledaddy" (Line 9), thereby making his mother laugh (Line 10). In the further conversation the family was negotiating names of playmates, using nicknames in a teasing way (Lines 13–20):

Excerpt 3 (Norwegian multiparty interaction. Participants: Mother, father, brother 6 years old, target child Per 3.2 years old)

(1)	Mother:	hvem andre er det du har lekt med a?	*(Who else did you play with?)*
(2)	Brother:	Liv.	*(Liv.)*
(3)	Per:	Liv.	*(Liv.)*
(4)	Mother:	jammen bortsett fra Liv?	*(yes but apart from Liv?)*
(5)	Father:	turtelduene?	*(the turtledoves?)*
(6)	Mother:	hn?	*(eh?)*
(7)	Father:	er dere turtelduer?	*(are you two turtledoves?)*
(8)	Per:	nei.	*(no.)*
(9)	Per:	turtelpappa.	*(turtledaddy.)*
(10)	Mother:	turtelpappa [=! med en latter].	*(turtledaddy [=! laughing])*
(11)	Per:	turtelpappa.	*(turtledaddy).*
(12)	Mother:	<hja> [>].	*(<oh yes> [>]).*
(13)	Per:	<e pingvin> [<].	*(<and penguin> [<]).*
(14)	Brother:	hva da?	*(what?)*
(15)	Mother:	hva heter det for noe Per?	*(what's it called again Per?)*
(16)	Per:	Plavin (exp: child in school).	*(Plavin).*
(17)	Mother:	ja.	*(yes).*
(18)	Brother:	Plavin og Planin.	*(Plavin and Planin).*
(19)	Mother:	Previn og Prenin.	*(Previn and Prenin).*
(20)	Brother:	Prenin og Pravin.	*(Prenin and Pravin).*
(21)	Mother:	nei Per # vi sitter ikke og griser sånn oppi suppa.	*(no Per # we don't sit and make a mess with our soup like you).*

Excerpt 4 illustrates how a typical multiparty school narrative, concentrating on unknown elements within a very well known event, gave children discursive experiences that might help their development of pragmatic skills such as identifying and differentiating pretence and teasing from more straightforward information questioning (editors' note: see also Fasulo et al., chap. 8, this volume, on similar practices in Italian multiparty family conversations). Cambridge school narratives included several examples of teasing and irony during multiparty interaction, though less related to the more typical Oslo style of negotiating over whom they were talking about. The next excerpt originates from one of the few preschool narratives that turned into a distant-future story. Sara had just told her family she did not want to go to school anymore, and the older sister and father asked if she wouldn't miss her best friend (Lines 5, 7, 9). The sister's response (Lines 13 & 16) to Sara's expectations of having her best friend with her at college (Line 12) was one of social distancing in addition to directly acknowledging what Sara had said. This meta-level of teasing or slight irony was also present in the sister's comment on Sara's way of speaking (Line 21), "talking about college already," as well as in the father's response (Line 22), "never hurts to plan ahead."

Excerpt 4 (American multiparty interaction. Participants: Mother, father, older sister, target child Sara 4.0 years old)

(1) Sister: <so how come you do'-nt want to og to school anymore because of that?> [>]
(2) Father: <you do-'nt have any xxx> [<]?
(3) Sara: well (be)cause he give me a headache.
(4) Sister: oh [=! laughs]?
(5) Sister: would-'ny you miss all your friends?
(6) Sara: huh?
(7) Sister: would-'nt you miss Michelle?
(8) Sara: xxx Michelle-'is there!
(9) Father: well if you did-'nt go there you would-'nt see Michelle.
(10) Sara: go where-!?
(11) Father: to your school.
(12) Sara: # then if I go to college-! and she-! goes to college then +\
(13) Sister: college [=! laughs]!
(14) Sara: um.
(15) Father: sure they might wind up going out together and going to college together.
(16) Sister: in twenty years [=! laughs]!
(17) Father: well.
(18) Sara: and then I can see her at college.

(19) Father: you could?
(20) Father: maybe you will grow up and you and her will go to the same college.
(21) Sister: xxx talking about college already.
(22) Father: hey never hurts to plan ahead.
(23) Mother: everybody probably goes someday right?
(24) Sara: umhmm.
(25) Sara: I like college.
(26) Sara: I know about college.
(27) Mother: umhmm.
(28) Mother: talk about going to school at daycare?
(29) Mother: talk about going to bigger schools?

Examples of teasing and pretence in school narratives, which were found only in multiparty interaction in either culture, may have prevented the low level of involvement that may otherwise be associated with mastering well-known conversational routines. Teasing, irony, and pretence addressed to a young child may, however, run the risk of threatening the child. Clearly, the mother in Excerpt 4 was doing some repair work to bring the narrative back to the matter-of-fact level the child was communicating on, making the daughter's future plans of going to college something "everybody" did (Line 23) and something they might have talked about at school (Lines 28 & 29).

This discussion about teasing and pretence took as its starting point school narratives that were more common in Oslo, as were narratives in general. Explanations were, in contrast, a more favored genre in Cambridge. A closer look into the Cambridge explanations might have revealed that explanations were as important as narratives for learning the pragmatics of teasing and pretence. In Excerpt 4, the first four utterances were categorized simultaneously as narrative and explanatory, and provide an example of irony or teasing developed within explanatory talk (Line 4). It may well be that the potential risk of threatening the child makes such meta-layers in communication appear in the first round within well-known and favored genres, as illustrated by these introductory comments at supper in Excerpt 5, with the grandfather requesting an explanation in a teasing way (Lines 2, 3, & 5):

Excerpt 5 (American multiparty explanation. Participants: grandfather, grandmother, mother, target child Bill 4.0 years).

(1) Bill: time for supper
(2) Grandfather: why?

(3) Grandfather: why should I have supper with you (tone is teas-
                   ing)?
(4) Grandmother: xxx.
(5) Grandfather: why?

Negotiating Accountability. Though parents were generally supportive of their children's narrative contributions, they demonstrated in several subtle ways that they did evaluate the accountability of their children's
stories. The mother in Excerpt 6 did not accept the story at once, but either returned the preceding utterance of her child in the form of questions (Lines 5, 7, & 9) or confirmed those parts of the preceding utterance
that she could make sense of through repeating it (Line 13), thus offering
an example of one way of evaluating accountability:

Excerpt 6 (Norwegian dyad. Participants: Mother, target child Mina
3.10 years old)

(1)	Mother:	hva sier du?	*(what's that you're saying?)*
(2)	Mina:	alle gutta vil'ke høre på # de som /er der.	*(all the boys listen to# those who/are here).*
(3)	Mother:	de voksne?	*(the adults?)*
(4)	Mina:	nn.	*(nn).*
(5)	Mother:	vil de det?	*(do they want to?)*
(6)	Mina:	nei # da får dem bare kjeft.	*(no # the they just get told off).*
(7)	Mother:	hja # noen kjefter på dem da?	*(aha # someone tells them off then?)*
(8)	Mina:	n # xxx # alle de voksne må # skal være på # når vi skal gå ut og sånn da # da # da må bare tre-åringer passe på at # nn # at xxx # ikke pass på # dem må bare passe på tre-åringene!	*(n # xxx # all the adults have to # have to be on # when we've to go out and things then # then # the just the three-year-olds look after that # nn # that xxx # not look after # they're only to look after the three-year-olds!)*
(9)	Mother:	hvem passer på tre-åringene?	*(who looks after the three-year olds?)*
(10)	Mina:	de store.	*(the big ones).*
(11)	Mother:	n.	*(n).*
(12)	Mina:	mens de tre-åringene passer på de små.	*(while the three-year-olds look after the little ones).*

(13) Mother: n # må passe på   *(n # got to look after each*
               hverandre # må være   *other # be nice to each other*
               snill mot hverandre og   *and look after each other).*
               passe på hverandre.

Though these types of subtle adult story evaluation were found in both
dyadic and multiparty interaction, more direct interlocutor validation was
found only in multiparty interaction. The next example, Excerpt 7, is
taken from a Cambridge multiparty narrative. The family had talked
about a boy in the target child's preschool who happened to be the son
of the classroom teacher and therefore stayed at home with her on the
weekends. The mother's metacomment in Line 7—"oh!"—evaluating the
child's contribution, might have been addressed more to the father than
the child. The example thus illustrates one way in which the communicative interrelationships between three persons may be considerably more
complex than in adult–child communication, offering the child opportunities to identify and acquire verbal tools for validating narrative accountability:

Excerpt 7: (American multiparty interaction. Participants: Father,
mother, target child Sam 3.9 years old)

(1) Mother: well <should-n't> [/] should-n't he have his Mummy
              home with him on one day a week?
(2) Mother: <or two?> [overlap>]
(3) Father: are-n't you sad when <your Mummy> goes to work?
              [<overlap]
(4) Sam: what?
(5) Father: are-n't you sad when your Mummy goes to work?
(6) Sam: no.
(7) Mother: oh!

The presence of an audience in multiparty interaction seemed to increase accountability demands. In Excerpt 8, target child Arne was invited
by his mother to talk about a trip to a nearby pond with his preschool
group that same morning. In Line 9, Arne mentioned a skipping rope,
following his mother's question of whether he had been sledging down the
ski-jumping hill, while his mother in Line 10 explicitly corrected this contribution, trying to stick to the school story. When his older sister interrupted his story (Line 23)—"do you know what?"—Arne tried to keep the
floor by giving his school narrative a dramatic turn (Lines 26, 28, and 29).
He did this by telling them that his class had met an elk, and that he drove

straight into this elk with his sledge, which had a steering wheel. Neither the mother nor the sister accepted this turn in the story, with the mother arguing that he could not possibly have sledged straight into an elk, and the sister by confronting him with the type of sledge he had been using. Sledges like that, she argued, did not have a steering wheel:

Excerpt 8 (Norwegian multiparty interaction. Participants: Mother, sister 10 years old, target child Arne 3.4 years old)

(1)	Mother:	var dere på tur i dag a?	*(did you have an outing to-day?)*
(2)	Arne:	nn.	*(nn).*
(3)	Mother:	hvor hen da?	*(where to then?)*
(4)	Arne:	på Østtjern.	*(to Østtjern pond).*
(5)	Mother:	og har dere vært på Østtjern # var det no gøy a?	*(so you were all at Østtjern then # was that anything fun?)*
(6)	Arne:	nn.	*(nn).*
(7)	Arne:	og så aka jeg xxx oppi dumpen.	*(and then I sledged # hill)*
(8)	Mother:	å # aka du på hoppet?	*(oh # were you sledging on the ski-jumping hill?)*
(9)	Arne:	hoppetau.	*(skipping rope).*
(10)	Mother:	nei ikke hoppe hoppe # du sa dumpen.	*(no not skip-jumping # you said the hill).*
(11)	Mother:	tenker du på det hoppet som er i bakken?	*(do you mean the ski jump slope?)*
(12)	Arne:	ja.	*(yes.)*
(13)	Mother:	aka du # så tørte du det a?	*(you were sledging # so you really dared to?)*
(14)	Arne:	nn.	*(nn).*
(15)	Mother:	gikk det fort da?	*(so you went fast then?)*
(16)	Arne:	nn.	*(nn).*
(17)	Mother:	kjempefort.	*(really fast).*
(18)	Arne:	n.	*(n).*
(19)	Arne:	xxx # rumpeakebrett.	*(xxx # sledging board).*
(20)	Mother:	å # dere hadde rumpeakebrett ja.	*(oh # so you had a sledging board).*
(21)	Mother:	n.	*(n).*
(22)	Arne:	<vet du hva> [>].	*(<do you know what> [>]).*

(23)	Sister:	<vet du hva> [<].	(<do you know what> [<]).
(24)	Arne:	der bakken?	(that slope)?
(25)	Mother:	nei?	(no?)
(26)	Arne:	jeg så en /elg der borte ved siden a hesten.	(I saw an /elk up there beside the horse).
(27)	Mother:	nei så du en /elg? [=! ler]	(never # you saw an /elk? [=! laughing])
(28)	Arne:	også kjørte jeg på den.	(and I drove into it).
(29)	Arne:	med ratt på.	(with steering weel).
(30)	Mother:	nei nå tuller du vel litegrann vel?	(aren't you maybe just being a bit silly now then?)
(31)	Mother:	kan ikke kjøre på elgen?	(cannot drive into the elk?)
(32)	Sister:	også er # det fins ikke rumpeakebrett med styring.	(and isn't # there aren't any sledging boards with steering wheels).
(33)	Mother:	nei det gjør det heller ikke nei.	(no there aren't either).
(34)	Sister:	det hadde vært rart.	(that would've been strange).
(35)	Sister:	vært kjemperart.	(would've been very strange).

In this case Arne did not defend his story when challenged. The next excerpt (9) offers another illustration of participant structures in story validation in which the target child Jim stuck to his propositions, supported by his brother. Jim's mother had introduced a school story by asking if his best friend had been in school today (Line 1). Jim answered that she was not; her back had been hurting because a cat had "opened her back" (Lines 2–12). By recasting Jim's utterance (Line 13) his mother responded to the accountability of the turn in the story, whereas Jim maintained and developed his version by giving an explanation (Line 16), still not accepted by the mother (Line 17), but developed further by the brother (Line 18):

Excerpt 9 (American multiparty interaction. Participants: Mother, older brother, target child Jim 3.8 years old):

(1)	Mother:	so was Lisa in today Jim?
(2)	Jim:	no.
(3)	Mother:	no?
(4)	Jim:	she-'is sick.
(5)	Mother:	she-'is sick.

(6) Mother: what-'is wrong with her?
(7) Jim: <she> [/] <she> [//] her back was hurting her.
(8) Mother: her back was hurting her?
(9) Jim: like Rudy-'s.
(10) Mother: like Rudy-'s?
(11) Mother: why what happened to Rudy?
(12) Jim: a cat opened her back.
(13) Mother: a cat opened [!] her back?
(14) Jim: yeah.
(15) Jim: yeah.
(16) Jim: (be)cause she had a cat.
(17) Mother: oh.
(18) Brother: <y(ou)> [/] <y(ou)> [/] you mean broke him in half?
(19) Jim: just a little bit.

Though the parents were mostly accepting of their children's contributions, they also offered subtle and varied ways of commenting on their narrative accountability. Though prompting narrative factuality is by no means a universal norm of pragmatic socialization, as shown by Heath (1983) in her study of the Black community of Trackton, several studies have documented the emphasis different cultural groups put on children's adherence to factuality. Georgakopoulou (chap. 2, this volume) found that Greek children's participation in familiar narratives was characterized by a preoccupation with factuality and eyewitnessed details as a way of confirming one's co-ownership of a story. Similarly, Blum-Kulka (1997) found that Israeli and Jewish American families challenged narrative accountability by metapragmatic comments (as also seen earlier in Excerpt 7, Line 7) and by directly questioning the accuracy of a story if it seemed counterfactual (as seen previously in Excerpts 8 and 9). Heath suggested that cultural groups with literate traditions will more often insist on narrative accountability. The White working-class parents in her study of Roadville expected their children to stick to the facts when retelling shared events, whereas the middle-class parents in addition encouraged such factuality in stories about events known only to the child. Parents in both Oslo and Cambridge encouraged narrative accountability through metacomments as well as by more direct questioning the factuality of school stories. Furthermore, as has been the main point here, they encouraged such accountability more explicitly and often in multiparty interaction in either culture. Multiparty interaction thus offered the children particular opportunities to learn pragmatic skills related to defending (Excerpt 9) and moderating, changing or leaving a point of view (Excerpt 8), as well as identifying how other interlocutors supported (Excerpt 9) or resisted (Excerpt 8) their narrative contributions.

CONCLUSION

In this chapter I have argued that to understand the impact of multiparty interaction as opposed to dyadic interaction for the learning of pragmatic skills in different cultures, we need to include the notion of genres as well as cultural codes for tellability. The findings that have emerged from this comparison of Oslo and Cambridge mealtime conversations in multiparty as opposed to dyadic interaction are the following:

1. In multiparty interaction, target children participated less, but on the other hand they seemed to gain experience of more complex participatory roles. These roles varied from listening to adult explanatory talk without participating to fighting to keep the floor in a narrative about a school event that they had primary ownership of (like Arne in Excerpt 7).

2. Though narrative talk was a more frequent genre in Oslo than in Cambridge dinner table conversations, multiparty interaction as opposed to dyadic interaction seemed to trigger narrative talk in both cultures. Narratives told in multiparty interaction most commonly would involve several tellers.

3. Though explanatory talk was a more frequent genre in the Cambridge than in the Oslo conversations, multiparty interaction generally did not result in more explanatory talk. Such talk tended to involve two participants also in multiparty interaction, quite commonly without the target child participating.

4. Multiparty interaction increased the possibility of some of the participants not having heard a story or knowing about the narrated event. In the Cambridge families, this lack of shared background knowledge in multiparty interaction resulted in more narratives about school. In the Oslo families, however, sharing scripted knowledge about a preschool event did not reduce its tellability, a finding that was also supported by the parental belief interview. The Oslo families had a narrative style that focused on unknown details of otherwise well-known events, lending tellability to everyday stories from school, also within dyadic interaction with much shared background knowledge. The developmental impact of participation in multiparty versus dyadic interaction in different cultures can therefore not be discussed separately from cultural codes of what is worth talking about.

5. School narratives in multiparty interaction had a particular form of complexity that was not found in dyadic interaction. The presence of an audience seemed to trigger more teasing and irony as well as more direct

forms of validating the story. These findings were based primarily on the Oslo school narratives as the Cambridge families rarely developed such narratives, though the few Cambridge school narratives in multiparty interaction did support this tendency.

The discussion has explored some specific pragmatic skills that children may acquire in narrative talk. Negotiating shared understanding in conversations about nonpresent persons, responding to meta-levels, and defending accountability are relatively mature pragmatic skills. Though documentation of such specific pragmatic skills in the target children was sporadic and primarily suggestive of potential or emergent competence, the discussion has highlighted some participant structures, particularly in multiparty interaction, that may help children learn such skills. Explanatory talk did not increase in multiparty interaction as did narrative talk. However, within multiparty explanatory discourse children did become exposed to more complex participant structures than in dyadic explanatory discourse. This finding suggests that a closer focus on how children learn to explain in everyday multiparty discourse would be relevant to the pragmatic skills needed in later collaborative forms of learning in school. Explanatory talk was most commonly a result of children requesting explanations or adults offering explanations, either spontaneously or as a response to a request, whereas narrative talk more commonly resulted from either adults or children offering a narrative spontaneously. Narrative interaction was more symmetrical in this regard, with school narratives in particular representing a group of narrated events of which the child had privileged knowledge. Questions of culturally molded tellability, which were found to influence ways of talking in dyadic and multiparty interactions, also influenced opportunities for learning pragmatic skills, mingled with problems of ownership of events narrated and of the specific ways a culture balances asymmetric with symmetric moves in adult–child interactions. Though narratives and explanations as speech genres appeared similarly in dyadic and multiparty mealtime discourse in certain respects across these two cultures, the primacy of narratives in general and narratives that the child had privileged knowledge of in particular in Oslo, as opposed to the primacy of the more asymmetric explanatory genre in Cambridge, may be related to the broader cultural parameters of relationships between the individual and the collective in cultures that differ in the dimensions of egalitarianism and homogeneity.

ACKNOWLEDGMENTS

I would like to thank the Norwegian Research Council and the Home-School Study of Language and Literacy Development at the Harvard Graduate School of Education for support on this project. I would also like to express my appreciation to the parents and children in Oslo and Cambridge who contributed their time and conversations to this study.

REFERENCES

Aukrust, V. G., & Snow, C. E. (1998). Narratives and explanations during mealtime conversations in Norway and the U.S. *Language in Society, 27,* 221–246.

Beals, D. (1993). Explanatory talk in low-income families' mealtime conversations. *Applied Psycholinguistics, 14,* 489–514.

Beals, D., & Snow, C. E. (1994). "Thunder is when the angels are upstairs bowling": Narratives and explanations at the dinner table. *Journal of Narrative and Life History, 4,* 331–352.

Bellah, R. N., Madsen, R., Sullivan, W., Swidler, A., & Tipton, S. (1985). *Habits of the heart: Individualism and commitment in American life.* New York: Harper & Row.

Blum-Kulka, S. (1997). *Dinner talk. Cultural patterns of sociability and socialization in family discourse.* Mahwah, NJ: Lawrence Erlbaum Associates.

Blum-Kulka, S., & Snow, C. E. (1992). Developing autonomy for tellers, tales, and telling in family narrative events. *Journal of Narrative and Life History, 2,* 187–217.

Bruner, J. (1983). *Child's talk. Learning to use language.* New York: Norton.

Bruner, J. (1996). *The culture of education.* Cambridge, MA: Harvard University Press.

Eriksen, T. H. (1993). Being Norwegian in a shrinking world. In A. C. Kiel (Ed.), *Continuity and change: Aspects of contemporary Norway* (pp. 11–37). Oslo: Scandinavian University Press.

Greenfield, P. M. (1994). Independence and interdependence as developmental scripts: Implications for theory, research, and practice. In P. M. Greenfield & R. R. Cocking (Eds.), *Cross-cultural roots of minority child development* (pp. 1–37). Hillsdale, NJ: Lawrence Erlbaum Associates.

Harkness, S., & Super, C. M. (1992). Parental ethnotheories in action. In I. E. Sigel, A. V. McGillicuddy-De Lisi, & J. J. Goodnow (Eds.), *Parental belief systems: The psychological consequences for children* (2nd ed., pp. 373–391). Hillsdale, NJ: Lawrence Erlbaum Associates.

Hart, B., & Risley, T. R. (1995). *Meaningful differences in the everyday experiences of young American children.* Baltimore: Brookes.

Heath, S. B. (1983). *Ways with words: Language, life and work in communities and classrooms.* Cambridge, England: Cambridge University Press.

Hornor, E. R. (1995). *Massachusetts municipal profiles 1994–95.* Palo Alto, CA: Information Publication.

Junefelt, K., & Tulviste, T. (1997). Regulation and praise in American, Estonian, and Swedish mother–child interaction. *Mind, Culture, and Activity, 4,* 24–33.

Kiel, A. (Ed.). (1993). *Continuity and change. Aspects of contemporary Norway.* Oslo: Scandinavian University Press.

Klausen, A. M. (1995). *Fakkelstafetten: En olympisk ouvertyre* [The torch relay race: An Olympic overture]. Oslo: Ad Notam Gyldendal.

Labov, W., & Fanshel, D. (1977). *Therapeutic discourse: Psychotherapy in conversation.* New York: Academic Press.

Lieven, E. (1994). Crosslinguistic and crosscultural aspects of language addressed to children. In C. Gallaway & B. Richards (Eds.), *Input and interaction in language acquisition* (pp. 56–73). Cambridge, England: Cambridge University Press.

Lightfoot, C., & Valsiner, J. (1992). Parental belief systems under the influence: Social guidance of the construction of personal cultures. In I. Sigel, A. McGillicuddy-DeLisis, & J.

Goodnow (Eds.), *Parental belief systems: The psychological consequences for children* (2nd ed., pp. 393–414). Hillsdale, NJ: Lawrence Erlbaum Associates.

Löfgren, O. (1993). The cultural grammar of nation-building: The nationalization of nationalism. In P. J. Anttonen & R. Kvideland (Eds.), *Nordic frontiers: Recent issues in the study of modern traditional culture in the Nordic countries* (pp. 217–235). Turku: Nordic Institute of Folklore.

MacWhinney, B. (1991). *The CHILDES project: Tools for analyzing talk.* Hillsdale, NJ: Lawrence Erlbaum Associates.

MacWhinney, B., & Snow, C. E. (1990). The Child Language Exchange System: An update. *Journal of Child Language, 17,* 457–472.

Ninio, A., & Snow, C. E. (1996). *Pragmatic development.* Boulder, CO: Westview Press.

Ochs, E., & Schieffelin, B. (1984). Language acquisition and socialization: Three developmental stories and their implications. In R. A. Shweder & R. A. LeVine (Eds.), *Culture theory: Essays on mind, self, and emotion* (pp. 276–320). Cambridge, England: Cambridge University Press.

Ochs, E., Taylor, C. Rudolph, D., & Smith, R. (1992). Storytelling as a theory-building activity. *Discourse Processes, 15,* 37–72.

Rabin-Jamin, J. (1998). Polyadic language socialization strategy: The case of toddlers in Senegal. *Discourse Processes, 26,* 43–65.

Rogoff, B., Mistry, J. J., Goncu, A., & Mosier, C. (1993). Guided participation in cultural activity by toddlers and caregivers. *Monographs of the Society for Research in Child Development, 58,* (7, Series No. 236).

Schwartz, S. H. (1994). Beyond individualism/collectivism: New cultural dimensions of values. In U. Kim, H. Triandis, S. Kagitcibasi, S. Choi, & G. Yoon (Eds.), *Individualism and collectivism: Theory, method, and application* (Cross-cultural research and methodology series, No. 18) (pp. 85–119). Thousand Oaks, CA: Sage.

Snow, C. E. (1995). Issues in the study of input, finetuning, individual and developmental differences, and necessary causes. In P. Fletcher & B. MacWhinney (Eds.), *Handbook of child language* (pp. 180–193). Oxford, England: Blackwell.

Statistics Norway. (1998). *Statistical Yearbook of Norway 1998.* Oslo: Grøndahl & Dreyers.

Tomasello, M. (1988). The role of joint attentional processes in early language development. *Language Sciences, 10,* 69–88.

Tomasello, M., Conti-Ramsden, G., & Ewert, B. (1990). Young children's conversations with their mothers and fathers: Differences in breakdown and repair. *Journal of Child Language, 17,* 115–130.

Vygotsky, L. (1978). *Mind in society: The development of higher psychological processes.* Cambridge, MA: Harvard University Press.

Wertsch, J. (1998). *Mind as action.* New York: Oxford University Press.

Chapter 4

"Do You Believe That Lot's Wife Is Blocking the Road (to Jericho)?": Co-Constructing Theories About the World With Adults

Shoshana Blum-Kulka
Hebrew University, Jerusalem

Dinner table conversations with children are rich in explanatory talk about how and why people behave and things happen the way they do. In this chapter, I focus on explanatory talk as a potential family arena for the co-construction of knowledge and the building of theories about the world.

Studies of dinner talk (see Pan, Perlman, & Snow, 2000, for a review) have repeatedly shown that dinner conversations are an intergenerational, language-rich activity type, an activity that fulfills a crucial role in language socialization in the broadest sense of the term. It is an activity type that provides explicit and implicit socialization for, sociocultural norms, preferred practices, interpretive framings, and expectations that relate language to context, thereby promoting the development of discourse skills and understanding (Ochs, 1990). Our study of Jewish-American and Israeli middle-class families (Blum-Kulka, 1997)[1] showed, for example, that in modern, middle-class families both the direct and indirect ratified participation of children in family discourse serves as a pri-

---

[1] The study involved three groups of middle-class, college-educated families: two Israeli groups (native Israelis and American-born Israelis) and a group of American-born Jewish Americans. All families came from an Eastern European background, and had at the time of the research two to three school-age children. Families were observed in their homes in Israel and the United States. An observer from the research team participated at three dinners, taped the conversation (twice by audio and once by video), and conducted in-depth ethnographic interviews with the families on a seperate occasion (see Blum-Kulka, 1997).

mary mode of mediation in their developmental passage to the adult discourse world. Dinner talk emerged as a critical social context in which children become socialized to local cultural practices regulating conversation, such as the choice of topics, rules of turn taking, modes of storytelling, rules of politeness, and choice of language (for bilingual families). Alexandra Georgopoulou's study of conversational storytelling in Greek families (chap. 2, this volume) and Vibeke Aukrust's study of narratives and explanations in Norwegian and American families (chap. 3, this volume) lend further support to the cultural embeddedness of narrative performances and explanatory discourse. Dinner talk is also a crucial arena for the joint, intergenerational celebration of verbal play that helps children attain speaker position (Fasulo, Liberati, & Pontecorvo, chap. 8, this volume) and cultivate cognition (Nevat-Gal, chap. 7, this volume). Mealtimes can provide a rich context for bilingual language development (Blum-Kulka, 1997; see also Kasuya, chap. 11, this volume) and the socialization of cultural modes for the expression of affect (Herot, chap. 6, this volume). A central feature of the discourse in the academic, middle-class Israeli and Jewish-American families we studied is its overreaching "modern" orientation to socialization. In Rogoff, Mistry, Goncu, and Mosier (1993) terms, this means that guided participation in these families relies heavily on verbal modes of communication. Furthermore, the underlying discourse norms held up are also modern in the sense that they conform to Western ideals of rational and individualistic thinking, promoting discourse that conforms to notions of cooperativeness and coherence derivable from such ideals. In this chapter, I argue that these same norms also extend to many facets of the dinner talk of less highly educated families, namely those in which parents have not had access to university.

The database for the study comprises 186 explanatory sequences extracted from dinner table conversations in the homes of eight Israeli families during the winter of 1990–1991. All the parents in these families are high school graduates and some have continued their education beyond high school in professional in-service training courses. Both parents work outside the home. The mothers mostly hold secretarial jobs; one works as housecleaner. The fathers' group includes a policeman, a fireman, an electronic technician, two drivers, a video technician, a salesman, and a plumber. All parents are native Israelis, with two to three Israeli-born school-age children. The families were recruited on the basis of demographic information provided by the children's schools. The families selected were pair-matched on family constellation with eight Israeli middle-class academic families.[2] We participated in and recorded three meals

---

[2]The matching was intended to allow for twofold group comparisons, for the effect of parental education on family discourse. Preliminary findings from the comparative analysis of

with each family (two by audio and one by video) and on a subsequent visit interviewed the parents at length about parental beliefs and practices. One meal from each family was fully transcribed, in the CHAT system (MacWhinney, 1991), and served as the basis for the analysis presented here.

What Do We Know about Explanatory Discourse?

Broadly defined, explanatory discourse is some stretch of talk that can be interpreted as a response to a problematic state of affairs, implicitly or explicitly perceived or pointed out by the potential explainer or an interlocutor in the course of the interaction (Antaki, 1994). Barbieri, Colavita, and Scheuer (1990) defined "explanations" more narrowly as follows:

> [An explanation is] an interactional move that occurs when one partner offers a piece of new information (explanans) referring to an object, event or piece of information of joint attention (explanandum). This information clarifies what was previously obscure. The partner may directly express the need for it by verbal or non-verbal means, or the speaker may presuppose such a need for the sake of his/her own goal related to the on-going interaction. (p. 248)

The important point shared by Barbieri et al. and Antaki for the approach adopted here is their respective emphases on explanations as interactional moves emerging in natural discourse in response to some need or problematic state of affairs. It follows that the study of explanatory discourse needs to pay attention both to the sequential emergence of this type of talk (why an explanation now) as well as to its function relative to a given speech event (what makes it an explanation in this event and for whom). Hence arguably, child language studies of explanations need to be informed by relevant work in social psychology, conversation analysis, and discourse analysis.

Historically, such work has not been well represented in child discourse studies. The cognitivist paradigm that dominated social psychology until recently (see Antaki, 1994, for a comprehensive review of mainstream attribution theory) largely inspired strongly the work on explanations in child language, essentially limiting much of its scope to causal explanations. Because the nature of causal links was identified as a cognitive developmental problem by Piaget, questions such as the passage from psychological to physical causality have been linked to stages of cognitive development, and research has been mainly concerned with the links be-

---

explanatory discourse in the two groups along the lines presented in this chapter reveal highly similar patterns in terms of the incidence of explanatory sequences, types of initiators and explainers, and variety of explanatory domains.

tween types of explanations and mental representations (e.g., M. Donald-son, 1978; M. L. Donaldson, 1986). Psycholinguistic studies of the development of causal connectives in child discourse give this line of research a linguistic turn: The interest here shifts to the linguistic markers and the types of cohesive text relations they represent, whether in explanatory (Peterson & McCabe, 1985) or narrative discourse (Berman & Slobin, 1994).

Yet to account for explanations in natural discourse, we need a theory that takes into account overall structures of explanatory discourse as well as its multifaceted functions. The first condition is partly met in research inspired by genre theory (e.g., Martin, 1989), which has spurred interest in the ability of young children to differentiate among genres (Hicks, 1990; Zecker, 1996) and in the macrostructures and genre markers differentiation of their written and oral explanations (Peled, 1994).

The second condition, recognizing the many functions of explanations, is met by discursive social psychology, as attribution theory has been refined and challenged by conversational approaches to explanatory discourse (Antaki, 1994; Edwards & Potter, 1992; Heritage, 1988). The view of explanatory discourse as an interactional achievement emerges in child language (only in the 1990s) in work on the effects of context (in an experimental design; Donaldson, 1986), the beginning of explanatory discourse in infants and preschoolers (Barbieri et al., 1989, 1990; Veneziano & Sinclair, 1995), and—most relevant for our purposes—in the study of mealtime explanations (Aukrust & Snow, 1998; Beals, 1993; Beals & De Temple, 1993; Beals & Snow, 1994; Keppler & Luckman, 1991) and child–adult "science process talk" in playing with a magnet (Snow & Kurland, 1995).

This last line of work expands the notion of explanation beyond causality (agency "why" explanations) to include both "what" (descriptive, defining, and clarifying explanations) and morality explanations justifying an action or warranting an argument. Furthermore, it allows us to consider the interrelation of various genres in natural discourse. The shift in the study of explanations from the lab to the real world has enriched the field with studies of explanations in natural discourse in which children participated. Such studies—as, for example, Keppler and Luckman (1991)—explore the conversational work required for setting up one party as the "teacher/explainer" and the fine-tuning employed by explainer and the audience to ensure reciprocity of perspectives throughout the explanatory exchange. But this line of research in child language is still in need of enrichment and refinement both in terms of the available data on natural explanatory discourse in different languages and cultures and in terms of theory.

In the study reported here, we looked for stretches of talk manifestly oriented to by the participants as "explanatory." In other words, we tried to define the text type, or genre, rather than the individual speech act. Two main trends emerge from this exploration:

1. The scope of issues dealt with at the family dinner table in families where parents have only high school education is extremely rich, ranging from physics to metaphysics (see also Beals, 1993, for similar findings for American working-class families). This richness lends support to our over-all claim regarding multiparty, intergenerational family discourse as a primary site for cognitive and discursive socialization.

2. As an interactional achievement, explanatory talk is collaborative and symmetrical, with children and parents alternatively being set up conversationally as the authoritative source of particular kinds of knowledge. In other words, through explanatory talk children learn from adults and adults learn from children.

EXPLANATORY DISCOURSE

Preamble: Is There a Genre of Explanatory Talk?

Antaki (1994) argued that all explanations have to do with "making plain" or "making intelligible," the general principle being that what counts as explanation is "some stretch of talk hearable as being a resolution to some problematic state of affairs" (p. 4). But how do we know that an informative stretch of talk is "hearable" as an explanation? In other words, can we distinguish between "just informative" from "informative and explanatory" types of talk? From the point of view of dinner talk with children, this question is important on two counts: first, because it leads us to consider the issue of knowledge transmission in general and its relation to the specific genre of explanatory talk; second, because it requires attention to the degree to which the specific features of the genre represent literate, decontextualized modes of language use. A consideration of these two aspects can pinpoint the contribution of dinner talk to socialization in terms of (a) content, specifying what domains of knowledge are transmitted and negotiated during dinner, and (b) in terms of form and function, exploring whether and how the discursive modes of the genre promote the use of extended discourse (Ninio & Snow, 1996).

The argument, then, is that we need to differentiate between the notion of *knowledge transmission* in family discourse as a by-product of different genres of talk, and the notion of *explanatory discourse* as a specific genre of talk. In family discourse, knowledge transmission (in the broad sense used by Keppler & Luckman, 1991) emerges as the by-product of conversational interaction in a variety of genres, such as control talk, gossipy talk, storytelling, and talk manifestly framed as explanatory talk. The knowl-

edge discussed or indirectly transmitted may include multiple domains of
reality, concern nature, technology, human beings, ways of thinking, and
norms of social behavior, as well as cultural norms for topic selection and
turn taking, metalinguistic knowledge, and discourse norms for extended
discourse construction.

Consider knowledge transmission focused on the principles of "rationality" and "verifiability," both notions associated with modern scientific
ways of thinking. As a guiding principle, rationality penetrates several
genres of family discourse. It occurs as a by-product of several genres of
talk, not necessarily of talk identifiable as explanatory or scientific. The
emphasis on the need for rational explanations goes beyond reasons and
justifications that accompany many requests; we also find it in the language of explanation and definitions provided in response to children's
questions, where it is expected, and in the types of parental questions that
guide parent–child co-construction of narratives, as well is in segments of
talk framed manifestly as concerning the transmission or clarification of
knowledge and/or understanding.

Explanatory talk as a specific genre has to do with sequences of talk that
problematize a perceived lack of knowledge or understanding relevant to
the topic of conversation. The prototypical case is the answer (and the discussion that may follow) to a question that poses something as problematic
and requires a solution. But the question may be implicit or be posed by
the explainers themselves, the range of puzzles and solutions offered very
broad, and the sequential organization of how such talk occurs highly varied. Thus the methodological issue of identifying explanatory sequences
in natural discourse becomes a theoretical issue of generic discourse analysis. This explains why, instead of relying on available definitions of "explanations" in family discourse (e.g., Beals, 1993; see also Aukrust, chap. 3,
this volume), we chose to redefine the genre as explanatory talk and set up
a list of discursive indicators for its identification.

In the following section, we discuss the set of criteria developed for identifying types of explanatory discourse, listing the discourse indicators that
justify each type's inclusion in the genre, and, where appropriate, we point
to the implications of its use in family discourse as an agent of socialization.[3]

Getting in: Identifying Explanatory Sequences

Operationally, the main difficulty in identifying explanatory sequences is
in singling them out from all other informative statements. To this end,

[3]The study was supported by Grant 289/93-2 from the Israeli Science Foundation. Nina
Kheimovitch was the research assistant in the project, aided in the last stages of the analysis
by Anat Shelley. I'm grateful to Nina for her meticulous coding and many good ideas.

we first examined all instances of message-oriented or transactional talk, namely talk primarily focused on the transference of information (rather than on interpersonal relations; cf. Brown & Yule, 1983). Examining this talk with the idea of explanations being the response to some problematic state of affairs, we formulated a set of specific criteria for identifying explanatory sequences. Explanatory sequences were defined as stretches of talk of any length (ranging from one utterance to a long exchange) that include any one of the following indicators:

1. *Talk provided as responses to "why" and "how" questions:* Explicit queries of "why" and "how" are clear and unambiguous indicators for identifying explanatory sequences. In the family conversations analyzed, such sequences relate to a rich spectrum of knowledge domains and behavior for all present. For example, in one case a mother responds to a child's query about why he cannot turn on the television during that specific dinner, by referring to the recording situation, "What did we decide? Today we don't watch television"; and in another case, a child responds in length to the observer's "why" query about the origins of her name. The difficulty in identifying such sequences arises when an implicit causal or process explanation is provided in the absence of a prior verbal move to justify its sequential appearance. The following three categories list cases when such justifications are derivable from the types of speech acts used.

2. *Talk provided in response to explicit or implicit accusations or complaints:* The explanations provided in this category are not necessarily targeted to the party who initiated the speech act. For example, in a family with three boys, when one of them complains that his brother Eran is "stealing" his food, the mother laughs and addresses her explanatory account to the observer: "He is taking food from Robi. He has an exaggerated appetite." In this case, a reason is given for verbally noted misconduct. In other cases, the account is offered as an apology for a presumed norm violation, as when the observer explains at length the difficulties she had finding the family's apartment concluding with "that is why I was a bit late."

3. *Self-initiated or responsive justifications to requests, apologies, and refusals:* Coming from parents, the provision of justifications to parental control acts and refusals has been associated in the literature with the elaborate, literate style of educated parents, presumably typifying their person-oriented attitude to education (e.g., Bernstein, 1996; Hasan, 1992). It is therefore revealing to note the occurrence of this type of elaborate style in the discourse of parents with high school education only: Parents in the families examined here provide rational explanations in justifying and refusing requests in similar ways to the patterns observed for middle-class families (Blum-Kulka, 1997). Thus in trying to elicit a story from her 4-year-old, one mother grounds the request in the observer's wish to hear it

("Why don't you tell Laura about your summer camp? Tell her. She wanted to know which summer camp you go to"); and another mother justifies her refusal to allow sweets before dinner with the expected "No, you can't have [chocolate] now. You won't eat [dinner] later."

4. *Talk provided as warrants for disagreements and claims:* The identification of explanations used as warrants for disagreements and claims requires attention to the unfolding of argument sequences; in other words, explanatory discourse of this type is closely embedded in sequential context. Consider the following (abbreviated) example[4]

(1)
Family 2, Liron (7.11 f).
The family are reminiscing about the dogs they had.

1.	Liron:	ABA, (0.9) aba=	DAD, (0.9) dad=
2.	Father:	=ma?=	=what?=
3.	Liron:	=ha-kalbat (0.3) pincer ha-zot shelan::u (0.7) keilu (0.5) ha-pincer shelanu ha-hu?	=The dog (0.3) that miniature pinscher of ou::rs (0.7) like (0.5) that miniature pinscher of ours ?

((9 turns omitted in which the parents try to figure out which dog she means

13.	Father:	nu (0.3) haya lanu kelev ka[ze?]	Well (0.3) did we have a dog like [that]?
14.	Mother:	[lo↑] haya lanu sh- p[incer kaze,]	[no↑] we didn't have pin[scher like this,]
15.	Liron:	[ken, hay]a lanu kmo ha-gur shelo,	[yes, we ha]d like his puppy,

---

[4] Transcription conventions follow conversation analysis conventions (e.g., Psathas & Anderson, 1990) expanded to include markers for prosodic shifts, modified from Couper-Kuhlen (1999): [words] – overlapping talk; = latching; (0.5) – timed intervals; (.) – intervals of less than 0.2 seconds; (. . .) – incomprehensible words; (words) – transcription doubt; . – a falling intonation at the end of an utterance;, - a 'continuing' intonation; -? rising intonation at the end of an utterance; • - a rising intonational shift; • - a falling intonational shift; WORD – high volume; • word• - low volume; *word* – stress on sylllable or word; wo::rd – sound sustention; word- - cut-off; >words< - fast rhythm; <words> - slow rhythm; {word} – unusual pronunciation; #words# - unusual tone, indicated in a comment; word/word/word – rhythmic pronunciation; "words" – direct quotation; ((comment)) – transcriber's comments. All examples (except Example 2) were translated from Hebrew.

16. Father: (1.0) lo, ani:ani lo   (1.0) no, I:I don't remem-
              zoxer.=   ber.=
17. Mother: =gam   =I [don't remember
              a[ni lo zoxeret.]   either.]
18. Liron: [ani yaxo-] yaxol le-   [I ca-] can show you
              har'ot lax ta-tmuna.   da'picture.
19. Father: lo, ani lo zoxer.   No, I don't remember.
              [haya lanu kelev]   [We had a dog]
20. Liron: [(ze) ba-albom] shel ima.   [(it's) in Mom's album].
((3 turns omitted))
24. Mother: a a a:a:a, hi codeket.   O o o:o:o, she's right. The
              ha-kelev, shyesh tmuna   dog, that there's a picture
              shel Liron)mishe-)   of Liron (fro-) when
              kshe-hi ktana im simla   she's little with a dress
              al ha-deshe, leyad ha-   on the lawn, near the-
              [im aba (shel'xa) ve-   [with (your) father and
              na'ama.]   Na'ama.]
25. Liron: [ve-im IM SABA   [And with WITH GRAND-
              L'YA]DI.   PA NEAR] ME.
26. Mother: (0.7) ve-na'ama. (0.3)   (0.7) and Na'ama. (0.3)
              codeket.=   right.=
27. Liron: =ve-na'ama.   =and Na'ama.
28. Father: (0.6) ze koker spanyal.   (0.6) it's a kokerspaniel.
((continued))

This example illustrates the high degree of context embeddedness in this type of explanatory discourse. Liron's claim that the family had once owned a rotveiler is first conceded by the father (Turn 13) but rejected by the mother (14). When Liron insists (15), the father aligns with the mother in categorically denying ever having had such a dog (16 & 17). Liron begins to build her strong counterargument in 18 ("I can show you da'picture"), and when met by further opposition (Turn 19) completes it by providing hard evidence ("it's in Mom's album"). Thus Turns 18 and 20 are explanatory only in response to the mother's denial of 14, and to both parents' claim in 16 and 17. In Turn 24, the mother concedes Liron's point, grounding her agreement in further explanatory talk concerning the picture and leading to a succession of brief turns in full concert between her and Liron (25, 26, 27), leaving the father alone to disagree (28). Thus a stretch of talk definable as "argument" provides for the emergence of explanatory sequences that function as such only within this particular sequential context.

5. *Talk provided as response to clarification questions and self-initiated clarifications:* Many of the clarification questions appear in family discourse in the course of dialogic interchanges between young children and parents. In such cases, they are used to help the child construct a coherent narrative or explanatory account, and are highly dependent for meaning on sequential context. The clear cases in this group include responses to straight queries for an explanation (Young child: "Mom, what's a 'melon dvash' [literally, "honey melon" in Hebrew]? Mother: "That it is sweet as honey"). We also considered as "explanatory" cases that included some kind of elaboration: namely, cases where the speaker provided information specifically attuned to the other person's presumed state of knowledge. At one of the dinners, while looking at the advertisement pamphlet for a amusement park the father has bought tickets for, the father points to a picture and says "this is this car="; his son (7) cuts in with a clarification query—"that collides?"—and the father explains: "Yes, two people sit in [the cars] and they turn the wheel and they turn around and they collide." The type of elaboration provided here marks the father's style as "literate" on two counts. It verbalizes informational content in accord with the child's assumed informational need, and it does so in an internally coherent fashion.

6. *Talk embedded in narratives to explain the motives of the protagonists, and narratives used to explain an overall principle:* This last item is actually comprised of two categories. These illustrate the liminality of explanatory talk as a specific genre. In narrative analysis, explanations embedded in the text might fall within "external evaluation" in the Labovian tradition, or be considered as indexing the "plan of consciousness" in Bruner's (1986) terms. In the family talk, such explanations emerge as warrants for action (or nonaction), as when during a story round about the family's visit to an amusement park, the mother explains why she did not join the others on the merry-go-round ("I'm scared stiff of heights"). Narratives may also be told to illustrate some overarching logical principle and explanations may embed brief illustrative narratives. This genre mixing is important in alerting us to the difficulties of delimiting genres in natural discourse. On the other hand, it also shows the richness of modes through which family talk can serve an overall explaining-the-world function for children, paving their way into culturally shared communities of knowledge.

The best example of such mixing of genres comes from the family dinner of a middle-class Jewish-American family (Blum-Kulka, 1997). It concerns the parental response to the story told by 10-year-old Samuel, who claims to have seen on his school trip "a giant turtle" on the lake. As the exchange opens, Samuel's use of the word *giant* as a description of the turtle immediately triggers doubt, which gradually and systematically builds up to the explicit expression of disbelief. For a while, Samuel holds his ground, but with repeated questioning his account begins to lose credibility: His mother's challenge gathers momentum, systematically undermining each of Samuel's claims, until the final collapse of his story. Finally, the mother takes it upon herself to dismiss the account in unequivocal terms, to formulate the scientific principle behind the dismissal in the elaborate code of literate language ("That's called an unconfirmed assumption"), and to illustrate the result of the lack of critical thinking through the story of the four blind men and the elephant, concluding with yet another explanatory didactic exposition of the principles involved. This extract follows a long interrogative sequence (Turns 1–40), which finally leads to Samuel's admission that he did not see the whole turtle, only his friend did:

(2) Jewish-Americans 3; Samuel (10m); Jeffrey (6m).

40.	Father:	Now we have more of an understanding.
> 41.	Mother:	**That's called an unconfirmed assumption.** You know what that's worth?
> 42.	Samuel:	What?
> 43.	Mother:	Nothing.
44.	Father:	( ).
45.	Mother:	Do you remember the story of the four blind men and the elephant? I was about to tell you a story as I tell you now ((tells the story, concluding)):

> **And they all came to a different conclusion based on what area they were touching because they didn't have the entire picture before them. Had they seen, which of of course they couldn't do, that if you see the entire picture that's one thing, and if you see parts of it, you can't assume from that a whole picture if you only have certain parts of it (0.5). So, if you see a head of a turtle and a little bit of its body, you can't assume that it's three feet (0.8), if you didn't see the whole turtle.**

@ End.
(Dinner Talk, 1997:192–194)

The example is extraordinary in its highly didactic tone. But it represents the discourse values that underlie many of the adult–child interactions in all the families studied, including those with less formal education.

Based on the criteria detailed in the last section, we identified 186 explanatory sequences. These were analyzed in terms of the domain of explanation (building on categories proposed by Aukrust & Snow, 1998) and the identity of initiators and explainers as mother, father, child, observer, or any combination thereof. Initially one person coded all the data. Blind double coding of 10% of the data showed that agreement was easily reached on the identity of explainer (83%), somewhat less so on the identity of initiator (67%), and problematic for the classification of explanations by domain (50%). This category was, therefore, double coded for all sequences and doubtful cases resolved through discussion.

Treasures Found: The Richness of Explanatory Domains

The range of domains covered by explanatory talk in dinner talk in these families is strikingly rich and varied. In decreasing order of frequency, it includes the following:

1. *Social conventions (28%):* The social conventions discussed include home routines, game rules, and general social norms, as in the talk that follows Mihal (5f) question "When does one get married?"
2. *Physical objects (25.8%):* Most explanatory talk in this category concerns definitions of objects and specification of their function, as in the response to a child's question about the tape recorder: "What does it do? It records your voice" (Riki 7f, and the observer).
3. *Internal state (13.4%):* This category includes talk about feelings, wishes, perceptions, and intentions, as in a child's expressed dislike for being recorded: "I don't like being recorded (.) because I have this funny voice on the radio" (Yosi, 8m).
4. *Behavior (10.2%):* Explanatory comments on behavior often take the form of justifications for requests, as in the mother's explanation about why on the first day of school the children have to go to sleep earlier than usual ("Tonight you go to sleep early in order to get used to . .[getting up in time for school])" (Mother to children).
5. *Personal characteristics (9.7%):* Conversations with and in the presence of an observer may have had an effect in triggering explanatory talk of this type, as when a father commented to the observer: "You see, she talks to you freely. It's interesting you know—with new people [usually] it takes her [a long] time until she opens her mouth" (Father about Noga, 4f).
6. *Politics (6%):* At dinner talk this category can emerge in response to children's queries, as in the conversation that ensues from a child's question concerning terrorists: "Mom, I want you to tell me what they [the terrorists] did to us and what we did to them" (Ronen, 9m).

7. *Family history (3.2%):* Name origins are a favorite topic for explanations in this domain as in ". . . why were you called Yakir? -Because grandpa eh I was dear (in Hebrew yakar) to him. ." (Observer and Yakir, 8m).

8. *Metaphysics (1.6%):* Though few in number, the three conversations that ensue around issues of metaphysics are all elaborate discussions that last for several minutes. One of these deals with reincarnation ("Dad, what does it mean in the next incarnation?"—Ronen, 9m), one with folk theories about Lot's wife, and the third with belief in God.

These domains represent variation along two axes: The first is on a continuum from the present and immediate to the nonpresent, spatially and temporally distant explanandums. This is the type of continuum that organizes the distribution of topics of talk at family dinner (Blum-Kulka, 1997). It is represented by the shifts in moving from talk about physical objects in the immediate surroundings, through issues of behavior, social conventions, and politics to issues of metaphysics. The most immediate explanandums have to do with the physical surroundings of the setting itself, such as bringing food to the table. Matters of behavior may be slightly more distant temporally, as when the mother explains why bedtime needs to be changed in anticipation of the school year. Social conventions, such as the age for marriage, are even more distant, by virtue of being of general cultural, timeless validity. Politics represents a further removal from here and now: Though the domain is typically triggered by recent happenings, it often involves discussions that span across long historical periods, as when, following a terrorist attack, a boy of 9 challenges his parents to justify governmental actions against terrorism in general. The most distant point on this continuum is occupied by topics with no apparent link to the here and now of dinner, or even the here and now of this world for that matter, as in the discussion of reincarnation.

The second continuum is represented by the move from internal, individual concerns to external ones with the personal characteristics of the "other," and shared family histories. Topics explained on this axis move from explanations concerning inner states, feelings, wishes, and intentions of the self (like why a child does not like being recorded), to attributed feelings, wishes, and intentions provided as explanations of the behavior of others, and to more generally shared explanations concerning the family as a whole, as in the case of name origins.

The significance of the distribution of explanation by domain lies in the width and breadth of the spectrum that emerges. Regardless of who the explainers are, dinner talk in these families seems to provide children with ample opportunities to participate in discussions concerning a rich variety of physical, emotional, and social phenomena. But the frequency distribution of explanatory talk by domain is only one of the indicators of this richness in opportunities. Because the amount of talk and the participation structure in any of these domains can vary greatly, we need to consider the actual talk in more detail to appreciate its mutual contributions to all present.

Getting There: The Emergence of Explanatory Discourse

The analysis of explanatory sequences by identity of initiators and explainers shows the active participation of all present in this genre. Not surprisingly, parents provide most explanations (49.5%); but there is also a substantial contribution (20%) from children. The rest of the explanations are provided by the observer (14.5%), by both parents (7.5%), or by some other dyadic collaboration of those present (see Table 4.1).

The role of the children is much more salient when considered in terms of initiation (see Table 4.2): Children initiate over a third (37%) of all explanations. We take this high proportion to indicate children's active participation in setting up slots for explanatory discourse. Parents' initiations exceed those of children only slightly (42%). The rest of the explanations are initiated either by the observer (19%) or by dyads of one of the adults and one of the children.

To understand how these sequences actually emerge we need to look at the sequential unfolding of explanatory discourse. From the conversational-analytic point of view we adopted for this analysis, the issues involve the way in which conversationalists set up explanatory slots for themselves and others. In this view, one's utterance is assigned with a certain function (i.e., considered an explanation, an account, an exoneration, etc.) by vir-

TABLE 4.1
Explainers: Proportion of Explanation
Sequences by Identity of Explainer

Explainer	Frequency	Percentage
Parent	92	49.5
Child	38	20.4
Observer	27	14.5
Two parents	14	7.5
Child & parent	8	4.3
Observer & parent	5	2.7
Two children	1	0.53
Observer & child & parent	1	0.53
Total	186	100

TABLE 4.2
Initiators: Proportion of Explanation Sequences
by Identity of Initiator(s)

Initiator(s)	Frequency (n)	Percentage (%)
Parent	78	41.9
Child	68	36.6
Observer	36	19.3
Observer & parent	3	1.6
Observer & child	1	0.5
Total	186	100

tue of its placement in a special slot arranged either by the speaker him or herself or by another participant. Once a slot has been created, the potential next speaker must fill it. This obligation is so strong that any utterance placed in it will be interpreted as the second element of the adjacency pair. Thus the very creation of the slot imposes on the next speaker a certain pattern of behavior. In case the next speaker infringes this pattern, the previous interlocutor's expectations are violated, although his or her statement(s) remain(s) undisputed. For explanatory talk, the most obvious slots are created by what, why, and how questions that seem to invite some type of account (father to son: "What's this pajama night..?"; child to parent: "What was awful?"). The point conversation analysts stress is that anything said in response in the next slot (unless opening up brackets for an inserted sequence) will be considered as an answer, and manifest a certain interpretation of the question. Thus if a mother asks her son "How did your shirt get so dirty?" and he answers her with "This is a great apple pie, Mom," this manifestly "nonanswer" might be considered as evidence for the question being taken as an invitation for an account that the speaker refuses to provide, as further evidenced by a next comment such as "Stop the compliment and tell me how your shirt got so dirty." For family discourse, it is particularly important that the act of creating explanatory slots and filling them with utterances is likely to influence the interlocutor's status in the conversation as the knowledgeable party (Antaki, 1994).

   In the explanations emerging in child–parent conversations, interlocutors hold a priori unequal social positions as children and adults, and may hold unequal knowledge positions relative to the domain of explanations. Consequently, for child–adult communication we posit four major (though not exhaustive) categories: slots set up by adults for children, slots set up by adults for themselves, slots set up by children for adults, and finally, slots set up by children for themselves. All of these possibilities are manifest at dinner.

Adults Set Up Children as Explainers.

(3) Family 8; Uzi (10m); Itamar (9m).

1.	Father::	ma ze ha-erev pijamot amarta?	Whats this pijama night you said?
2.	Uzi:	ze::e... (...) [ba::a].	I::its .. (...) [I::in]
3.	Father:	[ma] [be-pijama?	[what], in pijama?
4.	Uzi:	ken, ba::a-. ((general laughter)) baxeder shel Gay, az hu hezmin oti, ve-od shte yeladim ve-anaxnu (0.5)	Yes, i::in- ((general laughter)) in Guy's room, he invited me and two other kids and we- (0.5)
5.	Father:	nu? (0.9)	Nu? (0.9)
6.	Uzi:	ve-anaxnu mevi'im et ha-pijama shelanu= ((another child asks for Pepsi, overlapping Uzi's speech))	and we bring our own pijamas = ((another child asks for Pepsi, overlapping Uzi's speech))
7.	Father:	= ma, be- be-emca ha-yom? ((surprised tone of voice))	=What, in the middle of the day? ((surprised tone of voice))
8.	Uzi:	lo, be-yom shabat, shishi shabat.	No, on Saturday, Friday and Saturday
9.	Father:	ken? ve ima shelo marsha? (4.12)	Yes, and his mother agrees? (4.12)
10.	Itamar:	anaxnu na'ase erev e::eh (2.40) e:eh kita.	We shall have a class e::eh (2.40) e::eh evening.

In Example 3, the slot for Uzi to provide an explanation is set up by the father asking a question referring back to a topic mentioned earlier (Turn 1). As soon as the slot has been set up, Uzi proceeds to fill it with an explanation (Turns 5 and 7), thus fully observing the cooperative principle and circumventing the father's sarcastic keying in 4 and the other participants' gleeful response to this keying. Turns 6, 8, and 10 reinforce this slot, making sure that Uzi provides a satisfactory explanation. Interestingly, in this example it is the adult who orients to the child as having authority over a certain type of knowledge, setting him up as the authoritative source for matters that have to do with his social world.

Adults Set Up Themselves as Explainers.   According to Antaki (1994), when the speaker acts against his or her interlocutor's expectations, he or she often finds it necessary to set up a slot to account for this contradiction. This claim is illustrated by Example 3, where the slot not only is set up by the explainer herself, but seems to be "built into" her statement, because she is neither asked for an explanation nor indicates that she is going to provide one.

(4) Family 7. Yakir, (8m); Einat (11f).

1.	Mother:	Einat, tishmeu, hayom atem matxilim lishon muk<u>dam</u> kedey lehitragel hayom ve-maxar. ((to the observer))> kol yom hem yeshenim be-shte↑ym esre>	Einat, listen, tonight you go to sleep early in order to get used to it today and tomorrow. ((to the observer)) >Everyday (now) they go to sleep at twe?lve>.
2.	Observer:	ah ze be'emet meuxar (...)	Ah thats very late (...)
3.	Mother:	(...)lo maclixim lacet.	(...)They don't manage to get out.

The fragment opens with the statement that apparently contradicts the child's desires (Turn 1). Being aware of that fact, the mother attaches to her statement the explanation that seems to be intended to preempt arguing with her children (". . . in order to get used to it today and tomorrow"), and then goes on to expand the explanation in a way that takes into account the observer's perspective ("Everyday now [during holidays] they go to sleep at twelve"). This fragment can serve as an example of an elaborated code in which parents do not take children's compliance for granted, and rely on verbal means to justify their requests. In Bernstein's (1971) terms, it is a code "which is generated by a form of social relationship which does not necessarily presuppose . . . shared, self-consciously held identifications with the consequence that much less is taken for granted" (p. 90). As Example (4) illustrates, sometimes the speaker does not build a slot on his or her own, but rearranges the one set up by the interlocutor.

Slot Rearrangement.

(5) Family 7; Yakir (8m).

1.	Yakir:	ima, ani roce avokado.	Mom, I want some avocado.

2.	Mother:	od? bevaka<u>sha</u>.	More? Here you <u>are.</u>
3.	Yakir:	kama aba axal?	How much did Dad eat?
4.	Mother:	anaxnu lo sofrim kama oxlim, Yakir.	We don't count how much one eats, Yakir.
		Kol exad she-yoxal kama she-hu roce.	Everyone can eat as much as they want to.
		<u>labriut,</u> toxlu::u kama she 'tem ((atem)) rocim.	<u>Enjoy,</u> e::at as much as you ((plural)) feel like.

In family discourse, parents trying to transmit educational messages use the rearrangement option. Thus instead of answering Yakir's question in Turn 3 ("How much did Dad eat?"), his mother uses the slot, provided by him, to invoke the underlying familial social norms that actually make the question obsolete. Adults set themselves up as explainers for a variety of functions: to justify requests (Example 3) and to teach social norms (Example 4) and, more generally, to provide elaborations on any bit of knowledge considered important.

Children Set Up Adults as Explainers.

(6) Family 7; Einat (11f); Yakir (8m).

1.	Mother:	ze haya be-pesax, ze haya nora (3.1)	It was during pesach, it was awful (3.1).
2.	Yakir:	ima ma nora? (1.9)	Mom what's awful? (1.9)
3.	Mother:	be-argentina haya picuc.(2.1) mexablim pocecu et ha::a konsulya ha-israelit.	There was a bomb in Argentina. (2.1) terrorists blew up the:e Israeli consulate.
4.	Yakir:	ma ze "konsula"?	What's "consula"? ((mispronouncing the word))
5.	Mother:	kun<u>sulya</u>. be-kol medina she israel be-shalom ita az yesh- (0.5) kmo she-Yoshi haya be argentina? Yoshi ha-dod, ax shel aba, haya be argentina?	((kunsulya)) Con<u>sulate</u> ((correcting Yakir)). In every country Israel is at peace with there is- (0.5) Like Yoshi was in Argentine, uncle Yoshi, dad's brother, was in Argentina?
6.	Yakir:	nu	nu

7. Mother: yesh kol miney pkidim   And there are all kinds of
            bxirim she::eh garim   senior civil servants who
            kol arba shanim   live every four years
            be-ba-aracot ha-ele >ve   in these countries >and
            nikra'im diplomatim<   are called diplomats<
            she hem e::eh meka-   and they e:eh connect
            shrim beyn israel   Israel with other
            le-medinot >axerot<   >countries< °and all that°.
            °ve kol ze°. hevanta?   Do you understand?

((Einat initiates a topic shift))

Example 6 represents the prototypical case of a child asking an information question, thereby setting up a slot for his parent to explain. Thus the
traditional roles of parents as experts and children as novices are clearly
maintained (Keppler & Bergman, 1990), with the parent being the authoritative source of knowledge first on current events and next on the
structure of democracies. Note the fine-tuning of the mother to the child's
perspective: She begins with a general statement that is like a formal definition, and retracts to a concrete personal example she expects her son to
relate to (which he does in Turn 6), using it as a springboard to provide
the generalization in Turn 7.

Example 7 shows again that children's setting up of adults as explainers
may serve a variety of functions: Whereas in Example 6 it initiates a teaching sequence, in Example 7 it becomes the site of a negotiation about the
justification of a past parental decision concerning the child. The child is
the one who introduces the complainable item (Turn 3), and the parent is
expected to provide an account. The situation is complicated by the observer's involvement. It is she to whom Einat ostensibly complains about
spending an extra year at kindergarten, but the mother identifies herself
as the targeted audience. The mother is thus speaking to a double audience, phrasing her comments first in general terms (Turn 4) and then addressing them to the observer (Turn 6), but indirectly targeting the child
(Turn 6; "And I think she gained [from the delay]").

(7) Family 7; Einat (11f)

1. Einat: ani gam hayiti crixa   I also was supposed to go
            la'alot le::eh zayin,   into the::e seventh grade,
            aval ani ola le-[vav].   but I'm going to [sixth
                                          grade]
                                          ((addressing the
                                          observer)).

2. Mother: [lo], at lo   [No], you were
                     hayit <crixa<. at   not>supposed to>. You
                     noladt be yanuar   were born
                     ve ze ha-ta'arix shelax.   in January and thats your
                     hi- hi yaxasit gdola.   date. She-she is relatively
                                                      big.

3. Einat: >aval at hish'art oti   >But you left me for an
                     shana ba-gan.<   (extra) year in preschool.>

4. Mother: lo.(1.6) lo hayta brera,   No. (1.6) There was no
                     le-yelide yanuar, (2.16)   choice, those born in Janu-
                     >xayavim lehishaer°   ary (2.16) >must stay back
                     shana°<. ad december.   the °year°<. To the end of
                     ad sof december, ovrim   December, to the end of
                     shana.   December you go on to the
                                                      next year.

5. Observer: ah, az hi bidiyuk   Ah, so she's right on the
                     be-gvul.   borderline.

6. Mother: bidiyuk. <yelidat   Exactly, >she has been
                     yanuar<, ve le-   born in January<, and I
                     da'ati hi hirv↑ixa.   think she gained
                                                      (from the delay).

Children Set Up Themselves as Explainers.

(8) Family 6; Nimrod (7m)

1. Mother: > lo, Nimrod, ani micta   >No, Nimrod I'm sorry,
                     eret, lo axshav<.   not now.<
                                                      ((Nimrod is about to turn
                                                      on the TV))

2. Nimrod: lama?=   Why?=

3. Father: =lo [axshav].   =Not [now].

4. Mother: [kaxa]. ma hexlatnu?   [Because.] What
                     she-hayom anaxnu   have we decided? That
                     lo cofim ba- televi[zya].   today we don't watch [TV].

5. Nimrod: [ani]   [I]
                     yodea, ani yodea lama,   know, I know why, I know.
                     ani yodea. biglal hi (...)   Because she (...) will tape
                     taklit sratim mecuyarim.   cartoons.

6. Mother: [naxon.]   [Right.]

7. Observer: [naxon] ((laughs))   [Right.]((laughs))
              bidiyuk ha-inyan.   That's the point.
8. Father: ve-xuc mize (...)   And besides it's (...)

Example 8 represents a rather unusual situation whereby it is the child who seems eager to justify a parental prohibition. This example may be analyzed in two different ways: First, the child, willing to provide an explanation that is likely to be approved by his parents, creates a slot for doing so (Turn 2) and fills it successfully, though not very coherently, (turn 5), disregarding his parents' response. On the other hand, however, what Nimrod is doing might be classified as slot taking. In other words, he fills the slot set up by his mother initially meant for her to provide him an explanation. This explains why Nimrod works so hard to arrange the slot, by repeating three times "I know," as if he were asking for permission to provide an explanation that he is actually not expected to give. Its noteworthy that the mother and the observer fully cooperate with Nimrod's explanation, though besides being unclear (does he mean that she'll be using the TV, or does he mean that she'll tape the cartoons that he would have watched?) it is also obviously untrue.

(9) Family 6; Riki (6f); Nimrod (7m)

1. Nimrod: Ima rega ima ani asiti   Mom wait I've done
              (...)   (...)
2. Riki: [ana][shim kvar]   [Peo][ple already]
              (...)merov she ze::e   (...) because it i::is
3. Nimrod: [WAIT A
              [REGA::A!]   ima naxon   SECOND!]   Mom right I
              ani alalti ((aliti)) le-   got up on something
              mashehu meod mafxid.   very scary? You know
              At yoda'at ma ze?   what it is?
4. Mother: °ma?°   °What?°
5. Nimrod: at omedet betox nadne   You stand inside a swing,
              da, ze gavoa gavoa at   its high high up you see
              roa et kol ha-luna park   the whole Luna Park from
              me-lema'ala, boi tir'i   above, come see only there
              rak yesh min-   is a kind of-
6. Mother: => karusela<   =<Merry-go-round>
7. Nimrod: karusela kazot ve le-kol   such a merry-go-round and
              exad yesh xut yesh et   everyone has a string he
              ze=   has got it=
8. Mother: [=mitkan yeshiva].   [=a seat].

9.	Nimrod:	[koshrim otax be ze] ata tofes ve #pit'om hem ma'alim et ze lema'ala le[ma'ala lema-]#	[They tie you up] you hold on and ((shifts his tone of voice and tries to sound scary)) #suddenly they raise it high [high up-]#
10.	Mother:	[ve-moridim.]	[And bring it down]
11.	Nimrod:	(....)	(....)
12.	Riki:	IMA, ZE RAK ad gil shmone.	Mom IT'S ONLY only up to the age of eight.

Example 9 is illustrative again of how narratives and explanations can merge into each other. In telling about his experiences on the merry-go-round, Nimrod finds it necessary to describe in detail the way the ride is constructed. The child is clearly the one who sets himself up as the explainer by using a presequence to confirm that his mother really needs such explanation and is willing to accept it (Turns 3 and 4). In other words, as in other cases of openings for extended discourse, the child assigns his parent the task of setting up a slot for him to fill, and then accepts his or her cooperation in collaboratively constructing the explanatory/narrative discourse.

Examples 3 to 9 show four different configurations in the emergence of explanations: children and adults setting themselves up as explainers, and children and adults setting each other up as explainers. The larger significance of these patterns (and the usefulness of conversation analysis in revealing them) lies in what they tell us about the distribution of knowledge that gets discussed and clarified in family discourse and the shifting roles of expert and novice as a function of the types of knowledge concerned. Thus children are the experts on matters concerning their social world, like pajama parties, but adults are the experts on world knowledge, like consulates. So we can see that explanatory sequences are a rich resource for many types of learning. Nowhere is this more apparent than in cases where the explanatory sequence concerns epistemological issues of personal interest to the child. In the next section we analyze two such cases.

**Being There: Discussing Epistemological Matters
of Personal Concern**

(10) Family 2; Liron (7f); Matan (4m).

1.	Liron:	at- at ma'amina le-ze she-amru be- xadashot be-sof shavua	Do- do you believe what they said on the news this weekend about e::eh,

		al e::eh, be-derex le yam ha- melax?	on the road to the Dead Sea?
2.	Observer:	°ma amru? °=	°What did they say° ?=
3.	Liron:	=she-eshet lot e::eh a::ah nu (1.44) ha-pesel she-hafax le::eh-lihiyot e::eh (1.25) naciv melax?	=That Lot's wife, e::eh a::ah nu (1.44) this statue that became e:eh (1.25) a salt pellar?
4.	Mother:	<u>neciv</u> melax ((correcting her))	salt <u>pillar</u> ((correcting her))
5.	Liron:	<u>neciv</u> melax? az omrim she-hi zaza, ve lo notet ((notenet)) le - anashim lehikanes be-yam ha-melax.	salt <u>pillar</u>. So they said that she is moving and does not let people go into the Dead sea.
6.	Observer:	ah ken? ((laughs)) (4.25) at ma'amina le-ze? lo? (2.5)	Oh really? ((laughs)) (4.25) Do you believe that? You don't? (2.5)
. .			
7.	Liron:	ula- pa'am ani sha'alti ota ve hi amra ulay biglal (...) [aval ze lo yaxol lihyot]	Mayb- I've asked her and she told me, maybe it was because of (...) [but it can't be]
8.	Father:	[ulay ze biglal] ha-<u>saxaf</u> shel ha-mayim shel ha-geshem she haya.	[Maybe, it was because] of the <u>erosion</u> ((caused)) by the rain water.
9.	Liron:	(...)?	(...)?
10.	Father:	ze::eh	I::it's
11.	Mother:	HI LO MA'AMINA [SHE-ZE BE'EMET PESEL shel esh-eshet lot].	SHE DOESN'T BELIEVE [THAT IT IS INDEED LOT'S WIFE'S STATUE]. ((someone overlaps the mother's speech))
12.	Father:	aval ze::eh [(...)](...), lo?	But it's [(...)] (...), isn't it?
13.	Liron:	[ANI MA'AMINA she-ze-]	[I BELIEVE it is-]
14.	Mother:	VE YESH <u>DMUT</u> [SHE - SHE- NIR'ET KMO], AZ HI LO MA'AMINA [she-ze be'emet eshet lot]	AND THERE IS A <u>FIGURE</u> [TH---AT LOOKS LIKE] SO SHE DOES NOT BELIEVE, [that it's really is Lot's wife]

15.	Father:	[ken, dmut, barur] az bseder gam be- televizya kor'im le- ze eshet lot.	[There is a figure, it's obvious]. So OK, they also call it 'Lot's wife' on TV too.
16.	Liron:	LO, A[NI::I -]	NO, [I::I]
17.	Mother:	[ki ze] dom↑e. >amarti la she ze kmo mearat ha-netifim.gam be- mearat ha- netifim yesh <	[because] there is a resemblance. >I told her that it is like in a stalactite cave. In a stalactite cave as well there are<
18.	Liron:	lo, ima, ani ma'amina she ze eshet lot, aval ani lo ma'amina she hi yexola lo latet lahem lehagid le-anashim "al tikansu le [yam ha-melax."]	No, Mom, I believe that it's is Lot's wife, but I don't believe that she can hold people back, tell them "don't go into the [Dead sea".]
19.	Mother:	[lo, HA-KAVANA SHE-]	[No, THEY MEANT THAT-]
20.	Father:	[lo, hi lo notenet] me-bxinat ze she-omrim she- hi alula lehitmotet al ha-kvish. at mevina? ze ha- ze ha-kavana shelahem.	[No, she holds them back in the sense that they say she is likely to collapse onto the road. You see? Thats thats- what they mean.
21.	Mother:	kshe mexonit overet [ze alul lehitmotet al (...)]	When a car passes [it might collapse on (...)]
22.	Father:	[hevant? Lo, ze karov le- kvish], ve im ze be'emet yitmotet ze mesukan. ((topic shift))	[You see? No, it's close to the road], and if it really collapses, its dangerous.

This example requires some background. The coast of the Dead Sea is rich in various rock-salt formations. One of these resembles a human fig-ure, and is popularly known as "Lot's wife," invoking the biblical story of Sodom and Gomorrah. Lot's wife in the biblical story was punished for not obeying God's instruction not to look back while fleeing from Sodom: "He said: Escape for thy life; look not behind thee" (Genesis, 18:17), "but his wife looked back from behind him, and she became a pillar of salt" (Genesis 18:26). In contrast to the long monologue of Example 2, we have here an explanatory sequence unfolding in a diaologic mode, focused on clarifying for the child two issues related to folk beliefs: the folk identification of the salt pillar as embodying Lot's wife, and the personification attributed to this statue in blocking entrance to the Dead Sea (see Turns 3 and 4). The two issues are dealt with in turn by both parents; the father is active mainly in providing the logical explanation for the issue of blocking. He raises the possibility of erosion (Turn 7) as the possible background for the problem presumably referred to in what Liron heard on the radio. Later (Turn 19), he goes on to deconstruct the quote "she does not let people go into the dead sea" in two steps: First, he replaces the personified verb "she does not let," which suggests human intention with a nonvolitional term more associated with physical phenomena ("she might collapse on the road"), and second, he underscores the logical explanation by replacing the human reference term *she* with *it* ("It's close to the road and if it really collapses it will be dangerous"—Turn 21).

The mother is mainly concerned with the issue of differentiating between verisimilitude and reality or fact. She first casts doubt on the child's belief that the pillar is an embodiment of Lot's wife (Turn 10—"She doesn't believe that this is really Lot's wife statue"), and then goes on to substantiate the claim by elaborating the distinction between something that "is" and something that just "looks like" something else ("because there is a resemblance"—Turn 16), the explanation culminating by reference to the physical process by which such forms are created "it's like the stalactites cave" (Turn 16). Note that despite these combined efforts Liron persists in holding on to her belief identifying the pillar with the biblical persona, but she agrees to curtail its powers ("I believe that it's Lot's wife, but I don't believe she can hold people back, tell them "don't go into the Dead Sea") thereby at least partly embracing the scientific explanation provided (Turn 17).

This exchange juxtaposes two opposing epistemologies: that of the world of folk beliefs and fantasy, initially represented by the child, in which physical objects represent mythical figures endowed with human or superhuman powers, as against the world of objects and facts, represented by the parents, in which natural phenomena need to be explained by the logic of scientific processes. The meeting of these two epistemologies through talk at dinner opens up the possibility of change in initial positions. Though in this specific case it does not seem to completely convince the child to abandon her folk theory in favor of the theory of science, it does so partially, in the process involving her in thinking about the type of arguments needed to explain natural phenomena.

(11) Family 4; Ronen (9m); Mihal (5f). [218]

1.	Ronen:	[aba, slixa she-ani shoel- ABA, ma ze nikra] "ba gilgul haba"? (1.66)	[Daddy, excuse me for asking- DADDY, what does it mean] "in the next reincarnation" (1.66)
2.	Mihal:	[(...)]	[(...)]
3.	Father:	°ba gilgul haba °	°in the next reincarnation °
4.	Mihal:	gilgul haba.	next reincarnation. ((repeats))
5.	Ronen:	ah? (1.0)	ah? (1.0)
6.	Mother:	yesh emuna kazot (2.85)	There is a belief like that (2.85)
7.	Mihal:	[gilgul haba]	[in the next reincarnation]
8.	Ronen:	[(...)]?	[(...)]?
9.	Mother:	[SHE] BEN ADAM SHE-MET (1.0) xozer be cura axeret, o betor adam axer.	[THAT] ONE WHO DIES (1.0) comes back in a different form, or as another person.
10.	Ronen:	ken? (1.49) ze kaxa? (2.59) ima, ze kaxa [be'emet]?	Yes? (1.49) Is it so? (2.59) Mom, is it [really so]?
11.	Mother:	[ani lo yoda'at]	[I don't know]
12.	Father:	[yesh kaele she yomru] [af exad od lo (...)]	[there are those who will say] [no one has ever (...)]
13.	Mother:	[ani lo yoda'at. zot emuna]	[I don't know. It is a belief]
14.	Ronen:	ma?	What?
15.	Mother:	zot emuna.	It is a belief.
16.	Father:	hakol, gam be olam haba, mi [she ma'amin].	Everything, It's like someone who believes [in the afterlife].
17.	Ronen:	[mi ma'amin be-ze?]	[Who believes in that?]
18.	Father:	af exad od lo xazar me-sham=	Nobody has returned from there as yet=
19.	Ronen:	= ve-aba	=and Daddy
20.	Observer:	[Ronen (...)] ((laughs))	[Ronen (...( ]((laughs))
21.	Father:	[im hayu uvdot]	[if there were some facts]

22.	Ronen:	aba ve-yesh gam xelek lo katan she-coxek alehem. ((Mihal initiates a topic shift))	Daddy, and there are many who laugh at them.

Extract 11 presents a case of a less definitive commitment to the secular, rational view of the world. In response to Ronen's unusually polite and hesitant ("excuse me for asking") question, the mother provides an elaborate formal definition: "that one who dies comes back in a different form, as another person" (Turn 9). But despite the child's insistence, she refuses to reject this belief entirely, repeating "I don't know" three times (11, 13) in response to his question "Is it really so?" The father, on the other hand, adopts a critical and even mocking stance, considering reincarnation on a par with other nonprovable religious beliefs (note Turn 21—"if there were some facts").

FINAL REMARKS

Explanatory talk in the families studied here emerges in a variety of formats, topics, and participation structures. It ranges from brief one-item contributions to elaborate discussion sequences, from talk about food to theory building about the world, from dyadic exchanges between mother and child in the presence of others to truly multiparty discussions where all present participate. Though less easily definable than narratives, explanatory discourse is identifiable as a specific subgenre of family talk with considerable potential contributions to pragmatic development. It is a subgenre in which the interactional process is highly important and needs careful attention to details of sequential organization. Explanatory talk emerges at dinner in particular junctures of the conversation either as conversational responses to thematically relevant queries or as self-initiated moves aimed at closing perceived asymmetries of knowledge and understanding.

Dinner talk in the less educated families we examined here is in some aspects very similar to dinner talk in the college-educated families we studied previously. There is a modern consciousness shared by all the Israeli families studied that finds its expression in their reported attitudes to child socialization as well as in their discursive practices. Children are encouraged to have a voice in the family, are helped in maintaining the floor and developing their turns, and learn discursive norms by being held accountable for various aspects of their discursive performance.

To conclude, I consider the potential contribution of explanatory talk in the family to pragmatic development from three perspectives: in terms of the epistemological stance it might represent, in terms of its capacity in indexing an elaborate orientation to meaning, and in terms of its potential contribution to dialogism in family discourse and elsewhere. Details of these perspectives follow:

1. *Explanatory talk as indexing paradigmatic thinking:* Bakhtin's (1986) approach to speech genres is helpful in clarifying the way explanatory talk is related to epistemological stance. For Bakhtin, speech genres not only have structural integrity and independence, defined by specific interactions of form and content, but also embody a particular way of ordering and visualizing the world. He suggested that novels incorporate a variety of genres, some artistic and some from everyday life, and that these genres preserve their integrity within the novel. From this point of view, family discourse is like a novel; it too incorporates a variety of genres, such as verbal play, narratives, and explanations (Blum-Kulka, 1997; see also chaps. 2, 3, 7, and 8, this volume). Thus family discourse provides children with opportunities not only to engage in co-constructions of form and content typifying each genre, but also to experience the particular ways of ordering the world specific to each genre.

For explanatory discourse, this "ordering the world" function is closely linked to what Bruner (1986) called "paradigmatic ways of thinking." The paradigmatic way of thinking represents the logico-scientific mode of doing science. In this mode, the procedures used are geared toward principled hypotheses and formal categorization that can be verified through empirical testing, toward a language regulated by requirements of consistency and noncontradiction. The explanations of family discourse index this mode of thinking directly when verbalizing the logical principles involved in explaining the world, as in the case of the blind men and the elephant or in the case of Lot's wife. But they also index it, albeit less directly, with every explanatory utterance that provides justifications for action (in requests, refusals, and apologies), or for opinions (in arguments). Common to both is the epistemological stance to knowledge that requires rationality in explaining the world and human action within it. Thus the gains for socialization in this respect are as much in the wide scope of content areas and types of knowledge that can be touched upon, negotiated, and transmitted during dinner as in the modes of thinking potentially promoted through the process. Returning to the metaphor of the novel, it is also important to note that as in the novel, genres representing the paradigmatic mode of thinking are only one of the many genres that make up the fabric of dinner talk. Thus whatever is gained from explanatory talk is gained as much from the genre as such as from its contrast in form, function, and mode of thinking with other genres, like narratives.

2. *Explanatory talk as representing an elaborated orientation to meaning:* In the type of interaction between form and content it represents, explanatory talk is often considered as one of the manifestations of extended discourse (e.g., Ninio & Snow, 1996). The argument then is that children acquire the ability to construct autonomous extended discourse with experience in a variety of genres, such as definitions, narratives, and explanations. From this point of view, explanatory talk in the family is part of the discursive repertoire of "literate" language, namely language that indexes in Bernstein's terms (1971) an elaborated orientation to meaning. Two interrelated features of this elaborated orientation are particularly salient in explanations: verbal explicitness that is attuned to presumptions of reciprocity of perspectives, and internal coherence. Perhaps *the* major feast of pragmatic development is learning how to adapt the message, particularly over stretches of extended discourse, to the interlocutor's presumed state of knowledge. Practice in all types of explanations can help develop such skills first and foremost because taking into account asymmetries of knowledge is at the very core of the genre. Because explanations emerge in natural discourse as a response to such perceived or noted asymmetries, to be successful they need to continually attend to and respond to projected gaps of knowledge and tune the level of text's coherence accordingly. Issues of coherence building in explanatory talk will vary with the interlocutors, the complexity of the topic, and the degree to which it requires extended turns or can be dealt with in one brief utterance. But regardless of the length of the explanatory sequence (at least when self-initiated), its mere emergence seems indicative of an elaborated orientation to meaning.

3. *Explanatory talk and dialogism:* Building reciprocity of perspectives by engaging in explanatory talk also means shifts in what Drew (1991) called "the social distributions of authoritative access to bodies or types of knowledge" (p. 45). Though parents are (or at least are set up as or claim to be) the authoritative access of knowledge on a variety of topics, children can gain the status of authoritative access when it comes to matters of their social life, like pajama parties or merry-go-rounds. Thus in the family, queries for world and linguistic knowledge are typically initiated by children addressing adults, whereas queries concerning the children's world are initiated by adults addressing children. The multiparty, intergenerational participant structure of dinner conversations in the family allows for dialogical and reciprocal co-constructions of knowledge. The keying of such co-constructions, as we saw, is at times highly didactic and hierarchical and at other junctures conversational and egalitarian.

The conversational emergence of explanatory talk adds a further dimension to the issue of the authoritative sources of knowledge. We saw that both children and adults can set either themselves or each other up as explainers. Setting up oneself or the other as an explainer privileges one party as the one with "teaching" rights for at least one or several extended turns (Keppler & Luckman, 1991). From this perspective, the social distribution of explaining rights in the family is in principle egalitarian. As in narratives, the prospective explainer or prospective teller negotiates the rights for an extended turn, and such rights are available to all present, children included.

The multiparty structure of family dinners also allows for certain topics to be negotiated in a way that offers a spectrum of different perspectives, without granting any of these the status of the authoritative voice. A case in point is the conversation about reincarnation, where each of the parents takes a different stance, and the children are implicitly invited to choose between the father's categorical rejection of the possibility of such a phenomenon, against the mother's hypothetical acceptance of its existence. "Dialogism" (Linnel, 1998, building on Bakhtin) entails accepting reciprocity of perspectives and shifting distributions of authoritative sources of knowledge within a basically egalitarian participation structure. We saw manifestations of these features in the dinner talk examined, and argued that, as a result, children (and adults) can gain enormously from engaging with each other in explanatory talk.

REFERENCES

Antaki, C. (1994). *Explaining and arguing: The social organization of accounts*. London: Sage.

Aukrust, V. G., & Snow, C. E. (1998). Narratives and explanations in Norwegian and American mealtime conversations. *Language in Society, 27*(2), 221–247.

Bakhtin, M. (1986). *Speech genres and other late essays* (M. Holquist, Ed.). Austin: University of Texas Press.

Barbieri, M. S., Colavita, F., & Scheuer, N. (1989). Explanations: A pragmatic basis for early child competence. *IPrA Papers in Pragmatics, 3*(1), 130–155.

Barbieri, M. S., Colavita, F., & Scheuer, N. (1990). The beginning of the explaining capacity. In G. Conti-Ramsen & C. E. Snow (Eds.), *Children's language* (Vol. 7, pp. 246–271). Hillsdale, NJ: Lawrence Erlbaum Associates.

Beals, D. (1993). Explanations in low-income families' mealtime conversations. *Applied Psycholinguistics, 14*, 489–513.

Beals, D. E., & De Temple, J. (1993). Home contributions to early language and literacy. In D. Leu & C. Kinzner (Eds.), *Forty-second year book of the National Reading Conference* (pp. 207–275). Chicago: National Reading Conference.

Beals, D. E., & Snow, C. E. (1994). "Thunder is when the angels are upstairs bowling": Narratives and explanations at the dinner table. *Journal of Narrative and Life History, 4*, 331–352.

Berman, R., & Slobin, D. (Eds.). (1994). Relating events in narrative: A crosslinguistic developmental study. Hillsdale, NJ: Lawrence Erlbaum Associates.

Bernstein, B. (1971). Class, codes & control (Vol. 1). London: Routledge and Kegan Paul.

Bernstein, B. (1996). *Pedagogy, symbolic control, and identity*. London: Taylor & Francis.

Blum-Kulka, S. (1997). *Dinner talk: Cultural pattterns of sociability and socialization in family discourse*. Mahwah, NJ: Lawrence Erlbaum Associates.

Brown, G., & Yule, G. (1983). *Discourse analysis.* Cambridge, England: Cambridge University Press.

Bruner, J. (1986). *Actual minds, possible words.* Cambridge, MA: Harvard University Press.

Couper-Kuhlen, E. (1999). Coherent voicing: On prosody in conversational reported speech. In W. Bublitz, U. Lenk, & E. Ventola (Eds.), *Coherence in spoken and written discourse* (pp. 11–34). Amsterdam: John Benjamins.

Donaldson, M. (1978). *Children's minds.* Glasgow, Scotland: Fontana Originals.

Donaldson, M. L. (1986). *Children's explanations: A psycholinguistic study.* Cambridge, England: Cambridge University Press.

Drew, P. (1991). Asymmetries of knowledge in conversational interaction. In J. Markova & C. Foppa (Eds.), *Asymmetries in dialogue* (pp. 21–49). Avage, MD: Barnes & Noble.

Edwards, D., & Potter, J. (1992). *Discursive psychology.* London: Sage.

Hasan, R. (1992). Meaning in sociolinguistic theory. In K. Bolton & H. Kwok (Eds.), *Sociolinguistics today: International perspectives* (pp. 81–119). London: Routledge.

Heritage, J. (1988). Explanations and accounts: A conversation analytic approach. In C. Antaki (Ed.), *Analyzing everyday conversation.* London: Sage.

Hicks, D. (1990). Narrative skills and genre knowledge: Ways of telling in the primary school grades. *Applied Psycholinguistics, 11,* 83–104.

Keppler, A., & Luckman, T. (1991). "Teaching": Conversational transmission of knowledge. In I. Markova & K. Foppa (Eds.), *Asymmetries in dialogue* (pp. 143–166). Savage, MD: Barnes & Noble.

Linnel, P. (1998). *Approaching dialogue: Talk, interaction and contexts in dialogical perspectives.* Amsterdam: John Benjamins.

MacWhinney, B. (1991). *The CHILDES Project: Tools for analyzing talk.* Hillsdale, NJ: Lawrence Erlbaum Associates.

Martin, J. (1989). *Factual writing: Exploring and challenging social reality.* Oxford, England: Oxford University Press.

Ninio, A., & Snow, C. (1996). *Pragmatic development.* Boulder, CO: Westview.

Ochs, E. (1990). Indexicality and socialization. In W. J. Stigler, A. R. Scweder, & G. Herdt (Eds.), *Cultural psychology: Essays on comparative human development* (pp. 287–309). Cambridge, England: Cambridge University Press.

Pan, B. A., Perlman, Y. R., & Snow, E. C. (2000). Food for thought: Dinner table as a context for observing parent–child discourse. In L. Menn & N. Bernstein Ratner (Eds.), *Methods for studying language production* (pp. 181–205). Mahwah, NJ: Lawrence Erlbaum Associates.

Peled, N. (1994). *Between speech and writing: The production of oral and written texts between 3–9.* Unpublished doctoral dissertation, Hebrew University of Jerusalem, Israel.

Peterson, C., & McCabe, A. (1985). Understanding 'because': How important is the task? *Journal of Psycholinguistic Research, 14,* 199–218.

Psathas, G., & Anderson, T. (1990). The "practices" of transcription in conversation analysis. *Semiotica, 78,* 75–99.

Rogoff, B., Mistry, J., Goncu, A., & Mosier, C. (1993). Guided participation in cultural activity by toddlers and caregivers. *Monographs of the Society for Research in Child Development* (Vol. 58, No. 8).

Snow, C. E., & Kurland, B. (1995). Sticking to the point: Talk about magnets as a preparation for literacy. In D. Hicks (Ed.), *Child discourse and social learning: An interdisciplinary perspective* (pp. 189–221). Cambridge, England: Cambridge Univesity Press.

Veneziano, E., & Sinclair, H. (1995). Functional changes in early child language: The appearance of references to the past and of explanations. *Journal of Child Language, 22*(3), 557–581.

Zecker, L. B. (1996). Early development in written language: Children's emergent knowledge of genre-specific characteristics. *Reading and Writing, 8,* 5–25.

Chapter 5

Peer-Group Culture and Narrative Development

Ageliki Nicolopoulou
Lehigh University

Drawing on my analysis of a storytelling and story-acting practice that I have studied in a range of preschool classes, this chapter explores some of the ways in which peer-group activities can serve as a powerful context for promoting young children's language development, and in particular their narrative development. One implication of this analysis, I argue, is to reinforce a central organizing theme of the present volume: the need to rethink, refine, and broaden the conceptions of the "social context" of development now employed by most psychological research in this area. Explicitly or implicitly, this context tends to be conceived too exclusively in terms of adult–child interaction (usually dyadic), in which the more knowledgeable and capable adult takes on the role of instructing, guiding, correcting, and/or "scaffolding" the efforts of the less capable child. Even when interaction between children is studied, it is usually assimilated to the one-way expert–novice model, with the older sibling or other peer taking on the "expert" role.

The developmental significance of these kinds of interactions between unequals is undeniable; but this overly narrow focus on the model of dyadic adult–child (or, more generally, expert–novice) interaction has meant a neglect of other crucial dimensions of social context. These include the role of peers, and in particular of the peer *group*, in the process of development. In this respect, the role of peers is not limited to one-way transmission or facilitation, but also includes modes of genuine peer *collaboration*. Furthermore, such collaboration is not restricted to dyadic (or

117

even multiparty) interaction between individuals; children, like adults, also create, maintain, and participate in *fields of shared activity* that provide both resources and motivations for development, including narrative development.

The present chapter offers one concrete illustration of these processes. It presents evidence indicating that participation in a peer-oriented practice of spontaneous storytelling and story-acting contributed significantly to enhancing young children's narrative skills; and it seeks to delineate some of the ways that these effects were achieved. This discussion focuses on a study conducted in a Head Start class made up of children from poor and otherwise disadvantaged backgrounds, but these positive results are consistent with findings from preschools serving children from middle-class backgrounds where I have studied the use and effects of this storytelling and story-acting practice. In addition to confirming the potential value of peer-group practices in promoting narrative development, these results underline the need for developmental research to move, both conceptually and methodologically, toward a more fully sociocultural perspective.

The Social Context of Narrative Development: Adult–Child Interaction and Beyond

A great deal of developmental research is still conducted with little or no systematic consideration of the social context of development. In the field of language acquisition and development, however, major tendencies have long addressed the important role of "input" from the adult world (Galloway & Richards, 1994; Snow, 1995). A substantial body of research has sought to specify those features of adult–child interaction (in practice, most often mother–child interaction) that most effectively promote and facilitate the development of linguistic skills. Initially, this work focused primarily on very young children (for a useful review, see Snow, 1989), but it has increasingly been extended to language development in later years, including narrative development. One impetus for this kind of research has been a series of findings suggesting that the mastery of narrative skills by young children serves as a crucial foundation for their later acquisition of literacy and success in formal education (e.g., Snow, 1983, 1991; Snow & Dickinson, 1990, 1991; Wells, 1985, 1986). These studies have established the importance of social context for narrative development, and have begun to delineate the interactional styles that best facilitate it (e.g., Fivush, 1994; McCabe & Peterson, 1991; Peterson, Jesso, & McCabe, 1999).

But so far the focus of this research has generally been limited in two key respects: (a) it has dealt largely with "factual" narratives of past experiences and has neglected fictional or fantasy narratives (a point to which I return later); and (b) the "social context" of narrative development has, with some notable exceptions, been conceived narrowly in terms of modes of adult–child interaction.[1] Adult–child interactions obviously play an important role in children's development, education, and socialization. However, other researchers, including myself, have argued that this one-sided picture of the "social context" of development must be expanded to take systematic account of the complementary role of children's peer relations and group life (e.g., Corsaro, 1985; Davies, 1989; Nicolopoulou, 1996a, 1997a, 1997b; for a valuable overview of the role of the peer group in socialization, albeit one that excessively deemphasizes the impact of adult–child interaction, see Harris, 1995, 1998).

Narrative research that addresses the developmental significance of peer-group activity can draw on powerful theoretical resources, but these have not yet been exploited fully or effectively. A good deal of work on preschool children's peer interaction and its role in development has been inspired, directly or indirectly, by Piaget's seminal insight that the developmental significance of adult–child relations—necessarily asymmetric and hierarchical—is in important ways qualitatively different from that of peer-group relations, which are potentially more egalitarian and cooperative (Piaget, 1923/1959, 1932/1965; for endorsements and applications of Piaget's position, see Damon, 1984, 1988; for a useful critical overview of developmental peer-interaction research that compares the influence of Piagetian and Vygotskian perspectives, see Tudge & Rogoff, 1989; and for a more comprehensive overview that critically assesses the strengths and limitations of current approaches in cognitive research from a sociocultural perspective, see Rogoff, 1998). However, this Piagetian inspiration has so far generated more work on middle childhood than on the preschool years; and research on young children from this perspective has focused predominantly on children's play (e.g., Garvey, 1990; Stambak & Sinclair, 1993) and has rarely been integrated with the study of their narrative activity.

Some reasons why such integration would be useful are suggested by the work of Garvey, who has systematically examined both child–caregiver and child–child interaction, and has extended the concerns informing her play research to issues of language development and communication (1984). As Garvey's synthesis of the relevant research (1986) makes clear, children learn in different ways from each other—and develop different

---

[1]Nor is this second tendency restricted to narrative research; in a recent survey of work on language and socialization—that is, both socialization through language and socialization in the use of language—Ely and Gleason (1995) documented this basic pattern for the field as a whole, while also indicating some of the exceptions.

skills in the process—than when they learn from adults (see also Paley, 1986). More recently, Judy Dunn, studying young children in family contexts, has argued that interaction with siblings can play a distinctive and important role in promoting the development of communication and social understanding (Brown & Dunn, 1992; Dunn, 1988, 1989). However, even Garvey and Dunn do not systematically address *narrative* activity and development; and their analysis tends to stay largely at the level of dyadic interaction, with only scattered attention to group life and peer culture.

On the other hand, much of the research investigating the role of social context in narrative development has drawn theoretically on a Vygotskian perspective. Vygotsky was powerfully struck by Piaget's insight regarding the distinctive character of children's autonomous peer-directed activity, and in some respects he pushed it further, particularly in his seminal treatment of children's play (see especially Vygotsky, 1933/1967; for discussion, Nicolopoulou, 1993). Furthermore, Vygotsky's approach is more fully sociocultural than Piaget's, emphasizes the cognitive value of children's imaginative and symbolic activity, and offers a natural bridge between the study of play and of narrative (as I have argued in Nicolopoulou, 1993, 1996a, 1997a, from which I am drawing in the present discussion). In practice, however, much Vygotskian-inspired research, including narrative research, has utilized a weak and truncated conception of the sociocultural dimension in Vygotsky's theory. In particular, it has tended to interpret his key notion of the "zone of proximal development" rather narrowly, in terms of the direct effects of dyadic interaction between the developing child and adults—or, in some cases, more knowledgeable children. Even in research on peer collaboration linked with this paradigm, peer relations have usually, in effect, been conceptually assimilated to the dyadic adult–child model, being treated as another case of expert–novice interaction. (For some elaboration of the arguments behind these critical remarks, see Nicolopoulou, 1993, 1996a; Nicolopoulou & Cole, 1993. These points are also brought out by Rogoff, 1998.)

One partial exception that helps prove this rule is the valuable body of cross-cultural research, emerging at the intersection of anthropology, sociolinguistics, and developmental psychology, that has emphasized the distinctive role of siblings in socialization, including language socialization (two relevant collections are Schieffelin & Ochs, 1986; Zukow, 1989a). This research has an anthropological lineage going back to the work of Whiting and Whiting (1975) on sibling caregivers, but some key figures have also drawn explicitly on Vygotsky's theoretical approach (e.g., Ochs, 1988; Zukow, 1989b). It is therefore significant that most of this research has, once again, tended to view these sibling relationships in terms of an expert–novice model (for an especially clear and instructive example, see Zukow, 1989b).

Rethinking Social Context: The Limits of Interactional Reductionism

A less restricted vision is suggested by Vygotsky's (1933/1967) assertion—often noted, but insufficiently pondered—that, in the preschool years, "*Play* is the source of development and *creates* the zone of proximal development" (p. 16; emphases added). That is, it is a form of activity that pushes the child beyond the limits of development that have already been achieved and provides opportunities for further development. In saying this, Vygotsky was *not* referring to assisted problem solving in expert–novice interaction. Rather, the crucial feature of play from a developmental perspective is that in play children collaborate in constructing and maintaining a shared "imaginary situation" in an activity that is simultaneously voluntary, open to spontaneity, and structured by rules—but rules that are recognized and accepted as necessary by the children themselves rather than imposed from above by adults. That is, in play the child confronts a situation where the rules are not so much externally imposed as inherent in the structure of the activity itself, and are necessary in order to be able to carry out a practice or form of activity that is valued by its participants. The shared symbolic space of the play-world (Huizinga, 1938/1955) creates a field of activity for children's imagination that generates both opportunities and motivations for development.

This analysis offers a valuable starting point for building up an approach that can situate children's narrative development more effectively and comprehensively in sociocultural context. As I have argued (Nicolopoulou, 1996a, 1997a), what Vygotsky said of children's play also applies to their narrative activity: Both represent the union of expressive imagination with rule-governed cultural form. And in both, as Vygotsky emphasized with regard to play, the elements of imagination and fantasy are closely linked to the *cognitive* significance of the activity, in terms of both its motivations and its developmental value. It is through the creation and elaboration in imagination of a symbolic world dominated by meanings, with its own inner logic, that children are first able to emancipate their thinking from the constraints of their immediate external environment and thus, to take the first steps toward organizing thought in a coherent and independent way. At the same time, children *use* these symbolic activities to help them make sense of the world and their own experience, and to deal with themes and concerns that preoccupy them emotionally. These considerations indicate why we should avoid a one-sided concentration on children's "factual" narratives of past experience, which has marked the bulk of current narrative research conducted in naturalistic settings—important as these narrative genres undoubtedly are for children (Fivush, 1994; P. J. Miller & Moore, 1989). By fostering the development of children's symbolic imagination and providing a field for its exercise, pretend play and fictional narratives help prepare the way for the development of abstract thinking and "higher mental processes."

As children come to realize the possible purposes and satisfactions that can be pursued in narrative activity—which are symbolic, expressive, emotional, and social–relational as well as instrumental—they are driven to learn and appropriate the narrative forms culturally available to them and to turn these to their own ends; and they gradually discover that, in order to do so, they must attend to and grasp the (mostly implicit) rule-governed structures inherent in these narrative forms. Children are both impelled and enabled to do this through their participation in practices of shared symbolic activity that serve as collectively constituted fields within which to use and master these narrative forms, to explore and extend their inherent possibilities through performance and experimentation, and to push on to greater narrative range and proficiency. It is in these ways, if we follow up Vygotsky's insights, that certain types of peer-group activity can serve as especially powerful contexts for promoting development.

Two implications of the perspective outlined and advocated here are worth highlighting further. The first is the need to integrate the study of children's play and narrative more fully and effectively than is now generally done. In fact, it is probably most useful to see both pretend play and storytelling as falling within the field of narrative activity, on a continuum ranging from the discursive exposition of narratives in storytelling (full narrativity) to their enactment in pretend play. Of course, the analytical distinction between the two is important. For the issues considered in this chapter, a key difference is that storytelling represents a more fully *decontextualized* use of language, in the technical sense of this term emphasized by such scholars as Snow, Dickinson, and Wells (e.g., Snow, 1983, 1991; Snow & Dickinson, 1990, 1991; Wells, 1985, 1986). Language use is decontextualized to the extent that it involves explicitly constructing, conveying, and comprehending information in ways that are not embedded in the supportive framework of conversational interaction and do not rely on implicit shared background knowledge and nonverbal cues. For young children, stories, especially fictional stories, are an especially important example of decontextualized discourse in that they pose the challenge of explicitly building up a scenario or picture of the world using only words. To put it another way, free-standing stories are *self-contextualizing* (Wells, 1985, p. 253) to a considerably greater extent than other forms of discourse that young children typically experience and construct. On the other hand, play and storytelling are also closely interwoven and often mutually supportive in children's experience and development, and developmental research needs to grasp the ongoing interplay between them.

Second, more is at stake than simply adding child–child interactions to the analysis of adult–child interactions. Even more fundamentally, socially situated research needs to overcome its prevailing temptation to *reduce* the social context of development, conceptually and/or methodologically, to interactions between individuals (Nicolopoulou & Cole, 1993; Rogoff, 1998). To move from the isolated individual to the interactional pair (or even a sequence of interactional pairs) as the unit of analysis is a useful first step, but by itself it is incomplete and misleading. Interactions are themselves embedded in—and simultaneously help to constitute and maintain—various types of sociocultural context that enable and constrain them, and that structure their nature, meaning, and impact. At the most intimate or immediate level, these contexts may include families, peer groups, classroom minicultures, and socially structured practices and activity systems—for example, the shared symbolic space of the play-world. And these are in turn enmeshed in larger institutional and cultural frameworks ranging from organizations and communities to culturally elaborated images of identity, conceptual tools, and systems of meaning. (One justly celebrated analysis that captures these multiple layers of embedded contexts, situating culturally specific narrative styles and modes of socialization within the larger ways of life of different communities, is Heath, 1983.) These sociocultural contexts, both small- and large-scale, have to be understood as genuinely *collective* realities that, in manifold ways, shape the actions and experiences of those who participate in them. An effective approach to understanding development requires that we pay systematic attention to the ongoing interplay between three dimensions of the human world that are at once analytically distinct and mutually interpenetrating: individual, interactional or relational, and collective (for elaboration, see Nicolopoulou & Weintraub, 1998).

Toward a More Fully Sociocultural Perspective

As the work represented in this volume demonstrates, several tendencies in current research point the way toward a more comprehensive approach. One good example is the body of research that has studied the joint construction and uses of narratives in multiparty, multigenerational talk between family members during mealtime conversations (e.g., Aukrust & Snow, 1998; Blum-Kulka, 1997; Ochs, Smith, & Taylor, 1989; Ochs, Taylor, Rudolph, & Smith, 1992). Beyond its attention to the socializing role of multiparty (rather than exclusively dyadic) interactions, what is notable about this research is that it treats the narrative construction of reality as a collaborative enterprise, involving both adults and children; it situates these conversational practices and interactions in the context of the family group; and it examines how these practices are institutionalized differently in different national cultures, as well as different class and ethnic sub-cultures within particular societies. As Ochs et al. (1989) nicely put it, the "dinnertime" setting can be seen as an institutionalized *opportunity space* (pp. 238–239), culturally defined and collectively maintained, which enables and promotes certain forms of shared narrative and cognitive activity.

This line of research has continued to focus primarily on adult–child interactions (or conversations between adults witnessed by children). The research reported in this chapter seeks to broaden the picture further by examining peer-group relations among children themselves as a context for narrative activity, socialization, and development.

PEER-GROUP ACTIVITIES AS A MATRIX
FOR DEVELOPMENT: A CONCRETE EXAMPLE

The study on which I will focus was one of several that examined the operation and effects of a storytelling and story-acting practice pioneered by Vivian Paley (see Paley, 1986, 1988, 1990) that is integrated as a regular—but entirely voluntary—component of the curriculum in the preschool classes involved. At a certain period during the day, any child who wishes can dictate a story to a teacher, who records the story as the child tells it. (These are overwhelmingly fictional or imaginary stories, rather than "factual" accounts of personal experience of the sort one hears in "show and tell" or "sharing time.") At the end of the day, each of these stories is read aloud to the entire class at "group time" (or "circle time") by the same teacher, while the child/author and other children, whom he or she chooses, act out the story.

Several features of this practice are especially worth noting. One result of "group time" is that children tell their stories, not only to adults, but primarily to each other; they do so, not in one-to-one interaction, but in a shared public setting. In contrast to the artificial situations that predominate in much research on young children's narratives, here the children's storytelling and story-acting is embedded in the ongoing context of the classroom miniculture and the children's everyday group life. Their storytelling is also voluntary, self-initiated, and relatively spontaneous: The stories are neither solicited directly by adults nor channeled by props, story stems, or suggested topics. Furthermore, to a certain degree this practice combines two aspects of children's narrative activity that are too often treated in mutual isolation: the discursive exposition of narratives in storytelling and their enactment in pretend play. There is strong evidence that these conditions lead children to produce narratives that are richer, more ambitious, and more illuminating than when they compose them in isolation from their everyday social contexts and in response to agendas shaped directly by adults (Nicolopoulou, 1996a; Sutton-Smith, 1986).

Adults certainly play an important role in this storytelling and story-acting practice, but in terms of the narrative activity itself their essential role is indirect. In the classrooms I have studied, teachers who transcribe and read out the children's stories offer very little feedback, commentary, guidance, or other direct input as they do so. Instead, their key contribution is to establish and facilitate a child-driven and peer-oriented activity that develops its own autonomous dynamics, within which the children themselves can take an active role in their own socialization and development. This storytelling and story-acting practice creates a framework of shared symbolic activity that draws on preschoolers' emerging abilities to tell and enact fictional stories—and their enthusiasm for doing so—and helps these develop by serving as a collectively constituted field for narrative performance, experimentation, and cross-fertilization. To borrow the useful formulation of Ochs et al. (1989), this practice provides an institutionalized *opportunity space*. Its activation, and the realization of its developmental potential, depend on the engagement and enthusiasm of the children themselves. The role of adults is to help create and maintain the social framework within which these activities can flourish, rather than to intervene in them directly.

Research Sites and Data: An Overview

I have studied the use of this storytelling and story-acting practice in 12 preschool classrooms differing by geography and by social class background. The first stage of this line of research analyzed a body of 582 stories generated by a preschool class of 4-year-olds attending a half-day nursery school in northern California during the 1988–1989 school year. From 1992 to 1996 and (in collaboration with Elizabeth Richner) in 1999–2000, I collected an additional body of more than 3,000 stories from classes in two preschools in western Massachusetts, where I simultaneously conducted ethnographic observations of the classroom activities, friendship patterns, and group life of the children involved. (For some analyses based on material from these California and Massachusetts preschools, see Nicolopoulou, 1996a, 1997b; Nicolopoulou, Scales, & Weintraub, 1994; Richner & Nicolopoulou, 2001.)

In the preschools just mentioned, almost all the children in the classrooms examined came from middle-class or upper-middle-class families, largely professional or academic. In most cases, they lived with two parents, both of whom worked outside the home. During the 1997–1998 school year I was able to broaden the comparative scope of this research by collecting equivalent data—including 166 stories—from a Head Start class in western Massachusetts (ages 3 to 5); these children, of course, came from poor and otherwise disadvantaged backgrounds. In the present chapter, I focus primarily on this Head Start study. However, to establish some necessary background for that analysis, I will first outline some of the broad findings from my studies of middle-class preschools.

Spontaneous Storytelling in the Middle-Class Preschools: Narrative Development and the Uses of Narrative Activity

The key patterns have been strikingly consistent in all the middle-class preschool classes I have studied, in both California and Massachusetts. In all cases, the children became enthusiastically involved in this storytelling and story-acting practice, and brought considerable energy and creativity to their narrative activity. As the school year progressed, the children's stories became more complex and sophisticated, manifesting significant advances in both narrative competence and cognitive abilities. Within a short time, the stories of almost all the children involved displayed a degree of narrative complexity and sophistication that, according to the overwhelming consensus of mainstream research in narrative development (usefully summed up by Hudson & Shapiro, 1991), 4- to 5-year-old children should not be able to achieve (see Nicolopoulou, 1996a). In part, this substantial discrepancy is probably due to a tendency for research conducted in more or less isolated experimental settings to systematically underestimate young children's narrative capabilities. But the evidence strongly suggests that the children's participation in this storytelling and story-acting practice also significantly enhanced their narrative skills.

In the process, the children drew themes, characters, images, plots, and other elements from each other's stories; and they also incorporated elements into their narratives from a wide range of other sources including fairy tales, children's books, TV (and popular culture more generally), and their own experience. However, they did not simply imitate other children's stories, nor did they just passively absorb messages from adults and the larger culture. It is clear that, even at this early age, they were able to appropriate these elements *selectively*, and to *use* and rework them for their own purposes.

This process of active and selective appropriation is brought out especially well by patterns of differentiation in the children's narrative activity and development. Therefore, let me offer a brief and extremely schematic consideration of one important example: the emergence of systematic gender differences in the children's storytelling, linked to the formation of two gendered peer-group subcultures within the classroom that define themselves, to a considerable extent, against each other (see Nicolopoulou, 1997b; Nicolopoulou et al., 1994; Richner & Nicolopoulou, 2001). I should emphasize that all the preschools involved make strong and deliberate efforts to create an egalitarian, nonsexist atmosphere, and most of the children came from families that seemed to share this orientation. Furthermore, one of the teachers' intentions in using this storytelling and story-acting practice was to help generate greater cohesion and a common culture within the classroom group. The children did indeed use their narrative activities to help build up a common culture; but they also consistently used them to build up gendered subcultures within this common culture.

Although the stories were shared with the entire group every day, my analysis demonstrated that they divided sharply, consistently, and increasingly along gender lines. They were dominated by two highly distinctive gender-related *narrative styles,* differing in both form and content, that embodied different approaches to the symbolic management of order and disorder, different underlying images of social relationships and the social world, and different images of the self.

The girls' stories, for example, characteristically portrayed characters embedded in networks of stable and harmonious relationships, whose activities were located in stable and specified physical settings. One common genre revolved around the family and family activities. In contrast, the boys' stories were characteristically marked by conflict, movement, and disruption, and often by associative chains of extravagant imagery. Whereas the girls tended to supplement their depictions of family life by drawing on fairy-tale characters such as kings and queens or princes and princesses, boys were especially fond of powerful and frightening characters along the lines of large animals, cartoon action heroes, and so on. In short, the boys and girls developed and elaborated two distinctive styles of narrative representation that pointed to distinctive modes of ordering and interpreting the world, particularly the social world. Correspondingly, they presented two contrasting images of the self: in the girls' stories, a socially embedded and interdependent self, and in the boys' stories, an essentially isolated and conflictual self.

Furthermore, this narrative polarization was one aspect of a larger process by which two distinct gendered subcultures were actively built up and maintained by the children themselves. These subcultures were marked by the convergence of gendered styles in the children's narratives, gender differentiation in their group life, and increasingly self-conscious gender identity in the children involved. At the same time, the crystallization of these subcultures within the microcosm of the classroom provided a framework for the further appropriation, enactment, and reproduction of crucial dimensions of personal identity as defined by the larger society, including gender.

These findings suggest some broad conclusions that go beyond the specific subject of gender. The narrative construction of reality is not a purely individual process but a sociocultural one, whose cognitive significance is inextricably linked to the building up of group life and the formation of both individual and collective identities. Children participate—by way of narrative practices—in the process of their own socialization and development, and they do not do this *only* through the individual appropriation of elements from the larger culture. They also help to construct some of the key sociocultural contexts that shape (and promote) their own socialization and development.

Including Disadvantaged Children:
A Study of a Head Start Classroom

Until recently, I was able to conduct this kind of research only in preschools with children from predominantly middle-class families—and, with very few exceptions, this remains true of other research as well.[2] A major reason is that this type of spontaneous storytelling and story-acting practice is used relatively rarely in preschools serving poor and otherwise disadvantaged children (or even children from working-class backgrounds). However, in 1997–1998 I was able to study a Head Start classroom in Massachusetts where this practice was being introduced (Nicolopoulou, 1999). The central dynamics and results of this practice in the Head Start class were fundamentally consistent with those found in the middle-class preschools; in particular, the evidence strongly indicated that it promoted the narrative development of the children involved. On the other hand, the specific patterns also differed in several ways between these two kinds of preschool settings. Both the similarities and the differences are instructive.

One important difference in the background preparation that the two populations brought to this practice is worth emphasizing before we proceed: The Head Start children began the school year with significantly weaker narrative skills than did the corresponding middle-class children I have studied. Specifically, the Head Start children showed less familiarity with the basic conventions for telling a free-standing self-contextualized story and less mastery of the relevant language skills.[3] Thus, relative to the

---

[2]McNamee (1990, 1992) studied a Head Start program using this practice, but did not include a systematic examination of the effects on children's narrative and other language skills.

[3]I realize that the whole subject of social class differences in narrative skills is controversial, and in fact the overall picture is complex, but I will not attempt to engage that massive controversy directly. Suffice it to say that this contrast has emerged sharply in my research (as my later discussion should make clear) and that the kinds of social class differences in early narrative skills that I have just described have also been found in a substantial body of other research (e.g., Heath, 1982; Peterson, 1994; Snow & Dickinson, 1990).

middle-class children, they were much more in the position of building up the basic foundations for their participation in this narrative activity from scratch, rather than simply applying and expanding narrative skills they had already mastered. As a result, the analysis of the storytelling and story-acting practice in the Head Start setting brings out some of the basic developmental dynamics in especially illuminating ways.

A PEER-ORIENTED NARRATIVE PRACTICE AND ITS EFFECTS IN A HEAD START CLASS: DATA COLLECTION, EVALUATION, AND RESULTS[4]

The Classrooms, the Children, and the Site

The participants in this study were children attending two half-day preschool classes, consisting of 3- to 5-year-olds, in the same Head Start program in western Massachusetts during the 1997–1998 school year. That year the storytelling and story-acting practice was introduced into one class (the *target class*). (This was the first time that this practice had been used in any of the classes in this Head Start program.) This activity took place an average of 2 days out of the 4 days per week that the class met (59 days out of 120).[5] A second class, housed in the same building, was selected to serve as the *control class*. Except for the introduction of the storytelling and story-acting practice in the target class, the two classes used the same curriculum, and were even supervised by the same Education Coordinator.

Each class began and ended the school year with 17 students, but both had turnover in between (which is normal for Head Start classes), and only children present for the whole year were included in the analysis. In addition, four full-year children in the target class were not included for various other reasons.[6] The sample used for the analyses were 10 children from the target class (4 girls and 6 boys) and 15 from the control class (7 girls and 8 boys).

---

[4]For the sake of brevity, these are presented here in highly compressed form. For further details, explanation, and elaboration, see Nicolopoulou (1999).

[5]By contrast, in the middle-class preschools I have studied this practice generally took place almost every day. The fact that this practice was operating at only half-capacity, so to speak, in this Head Start class helps make the positive results described later especially impressive.

[6]One suffered from microcephalia and had minimal language skills; one was Spanish monolingual and therefore not suitable for comparison; one child was mistrustful of adults in general, and refused to be tested; and one child was not tested in the fall due to a tester's oversight.

All the children in both classes came from poor families that qualified for Head Start assistance, with reported annual incomes ranging from $5,000 to $10,000. In most cases, there appeared to be some degree of family difficulty or instability. Slightly less than a third of the children in each class lived in a household with two married parents; the majority lived with mothers who were single, separated, or divorced. With regard to ethnic and racial background, about three fourths of the children in these two classes were non-Hispanic White (a category that made up 97% of the community as a whole), mostly born and raised in Massachusetts. In the target class, about one third of the children included in the analysis were Hispanic (meaning that one or both parents were immigrants from the Caribbean), but all of these spoke English. There were no non-Hispanic Black children in either class.

Data Collection

Three main types of data are reviewed here. The first consisted of the spontaneous stories generated by the storytelling and story-acting practice—a body of data pertaining, by definition, only to the target class. The children in the target class generated a total of 166 stories during the school year, of which 118 were included in the analysis. As explained earlier, these stories were transcribed by the teacher as part of the practice itself. (She also recorded which children acted in each story performance and what roles they played.)

To allow systematic comparison between the target and control classes, two tests were administered to children in both classes at the beginning and end of the school year: the Expressive Vocabulary Test (EVT)[7] and a story-production task devised for this study, the Figurine-Based Narrative Task (FBNT). The EVT was included because there are good reasons to believe that the productive vocabulary skills it measures are, along with narrative skills, part of an interconnected and mutually reinforcing cluster of decontextualized oral-language skills that provide critical preparation for literacy and long-term school success (Dickinson, Cote, & M. W. Smith, 1993; Snow, 1991).

Evaluating Children's Narrative Development

The overall hypothesis informing this study centered on two key expectations: First, regular participation by young children in this storytelling

---

[7]The version of the Expressive Vocabulary Test provided by the American Guidance Service (Williams, 1997) was used.

and story-acting practice should promote the development of their narrative abilities; and, second, it should also (directly and indirectly) promote the development of a broader range of decontextualized language skills, specifically including productive vocabulary skills. Analysis of the three types of data just outlined strongly confirmed these expectations. By a range of criteria, the narrative skills manifested in the spontaneous stories of the children in the target class improved quite significantly over the course of the year. And the comparisons between the target and control classes linked the advances by the children in the target class to their participation in the storytelling and story-acting practice. The scores of the children in the target class on both the EVT and the FBNT increased significantly more between September and May than did those of the children in the control class. In fact, on both measures the children in the target class began the year with lower mean scores than those of the children in the control class, but they improved sufficiently that by the end of the year their mean results were significantly higher than those of the children in the control class.

In short, the analysis yielded three mutually supportive types of evidence for the developmental benefits of the storytelling and story-acting practice. I briefly discuss each in turn.

Promoting Narrative Development: Analysis of the Children's Spontaneous Stories

The stories composed by each child in the fall and in the spring were compared using five measures I constructed (in collaboration with Elizabeth Richner) to capture various dimensions of narrative development.[8] These fell into two broad categories:

1. The first two measures (loosely adapted from work in functional linguistics and sociolinguistics) attempted to capture the *linguistic complexity and sophistication* of the children's storytelling.

2. The other category focused on the *representation of character* in the children's narratives; ongoing work suggests that examining the selection, portrayal, and coordination of characters is especially useful for capturing the development of specifically narrative sophistication and coherence in young children (Nicolopoulou, 1998; Nicolopoulou & Richner, 1999; Richner, 1999).

---

[8]Fully satisfactory standard measures still need to be designed for capturing *young* children's narrative abilities and development, and particularly for assessing their spontaneous stories. For some discussion of the limitations of currently predominant approaches, see Nicolopoulou (1996b, 1997a, 1998).

Linguistic Complexity and Sophistication.

• *Types of Utterances: Clauses vs. Non-Clauses.* For this analysis, each story was broken down into its basic expository units, or *utterances* (loosely adapting the terminology of Berman & Slobin, 1994). Utterances can be *clauses* (which contain a verb) or *non-clauses* (which do not). (Examples of non-clause utterances include disconnected names and other nouns, simple lists of characters, and more complex but still incomplete fragments of clauses—e.g., "A whole bunch of big dinosaurs," "Then the wedding boy again," etc.) One dimension of narrative development is that young children should be able to handle an increasing number of clauses effectively within a single story; furthermore, narratives should increasingly be made up of clauses, as opposed to non-clauses. The results (see Table 5.1) indicated that the number of clauses per story per child did increase significantly during the year. The mean proportion of clauses vs. non-clauses per story also increased, although this increase was not statistically significant.

• *Types of Clauses: Narrative vs. Non-Narrative.* This distinction is loosely adapted from one introduced by Labov and Waletzky (1967/1997). Essentially, *narrative clauses* move the narrative ahead by depicting a series of events in temporal sequence. *Non-narrative* clauses may be of several

TABLE 5.1
Development of Spontaneous Stories Produced
by Children in Target Class (Mean Proportions)

	Fall	Spring
Linguistic Complexity and Sophistication		
• *Types of Utterances:*		
Number of Clauses	4.67	7.73*
% Clauses vs. Non-Clauses	63 vs. 37	77 vs. 23**
• *Types of Clauses:*		
Number of Narrative	2.32	6.23**
% Narrative	51	83**
% Narrative vs. Non-Narrative	51 vs. 49	83 vs. 17***
Representation of Characters		
• *Types of Characters:*		
% Active	35	62***
% Passive	13	24
% Inactive	51	14***
% Active vs. Passive	35 vs. 13*	62 vs. 24***
% Active vs. Inactive	35 vs. 51	62 vs. 14***
• *Depth and Complexity:*	1.79	3.45***
	(Level 2)	(Level 4)
• *Interaction and Coordination:*	1.82	3.09**
	(Level 2)	(Level 3)

*$p < .01$. **$p < .001$. ***$p < .0001$.

types. In this sample, the non-narrative clauses were overwhelmingly simple descriptions, stage directions, and random comments tangential to the story—varieties of what might be termed "junk" clauses. Thus, an increasing proportion of narrative clauses in the children's stories would be an indicator of development. The results indicate that this development did occur (see Table 5.1). The mean proportion of narrative clauses per story increased quite significantly during the year.

Representation of Character.

• *Types of Characters: Active vs. Passive vs. Inactive.* The results (Table 5.1) again show clear and significant improvement. From fall to spring semester, the mean proportion of inactive characters per story decreased dramatically (fall $M = 51\%$, spring $M = 14\%$), whereas the mean proportion of active characters increased (fall $M = 35\%$, spring $M = 62\%$). In the fall, inactive characters were most frequent; in the spring, there was a low proportion of inactive characters, and a higher proportion of active than of passive characters.

• *Character Depth and Complexity.* This analysis focused on the *depth and sophistication* with which children portrayed characters in their stories. A scale with seven levels was constructed, ranging from simple actions (Level 1) and purely external descriptions (Level 2) to an increasing depiction of internal states and motivations (Levels 3–4) and the explicit depiction of intentions, desires, and beliefs mediating characters' actions (Levels 5–7). (For a more detailed presentation of the coding scheme, see Nicolopoulou, 1999; Nicolopoulou & Richner, 1999; Richner, 1999). This conceptual scheme draws, in part, on research dealing with children's social understanding and their "theories of mind" (for useful overviews, see Astington, 1993; Flavell & P. H. Miller, 1998).

The results (Table 5.1) indicated that the children significantly improved their level of character representation over the course of the year. In the fall, most children's level of optimal character depiction did not go beyond simple external descriptions (Level 2); by the spring, most children were capable of depicting characters who exhibited a perspective on the world (Level 3), and half were able to depict characters who also reacted emotionally and evaluatively to other characters (Levels 4–5).

• *Character Interaction and Coordination.* This measure attempted to capture one aspect of structural complexity and coherence in the narratives, by examining children's ability to *coordinate* characters in an effective way. A scale with six levels measured whether characters in a story interacted with other characters (Levels 2–4) and whether these interactions were fully coordinated to each other so that a coherent plot began to emerge (Levels 5–6).

The results (Table 5.1) indicated that the children significantly improved their abilities to manage character interaction during the year. In the fall, most of the children depicted character interaction at Level 2, at best (from no interaction to low interaction between characters), and only two children achieved Level 3 (medium interaction: some interaction among some of the characters). By the spring, almost all the children in the sample had achieved either Level 3 or Level 4 (high interaction). Most of these children still needed to go further before they could produce narratives with coherent and well coordinated sets of characters; but their improvement was significant.

Summary. Over the course of the year, the narrative capabilities of the children in the target class improved consistently and significantly along four of the five dimensions I have just discussed (with positive but less decisive results on the remaining dimension). It is necessary to add a cautionary note. In terms of the narrative competence and sophistication they displayed, the stories told by the children in this Head Start class in the spring were still considerably less advanced than the stories I have collected from children of equivalent ages in middle-class preschools. Despite the progress these children made in developing their narrative skills during the year, they still had a substantial amount of catching up to do in this respect. But the key point here is that the children in the target class did show a clear and significant pattern of narrative development.

Promoting Narrative Development: Figurine-Based Narrative Task

Did the use of the storytelling and story-acting practice in the target classroom help to promote this development? To address this question more directly, I now turn to evidence that allows for systematic comparison between the target and control classes: the children's performance on the FBNT.

This task was administered individually to each child in both the target and control classes in September (*pretest*) and in May (*posttest*). During a session, an adult tester sought to elicit two stories from the child. In each case, the tester began by suggesting an orienting theme and presenting a set of small figurines to illustrate the theme. One set of figurines represented a family, the other several big and powerful animals; the corresponding themes are ones I have found to be especially popular in children's own spontaneous stories (with girls particularly favoring family life, and boys the actions of powerful animals).[9]

---

[9]Of course, this procedure remains subject to some of the methodological limitations of constrained story-elicitation tasks that I mentioned earlier. However, it seemed necessary to

All children included in the sample eagerly produced responses to this task, often lengthy ones, but these were not always narratives. For purposes of analysis, each response was divided into discourse units, which were classified into three categories: *narrative, pretense,* and *other non-narrative.* "Narrative" and "pretense" discourse units both present (more or less) coherent fictional scenarios through symbolic means. What distinguishes them is the extent to which they constitute decontextualized discourse, in the sense referred to earlier in this chapter. A *narrative* discourse unit builds up a complete scenario (or portion of it) using words—a scenario that a listener could (in principle) understand without seeing the gestures of the child or physical manipulations of the figurines. To draw again on a formulation by Wells (1985), it is effectively "self-contextualizing" (p. 253). A *pretense* scenario is verbally incomplete in this sense. The child uses the figurines and other nonverbal elements to demonstrate (not merely illustrate) the actions, events, or characters being described; a significant number of elements are left implicit in the verbal account. *Other non-narrative* is a heterogeneous residual category that includes conversational interactions irrelevant to the task, nonsymbolic comments about figurines, simple counting or description, and so on. The analysis examined the mean proportions of different types of discourse units in each response—and, specifically, the relative proportions of narrative vs. non-narrative discourse units.

The results (see Table 5.2) showed a clear contrast between the target and the control classes. In the target class, the children's responses to the FBNT moved significantly and substantially in the direction of greater narrativity between the fall and the spring; the responses of the children in the control class did not. In the target class, the mean proportion of "narrative" discourse units increased dramatically (from 5% to 34%), and the proportion of "other non-narrative" units decreased correspondingly (from 69% to 33%), with a slight (and non-significant) increase in the proportion of "pretense" units. In the control class, by comparison, the proportion of "narrative" units increased only slightly (from 9% to 16%), and the change was not statistically significant; the decrease in the proportion of "other non-narrative" units was somewhat greater (from 60% to 43%), but still not quite significant; and there was a non-significant increase in the proportion of "pretense" units. In short, the children in the control class, unlike those in the target class, showed no significant improvement in the narrativity of their responses. Thus, these results strongly support

---

complement the analysis of the spontaneous stories with data that allowed for controlled comparison between the two classes; and it seemed plausible that any bias in the results toward underestimating the children's narrative capabilities should affect both classes roughly equally.

TABLE 5.2
Mean Proportions of Discourse Types Per Story-Elicitation
Response (Figurine-Based Narrative Task)

	Pretest (September)			Posttest (May)		
	%N	%P	%O	%N	%P	%O
Target Class	5	27	69	34	34	33
Control Class	9	31	60	16	42	43

Note. N = Narrative, P = Pretense, O = Other Non-Narrative.

the conclusion that participation in the storytelling and story-acting practice significantly enhanced the children's narrative development.

Building Decontextualized Language Skills: Expressive Vocabulary Test

Of the range of vocabulary tests available for use with young children, the EVT was selected because it focuses on vocabulary production rather than just comprehension, and it tests the ability of children to retrieve appropriate words, apply them, and provide synonyms for them rather than merely to recognize them. Like the FBNT, the EVT was administered to children in both the target and control classes at two times during the school year, in September and May. The scores reported here for both pretest and posttest are age-adjusted scores standardized on the basis of national norms according to the usual practice.

The results were both striking and statistically significant. In September, the mean standardized scores for the control class were significantly higher than for the target class (target $M = 92$, control $M = 96.26$). But over the course of the year, the performance of the children in the target class increased sharply, and that of the children in the control class did not, so that in May the relative positions of the two classes had actually reversed themselves (target $M = 95.33$, control $M = 92.94$).

Overall Results

Taken together, the results of these three analyses strongly support the conclusion that participation in this spontaneous storytelling and story-acting practice promoted the development of children's narrative skills (and of related decontextualized oral-language skills). As noted earlier, these positive results are consistent with those I have found in middle-class preschools where this practice is used.

EXPLAINING THE BENEFITS OF THIS PRACTICE: PEER-GROUP CULTURE AND THE DYNAMICS OF NARRATIVE COLLABORATION

In short, the evidence indicates that this storytelling and story-acting practice can significantly advance young children's narrative development. The next questions to be addressed are *how* and *why* it achieves these effects. It is clear that the kinds of mechanisms usually emphasized in the context of expert–novice interaction, such as scaffolding, expert guidance, or conversational fine-tuning, do not play an important role here. So how should the developmental benefits of children's participation in this practice be explained? Let me offer a brief, incomplete, and partly exploratory response.

As I have argued throughout this chapter, the heart of the matter is that this storytelling and story-acting practice provides the framework for an ongoing, socially structured, and collectively constituted field of shared symbolic activity. The children themselves help to generate and sustain this activity system through their participation in the storytelling and story-acting practice; and it serves, in turn, as a sociocultural context that shapes their activity and offers them opportunities, resources, and motivations for narrative development. In this respect, several (interconnected) features of this practice seem especially critical.

The first is the public, peer-oriented, and peer-evaluated character of the children's narrative activity. The stories are presented to the class as a whole, and at one point or another all the children also participate in acting out their own stories and each other's. As a result, this activity engages the children and creates a public arena for narrative collaboration, experimentation, and cross-fertilization. Let me make it clear that when I speak of collaboration here I am not referring primarily to forms of direct cooperation, such as multiauthored stories. These are common enough in the middle-class preschools I have studied (though, as it happens, there were no jointly authored stories in this Head Start class), but they are not the main point. Rather, the key vehicle for narrative collaboration in this context is the children's participation in the public arena of the storytelling and story-acting practice itself. Even in a small class of children from similar backgrounds, different children come with distinctive experiences, knowledge, skills, concerns, and temperamental styles. This practice allows these individual skills and perspectives to be transformed into shared and publicly available narrative resources, so that each child can benefit from the variety of these resources that the other children bring with them. Also, to borrow a phrase from Paley (1986), this public arena offers children an "experimental theater" (p. xv) in which they can reciprocally try out, elaborate, and refine their own narrative efforts while getting the responses of an engaged and emotionally significant peer-group audience.

Therefore, this practice can effectively integrate individual spontaneity with peer-group collaboration and mutual support. As children participate in it, they contribute to, draw on, and work with a growing common stock of themes, characters, images, plots, and other cognitive, symbolic, and linguistic resources. But at the same time, individual children can participate in this field of shared activity according to their own pace, rhythm, and inclination. Because the children are given control over what stories to tell, when to tell them, and who should act in their stories, it provides them with the opportunity to use and elaborate their narratives for their own diverse purposes—cognitive, symbolic, and social–relational.

Furthermore, the public arena of this storytelling and story-acting practice is itself enmeshed in the more general framework of the children's peer relations and group life. Again, a mutually reinforcing dynamic is at work. On the one hand, this practice helps to form and sustain a common culture in the classroom (while also facilitating the expression and articulation of differences within this common culture); and, simultaneously, this practice is shaped, supported, and energized by its embeddedness in that peer-group culture. In all the preschool classes I have studied, the emotional significance of the peer group and peer relations for young children is clearly part of what draws children into this practice and fosters their intense engagement with it.

Finally, the developmental value of this practice is greatly enhanced by the fact that its mode of combining story*telling* with story-*acting* effectively integrates elements of narrative discourse and of pretend play. I argued earlier that we need to recognize the close affinity and interdependence between the two in children's experience and development. This practice is able to utilize the interplay between them in a manner that promotes and facilitates narrative development. It does so, I would argue, in two important ways that are analytically distinct but ultimately interconnected.

First, the storytelling and story-acting portions of this practice represent two forms or dimensions of narrative activity that involve complementary cognitive and linguistic skills: (a) the highly *decontextualized* use of language in composing and dictating the stories, and (b) highly *contextualized* narrative enactment, which is characteristically a central feature of children's pretend play. The contribution of this practice lies in the way that it links these two dimensions. On the one hand, the storytelling component of the practice poses for the child an exceptionally challenging demand for decontextualized discourse, because the child is called on to construct a complete, self-contextualizing fictional narrative using only words. The child's storytelling is not embedded in an immediate framework of conversational interaction and response (which means that in certain respects the demand for decontextualized use of language here is greater than, for example, in the conversational elicitation and construction of narratives of past experience), and the composition of the story is typically several hours removed from its enactment. On the other hand, my analysis of this practice has made it clear that the reading out and enactment of the children's stories not only helps to motivate the children's storytelling, but also serves some important educative functions. In particular, it helps bring home to the child in a vivid way what is required for a narrative scenario to be effectively complete, self-contextualizing, and satisfying.

The second major implication of this integration of narrative discourse and enactment brings us back to some key factors we have already discussed. The story-acting portion of this practice puts the children's storytelling into a public arena and embeds the practice as a whole in the framework of the children's peer relations and group life. For example, choices about who acts in whose stories, and which roles they are given, express and help structure patterns of friendship, affiliation, and group inclusion; and one concern that influences the children's storytelling is the effort to provide roles that actual and potential friends will find desirable, or that can give the author a claim on desirable roles in the future. In these and other ways, the children's engagement in the activity is reinforced and partly channeled by a range of powerful social–relational motivations.

In combination, these features help explain why this storytelling and story-acting practice can be a powerful context for promoting the narrative development of young children. To flesh out this analysis a bit, I offer a brief and selective account of how some of these dynamics operated in the concrete setting of the Head Start class.

The First Phase: Searching for Narrative Form

As soon as the storytelling and story-acting practice was initiated in the target class in early October, most of the children were immediately eager to tell stories and all were eager to participate in acting them out. Within a short time, almost all the children were participating enthusiastically in both components of this activity, and their enthusiasm remained undiminished throughout the year. During a storytelling session, there were always several children gathered around the story table, waiting their turns fairly patiently while other children dictated (and these were not, on the whole, very patient children). When characters were being chosen, many children vigorously advertised their desire to be picked, even waving their hands and shouting "me, me" to request desired roles.

At first, however, their enthusiasm outran their narrative competence. As noted earlier, by comparison with the children in the middle-class preschool classrooms I have studied these children began the year considerably less prepared to compose free-standing fictional narratives. This was not entirely surprising, though I was a little surprised by the extent to which it was true for this sample. Whitehurst et al. (1994) cited other studies estimating that "a typical middle-class child enters first grade with [previous experience of] 1,000 to 1,700 hr of one-on-one picture book reading, whereas the corresponding child from a low-income family averages 25 such hours" (p. 679). And Peterson (1994) found that young children with the weakest narrative skills tended to come from households that combined low income with "family disorganization," which was true for almost all the children in both the target and control classes. This chapter has argued against a one-sided focus on the role of adult–child relations in children's socialization and development, but it would also be foolishly one-sided to overlook their importance. In terms of their narrative capabilities, these Head Start children started out at a disadvantage due to weaknesses in narrative knowledge and skills that the corresponding middle-class preschoolers had acquired more fully in their earlier years, primarily (one can assume) in the context of relations with adult caregivers.

Thus, at the beginning of the year, most of the children did not display effective familiarity with many of the basic, minimal conventions of telling a story, such as beginning with a setting statement, explicitly relating events in temporal sequence, and so on. Even more fundamentally, most of them did not seem to fully grasp the principle that their stories needed to be explicitly self-contextualizing—that is, that they needed to construct a complete narrative scenario using words. In their first attempts at storytelling, the children simply listed a string of characters (and sometimes mentioned other potentially relevant elements), usually without providing any actions or descriptions for the characters, let alone relating them to each other or integrating them into plots. For the first 3 weeks of storytelling, all the "stories" were of a type captured by this example:

> That is a book. The Rex, Tyrannosaurus Rex. A longneck, tigers. Now bear, fish. Now alligator. Big fish. Now polar bears. Next is butterflies, flower, and—I know it's a secret—a Rex, two Rexes. And that's how much animals, and another. A tiger, a boy. (Darren, 4-4)[10]

At times, the teacher transcribing these protostories tried to elicit some elaboration from the child, by asking, for example, "What does this character do?" But in most cases the children answered "I don't know" or ignored her questions. The few who did respond seemed to understand this question as a request to describe a characteristic or stereotypical action of the character (e.g., the snake goes "ssss," the frog goes "ribbit," the dino-

---

[10]Pseudonyms are used for all children quoted or otherwise discussed here.

saur wags his tail), and they usually demonstrated these actions rather than explaining them verbally—that is, they were showing rather than telling. The teacher's interventions did not seem to move the stories toward an adequate narrative form.

However, the story-acting component of this practice appears to have played a major role in helping the children move toward more fully self-contextualizing discourse in composing their stories. This was true in part because the enactment of the children's stories often brought home to them why listing characters was not enough to create a satisfying story. For example, one child, whose dictated "story" had consisted only of a set of characters with no actions, became upset when the teacher asked her and the other child-actors to sit down after this list had been read out (Deena, 4–6). The child turned to the teacher with surprise and said emphatically, "But we didn't do it!" She had obviously envisioned her characters performing some actions, even though she had not explicitly given them any. When the teacher let them proceed, the children acted out stereotypic actions associated with each character role. Another child (Bianca, 3-4), in her first storytelling attempt, listed a set of characters and other story elements ("a frog, a log") without indicating how they were related. However, when the teacher read the story to the class for its enactment, and Bianca was preparing to act out her own role as frog, she turned to "correct" the teacher's reading of her story by announcing what had originally been implicit: "The frog *sits* on the log." In short, the acting-out of their stories helped the children to understand the need to construct a complete and explicitly self-contextualizing narrative scenario when they composed the stories.

But the most crucial feature of the story-acting was its role in making the children's storytelling a public and peer-oriented activity; this allowed the children to use the storytelling and story-acting practice as a shared public arena for narrative collaboration and cross-fertilization.

Finding the Story: The Emergence of a Shared Genre Through Narrative Collaboration

The dynamics of this peer collaboration become apparent when we consider the process by which the children were able to move beyond their initial phase of protonarrative groping. About 3 weeks after the initiation of this practice, one of the girls, April, produced a story that for the first time met the minimal standards for a free-standing fictional story.

> Wedding girl and wedding boy, and then there was a baby. And then there was the person that brought out the flowers. And then there was some animal that wrecked the house, the church house that people were getting married in. And a person was listening to a wedding tape. And that's all. (April, 5–1).

Clearly, this story was not yet very sophisticated. It lacked such basic devices as a formal beginning, and the sequence of events was laid out in a loose and partly implicit way, by bringing in a series of characters and assigning actions to each in turn. However, in comparison with the stories that preceded it, this one displayed some important strengths. It constructed a relatively coherent and explicit scenario, presenting a set of interrelated characters and integrating them within a sketchy but readily discernible plot. In the process, it introduced, and combined, a set of organizing themes that were to prove powerfully appealing to other children in the class: first, a wedding, featuring the two linked characters of Wedding Boy (WB) and Wedding Girl (WG); and second, animal aggression.

The major significance of April's story is that this story paradigm was gradually taken up, with variations, by other children in the class, until it became pervasive in the children's storytelling. But it is worth noting that April herself did not immediately repeat or elaborate this storyline. It was first taken up and reused, with variations, 3 weeks later by Anton, a boy who had been given the role of WB in April's first story; in Anton's story, the wedding couple got married and then went on to have children (an event that, incidentally, happens very rarely in boys' stories). It was not until the day after Anton's story, following this recognition and appropriation of the storyline by a classroom peer, that April told a second story. She again used the WG/WB + animal aggression model, but with her own variations; most notably, the animal aggression was directed explicitly against one of the wedding couple: "And the animal wrecked the house that people were getting married were dancing in. And the animal ate the wedding girl." April's second story was part of a flurry of similar stories by other children, and stories using this cluster of themes became increasingly popular as the year went on.

This story paradigm thus became the common property of the classroom peer group. By the end of the fall semester, it had become a hegemonic model for the children's storytelling, and a shared point of reference even for stories that used different themes wholly or in part. By the spring semester, all children who told stories had used versions of this model, or at least some of its elements, in a number of their stories (see Fig. 5.1); and the overall proportion of stories that incorporated this model and/or drew on its central themes, in various configurations, was quite high (100% for some children; see Fig. 5.2).[11] Furthermore, within a short time following the group's adoption of this model in the fall, the

---

[11]One of the children included in these figures, Marcus, was a newcomer who joined the class in the spring; for this reason, his stories were not included in the statistical analyses discussed earlier. (The stories by Lettrice were also not included in the previous analyses, because she was not administered the EVT and FBNT in the fall due to a tester's oversight.)

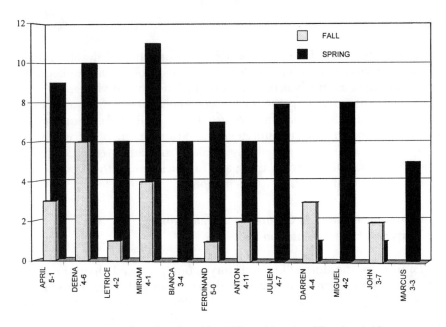

FIG. 5.1.   Number of stories with wedding girl and wedding boy (with or without animal aggression).

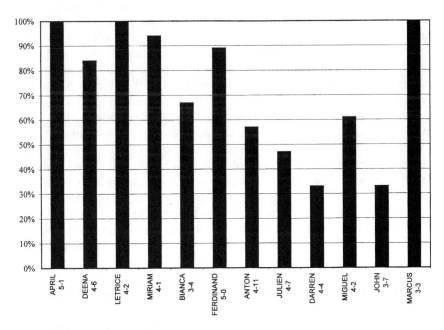

FIG. 5.2.   Percentage of stories with wedding girl and wedding boy (with or without animal aggression).

143

children largely ceased to dictate protostories consisting of simple strings of inactive characters; with a very few exceptions, all their stories became more advanced, even when they used other kinds of storylines.

In short, this narrative paradigm became a cultural tool that was shared and elaborated by the classroom peer group as a whole. This is a major example of the way in which the storytelling and story-acting practice helped to create a shared body of publicly available narrative resources from which different children could draw, and to which in turn they could contribute, in the course of their participation.

Constructing a Common Culture as a Framework for Narrative Experimentation

In the process, the storytelling and story-acting practice helped the children to build up a common culture in the classroom, and the shared narrative paradigm just described became a key unifying feature of their common culture. This process was reinforced by the fact that children who joined the class during the year were almost always included in the classroom peer group by being given parts in story-acting performances, and then usually made their own bids for inclusion by drawing on versions of the dominant story paradigm to compose their first stories. At the same time, this common culture, and the narrative activity with which it was enmeshed, provided a framework for narrative experimentation and diversity. Children drew elements from each other's stories, but they also used and developed them in somewhat different ways, and generally managed to put their personal stamp on them. Even when children told stories using this central narrative paradigm, they developed variations on it over time—which could then be used and elaborated by other children.

These patterns of elaboration and reshaping were complex, and can only be touched on here. For example, whereas April's first stories had described a generic "animal" as the source of violence, a tendency soon developed to give the aggressing animal greater specificity. This took several forms. Darren, one of whose primitive protostories was quoted earlier, was the first child to tell a WB/WG + aggression story in which the aggressing animal was identified as a dinosaur; the dinosaur motif became sufficiently popular that dinosaur aggression emerged as a major shared theme in its own right (see Table 5.3). Other animals (T-Rex, tiger, shark, elephant) also came to be used for this purpose, in a range of variations and combinations, sometimes fighting each other as well as attacking the wedding couple. Some children, primarily girls, gradually elaborated the description of the wedding ceremony, adding new details and characters. Other children, primarily boys, elaborated the themes of violence, aggression, and disorder, sometimes with only a perfunctory mention of WB and WG.

TABLE 5.3
Mean Proportions of Some Common Themes
in Stories Told by Children in the Target Class

	Girls	Boys
Wedding Girl & Wedding Boy	80%	51%
WG & WB + Aggression	68%	49%
Dinosaur Aggression	52%	62%

(For some patterns of variation in the use of the different themes, see Table 5.3). In stories expressing this tendency, the configurations of conflict and disruption became more detailed, complex, and imaginative.

Here is one example from the spring (3/24/98), which displays considerable narrative exuberance, though not much formal elegance:

> The police. And the wedding girl and the wedding boy get married. And the police get the wedding girl, and the people were there and killed the wedding girl. And then they put her in the dirt. And then they turn like vampires. And then the police put the girl in the water. And then the dad with the gun killed the police. And then the grandma comes, and she opened the house, and the girl goes upstairs, and they close the door. And then the bad guys kill the police—all of the police. The bad guy gets the girl in the car, and then the ambulance comes, and the fire at home, and they went walking through the water at home. (Ferdinand, 5–5)

Note that Ferdinand begins the story with a fairly compact and coherent scenario, but he then cannot resist elaborating further, mostly by multiplying images of violence and disruption, and this elaboration pulls the coherence of the story apart. Despite these and other weaknesses, the ambition and the quality of this story contrast sharply with those of the proto-stories that predominated in the first phases of the children's storytelling (including Ferdinand's first attempts, which consisted of very simple lists).

Thus, the processes of narrative collaboration and variation were intertwined and mutually supportive. One of the key features that helped make this peer-group practice such a powerful context for promoting the children's narrative development, I would argue, is precisely the way it allowed and encouraged this interplay.

Narrative Elaboration, Development—and Limitations

The thread I have followed in this account, centering on the role of this key story paradigm within the peer-group culture of the class, captures only a portion of the overall picture. But it does bring out some important dynamics. It is worth reemphasizing that the process just outlined was not initiated or directly furthered by the adults in the classroom—who, in fact, were surprised and puzzled by the appeal of the WB/WG/animal aggression story model. Nor can it be attributed directly to the child who first used this storyline, April. She did introduce this narrative paradigm into the classroom miniculture, but then other children took major roles in its diffusion and elaboration; and within a short time it had become the common property of the peer-group culture as a whole. It thus became a shared resource that was used as a basis for continuing narrative experimentation and cross-fertilization. Different children were able to appropriate the themes it provided and to work them over and elaborate them in their own ways. The pattern of repetition, variation, and elaboration that this involved appears to be one of the important tools that children use to gain a sense of the possibilities inherent in narrative form and to achieve a greater mastery of these possibilities.

In the process, the overall quality of the stories produced by the children in this Head Start class improved significantly over the course of the school year (as demonstrated by the results presented earlier). The stories became more ambitious, complex, coherent, and effective. Characters were portrayed more sharply and substantially; and both the characters and their actions were coordinated more effectively. Of course, some children were more successful than others; and the patterns of improvement in the stories of individual children were invariably complex rather than simple or unilinear, not least because they reflected an interplay of partly competing priorities. In some cases, for example, when children had mastered the ability to compose simple but fairly coherent stories, they would begin pushing their stories further, adding more characters, themes, and actions, and in some cases trying to move from single- to multiple-episode stories. When this happened, the result was usually increased tension between the richness and complexity of the stories and their coherence, with the coherence of the stories temporarily losing ground. But, overall, the children's pattern of narrative improvement was clear and significant.

It is important to recognize the continuing weaknesses and limitations in the narrative skills of the children in this class, even at the end of the year. Compared to middle-class preschool children I have studied, they still displayed considerably less ability to use narrative in flexible, confident, and sophisticated ways. This was not only true in terms of criteria of linguistic and structural complexity and sophistication. It was also reflected in the narrower range of themes, plots, and other cultural elements that the Head Start children were able to incorporate and use effectively in their stories. It is striking that this Head Start class developed only one powerful shared genre, whereas the classes I have studied in middle-class preschools invariably develop and elaborate a number of such genres.

The relative weakness in the Head Start children's mastery of narrative skills and resources probably also helps account for the curious fact that the themes used in their stories were less sharply polarized along gender lines than in those of the middle-class children. Although this matter requires a more extended analysis than can be offered here, it is likely that one crucial reason for this result was that the children in the target class were simply not yet able to elaborate fully distinctive narrative styles of this sort. (It would be intriguingly counterintuitive if the reason were that the worldviews of the Head Start children were less gender-differentiated and gender-stereotyped than those of the middle-class children. But a substantial amount of evidence, from classroom observations and other sources, renders this interpretation quite implausible.) The experience of this Head Start class suggests that it is first necessary for the children to establish a common culture as a framework for narrative experimentation and collaboration, before they can go on to articulate and elaborate narrative subcultures within the group; these children were presumably still working in the first stage.

But despite these reservations and limitations, it remains true that participation in the storytelling and story-acting practice promoted a quite significant improvement in the narrative skills and performance of the children in this Head Start class. This is especially impressive given the children's relatively weak mastery of narrative skills and conventions at the beginning of the year. Because these children did not begin with a strong foundation of narrative skills and resources, one might have expected that they would be especially dependent on further adult input and scaffolding—and, of course, such forms of adult–child interaction can play an important role in promoting their development. But in fact, the children contributed quite effectively to promoting each other's narrative development through a process of collaboration in the context of this peer-oriented narrative activity.

CONCLUSIONS AND IMPLICATIONS

The research reported in this chapter has demonstrated that a peer-oriented storytelling and story-acting practice of the type analyzed here can serve as a powerful context for promoting young children's narrative development. I submit that these findings have important implications, both theoretical and practical.

First, they provide strong evidence that certain forms of peer-group activity, when carefully and appropriately integrated into the preschool curriculum, can contribute to young children's development and education in ways that usefully complement the role of more direct adult–child interactions. This opens up valuable possibilities for early childhood education.

For example, Peterson et al. (1999) reported that an intervention program aimed at changing mothers' styles of conversational interaction with their children in poor families increased the children's narrative skills, but when similar intervention programs were attempted in preschools, "None of them had any effect" (p. 65). The reasons, they argued, are that effecting such changes requires a much greater frequency of sustained adult–child interaction than teachers or other school professionals can realistically provide, and that teacher–child interactions lack the emotional importance of the mother–child relationship. This failure "suggests that it is very difficult to change narrative skills in school-based programmes" (p. 65). This may be true if one focuses exclusively on modes of dyadic adult–child interaction. But precisely the two factors they mentioned are among the most important that help explain the success of the storytelling and story-acting practice in improving children's narrative skills. Because it utilizes a resource that is plentiful in the classroom (other children) rather than one that is relatively scarce (adults and their time), it can generate a very high volume of peer-oriented participation, interaction, and collaboration; and the emotional importance of peer-group relations for young children heightens their engagement in this activity, its impact on them, and its developmental value.

More generally, this chapter has sought to suggest some concrete ways that developmental research can, and should, move beyond an exclusive focus on dyadic adult–child interaction for understanding the role of social context in development. Both narrative research and educational practice should treat children's group life as a developmental context of prime importance and great potential, and should seek to identify, understand, and facilitate those forms of peer-group activity that can most effectively engage children in ways that promote their narrative development.

ACKNOWLEDGMENTS

The research discussed in this chapter was partly supported by a Spencer Foundation Small Grant and a Junior Faculty Fellowship from Lehigh University; and portions of it were carried out in collaboration with Elizabeth Richner. I am grateful to the editors of this collection, Shoshana Blum-Kulka and Catherine Snow, for their useful comments, queries, and suggestions. And I am indebted to Jeff Weintraub for extensive advice, constructive criticism, and theoretical guidance.

REFERENCES

Astington, J. W. (1993). *The child's discovery of the mind*. Cambridge, MA: Harvard University Press.

Aukrust, V. G., & Snow, C. E. (1998). Narratives and explanations during mealtime conversations in Norway and the U.S. *Language in Society, 27,* 221–246.

Berman, R., & Slobin, D. I. (Eds.). (1994). *Relating events in narrative: A crosslinguistic developmental study.* Hillsdale, NJ: Lawrence Erlbaum Associates.

Blum-Kulka, S. (1997). *Dinner talk: Cultural patterns of sociability and socialization in family discourse.* Mahwah, NJ: Lawrence Erlbaum Associates.

Brown, J. R., & Dunn, J. (1992). Talk with your mother or your sibling? Developmental changes in early family conversation about feelings. *Child Development, 63,* 336–349.

Corsaro, W. A. (1985). *Friendship and peer culture in the early years.* Norwood, NJ: Ablex.

Damon, W. (1984). Peer education: The untapped potential. *Journal of Applied Developmental Psychology, 5,* 331–343.

Damon, W. (1988). *The moral child: Nurturing children's natural moral growth.* New York: The Free Press.

Davies, B. (1989). *Frogs and snails and feminist tales: Preschool children and gender.* North Sydney, Australia: Allen & Unwin.

Dickinson, D. K., Cote, L., & Smith, M. W. (1993). Learning vocabulary in preschool: Social and discourse contexts affecting vocabulary growth. *New Directions for Child Development, 61,* 67–77.

Dunn, J. (1988). *The beginnings of social understanding.* Cambridge, MA: Harvard University Press.

Dunn, J. (1989). Siblings and the development of social understanding in early childhood. In P. G. Zukow (Ed.), *Sibling interaction across cultures* (pp. 106–116). New York: Springer-Verlag.

Ely, R., & Gleason, J. B. (1995). Socialization across contexts. In P. Fletcher & B. MacWhinney (Eds.), *The handbook of child language* (pp. 251–270). Cambridge, MA: Blackwell.

Fivush, R. (1994). Constructing narrative, emotion, and self in parent–child conversations about the past. In U. Neisser & R. Fivush (Eds.), *The remembering self: Construction and accuracy in the self-narrative* (pp. 136–157). New York: Cambridge University Press.

Flavell, J. H., & Miller, P. H. (1998). Social cognition. In W. Damon (Gen. Ed.) & D. Kuhn & R. Siegler (Vol. Eds.), *Handbook of child psychology: Vol. 2. Cognition, perception, and language* (5th ed., pp. 851–898). New York: Wiley.

Galloway, C., & Richards, B. (1994). *Input and interaction in language acquisition.* London: Cambridge University Press.

Garvey, C. (1984). *Children's talk.* Cambridge, MA: Harvard University Press.

Garvey, C. (1986). Peer relations and the growth of communication. In E. C. Mueller & C. R. Cooper (Eds.), *Process and outcome in peer relationships* (pp. 329–345). Orlando, FL: Academic Press.

Garvey, C. (1990). *Play* (2nd ed.). Cambridge, MA: Harvard University Press. (Original work published 1977)

Harris, J. R. (1995). Where is the child's environment?: A group socialization theory of development. *Psychological Review, 102,* 458–489.

Harris, J. R. (1998). *The nurture assumption: Why children turn out the way they do.* New York: The Free Press.

Heath, S. B. (1982). What no bedtime story means: Narrative skills at home and school. *Language in Society, 11,* 49–76.

Heath, S. B. (1983). *Ways with words: Language, life, and work in communities and classrooms.* New York: Cambridge University Press.

Hudson, J. A., & Shapiro, L. R. (1991). From knowing to telling: The development of children's scripts, stories, and personal narratives. In A. McCabe & C. Peterson (Eds.), *Developing narrative structure* (pp. 89–136). Hillsdale, NJ: Lawrence Erlbaum Associates.

Huizinga, J. (1955). *Homo ludens: A study of the play element in culture.* Boston: Beacon Press. (Original work published in Dutch in 1938)

Labov, W., & Waletzky, J. (1997). Narrative analysis: Oral versions of personal experience. *Journal of Narrative and Life History, 7,* 3–38. (Original work published 1967)

McCabe, A., & Peterson, C. (1991). Getting the story: A longitudinal study of parental styles in eliciting narratives and developing narrative skill. In A. McCabe & C. Peterson (Eds.), *Developing narrative structure* (pp. 217–253). Hillsdale, NJ: Lawrence Erlbaum Associates.

McNamee, G. D. (1990). Learning to read and write in an inner-city setting: A longitudinal study of community change. In L. C. Moll (Ed.), *Vygotsky and education: Instructional implications and applications of sociohistorical psychology* (pp. 287–303). New York: Cambridge University Press.

McNamee, G. D. (1992). Vivian Paley's ideas at work in Head Start. *The Quarterly Newsletter of the Laboratory of Comparative Human Cognition, 14,* 68–70.

Miller, P. J., & Moore, B. B. (1989). Narrative conjunctions of caregiver and child: A comparative perspective on socialization through stories. *Ethos, 17,* 428–449.

Nicolopoulou, A. (1993). Play, cognitive development, and the social world: Piaget, Vygotsky, and beyond. *Human Development, 36,* 1–23.

Nicolopoulou, A. (1996a). Narrative development in social context. In D. I. Slobin, J. Gerhardt, J. Guo, & A. Kyratzis (Eds.), *Social interaction, social context, and language: Essays in honor of Susan Ervin-Tripp* (pp. 369–390). Mahwah, NJ: Lawrence Erlbaum Associates.

Nicolopoulou, A. (1996b, July). *Problems, strategies, and intentions in young children's narrative genres.* Paper presented at the annual meeting of the International Congress for the Study of Child Language, Istanbul, Turkey.

Nicolopoulou, A. (1997a). Children and narratives: Toward an interpretive and sociocultural approach. In M. Bamberg (Ed.), *Narrative development: Six approaches.* Mahwah, NJ: Lawrence Erlbaum Associates.

Nicolopoulou, A. (1997b). Worldmaking and identity formation in children's narrative playacting. In B. D. Cox & C. Lightfoot (Eds.), *Sociogenetic perspectives on internalization* (pp. 157–187). Mahwah, NJ: Lawrence Erlbaum Associates.

Nicolopoulou, A. (1998, June). *The elementary forms of narrative coherence in young children's storytelling.* Paper presented at the 1998 Annual Meeting of the Jean Piaget Society, Chicago.

Nicolopoulou, A. (1999). *Mobilizing the untapped potential of peer-group practices in preschool settings to promote narrative development and emergent literacy in low-income children* (Final Report to the Spencer Foundation). Unpublished research report, Lehigh University, Bethlehem, PA.

Nicolopoulou, A., & Cole, M. (1993). The generation and transmission of shared knowledge in the culture of collaborative learning: The Fifth Dimension, its play-world, and its institutional contexts. In E. A. Forman, N. Minick, & C. A. Stone (Eds.), *Contexts for learning: Sociocultural dynamics in children's development* (pp. 283–314). New York: Oxford University Press.

Nicolopoulou, A., & Richner, E. S. (1999, September). *Narrative development and emergent literacy in social context: Integrating peer-group practices in the education of low-income children.* Paper presented in an invited symposium on "The collaborative classroom as a context for development" at the IXth European Conference on Developmental Psychology, Spetses, Greece.

Nicolopoulou, A., Scales, B., & Weintraub, J. (1994). Gender differences and symbolic imagination in the stories of four-year-olds. In A. H. Dyson & C. Genishi (Eds.), *The need for story: Cultural diversity in classroom and community* (pp. 102–123). Urbana, IL: NCTE.

Nicolopoulou, A., & Weintraub, J. (1998). Individual and collective representations in social context: A modest contribution to resuming the interrupted project of a sociocultural developmental psychology. *Human Development, 41,* 215–235.

Ochs, E. (1988). *Culture and language development: Language acquisition and language socialization in a Samoan village.* Cambridge, England: Cambridge University Press.

Ochs, E., Smith, R., & Taylor, C. (1989). Detective stories at dinnertime: Problem-solving through co-narration. *Cultural Dynamics, 2,* 238–257.

Ochs, E., Taylor, C., Rudolph, D., & Smith, R. (1992). Storytelling as a theory-building activity. *Discourse Processes, 15,* 37–72.

Paley, V. (1986). *Mollie is three: Growing up in school.* Chicago: University of Chicago Press.

Paley, V. (1988). *Bad guys don't have birthdays.* Chicago: University of Chicago Press.

Paley, V. (1990). *The boy who would be a helicopter: The uses of storytelling in the classroom.* Cambridge, MA: Harvard University Press.

Peterson, C. (1994). Narrative skills and social class. *Canadian Journal of Education, 19,* 251–269.

Peterson, C., Jesso, B., & McCabe, A. (1999). Encouraging narratives in preschoolers: An intervention study. *Journal of Child Language, 26,* 49–67.

Piaget, J. (1959). *The language and thought of the child.* London: Routledge. (Original work published in French in 1923, 3rd ed. 1945)

Piaget, J. (1965). *The moral judgment of the child.* New York: The Free Press. (Original work published in French in 1932)

Richner, E. S. (1999). *From actors to characters to persons: The development of character representation in young children's narratives.* Unpublished master's thesis, Lehigh University, Bethlehem, PA.

Richner, E. S., & Nicolopoulou, A. (2001). The narrative construction of differing conceptions of the person in the development of young children's social understanding. *Early Education and Development, 12,* 393–432.

Rogoff, B. (1998). Cognition as a collaborative process. In W. Damon (Gen. Ed.) & D. Kuhn & R. S. Siegler (Vol. Eds.), *Handbook of child psychology: Vol. 2. Cognition, perception and language* (5th ed., pp. 679–744). New York: Wiley.

Schieffelin, B. B., & Ochs, E. (Eds.). (1986). *Language socialization across cultures.* New York: Cambridge University Press.

Snow, C. E. (1983). Literacy and language: Relationships during the preschool years. *Harvard Educational Review, 53,* 165–189.

Snow, C. E. (1989). Understanding social interaction and language acquisition: Sentences are not enough. In M. H. Bornstein & J. S. Bruner (Eds.), *Interaction in human development* (pp. 83–103). Hillsdale, NJ: Lawrence Erlbaum Associates.

Snow, C. E. (1991). The theoretical basis for relationships between language and literacy in development. *Journal of Research in Childhood Education, 6,* 5–10.

Snow, C. E. (1995). Issues in the study of input: Finetuning, universality, individual and developmental differences, and necessary causes. In P. Fletcher & B. MacWhinney (Eds.), *The handbook of child language* (pp. 180–193). Cambridge, MA: Blackwell.

Snow, C. E., & Dickinson, D. K. (1990). Social sources of narrative skills at home and at school. *First Language, 10,* 87–103.

Snow, C. E., & Dickinson, D. K. (1991). Skills that aren't basic in a new conception of literacy. In E. M. Jennings & A. C. Purves (Eds.), *Literate systems and individual lives: Perspectives on literacy and schooling* (pp. 179–191). Albany: State University of New York Press.

Stambak, M., & Sinclair, H. (Eds.). (1993). *Pretend play among 3-year-olds.* Hillsdale, NJ: Lawrence Erlbaum Associates.

Sutton-Smith, B. (1986). The development of fictional narrative performances. *Topics in Language Disorders, 7,* 1–10.

Tudge, J., & Rogoff, B. (1989). Peer influences on cognitive development: Piagetian and Vygotskian perspectives. In M. H. Bornstein & J. S. Bruner (Eds.), *Interaction in human development* (pp. 17–40). Hillsdale, NJ: Lawrence Erlbaum Associates.

Vygotsky, L. S. (1967). Play and its role in the mental development of the child [Translation of a stenographic record of a lecture given in Russian in 1933]. *Soviet Psychology, 12,* 6–18.

Wells, G. (1985). Preschool literacy-related activities and success in school. In D. R. Olson, N. Torrance, & A. Hildyard (Eds.), *Literacy, language, and learning: The nature and consequences of reading and writing* (pp. 229–255). New York: Cambridge University Press.

Wells, G. (1986). *The meaning makers: Children learning language and using language to learn.* Portsmouth, NH: Heinemann.

Whitehurst, G. J., Arnold, D. S., Epstein, J. N., Angell, A. L., Smith, M., & Fischel, J. F. (1994). A picture book reading intervention in day care and home for children from low-income families. *Developmental Psychology, 30,* 679–689.

Whiting, B., & Whiting, J. (1975). *Children of six cultures: A psycho-cultural analysis.* Cambridge, MA: Harvard University Press.

Williams, K. (1997). *Expressive vocabulary test.* Circle Pines, MN: American Guidance Service.

Zukow, P. G. (Ed.). (1989a). *Sibling interaction across cultures.* New York: Springer-Verlag.

Zukow, P. G. (1989b). Siblings as effective socializing agents: Evidence from central Mexico. In P. G. Zukow (Ed.), *Sibling interaction across cultures* (pp. 79–105). New York: Springer-Verlag.

Part II

THE LANGUAGE OF AFFECT AND HUMOR: PRAGMATIC DEVELOPMENTAL PERSPECTIVES

Chapter 6

Socialization of Affect During Mealtime Interactions

Christine Hérot
Massachusetts General Hospital, Boston

Gathering around the table to share a meal may, for some families, be a daily routine that follows ritual patterns and provides children with a context where they can learn the idiosyncratic norms and affective inner-workings of their family. For some (fragmented) families, however, mealtimes may not be an organized and entirely predictable event: Family constellations can defy our societal and cultural expectations. Yet, even if the cast of family members that sits at the table fluctuates in size and membership, the verbal and nonverbal interactions that take place during mealtimes remain embedded in the affective fabric unique to each family.

The socialization of affect within families is a complex process through which parents can help their children understand their own emotions (Eisenberg, 1992), develop a sense of empathy for others, and function as competent "emotional" beings in their culture.

Children's affective development occurs along several pathways that include verbal and nonverbal domains of affect and requires the learning of appropriate emotional displays, the recognition of emotions (one's own as well as those of others), and the management and regulation of one's emotions. The acquisition of verbal expressions of affect includes the learning of emotion words and concepts and the ability to map these words onto feeling states. The capacity to recognize one's emotions and the variety of emotions one can experience evolves as children become more mature "feeling" beings. For instance children who are 5 years old usually deny the coexistence of two feelings but by age 10 they are capable of appreciat-

155

ing the possibility of experiencing conflicting feelings simultaneously, such as regret and relief or anger and love. The development of nonverbal affect also follows developmental milestones. Children learn to recognize other's nonverbal displays of affect as they learn the social rules of congruent nonverbal affective expressions (e.g., smiling and expressing positive affect while receiving a disappointing gift).

The impact of expressed parental affect on children's emotional development is far-reaching. Warmth and praise, for instance, have positive effects on children's self-image and socioemotional competence (Denham, Renwick, & Holt, 1991). Parental warmth is correlated to children's empathy, altruism, and nurturance (Mac Donald, 1992). Mothers' empathic, warm caretaking has been associated with 1- and 2-year-olds' prosocial behaviors directed to others in distress (Zahn-Waxler, Radke-Yarrow, & King, 1979).

In this chapter we report on a qualitative analysis of expression of affect (verbal and nonverbal) in various family interactions during mealtimes. We looked at the verbal expression of affect, the nonverbal tone of voice of the mother, and how these varied as a function of the actual family configurations: mother–child dyads, triads, and multiparty family interactions. Engaging in interaction with several rather than just one interlocutor clearly may expand the variety and frequency of emotions expressed and expected, thus perhaps constituting a richer context for the socialization of emotion. Conversely, the presence of several interlocutors may increase the felt need to modulate emotional display in the interests of politeness thus constituting a rich context for the socialization of emotional expression. We were interested in (a) whether there was any verbal communication of affect during mealtimes, (b) the overall quality of mother's nonverbal expression of warmth and patience, and (c) whether family configurations (dyads vs. triads. vs. multiparty) seems to influence the verbal and nonverbal expression of positive affect.

LITERATURE

Socialization of Verbal Affect in the Family

Socialization of affect in the family occurs through modeling of behaviors as children observe, learn about, and tend to imitate the behaviors of other people who play an important and powerful role in their lives (Eisenberg, 1992). Affect can be socialized through the use of words. Symbolic modeling such as preaching—talk about the importance of being kind and generous to others—appears to have an impact on children. But some socialization techniques are more successful than others. For instance Eisenberg (1992) showed that "general" statements such as "people should give" may be less effective than empathy-inducing statements. That is, children who hear empathy-inducing statements seem to be more receptive to the statements and are more likely to engage in empathic behaviors themselves than those who are simply told to act prosocially.

Other socialization strategies such as prosocial attributions—a parent telling a child that he is a gentle person—may also promote prosocial behaviors, as can some disciplinary techniques such as reasoning and inducements, as opposed to punishment.

The effective socialization of affect is also influenced by the quality of the parent–child relationship. Children are more likely to imitate a model if they have a positive relationship with the adult and if the adult has displayed contingent and consistent warmth. In cases where parents express noncontingent warmth, the children simply seem to do as they please (Eisenberg, 1992).

Culture and Socialization of Affect

The pragmatic rules of appropriate affective displays are culturally bound and defined. Ninio and Snow (1996) pointed out that the pragmatic linguistic development in children not only includes the acquisition of communicative intent but also the acquisition of rules of politeness and other culturally determined rules for using speech. In parallel, children have to acquire the cultural pragmatics of emotional displays both linguistically and nonverbally. In the United States communication of affect is linguistically marked by the use of lexical terms such as emotion words (happy, sad), terms of endearment (honey, sweetie), or verbs (cry, laugh) etc. The use of such linguistic markers is governed by the situational context and the power differential, closeness, and intimacy between interlocutors. Moreover, within the U.S. culture, socioeconomic status and minority status also play a role in determining the frequency and situational use of lexical markers of affect.

Similar culturally specific rules influence the display of nonverbal affect and children are socialized to express the emotions that are valued not only within their society but also within their family. The emotional scripts that have to be acquired by the children for them to be considered emotionally competent may sometimes be nonuniversal and idiosyncratic (Lewis, 1989). Ochs (1988), for instance, reported that Samoan has a rich system of encoding positive affect: grammatically through the use of interjections, pronouns, changes in phonological registers and pragmatically through the use of intensifiers, specifiers, and turn-taking constraints. Ochs (1988) also stated that in Samoan "affect once encoded is a powerful means of securing some desirable response from others, constraining

what will be said next and what will be done next; and young children understand this cause–effect quite early in Western Samoa and use language
to this end from the start" (p. 183). The socialization of affect in the Samoan culture points to the valued social displays that parents expect from
their children. Samoan caregivers use empathy as a control strategy to invoke specific feelings in a child who has done something wrong. Instilling
fear is another means to control children as well as shaming and the use of
derogatory nicknames. Socializing children to behave respectfully is of ut-
most importance. Respectful behaviors are defined in part as being attentive to others through greeting and serving and through the ability to take
the perspective of others.

Within each culture affective expressions can take various linguistic and
nonverbal forms and the socialization of affect reflects the values given to
specific emotions and to their appropriate social display. The socialization
of affect follows a complex pattern of culturally determined pathways
learned very early on by young members of the culture and transmitted
intergenerationally.

Socialization of Affect and the Development
of Perspective-Taking Skills

Emotionally competent children and adults in the U.S. culture are expected to express certain kinds of emotions in specific situations and be
able to read and respond to affective displays in others. The inability to
read affective cues in others or to express congruent affect can be a sign of
psychopathology (Camras, Grow, & Ribordy, 1983; McCown, Johnson, &
Austin, 1986; Zabel, 1979). Perspective-taking is essential in the understanding of emotions expressed by others and follows a developmental
pathway that enables young children to attend to more subtle cues in affective expressions in others as their perspective-taking skills mature
(Eisenberg & Strayer, 1987).

Dunn (1999) suggested that mind-reading and attribution of intention
begins in the family where infants and children, through their early interactions with their parents, acquire the ability to communicate intentionally. Emotions are usually at the core of these interactions. A parent will
respond to the cries or distress signals of a child thus teaching the child
that this behavior elicits a reaction from the caregiver. The child becomes
aware that others attend to these behaviors and emotions and they in turn
learn to recognize others' emotions and start attributing intentions and
causality to displays of affect.

Other parental behaviors enhance the development of perspective-
taking skills in children. Conversations about feelings between parents
and children or among siblings have indeed been shown to sensitize children to the emotions and feelings of others (Dunn, 1989, 1992). Dunn,

Creps, and Brown (1996) also reported that with children's development of communicative skills and social understanding between the ages of 2 and 5 years there is an increase in siblings interactions and a decrease in interactions with the mothers. This shift is explained in part by the children's ability to join in pretend play and in more interesting interactions with their older siblings. The influence of sibling interactions on a young child's perspective skills and prosocial development is not negligible because during childhood siblings spend much time interacting with one another (Dunn, 1992).

Impact of Nonverbal Affect on Child Development

Warmth, which represents such a central tenet in successful childrearing, is expressed not only verbally but also through important communicative paralinguistic features such as body language and tone of voice. The affect expressed in parental tone of voice during mealtimes is an important indicator of the warmth or coldness of the environment that children are raised in. Parental warmth has been described as having tremendous impact on the development of children's cognitive and socioemotional development. For instance, the witnessing of positive or negative parental affect can induce parallel affective reactions in the child. Bugental, Cortez, and Blue (1992) have underlined the power of emotional contagion at all ages whereby the affect expressed by others may lead to information-processing changes or behavioral action in the observer. The negative affective state a child may experience as a result of emotional contagion at perceiving maternal expression of anger, impatience, or other negative affect can potentially lead to a depletion of the child's cognitive functioning, a reduction in processing capacity, biased access to memory, and selective encoding processes (Bugental et al., 1992). Positive affect, on the contrary, seems to be associated with an increase in the child's internalized sense of control (Kuczynski, 1984). Moreover, children who come from warm, supportive homes tend to be relatively empathic and prosocial (Eisenberg, Fabes, Carlo, & Karbon, 1992).

There is evidence that supports an association between social competence and nonverbal behavioral skills. For instance, a group of adolescent male delinquents and a group of high-school aged children with emotional problems who were shown slides of Facial Affect were significantly less accurate in decoding facial expressions than were the control groups (McCown et al., 1986; Zabel, 1979). Similar findings were provided in a study of young physically abused or neglected children who were less accurate in identifying affect than nonabused children (Camras et al., 1983).

Finally, behavioral problems in young children (toddlers and preschoolers) such as chronic oppositional and disruptive behavior have been associated with the temperament of the children but also with "ineffective, lax, punitive, and erratic parenting" (Zahn-Waxler, Cole, Richardson, Friedman et al., 1994).

The Affective Experience of the Child in Dyadic Versus Triadic Relationships

The affective experience of the child in a dyadic relationship with his or her mother compared to a triadic relationship with his or her mother and father functions in qualitatively different modes. A triad brings new factors into the relationship such as competition, repetition, and the quality of the relationship between father and mother; the nature of the marital relationship clearly has an impact upon the child's experience (Webster-Stratton & Hammond, 1999). Indeed closeness and intimacy in the marriage has been shown to predict warmer, more sensitive parenting (Cox, Owen, Lewis, & Henderson, 1989) whereas hostile–competitive coparenting processes (during infancy) forecast children's aggressiveness and hostility during preschool (McHale & Rasmussen, 1998). The infant in the triadic relationship is thus exposed to different affective modes and is the recipient of more complex interpersonal input.

Moreover positive relationships within families have been reported by Emde (1988) to have a potentially positive influence on the breaking of cross-generational patterns of continuity with respect to maladaptive functioning and insecure attachment. That is, the presence of a supportive spouse allowed mothers who had been insecurely attached to their own caregivers to stop maladaptive patterns from repeating themselves. These patterns of discontinuity occurred when mothers were able to talk about their own adverse child-rearing experiences and did not idealize their parents. In most of these cases the spouse had provided the positive affective modeling that the mother had never received as a child.

The literature on dyadic versus triadic relationships is fairly recent and has mostly focused on the affective experience of infants. However the conceptual issues that have emerged form this research will undoubtedly extend beyond infancy and into childhood.

The affective experience of the child in dyadic versus multiparty interactions is bound to be qualitatively different since the presence of several adults during mealtimes (grandparents, uncles, and neighbors) during mealtimes or other focused interactive settings provides the child with diverse affective, cognitive, linguistic, and pragmatic input. The child is thus exposed to a variety of adult's attitudes, beliefs, and personal histories. The purpose of the analyses presented here is to describe how emotions are expressed, regulated, and socialized during mealtime conversations in North-American low-income families.

LONGITUDINAL STUDY: THE HOME–SCHOOL
LANGUAGE AND LITERACY PROJECT

Forty-six families who have been part of the Home–School Study of Language and Literacy Development provided us with audiotapes of their mealtime interactions. The Home–School Study of Language and Literacy Development followed 80 children from low-income families in the Boston area, starting when the children were age 3, to study the social precursors of successful literacy achievement. One aspect of the study concentrates on the home environment. During yearly home visits when the children were between 3 and 5, the home visitors interviewed the mothers, had the mother and child complete several literacy tasks, and left a tape and tape recorder with the mother, so she could record a mealtime when other members of the family were present. These mealtime interactions were then transcribed. These are the data that were analyzed for this study.

Family Configurations

We divided the 46 families into four groups to separate the dyadic relationships from the multiparty family dinners. We then subdivided the multiparty family dinners according to the presence or absence of another adult (other than the mother). Three groups emerged: the nuclear family that includes the mother, father, and children. A second group with the mother, one or more children, and another adult other than the father (grandparent, friend, etc.). The third group includes mother and children with no other adults. All the target children were age 5 at the time of the home visit and taping of the mealtime. The configurations of participants in the mealtimes analyzed are presented in Table 6.1.

Method

The expression of affect was assessed in two ways:

1. *Verbal expression of affect.* From the transcripts of the audiotaped mealtime conversations we looked at the verbal expressions of affect. Based on studies about socialization of prosocial behavior (Barnett, 1987; Eisenberg, 1992) verbal expressions of affect were identified by two re-

TABLE 6.1
Family Configurations

Mother–Child Dyads N (%)	Mother + Father + Child(ren) N (%)	Mother + Adults + Child(ren) N (%)	Mother + Child(ren) (no adults) N (%)
5 (11%)	15 (33%)	8 (17%)	18 (39%)

searchers: use of emotion labels (I am/he is happy, sad, angry, upset, jealous), empathic inductions (instructing children to take the perspective of another), praise, prosocial attributions, disciplinary techniques, and parental modeling. The two researchers working independently underlined in each transcript any statement by any family member that corresponded to our definition of verbal affect.

2. *Nonverbal expression of affect.* Each mother's tone of voice was assessed for characteristics of warmth and patience. A recently developed coding system that measures these features in the tone of voice has been reliable on two studies (Hérot, 1996).

We only assessed the mother's tone of voice as she was the primary caretaker who was consistently present during mealtimes in our sample of 46 families. The warmth and patience of her tone of voice was a good indicator of her own way of modeling affect, and of her own affect during mealtime. Tone of voice coding provided information necessary to complement maternal verbal expressions of affect.

This twofold approach to the assessment of expressed affect (verbal and nonverbal) presented in this chapter thus provides an unprecedented method to assess the socialization of affect and offers two complementary vantage points into the affective environment that surrounds children.

Ethnicity

This sample comes from a low-income, low-SES stratum of society consisting mainly of Caucasian households with a few Hispanic and African-American families.

Previous research has shown that low-income families may be less expressive or less positive in their expression of affect (Alvy, 1987). Verbal affect may then be less prominent during parent–child exchanges as a result. A microanalysis of verbal and nonverbal expressions of affect in a sample of low-income African-American mothers (Hérot, 1996) showed that there was no homogeneity in the presence or absence of affective expressions (i.e., a wide spectrum of affective behaviors was demonstrated). Warmth was often expressed nonverbally (tone of voice, facial, and physical expressions). However, the majority of mothers did not use praise or verbal expressions of affect while interacting with their young child on a challenging task. This finding was consistent throughout the interactions among mothers who expressed a lot of warmth nonverbally as well as among mothers who did not express positive affect nonverbally.

Due to the very limited number of Hispanic and African-American families in the sample we studied for this analysis we did not try to distinguish among ethnic groups in our assessments of socialization of affect (35 Caucasian, 6 African-American, and 5 Hispanic) although we realize the importance of further study in that domain.

Presentation of the Results

Because we divided our 46 families into four groups we present a description of each of the four groups separately with results of the nonverbal expressions of affect for the mothers in each group. We also provide excerpts from the mealtime conversations to illustrate the various types of verbal socialization of affect that were expressed.

In order to respect the confidentiality of the families we have changed the children's names and refer to the mother as mother, father as father, brother as brother, etc. Moreover when reference to another person's name was made in the conversation we have changed that name as well.

A. Dyadic Mother–Child Interactions

Only five families where mother and child shared a meal alone provided us with an audiotape of their conversations. At two mealtimes, the mothers (40%) expressed warm and patient nonverbal affect. There was no consistent negative, cold, impatient affect in the other three families; they were showing instead inconsistent affect. That is, the mother at times expressed warm, positive affect but at other times expressed somewhat negative, cold nonverbal affect.

It is rare to see mothers who are both very warm and very cold in their nonverbal affect and it is more common to see general affective tendencies toward warmth and patience or the opposite kind of affect. But inconsistent affect is noticeable as it is highly disturbing for children's optimal affective development.

In the following dinner conversation, Example #1, between mother and son the inconsistent nonverbal affective messages matched the verbal affective duel taking place as the interactions oscillated between expressions of love and threats:

Example 1 (Participants: Mother, target child Mark, age 5)

(1) Mother: You are not paying attention to what I am saying.
(2) Mark: I'll pick up this table if you don't leave me a bite.
(3) Mother: Now you're threatening me? Ha!
(4) Mark: I can.
(5) Mother: I bet you can.
(6) Mark: And I did.
(7) Mark: I'm gonna pick it up real high.
(8) Mother: Well, I don't give in to threats. Sorry.

The confrontational behavior of this child bounced against the mother's sarcastic and seemingly indifferent behavior. The dyad alternated between threats from the child and his requests for affection (7). There was no third party present to intervene and release some of the mounting tension between the child and his mother. Yet, in Example #2, both mother and child also expressed their love for each other (11) (12), thus reaching an acceptable end to the verbal affective tug of war that had taken place:

Example 2 (Participants: Mother, target child Mark, age 5)

  (1) Mother: What were you making in the sandbox when I picked you up today?

  (2) Mark: A deep hole.

  (3) Mother: Oh.

  (4) Mark: So if Matthew is not my friend he could step on it and trip.

  (5) Mother: Oh that's sweet. (sarcastic)

  (6) Mother: What do you want?

  (7) Mark: I want a hug.

  (8) Mother: What?

  (9) Mark: A hug.

(10) Mother: You want a hug? Why?

(11) Mark: Because I love you.

(12) Mother: I love you too.

In contrast, in this next family's interactions, Example #3, characterized by positive nonverbal maternal affect, we see the 5-year-old child initiate praise (1) (13) as he points out how cute his dog is and underlines the positive qualities of the pet. Praise and positive attributions are signs of prosocial behavior and internalization of positive affect in this child whose mother also shows concern and love. The dyadic exchanges are full of expressions of caring affect (4) and reflect a mother–child unit that is consistently respectful and altruistic.

Example 3 (Participants: Mother, target child: Kevin, age 5)

  (1) Kevin: My puppy's gonna have something of mine, right baby? Ain't he cute?

  (2) Mother: mmhm. He is adorable. Want me to cut your meat up?

  (3) Kevin: No.

  (4) Mother: Don't try to put it all in your mouth honey, it's hot.

(5) Kevin: Mom, know something?
(6) Mother: What?
(7) Kevin: Have you ever seen (?) the flip she did for me?
(8) Mother: Who?
(9) Kevin: The dog.
(10) Mother: What he flips over?
(11) Kevin: Yeah. I told her to flip over and she did.
(12) Mother: hmm.
(13) Kevin: That's a nice dog.

Another aspect of affect socialization is to teach children to recognize bad behaviors in others and learn to set limits (3) (5) as is demonstrated in this mother–child interaction (Example #4):

Example 4: (Participants: Mother, target child Beth, age 5)

(1) Mother: Didn't you go to Mary's house?
(2) Beth: I don't like that little girl.
(3) Mother: Okay. The next time she comes when she starts scratching you have to tell her okay? Next time you tell her.
(4) Beth: No.
(5) Mother: Tell her "stop doing that. I don't like that. That's not nice."

The mother, whose nonverbal affect was very warm and patient throughout the mealtime conversation, is offering her daughter a mature and respectful way to deal with others' aggressive behavior. Through modeling this mother is teaching her child how to treat others and how to express verbally how she feels about the other's behavior as well as set her limits. This 5-year-old is thus being socialized to become a good communicator of affect.

B. Mother, Father, and Children Interactions

The presence of both parents during mealtimes can provide children with multiple viewpoints and a range of affective responses. The positive or negative quality of the experience will in part depend on the quality of the marital relationship.

In this group of families ($N = 15$) the maternal nonverbal affect was positive (warm and patient mother's tone of voice) in 10 families (71%) whereas negative affect (cold and impatient mother's tone of voice) only occurred in one family (6%). The mothers' nonverbal affect in the four remaining families was fairly neutral, neither really positive nor negative. A large majority of mothers in this configuration expressed nonverbal positive affect and in the one family where the mother expressed cold, impatient nonverbal affect there was no expression of verbal positive affect either (Example #5). Rather, the mother appeared impatient and somewhat indifferent to the possibility that her child could burn herself with food that was too hot to eat (3):

Example 5 (Participants: Mother, Sister)

(1) Mother: Now you eat your potatoes. Here wipe your hands.
(2) Sister: They're too hot.
(3) Mother: They'll cool off.

On the other hand, in the 10 families where the nonverbal maternal affect was warm and patient, the socialization of affect took many forms. It is for instance clear that during mealtimes getting a child to eat and finish his dinner represents a challenge that sometimes requires creativity from the parent and where affective ploys may prove more or less successful. In the following interaction (Example #6), both the mother and father are trying to get their child to finish his dinner by invoking the plight of others who are starving and by appealing to the child's sense of empathy (4) (9):

Example 6 (Participants: Mother, Father, Visitor, target child Pete, age 5)

(1) Father: Pete you're gonna eat your food.
(2) Pete: www. (grunting)
(3) Father: Sit down and eat your food.
(4) Mother: There are people starving in the world.
(5) Pete: Well I'm not. I'm full.
(6) Visitor: We got our progress reports back.
(7) Father: mmm.
(8) Pete: I'm full.
(9) Father: Well think of all the Kurds Pete.
(10) Pete: O. (laughs).

In this next family, Example #7, the father teaches the child the rules of politeness regarding age and appearance by pointing out that it is not nice to tell someone that they look older than their age (6). The socialization of affect in our culture includes teaching children not to hurt others' feelings. Children thus have to learn early on our societal parameters for being nice to others. If comments about some physical traits such as youthfulness, beauty, thinness can be expressed, other truths about old age, homeliness, and weight are to be kept for oneself:

Example 7: (Participants: Mother, Father, target child John, age 5)

  (1) John: Mama is thirty-one. I mean Mama is thirty years old.
  (2) Father: Yep. Does she look any different?
  (3) John: Um she looks like sixty-two.
  (4) Mother: Oh God John. (laughs)
  (5) Father: aw (laughs)
  (6) Father: That's not nice John.
  (7) John: Oh yeah? Oh yeah? Well Linda's father is sixty-two.
  (8) Father: No he is not honey.
  (9) John: uhhuhh. I said "how are old are you?" "Sixty-two."
 (10) Father: He was teasing. He was funning you.
 (11) Mother: I think he was only kidding you.

Conversations between parents in front of children can also serve as (good or bad) models that children learn from. In the following triadic interactions, Example #8, empathic concern about others is at the core of the conversation between the mother and father (1) (3) (8) (9) in the presence of the child, who, although he is not actively participating in the conversation, is the recipient of his parents' empathic concern for others:

Example 8: (Participants: Mother, Father, target child Jim, age 5)

  (1) Mother: Those poor students at city hospital honey . . .
  (2) Father: Yeah.
  (3) Mother: They want to close the program and the girls that are gonna graduate next year. What are they going to do?
  (4) Father: Honey right there.
  (5) Mother: Honey.
  (6) Father: Got to find another program, I suppose, that will accept them.
  (7) Mother: Yeah.
  (8) Father: That's the least they could do for them find another school that took their accreditation.
  (9) Mother: I know it's just sad you know they work so hard.

(10) Father: What's the matter honey? You don't feel good?
(11) Jim: Full.

A little while later, Example #9, physical expressions of affection
(kisses) (5) and caring for family pets (9) are also apparent in the following
exchanges:

Example 9: (Participants: Mother, Father, target child Jim, age 5)

  (1) Mother: Well Jim and I are going to head for the market this
               morning. To market to market.
  (2) Father: Okay. Do you need anything?
  (3) Jim: Yes.
  (4) Father: xxx.
  (5) Mother: He needs kisses.
  (6) Mother: Oh daddy said he wanted popcorn seeds.
  (7) Jim: Yes.
  (8) Jim: Oh! Birdseed.
  (9) Mother: You're right. Those poor birds they're going to think
               that we forgot them aren't they?
(10) Jim: Yes.

Next, in Example #10, Jim learns a valuable lesson from his mother
about competition (comparing oneself to others), self-esteem, and a certain philosophy of life (9):

Example 10: (Participants: Mother, target child Jim, age 5)

  (1) Mother: What's that new little boy we met?
  (2) Jim: uhhuh.
  (3) Mother: How old is he?
  (4) Jim: Five and a half and a nickel. Is that bigger mom?
  (5) Mother: You're five and a half.
  (6) Jim: But he is five and a half in nickels.
  (7) Mother: Five and a half in nickels. I never heard of that honey.
               A nickel is a form of money. Five is a form of years and
               a half would be a half year six months. You can't be five
               and a half and a nickel. That's silly.
  (8) Jim: Maybe he's just five but he seems to go faster than me
               with those sneakers.

(9) Mother: Well you know honey there's gonna be people who are gonna go faster than you through your life and there's gonna be people that go slower than you through your whole life. God didn't make everybody to do the same thing the same way. We're all our person and we're supposed to be the best we can be. You're the best I think.

Surrounded by caring and empathic parents Jim appears to be a thoughtful and caring child (4):

Example 11 (Participants: Mother, target child Jim, age 5)

(1) Mother: Jim where did you get this honey?
(2) Jim: Um, on the ground.
(3) Mother: Oh.
(4) Jim: For the flowers I thought it would be nice.

This little boy may have internalized empathic behavior from his very empathic parents and is thus able to show thoughtfulness and sensitivity for others, even for flowers.

C. Mother–Children Interactions

In our sample a fairly large number of families ($N = 18$) included the mother as the only adult figure sharing a meal with more than one child. The absence of the father, whether it was due to a family breakdown (divorce, death) or a temporary absence puts a heavy responsibility on the mother to handle dinner with several children. On the one hand children may be more unruly as they outnumber the adult and the mother cannot count on any one to take over or relieve her briefly of her duty. Not surprisingly, the nonverbal expression of affect was somewhat more negative in this group of mother–children than in other family configurations. That is, this group had the highest number of cold, impatient mothers of any group ($N = 6$, 33%). There were however nine families (50%) where the mother expressed positive nonverbal affect consistently throughout the meal regardless of the burden of being the sole adult care-taker of a group of children.

These seemingly disparate findings may indicate that the ability to express positive affect may be an internal personality trait that allows some mothers to withstand stressful and difficult family situations and remain warm and patient regardless of the family configurations. We can hypothesize that the more negative mothers may in general be more cold and impatient but we need more data and more instances of interactive situations to verify this assumption. We cannot disregard the possibility that the more "negative" mothers were simply more irritable that particular evening.

In families with several children the role that siblings play in the socialization of affect cannot be overlooked. By kindergarten the amount of time children spend with their siblings is greater than the time spent with their parents. The quality of the sibling relationships is different from parent–child relationships; siblings are more equal in status and sibling relationships are characterized both by negative behaviors such as aggressive, competition, and rivalry and by cooperative, prosocial interactions. Sibling relationships are embedded in the interactions of the larger family unit and are influenced by and parental attitudes and behaviors (Eisenberg, 1992).

Competition and comparison among siblings can foster low self-esteem, resentment, and overall negative affect. But in the following exchanges, Example #12, the mother effectively deflected the conflict between siblings (1) by praising the children, showing concern, and appealing to the children's sense of empathy (2):

Example 12 (Participants: Mother, brother Matt, target child Jack, age 5)

(1) Jack: I worked longer than Matt that's why I'm so hungry.
(2) Mother: You worked longer than Matt? Yeah! You've been working most of the afternoon. You did a nice job. But poor Matt he was in school all day that makes you tired too.
(3) Matt: Very tired doing work.
(4) Mother: He got a hundred on his spelling test! You should see his spelling words.

Jack is then invited to read out loud challenging "color" words with the support of his mother (Example #13). His older brother Matt is not impressed (14) and the mother reminds him that 5-year-olds do not have the same reading abilities as older children (15):

Example 13 (Participants: Mother, brother Matt, target child Jack, age 5)

(1) Jack: Yellow
(2) Mother: Say them out loud.

(3)	Jack:	Red yellow blue . . .
(4)	Jack:	zzz (laughs)
(5)	Matt:	And buh . . .
(6)	Jack:	Black!
(7)	Jack:	White?
(8)	Mother:	Excellent. Keep going.
(9)	Jack:	Pink?
(10)	Mother:	That's a hard one. Pur . .
(11)	Jack:	Purple! Orange.
(12)	Mother:	Excellent
(13)	Jack:	That's hard.
(14)	Matt:	Cinch
(15)	Mother:	He's five years old it's hard Matt. And buh . . .
(16)	Jack:	Brown
(17)	Mother:	Brown very good.

In this next family, Example #14, the mother throughout the meal is very involved in discussion with her children, and teaches them empathy, and appropriate behavior (2). The older siblings also play an important role in the socialization of affect within the family as they sometimes adopt an "authoritarian" parenting role that the mother does not condone:

Example 14 (Participants: Mother, target child Tom, age 5)

(1)	Tom:	Nathan keep quiet.
(2)	Mother:	I don't think that it's very nice to say that.

Tattle telling is not uncommon among siblings (3) but in this instance (Example #15) the exchange ends with an intervention from sister 2 who demonstrates a certain wisdom mixed with empathy (7):

Example 15 (Participants: Mother, Sister 1 Mary, Sister 2 Ellen, target child Tom, age 5)

(1)	Tom:	I want all the bacon.
(2)	Mother:	No you can't have anymore it's not that good it's not even good for you really.
(3)	Mary:	Tom wants all the bacon in the world.
(4)	Mother:	Hmm?
(5)	Mary:	Now he's saying he wants all the bacon in the world.

(6) Tom: Of course I don't.

(7) Ellen: You could get sick because of bacon.

Sibling interactions are not always dominated by older siblings "teaching" their less experienced brothers or sisters. Here, in Example #16, the younger child offer the older sister some words of advice (17):

Example 16 (Participants: Mother, Sister 1 Mary, Sister 2 Ellen, target child Tom, age 5)

(1) Ellen: Yeah but the twins are the ones that love me.

(2) Mother: They love you Ellen?

(3) Ellen: Yeah.

(4) Mother: Did they tell you that?

(5) Ellen: Yep.

(6) Mother: Did they?

(7) Tom: They try and kiss her all day long.

(8) Mother: Really?

(9) Ellen: They do and every time they try I spit at them.

(10) Mother: Oh that's not nice you just . . .

(11) Mary: Didn't you get in trouble for that?

(12) Mother: You just tell them you don't want them to do that or you won't play with them.

(13) Tom: She does.

(14) Mary: They don't chase her.

(15) Tom: Just Ellen just kiss them back just kiss them back they'll stop it.

(16) Ellen: Why?

(17) Tom: Kiss them back they'll stop it.

(18) Ellen: No way!

(19) Mother: That's true. You could try it.

(20) Ellen: No!

Love in its many expressions seems to be a recurring topic of conversation in this family. Emotions and affect are directly discussed and every member of the family shares their own insight based on their experience. The ability to talk about affect is in itself a sign that this family cares about feelings and emotions. The next interaction (Example #17) concerns love and spelling. The 5-year-old child wishes to learn the spelling of a very endearing and meaningful phrase (1):

Example 17 (Participants: Mother, Sister 1 Mary, Sister 2 Ellen, target child Tom, age 5)

(1) Tom: Momma how do I spell "I love you"?
(2) Tom: I L
(3) Mother: mmhm.
(4) Tom: I L
(5) Mary: I L
(6) Mother: Let him do it SIS1. And what? I L what?
(7) Tom: "I love you." I. L.
(8) Mother: Mmhm.
(9) Tom: O. L. that's the only thing I know.
(10) Ellen: No. It goes.
(11) Mother: I. L. O.
(12) Ellen: It goes I. L.
(13) Mary: I. L. O.
(14) Mother: ssh!
(15) Ellen: I. L. O. V. E.
(16) Mother: L.O.V.E spells love.
(17) Tom: L.O.V.E
(18) Mother: Sound it out.
(19) Tom: "I love you."

Teaching empathic behavior to one's children involves teaching them to respect and care about not only people but animals as well (1) (3) (8). In the following example (#18) the mother teaches her child to imagine what the kitten is experiencing and feeling (6) (8) to make the child understand that he is hurting the pet. His 5-year-old sister shows understanding and empathic concern as well (5):

Example 18 (Participants: Mother, Brother John, target child Tanya, age 5)

(1) Mother: Oh John don't do that to the kitten!
(2) John: Why?
(3) Mother: Because it might hurt him.
(4) John: I know what.
(5) Tanya: He is only a baby.
(6) Mother: Would like me to push your neck down like that?
(7) John: No.
(8) Mother: I didn't think so. Well the kitty doesn't like it either.

The mother then goes on to explain to her 5-year-old that a sense of identity is in part based on one's name and its consistency over time (4). Again, in Example #19, she uses empathic induction (4) to help her daughter take another's perspective:

Example 19 (Participants: Mother, target child Tanya, age 5)

(1) Tanya: Can I name the kitty "Bobby"?
(2) Mother: No you already named it "Daisy".
(3) Tanya: Oh yeah.
(4) Mother: What if Sarah kept changing Sophie's name and then she wouldn't know what her name was. She would be all confused.
(5) Tanya: Is the kitty all confused now?
(6) Mother: She might be because when we got her she had a different name.

If some mothers showed positive nonverbal affect and talked about love and expressions of affect, other mothers on the other end of the affective spectrum were less empathic and more impatient both in their verbal and nonverbal expressions. In the following family (Example #20) the mother restricts the amount of chocolate that her child can eat (2) but does not offer any explanation as to why the child should not have more chocolate. When her child asks for an explanation (3) she tells him that he should not have any more sugar without explaining the possible deleterious effect of eating too much sugar. She appears to have a lower threshold of tolerance for children's failure to comply and expresses that she does not want to engage in a discussion ("you're not going to drive me nuts") (4):

Example 20 (Participants: Mother, Brother Sam, target child Emily, age 5)

(1) Sam: Can I have chocolate momma?
(2) Mother: This is it though. You are not having any more sugar.
(3) Sam: Because we'll eat it all?
(4) Mother: You are just having one glass of chocolate milk because there is sugar in it and you're not going to drive me nuts.
(5) Emily: Sam you talk too. Say delicious.
(6) Mother: Emily! You want more?
(7) Emily: Not yet.
(8) Mother: Are you going to want more? (angry)

(9) Emily: Yes.

(10) Mother: Yeah. I'm not waiting all day to wait on you.

(11) Emily: All right. Well. Time's up.

(12) Sam: Mama. Can I talk too?

(13) Emily: Talk.

(14) Mother: Oh shut up.

The mother's use of the words "shut up" sends an implicit message about her authority. Her decisions are final and not to be discussed. This mother also seems to see herself as her children's "maid" ("I am not waiting all day to wait on you") and expresses impatience and dissatisfaction about her role. She may be unaware that she is negatively socializing her children by modeling disrespect and by showing that adults have complete power over children.

D. Mother, Adults and Children

This fourth group ($N = 8$) included the mother and child, siblings, and adult friends or grandparents. At three mealtimes the mothers (38%) expressed positive nonverbal affect and one mother (12.5%) showed clear negative nonverbal affect. The presence of other adults, especially grandparents, provided other topics of discussion and added more ways of modeling the expression of affect. Moreover, grandparents shared with their grandchildren a sense of family history, family memories, knowledge of the grandchildren's parents as they bring in their own parenting beliefs.

In this family (Example #21) were the expression of nonverbal affect was positive it is clear that the entire family is very empathic (10):

Example 21 (Participants: Mother, Grandmother, target child Susan, age 5)

(1) Mother: What else did we do today? What did we write out?

(2) Susan: Valentine cards for all my friends and their friends at school.

(3) Grandmother: oh.

(4) Susan: And we mailed them.

(5) Mother: Catherine.

(6) Susan: And Samantha.

(7) Grandmother: And you mailed them to them right?

(8) Susan: Yep.

(9) Mother: We mailed one to Stephanie.

(10) Grandmother: Oh she'll be happy.

Discussion

Socialization of Affect. The qualitative microanalysis presented here shows that the socialization of affect between parents and children did occur during mealtime conversations through both verbal and nonverbal processes regardless of the family configurations. That is, the socialization of affect occurred in dyadic exchanges between mother and child as well as in multiparty families. However, exposure to a variety of socialization techniques was more likely and frequent in multiparty families. The presence of the father for instance increased the likelihood that modeling of affect would take place between mother and father in front of the child as well as between parent and child. Moreover, the presence of other adults (father, grandparents, or friends) usually provided other types of affective reinforcements and alleviated the burden and parental responsibility placed on the mother.

More often than not affect was a topic of conversation and parents used affect modeling, preaching, empathy-inducing statements to teach their children about their own emotions and those of others'. A lot of implicit and explicit teaching of affective rules and norms also took place during dinner.

Nonverbal Affect. The nonverbal expression of affect measured in the mothers' tone of voice was overall more positive than negative in our sample of 46 mealtimes. The mother's tone of voice was rated as warm and patient in 25 family meals (54%). Within our family subgroups, it was interesting to note that the highest percentage of positive nonverbal affect took place in the nuclear families (mother, father, and children). The highest percentage of negative affect (cold and impatient tone of voice) was found in the family meals where the mother was the only adult dealing with more than one child. This is not surprising as the demands on the mothers to get every child to eat and behave are more burdensome. However, a large number of mothers in this more demanding family configuration still showed consistent positive nonverbal affect.

Eisenberg (1992) identified successful and optimal verbal socialization techniques that were frequently embedded in warm and patient nonverbal maternal affect, which we found to be true in our sample for the majority of our family meals. For instance families where parents used empathy-inducing statements also praised their children, showed empathy toward others, and the mothers' tone of voice was warm and patient. In contrast, when maternal nonverbal affect was cold and impatient, little socialization of affect took place verbally and interactions between parents and children were characterized by lack of respect and authoritarian attitudes.

Positive nonverbal affect was, however, also present in families where there was no verbal socialization of emotions. That is, conversations did not have to revolve about particular affective topics, nor was there any empathy-inducing statement or praising but the conversations nonetheless were characterized by very warm, positive maternal nonverbal affect. The expression of warmth and patience in the mothers' tone of voice was in itself a form of socialization of affect. The environment created by a nurturing and warm mother is conducive to the socialization of nonverbal affect. Verbal exchanges that do not revolve about affect or empathy can still transmit positive affect from parents to children albeit in an implicit way.

Cultural Aspects of Affect Socialization

One of the most basic cultural characteristics prevalent in this sample of low-SES American families is the actual discussion and expression of affect among family members. Love is expressed verbally ("I love you," sending Valentine cards) and nonverbally between mother, father and children, between friends, etc. Other cultures do not express love quite as explicitly and as frequently as Americans do. Thus one challenge to American children is to learn how to express love explicitly, and what limits to put on such expressions.

From these mealtime conversations it is also obvious that the displayed emotions valued in our culture include empathy, love, and concern about others. Praising and treating others respectfully while asserting one's rights and setting one's limits are important affective behaviors learned within the family. Threatening one's parents is unacceptable and complying with parents' requests is expected of all children. To convey these culturally important values parents used empathy-inducing statement showing that they expect their 5-year-old children to be able to take the perspective of others and reflect about other's emotions and feelings.

Conclusion

Even though our sample was fairly small and our qualitative observations were made on a single mealtime event the richness of the data prevails and the twofold approach presented here provided a new way to assess expressions of affect both verbally and nonverbally. Dinner conversations proved to be rich with affective input (verbal or nonverbal) and with affectively laden topics of discussion where parents did transmit affective values implicitly or explicitly.

Further work is required in our understanding of parental socialization of affect during mealtimes. An analysis of additional mealtime conversations for each family would provide further data about the consistency or fluctuation of affect within each family over time. This would also further our understanding of the development of parental socialization of affect as the children get older and become more competent in the management, recognition, and expression of their emotions.

REFERENCES

Alvy, K. T. (1987). *Black parenting*. New York: Irvington.
Barnett, M. A. (1987). Empathy and related responses in children. In N. Eisenberg & J. Strayer (Eds.), *Empathy and Its Development* (pp. 146–162). Cambridge, England: Cambridge University Press.
Bugental, D. B., Cortez, V., & Blue, J. (1992). Children's affective responses to the expressive cues of others. In N. Eisenberg & R. Fabes (Eds.), *Emotion and its regulation in early development. New directions for child development* (pp. 75–89, No. 55). The Jossey-Bass education series, San Francisco, CA: Jossey-Bass.
Camras, L. A., Grow, J. G., & Ribordy, S. C. (1983). Recognition of emotional expression by abused children. *Journal of Clinical Child Psychology, 12,* 325–328.
Cox, M. J., Owen, M. T., Lewis, J. M., & Henderson, V. K. (1989). Marriage, adult adjustment, and early parenting. *Child Development, 60*(5), 1015–1024.
Denham, S. A., Renwick, S. M., & Holt, R. W. (1991). Working and playing together: Predicting socio-emotional competence from mother-child interactions. *Child Development, 62,* 242–249.
Dunn, J. (1989). Siblings and the development of social understanding in early childhood. In P. Zukow (Ed.), *Sibling interaction across cultures. Theoretical and methodological issues* (pp. 106–116). New York: Springer Verlag.
Dunn, J. (1992). Sisters and brothers: Current issues in developmental research. In F. Boer & J. Dunn (Eds.), *Children's sibling relationships: Developmental and clinical issues* (pp. 1–17). Hillsdale, NJ: Lawrence Erlbaum Associates.
Dunn, J. (1999). Making sense of the social world: Mindreading, emotion, and relationships. In P. Zelazo, J. Astington, & D. Olson (Eds.), *Developing theories of intention. Social understanding and self-control* (pp. 229–242). Mahwah, NJ: Lawrence Erlbaum Associates.
Dunn, J., Creps, C., & Brown, J. (1996). Children's family relationships between two and five: Developmental changes and individual differences. *Social Development, 5*(3), 230–250.
Eisenberg, N. (1992). *The caring child*. Cambridge, MA: Harvard University Press.
Eisenberg, N., Fabes, R., Carlo, G., & Karbon, M. (1992). Emotional responsivity to others: Behavioral correlates and socialization antecedents. In N. Eisenberg & R. Fabes (Eds.), *Emotion and its regulation in early development. New directions for child development* (pp. 57–73, No. 55). San Francisco, CA: Jossey-Bass.
Eisenberg, N., & Strayer, J. (1987). *Empathy and its development*. Cambridge, England: Cambridge University Press.
Emde, R. N. (1988). The Effects of relationships on relationships: A developmental approach to clinical intervention. In R. Hinde & J. Stevenson-Hinde (Eds.), *Relationships within families: Mutual influences* (pp. 354–367). London: Clarendon Press.

Hérot, C. (1996). *The wheels on the bus go round and round: A portrait of African American teenage mothers' verbal and nonverbal behavior with their children.* Unpublished Doctoral Dissertation. Harvard Graduate School of Education.

Kuczynski, L. (1984). Socialization goals and mother-child interaction: Strategies for long-term and short-term compliance. *Developmental Psychology, 20,* 1061–1073.

Lewis, M. (1989). Cultural differences in children's knowledge of emotional scripts. In C. Saarni & P. Harris (Eds.), *Children's understanding of emotion* (pp. 350–373). Cambridge, England: Cambridge University Press.

McCown, W., Johnson, J., & Austin, S. (1986). Inability of delinquents to recognize facial affects. *Journal of Social Behavior and Personality, 1*(4), 489–496.

MacDonald, K. (1992). Warmth as a developmental construct: An evolutionary analysis. *Child Development, 63,* 753–773.

McHale, J. P., & Rasmussen, J. L. (1998). Coparental and family group-level dynamics during infancy: Early family precursors of child and family functioning during preschool. *Development and Psychopathology, 10*(1), 39–59.

Ninio, A., & Snow, E. C. (1996). *Pragmatic development.* Westview Press.

Ochs, E. (1988). *Culture and language development.* Cambridge, England: Cambridge University Press.

Webster-Stratton, C., & Hammond, M. (1999). Marital conflict management skills, parenting style, and early-onset conduct problems: Processes and pathways. *Journal of Child Psychology and Psychiatry and Allied Disciplines, 40*(6), 917–927.

Zabel, R. H. (1979). Recognitions of emotions in facial expressions by emotionally disturbed children and nondisturbed children. *Psychology in the Schools, 16,* 119–126.

Zahn-Waxler, C., Radke-Yarrow, M., & King, R. A. (1979). Child Rearing and children's prosocial initiations towards victims of distress. *Child Development, 50,* 319–330.

Zahn-Waxler, C., Cole, P. M., Richardson, D. T., Friedman, R. J., et al. (1994). Social problem solving in disruptive preschool chikren: Reactions to hypothetical situations of conflict and distress. *Merrill-Palmer Quarterly, 40*(1), 98–119.

Chapter 7

Cognitive Expressions and Humorous Phrases in Family Discourse as Reflectors and Cultivators of Cognition

Ruth Nevat-Gal
Hebrew University, Jerusalem

This chapter focuses on two linguistic phenomena found in the discourse of Israeli families: the multiple usage of cognitive expressions and versatile linguistic usage to create a humorous effect. Both kinds of expressions reflect the participants' cognitive processes and serve as devices for cultivating the cognition of the participating children.

Vygotsky's sociocognitive approach connects intellectual development to the ability to control the social means of thinking, that is, language (Vygotsky, 1962). Language as a semiotic system serves as a focusing means and as an indicator of reaction and relation in both abstract and concrete situations. As an organized system of signs, it also broadens the human abilities of organization, flexibility, and creativity (Vygotsky, 1978). Speech acquired by interpersonal relations becomes an internalized pattern for intrapersonal self-direction. This process is well demonstrated in the egocentric speech used by young children, which, according to Vygotsky (1987), is a transitional stage between social and internal speech. Bruner (1983) also regarded the child's growing command of language in routine procedures as being simultaneously a process of acquiring mastery of the foundations of culture.

Interest in social thinking, and particularly in everyday thinking, has been the basis of works such as those by Rogoff and Lave (1984), Rogoff and Wertsch (1984), Rogoff (1990), and Goodnow and Collins (1990), in which the nature of cultural structures transmitted by interactions and the processes of transition are investigated. Ochs, Taylor, Rudolph, and

181

Smith (1992) discarded the old notion of family discourse "as a breeding ground for restricted codes, egocentric discourse and concrete low level thinking" (p. 67) and saw the family dinner as a social situation that fosters intellectual development "by the very nature of the family dinner [with] its familiarity, its captive audience over time, and its generally shared expectation that daily experience and perspectives will be aired" (p. 38).

In discussing enculturation, Swartz and Perkins (1990) and Perkins (1993) maintained the centrality of creating a culture of thinking in which tendencies or dispositions are cultivated. Such environments mean creating, encouraging particular thinking modes, and instilling a preference and a motivation to participate in the thinking modes of a given culture.

The argument of this chapter is that the enculturation of thinking modes occurs through routinely recurring patterns of discourse during family meals.

METHOD

Presented here is part of a project dealing with the enhancement of cognitive development through dinner talk, based on 32 dinner conversations of 16 Israeli families, involving 8 college-educated parents and 8 high-school-educated parents.

This project is based on two sets of data collected by Shoshana Blum-Kulka. Data for the first set, from college-educated Israeli and Jewish-American families, were collected during 1985–1986 by Blum-Kulka and Snow and served as the basis for *Dinner Talk* (Blum-Kulka, 1997). Data for the second set, from high-school-educated Israeli families, were collected during 1991–1997 and have been incorporated in the analyses of family explanations (see Blum-Kulka, chap. 4, this volume).

The conversations were recorded during dinnertime and later transcribed and closely analyzed both qualitatively and quantitatively. Two components of the larger project are presented here: the usage of cognitive expressions and the usage of humorous language. The cognitive expressions were selected following the technique used in Snow (1991) for identifying reminiscences: All occurrences of the item of interest were marked. Thus cognitive verbs in any tense or declension, such as *know, recognize, understand, think, intend, remember,* and *describe,* were analyzed, as were nouns pertaining to thought, such as *problem, experiment,* and *plan.* When marking the humorous expressions, judgments had to be made about the intention of the expressions, for example, and their illocutionary force.

The analysis was performed on all expressions of all the participating members of the family and in all speech acts. Both cognitive and humorous expressions may be found in narratives and directives and in negotiation, problem solving, explanations, planning, and exchanging ideas on matters close and distant.

Each dinner conversation served as a unit of analysis, based on the assumption that discourse socializes whether the children are participants as talkers or whether they are participants as listeners and eavesdroppers: Children learn both from active participation and from a socializing model (Cazden, 1983).

COGNITIVE EXPRESSIONS

Cognitive Expressions, Involvement, Distancing, and Practical Thinking

In his discussion of the characteristics of spoken versus written language, Chafe (1985) specified three types of involvement that participants nurture: the involvement of the speaker with her or himself ("ego involvement"), social involvement, and content involvement. As cognitive expressions often serve to initiate a dialogue, denoting hesitation or uncertainty, and the dialogue that ensues may be ideational or content focused, cognitive verbs may then be active in supporting a more complex idea of reality. Hence, Chafe's three types of involvement are integrated in cognitive expressions, being not only polite formulas, but also facilitators of negotiation and idea exchange.

In the following directive, the father is initiating a combined involvement with Dafi over a practical matter that is of concern to him. He indicates his uncertainty by using a cognitive expression. Dafi's response is meant to test her father's speculation:

(1) Family 10: Dafi (12 F), Noga (8 F), Yaron (4 M).

Father: *Dafi, tir-i im yesh od kerax.*   *Dafi, see if there is any more*
          nidme li she-eyn kvar.   *ice. I don't think there is any*
                                               left.

Cognitive expressions may transform conative speech (Jakobson, 1960) into a plan of action, thus distancing the discourse from immediate concerns. Sigel (1982) and Sigel, Stinson, and Flaugher (1991) defined distancing behavior as communication intended to distance oneself consciously from the present and create a cognitive environment, a mental representation. According to Sigel (Sigel, 1979, 1982; Sigel & Saunders, 1979), high levels of distancing and developed verbal communication positively affected the children's recall ability, their ability to predict, and their academic success in scholastic domains that require a high level of representation.

Consider the following conversation, in which the mother expresses her wish to replace one set of dishes with another and uses a subjective evaluation to do so:

(2) Family 1: Nadav (11 M), Yoram (10 M).

Mother:	*Motekle leda'ati <ata asita taut.*	*Sweetie, in my opinion you made a mistake.*
Father:	*ve ma xx be'ecem?*	*And what xx in fact ?*
Mother:	*Asita taut she samta calaxot ktanot ki anaxnu rocim lasim +*	*You made a mistake when you put out the small plates because we want to put +*
Father:	*Aval en xx*	*But there aren't any xx*
Mother:	*ma zot omeret en zalaxot gdolot? lo yitaxen efo hen?*	*What do you mean there aren't any large plates? That can't be. Where are they?*

Interlocutors participate in a multilogical process of critical thinking, in which claims and arguments are evaluated, findings are analyzed, and significant knowledge is predicted and applied. They also refer to each other's strategies for thinking.

Ennis (1987) referred to critical thinking as "balanced and reflective thinking focused on the decision of what to believe and what to do" (p. 9), and it is logical and analytical skills that constitute the center of the definition. On the other hand, McPeck (1990) insisted that in daily discourse, critical thinking mainly involves not the analysis of conclusions, but understanding information and evaluating data, information, and facts.

Here is an example of evaluating information:

(3) Family 6: Iris (6 F), Lilach (6 F), Rami (1 M).

Mother:	*Taxtexi yoter katan iris, ze gadol miday. ani xoshevet sheze yoter ta- im kaze katan, lo?*	*Cut it a little smaller, Iris, it's too large. I think it's tastier smaller, don't you?*

Presenting opinions in a subjective form facilitates critical discussion and signifies the need to express a degree of evidentiality. Because information about the world is never absolute, dialogical-critical thinking is necessary, and so opinions are presented for testing, adaptation, and completion, as in the following example:

(4) Family 8: Merav (11 F), Ran (8 M).

Father:	Yesh po mashehu basalat she-hu noten ta'am mar.	There is something in the salad that is giving it a bitter taste.
Merav:	ze shemen zayit.	It's olive oil.
Mother:	ze kruv <u>ani xoshevet</u>.	It's the cabbage, <u>I think.</u>
Father:	ze hashemen zayit, betax lo hakruv . . .	It's the olive oil, certainly not the cabbage . . .

Most of the cognitive expressions used during the meals clarified information. Others mitigated directives and opened them to discussion, at least theoretically. Cognitive expressions were also used to get and hold attention and as intensifiers to express strong conviction.

In brief, cognitive expressions may be used for referential, conative, phatic, or expressive functions of discourse (Jakobson, 1960). When dealing with the referential function, interlocutors in a family meal setting strive to adhere to the maxim of quality (Grice, 1975) prescribed by their culture for dealing with different topics.

Relations Between Reality and Cognition

What are the relations between our perception and the reality perceived? Interlocutors debate this question and use cognitive expressions to indicate their findings.

Incompatibilities.   The father in Example 5 is commenting on Oshrit's request for some tea:

(5) Family 14: Yaniv (7.7 M), Oshrit (6.5 F).

Father:	<u>Xashavti</u> she'at roca shokolit.	<u>I thought</u> you wanted some chocolate milk.

Inferences.   The smell of rolls baking in the oven triggers the following remarks:

(6) Family 2: Shlomit (12 F), Riki (10 F), Mira (5 F).

Shlomit:	ima, <u>lo nir'a li</u> shenoxal harbe laxmanyot.	Mummy, <u>it doesn't seem to me</u> that we'll eat many rolls.
Mother:	lama? halaxmanyot kevar nisrafot?	Why? Are the rolls already burnt?
Shlomit:	ken. yesh gam bli afiya.	Yes. There're also some unbaked ones.

Father:	keshe'omrim laxmanya batanur.	When one says a bun in the oven.
Mother:	nu, <u>ata mevin</u> axshav et <u>hamusag</u> lefi ha're'ax.	Well, now <u>you understand</u> the term <u>according to the smell.</u>

%Comment: referring to an idiom describing a pregnant woman.

Actual sensual impressions are the basis for inference about a future scenario or about the meaning of an idiom. The connection is made through the use of cognitive expressions.

Cognitive Expressions as Signifying Metacognitive Activity

Metacognitive behavior indicated by the use of cognitive expression is part of the attempt to monitor the quality of information. According to Vygotsky (1962), information acquired through conscious activity is of a higher level of knowledge than information acquired automatically. One of the important characteristics of modern knowledge, according to Feurstein and Feurstein (1996), is the fact that it has been distanced from reality.

Flavell (1978) distinguished between two focuses in the metacognitive system:

1. The information focus is knowledge that one possesses regarding (a) one's ability, knowledge, and preferences, (b) tasks and subject matter, and (c) strategies for task performance.
2. The application focus is the ability to regulate and monitor processes and products, meaning skills in applying knowledge about self, task, and strategies.

Thinkers' Awareness of Their Own Cognition. In the following example, the father is reporting his lack of understanding, remarking on the attendants in the nearby gas station:

(7) Family 6: Lilach (6 F), Iris (6 F) Rami (1 M).

Father:	hem meramim kol hazman, az lif'amim yesh lahem eyze pat-ent <u>shelo hiclaxnu lehavin</u> oto, shehem maclixim lehavi et hamisparim shama lesxum mesuyam bli shehem yaxnisu et hadelek befnim.	They always cheat, they have some kind of "patent" that <u>we can't understand,</u> where they are able to bring the digits to a certain sum without filling the tank at all.

The use of the word *patent* indicates an evaluation of the activity as a sophisticated one, thus making it difficult to follow.

Here, in Example 8, taken from the same family, the mother is marking a piece of knowledge as a familiar one, in a process of scaffolding:

(8) Family 6: Lilach (6 F), Iris (6 F) Rami (1 M).

Father:	*aval eyzo xagiga mishpaxtit naxgog be'tu bishvat?*	*So what kind of a family cele-bration will we have on the 15th of Shvat?*
Mother:	*mi nolad be'tu bishvat? atem yod'im?*	*. Who was born on the 15th of Shvat? Do you know?*

Note that Shvat is the name of a Hebrew month.

Awareness of the Existence of a Problem. Defining a situation as a problem requires careful deliberation. For instance, in Example 9, Noga skipped school and claims she doesn't ever want to go back to school. Defining Noga's problem is an opener in an effort to convince Noga that her course of action is not acceptable and that an alternative course has to be found:

(9) Family 10: Dafi (12 F), Noga (8 F), Yaron (4 M).

Father:	*axshav ze be'aya, mipney she: baxayim yesh devarim she'osim bli sherocim la'asot otam veyesh siba tova la'asot otam, aval . . .*	*Now it's a problem, because there are certain things in life that you have to do without wanting to do them, and there's a good reason to do them, but . . .*

Thinking Management. Instructions about the steps to be taken to solve the problem follow the definition, as in the following example:

(10) Family 10: Dafi (12 F), Noga (10 F), Yaron (4 M).

Father:	*rega, Dafi, kodem menatxim et hamikre ve'axar kax magi'im le'maskanot.*	*One moment, Dafi, first we have to analyze the situation and then we can draw conclu-sions.*

Using a variety of expressions for different thinking forms helps to distinguish between the different modes of thinking:

1. *Defining goals.* The need to clarify the purpose for actions is modeled in Example 11 by the father's interrogation following Nadav's story about the trip his class has taken to a nearby teacher's college:

(11) Family 1: Nadav (11 M), Yoram (10 M).

Father: *hisbiru laxem et hamatara?*   *Did they explain the aim to*
          lama lakxu otxem?   *you? Why did they take you?*

2. *Inquisitive thinking.* In Example 12, the father asks his 6-year-old twin girls about a school nature outing. One should note the use of the verb *gilitem*—discover—instead of *macatem*—found, or *ra'item*—saw:

(12) Family 6: Lilach (6 F), Iris (6 F) Rami (1 M).

Father: *ve'eyze xarakim gilitem?*   *And what kind of insects did*
                                       you discover?

3. *Awareness and responsibility.* In Example 13, the mother and Rami discuss students' and teachers' responsibilities. Both hold the assumption that one should be aware of one's own difficulties in understanding and define them in order to learn. Rami believes that an immediate response to students is a helpful one:

(13) Family 4: Rami (16 M), Xagit (12 F), Dani (8.5 M).

Mother: *az lama lo kamta ve'amarta,*   *So why didn't you get up and*
          mixa ani lo mevin.   *say, Micha, I don't under-*
                                          stand.

Rami: *Kol hazman kamu ve'amru*   *We constantly got up and told*
          veze hafashlot shelo. hu lo   *him, and that's his mess-up. He*
          metaken ta'uyot, hu lo, hu   *doesn't correct mistakes. He*
          melamed lefi misgeret lo   *teaches according to an rigid*
          gmisha. im hu haya makshiv   *framework. If he had listened to*
          lanu mehahatxala ad hasof   *us from beginning to end, and*
          ve'az haya . . . harbe shgi'ot *then . . . many of our mistakes*
          shelanu hayu metukanot.   *would have been corrected.*

4. *Precision, concentration.* The mother fails to follow Nadav's story. Here, in Example 14, she asks for specific details and instructs her son to concentrate and use his memory:

(14) Family 1: Nadav (11 M), Yoram (10 M).

Mother: *ani roca bediyuk le'havin,*   *I want to understand exactly,*
          tenase lizkor.   *try to remember.*

5. *Originality.* In Example 15, the mother pleads for more originality:

(15) Family 5: Niva (13 F), Yoav (11 M), Tama (4 F).

Mother: *Hine, hine* <u>*tiheye kecat yoter*</u>   *Here, here,* <u>*be a little more*</u>
         <u>*mekori,*</u> *bapa'am she'avra*   <u>*original,*</u> *you already said that*
         amrta et ze.   *last time.*

Also used in the conversations studied were such expressions as *"ten-axashu"*—guess, *"kulam hexlitu al ze"*—everybody decided on that, and *"anaxnu crixim le'hamci nose"*—we have to think up a subject. Each of these phrases refers to a different mode of thinking, including speculating, collaborative thinking, and inventive thought.

Reflection

Actions, thoughts, and emotional states are interconnected, according to interlocutors.

Applegate et al. (1992) define messages that encourage recipients to consider causes and consequences of actions as reflection-enhancing messages. These messages are part of a person-centered orientation to communication, presenting complex reasoning behavior.

Rami (Example 16) can see how thoughts can cause an emotional reaction:

(16) Family 4: Rami (16 M), Xagit (12 F), Dani (8.5 M).

Father: *at mefaxedet mi . . . ?*   *You're afraid of . . . . ?*
Observer: *lo, aval keshe'hazanav shelo*   *No, but when its tail touches*
           noge'a bi, ani <u>*mefaxedet.*</u>   *me,* <u>*I'm afraid.*</u>
Rami: <u>*at xoshevet*</u> *she-ze xatul.*   <u>*You think*</u> *it's a cat.*

The mother (Example 17) attributes her sister Hanna's sudden interest in football to her emotional attachment to her son:

(17) Family 10: Dafi (12 F), Noga (8 F), Yaron (4 M).

Mother: *xana matxila lehavin*   *Hanna is beginning to under-*
         bekaduregel. <u>*haben shela nora*</u>   *stand football.* <u>*Her son is very*</u>
         <u>*mit'anyen baze, gam hi pit'om*</u>   <u>*interested in it, she suddenly*</u>
         <u>*yoda'at.*</u>   <u>*knows too.*</u>

Cognitive Expressions for Communication Management

Evaluating. The attempt on the part of interlocutors to adhere to the maxims of quantity and relevance forces them to evaluate the degree of common knowledge, so that they can supply the necessary information but avoid being overbearing by being too verbose. For instance, in Example 18, because the guest doesn't know the story, the mother can go on telling it:

(18) Family 4: Rami (16 M), Xagit (12 F), Dani (8.5 M).

Mother:	Makira et sipur ha'arnav shel li'ora?	You _know_ the story of Liora's rabbit?
Guest:	Lo.	No.
Mother:	Ken be'yom rishon she'avar . . .	Yes, last Sunday . . .

And, in Example 19, Yoav is reluctant to supply information he considers already shared:

(19) Family 5: Niva (13 F), Yoav (11 M), Tama (4 F).

Yoav:	Anaxnu asinu yoter po+.. ani hayiti.	We did more here+.. I was.
Mother:	Ma?	What?
Observer:	Ma. ma hayita?	What, what were you?
Mother:	Ma?	What?
Yoav:	Ke'ilu at lo yoda'at	As if you don't know
Mother:	Ma?	What?
Yoav:	At lo yoda'at?	You don't know?
Father:	Ah, katav, katavenu mimodi'in.	Oh, a reporter, our reporter from Modi'in.

Recruiting. Whereas in the previous examples cognitive expressions were used in interrogatives, with rising intonation, here they are used as comments, with flat intonation. The speakers are relying on the listeners' knowledge, and this knowledge is stated as a basis for agreement, allowing for less specification.

Here, in Example 20, they talk about shopping for furniture:

(20) Family 9: Sivan (8 M), Carmel (5.6 M).

Mother:	Ze beyn agripas leyafo. Yesh kol miney simta'ot ka'ele.	It's between Agripas and Jaffa. There are many such alleys.
Observer:	Ah.	Oh.
Mother:	At _yod'at_, yesh sham simta im gan kaze nexmad. mamash gan misxakim.	You _know_, there's an alley there with such a nice park. A real playground.

In Example 21, the father describes his work to the observer:

(21) Family 14: Yaniv (7.7 M), Oshrit (6.5 F).

Father: *Anaxnu sho'avim rak im yesh*   *We only pump if there's any*
           sakana, ata <u>mevin</u>?   *danger, do you <u>understand</u>?*

In Example 22, the mother (in the same family) discusses the rich meals they used to eat in her family of origin. She speaks in a fragmented manner and allows the listener to fill in the gap by using a cognitive expression:

(22) Family 14: Yaniv (7.7 M), Oshrit (6.5 F).

Mother: *Hayom keshe'ani ro'a et ze*   *Today when I see this I say*
           ani omeret eyx yaxolnu le'exol.   *how could we eat. It's lucky*
           mazal she'anaxnu lo shmenot   *that we're not fat, all of us.*
           kulanu. at <u>yoda'at</u> ze le'exol   *You <u>know</u> this means to eat xx*
           xx ze lexem.   *it's bread.*

Shifting.   In Example 23, Yakir, who has been discussing with his family the desirable amount of his donation to the Society for the Deaf (which his sister is raising money for), changes his mind and decides not to donate at all. His change of mind is signaled by a cognitive expression:

(23) Family 15: Hilla (10.7 F), Yakir (6.11 M).

Yakir: *<u>at yoda'at ma</u>, ani lo torem.*   *<u>You know what</u>, I'm not do-*
                                                   nating at all.

Mitigating Disagreements.   Blunt disagreement might be face threatening (Goffman, 1967). The expression of disagreement with an opinion may be mitigated by the use of cognitive expressions.

In both of the following examples, the validity of a comparison is challenged politely. In Example 24, the mother takes issue with the comparison that Rachel, the observer, is making between two Jerusalem neighborhoods:

(24) Family 1: Nadav (10 M), Yoram (10 M).

Mother: *ani lo <u>yoda'at</u> im ze oto*   *<u>I don't know</u> if it is the same*
           hadavar mibexinat herkev   *as far as the make-up of the*
           ha'oxlosia.   *population is concerned.*

In Example 25, the observer brought some ice cream for dessert. The father rejects the comparison between two brands of ice cream:

(25) Family 5: Noga (13 F), Yoav (11 M), Tama (4 F).

Noga:	ma, kanit lanu glida amerika'it?	What, you bought us American ice cream?
Yoav:	lo, kanta, bo'i tir'i, at xayevet.	No, she bought, come and see, you must.
Father:	ha'amerika'im yesh lahem glida nehederet.	The Americans have great ice cream.
Observer:	haglida ha'argentina'it hazot shel hame'anolitus gam ken lo ra'a bixlal.	This Argentinian ice cream from the Menaolitus isn't bad at all either.
Noga:	ta'im.	Tasty.
Father:	lo yode'a.	I don't know.

Presenting disagreement as lack of knowledge or uncertainty serves to save face.

Expressive Goals and Cognitive Expressions

Marking information as subjectively significant or insignificant is also achieved by the use of cognitive expressions.

Examples 26–28 were recorded in the same family. In Examples 26 and 27, the mother emphasizes information by using cognitive expressions. Here, the mother turns to the observer and starts a new topic of discussion:

(26) Family 15: Hila (10.7 F), Yakir (6.11 M).

Mother:	at yoda'at she'hem kiblu te'udot ha'shavu'a. at yoda'at laura?	You know that they [the children] got their report cards this week. Did you know, Laura?
Observer:	Lo.	No.
Hila:	Ken.	Yes.
Mother:	te'uda yafa me'od.	very nice report card.
Observer:	Ahh.	Oh.
Mother:	te'udot yafot me'od. axar-kax nar'e lax et hate'udot.	Very nice report cards. Later, we'll show you the report cards.

Obviously, the observer has no notion of the new information, and the question "Did you know?" serves to focus both her and the overhearing children's attention. By paying an indirect compliment to the shy children, the mother is trying to involve them in the conversation.

Here, in Example 27, while discussing a popular TV show that the mother and daughter are watching, the mother turns to the observer and says:

(27) Family 15: Hila (10.7 F), Yakir (6.11 M).

Mother:	*hem ro'im sport ve'anaxnu nixnasim lexeder xxx, ze mashe'hu [///], kol medinat is-rael, sheted'i lax.*	*They're watching [the father and Yakir] sports and we [the mother and Hila] come into the room xxx, It's something [///], the whole of the State of Israel, you should know.*

Note that the mother means that *everybody in Israel* is watching.

In Example 28, Nadav signifies lack of interest using the same expression as the mother did:

(28) Family 1: Nadav (11 M), Yoram (10 M).

Observer:	*agav mi hamora hamaxlifa shelaxem axshav?*	*By the way, who's your substitute teacher now?*
Nadav:	*ma ani yode'a. axat shekor'im la rina.*	*I don't know [literally: What do I know]. Somebody called Rina.*

HUMOROUS EXPRESSIONS

The use of both literary and colloquial language aims at creating involvement and sustaining it (Tannen, 1989). The emotive-expressive and the poetic functions jointly create a style that consists of sound play, double meaning, picturesque images, and metaphors. A variety of the means mentioned by Tannen can be detected in humorous phrases used by the families observed.

Humor enables the expression of individuality in creative and unique ways. It brings children and adults closer and turns aggressiveness into an event that highlights solidarity, pleasure, and cleverness. Humorous frames are part of sociable conversation (Blum-Kulka, 1997).

Humorous expressions are usually welcomed, as can be observed in the joint participation of children and adults in creating them and in the expressions of satisfaction on the part of the adults. Attempts to control children's expressions, even when wild, are cautious, as in the following example, in which the rational reaction of the father puts an end to the children's playful mood:

(29) Family 6: Iris (6 F), Lilach (6 F), Rami (1 M).

Lilach:	at titxatni im ha, at titxatni im iris im iris.	[to the observer] You'll marry the, you'll marry Iris Iris.
Iris:	ken vedalya titxaten.	Yes, and Dalya [the mother] will marry.
Lilach:	im dubi, dubi.	Dubi [the dog] Dubi.
Iris:	ken ve'ehud yitxaten im rami.	Yes, and Ehud [the father] will marry Rami [the baby].
Lilach:	vedubi yitxaten im miriam ve'ehud yitxaten im harosh shelo.	And Dubi will marry Miriam and Ehud will marry his head.
Father:	rega, im dalya titxaten im dubi, az eyx miriam yexola le'hitxaten im dubi?	One moment, if Dalya marries Dubi, then how can Miriam marry Dubi?

Exposure to humor affects creativity (Ziv, 1989). Creative people are aware of humor, create humor, and are receptive to humor (Ziv, 1984). Humor and creativity are derived from the same mental set, which consists of what Ziv called "playfulness." Playfulness is manifested emotionally in pleasure, devotion to the process, and a feeling of relative freedom in adhering to truth values. Cognitively, playfulness derives from lateral thinking and can be detected in creative processes in any domain, as well as in humorous expressions (De Bono, 1977).

Both humor and insight derive from lateral thinking, which creates new ideas and constructs new patterns. Both are, according to De Bono (1977), temporary alternative organizations of information. If that organization is sudden, it arouses humor, whereas if it is permanent, it arouses understanding. Ziv and Gadish (1988) found a high correlation between creativity and humor, and also between creativity and the low need for social acceptance. Perkins (1993) saw a close relation between creativity and values such as autonomy, objection to conformity, pleasure deriving from originality, the willingness to put effort into creation and motivation for creation, tolerance to ambiguity, disarray, and lack of symmetry. It may be maintained that creative humor, which is part of family talk, is cultivated in an environment that encourages such thinking values.

Distance from the immediate situation is another feature of humor and makes humorous phrases part of extended discourse. Even the undeveloped humor of infants demonstrates an understanding that intending a humorous effect allows for more freedom of play and for unusual combinations. Infants' humor is expressed in playful games in which children spontaneously create sound games and enjoy rhyming, repetitions, and violations of norms. The violation of norms itself is amusing to the young: They make no attempt to create ambiguities or surprising shifts.

The twin sisters in Example 30 tease their baby brother and talk simultaneously, using rhymes, repetition, and violations of norms:

(30) Family 6: Iris (6 F), Lilach (6 F), Rami (1 M).

Girls:	*xamor exad, tipesh exad,*	
	zanav	*Ass, stupid, tail*
	likluk xalav	*Milk-licker*
	tapu'ax adama	*Potato*
	Meluxlaxim	*Dirty*
	im lexem im xem'a	*With bread, with butter*
	tapu'ax adama	*Potato*
	lexem im xem'a	*bread and butter*
	para aduma	*Red cow*
	ozen aduma	*Red ear*

In Example 31, the young sisters continue with their fun by repeating words in a playful dialogue:

(31) Family 6: Lilach (6 F), Iris (6 F), Rami (1 M).

Iris:	*ma ze gadol?*	*What is big?*
Lilach:	*Gadol.*	*Big.*
Iris:	*ma ze gadol?*	*what is big?*
Lilach:	*Katan.*	*Small.*
Iris:	*Benoni.*	*medium size.*
Lilach:	*Benoni?*	*medium size?*
Iris:	*Rami katan [/] katan.*	*Rami is small [/] small.*
Lilach:	*Katan.*	*Small.*
Iris:	*katan kaze.*	*so small.*

Nonsense fun is also present in the following lines:

(32) Family 2: Shulamit (12 F), Riki (10 F), Mira (5 F).

Mother:	*xaverim bete'avon.*	*friends, bon appetite.*
Mira:	*ani oxelet et hashulxan.*	*I'm eating the table.*

The ability to participate in adult humor develops with age. Following is an example of a joke told by Dafi (12):

(33) Family 8: Dafi (12 F), Noga (8 F), Yaron (4 M).

Dafi:		

Dafi: *yesh bedixa al xaver exad shepogesh et hasheni barexov ve'omer "hamishpaxa sheli mishpaxa shel si'anim . . . axoti hayta rishona hi kafca mimatos migova shel 25 meter, ve'ima sheli axarey ze migova shel 500 meter, ve'aba sheli migova shel 600 meter ve'ani mitkonen likfoc migova shel 1000 meter". az omrim lo "uma omeret hamishpaxa al kax?" az homer: "eyzo mishpaxa?"*

There's a joke about a fellow who meets another fellow on the street and tells him, "My family is a family of record breakers . . . my sister was the first, she jumped out of a plane from a height of 25 meters, and my mother jumped after that from 500 meters, and my father jumped from 600 meters, and I intend to jump from 1000 meters". So they ask him, "And what does the family say about all this?" and he answers, "What family?"

This is a well-formulated joke that gradually builds up the humorous effect. The point is made by what is omitted and must be inferred.

The humor of adolescents and adults is based on the tension or a gap between what is known about reality, or is acceptable in reality, and what is presented or described in humorous expressions. Here are some examples.

Incompatibility

In Example 34, the mother addresses Tama in a humorous way:

(34) Family 5: Niva (13 F), Yoav (11 M), Tama (4 F).

Mother: *tikxi xalav geveret.*   *Have some milk, madame.*

In Example 35, Niva spells out the humorous comparison implied by her mother's words:

(35) Family 5: Niva (13 F), Yoav (11 M), Tama (4 F).

Mother: *ah ken? aha. ata yaxol lish'ol et ze bekol ram ve'ani lo agid lexa im lo teshev vetedaber. dessert ze sxar tirxa.*

[to Yoav] Oh yes? oh. You can ask that out loud, and I won't tell you I f you don't sit down and talk. Dessert is your honorarium.

Observer: [laughs]

Mother: *dessert ze sxar tirxa.*   *Dessert is your honorarium.*

| Niva: | *halevay velitro'ax haya le'exol.* | *I wish laboring would be eating.* |

"Sxar tirxa" is a legal expression. There is a mismatch between the register and the situation.

Exaggeration

Here the humorous effect lies in the playful overestimation of the mother's practical idea:

(36) Family 6: Iris (6 F), Lilach (6 F), Rami (1 M).

Mother:	*xashavti shenerasek od gvina cehuba im agvania kmo she'ani osa layeladot.*	*I thought we'd grate some more hard cheese with a tomato, just like I do for the girls.*
Father:	*ken, ze haya ra'ayon tov.*	*Yes, that was a good idea.*
Mother:	*ze ra'ayon ge'oni.*	*It's an ingenious idea.*
Father:	*Geoni.*	*Ingenious.*
Mother:	*lo paxot mige'oni.*	*Not less than ingenious.*

Images

The same parents describe the way their baby is eating, using exaggeration and imagery:

(37) Family 6: Lilach (6 F), Iris (6 F), Rami (1 M).

| Father: | *kmo pompa.* | *Like a pump.* |
| Mother: | *maxon she'iva.* | *A pumping plant.* |

Imagery and cumulative exaggeration enrich the immediate event. The humorous discourse has been distanced from its original stimulus.

Impersonation

In Example 38, Nadav impersonates a government minister and then "interviews" his brother Yoram:

(38) Family 1: Nadav (11 M), Yoram (10 M).

| Nadav: | *kan medaber sar haxakla'ut.* | *This is the Minister of Agriculture speaking.* |
| Nadav: | *Bevakasha ledaber la'inyan. ha'im leda'atxa peres rosh* | *Please talk to the point. Do you believe that Peres is a* |

	memshala ra'uy. Namek!	*worthy Prime Minister? Jus-*
	hasber! paret!	*tify! Explain! Specify!*
		[everybody is laughing]
Yoram:	*hu lo yoter tov miviktor*	*He isn't better than Victor*
	atyar,aval hu gam kaxa kaxa.	*Atyar, but he is also so, so.*
Nadav:	*mi ze viktor atyar. ma at*	*Who is Victor Atyar. What do*
	yoda'at al viktor atyar?	*you know about Victor Atyar?*
	namek! hasber! paret!	*Justify! Explain! Specify!*
		(laughter)
	ani mevakesh lo lecaxkek	*I ask the audience to refrain*
	bakahal. ani medaber po im	*from laughing I am here talk-*
	geveret me'od mexubedet veze	*ing with a distinguished lady,*
	shehi zkena ukmate'ha	*and the fact that she is old*
	mamash kmutim, eyn	*and really wrinkled, there's*
	ma ledaber, lo carix licxok.	*nothing to talk about, no need*
	busha vexerpa, bador shel	*to laugh. Shame on you. In*
	yameynu hayu xalucim.	*our generation people were*
		still pioneers.

Pretend play enables Nadav to express emotions and aspirations of self-aggrandizement linguistically. Nadav uses a mixture of registers: formal school register and political interview register. Both registers are higher than the common use of language in family discourse. The make-believe situation is by nature detached from the present and cognitively serves as a distancing device.

Humor for Amusement—Hypothetical Absurd Situations

Playful joyous thought can produce imaginary scenarios that totally contradict familiar scripts and our common knowledge about events and objects.

For instance, in Example 39 a mother playfully constructs an absurd situation as she talks about the recording during the meal:

(39) Family 5: Niva (13 F), Yoav (11 M), Tama (4 F).

Mother:	*naklit ma she'amarnu az*	*We'll record what we said*
	hayinu yexolim lehit'amen al	*then [i.e., the previous record-*
	ze ukshemiryam (hamaklita)	*ing] we could have practiced*
	hayta ba'a hayinu medabrim	*on it, and when Miriam (the*
	oto davar.	*observer) came, we would say*
		the same things.

Miriam:	*lama?*	*Why?*
Mother:	*nagid yesh lax tayprecorder, nagid pa'am ba'a sheyavo hacalam nilmad be'al pe.*	*Let's say you have a tape-recorder, let's say the next time the photographer comes we will learn by heart.*
Miriam:	*lo!*	*no!*
Mother:	*Bediyuk. shehu yavo nedaber bul oto davar.*	*Exactly. when he comes we will say exactly the same thing.*

Each member of the family in Example 40 likes his or her salad in a different way, and each one has one ingredient that he or she dislikes:

(40) Family 4: Rami (16 M), Xagit (12 F), Dani (8.5 M)

Mother:	*az exad hara'ayonot sheracinu limco, haya magnet la'salatim.*	*So one idea we were looking for was a salad magnet.*

Violations of Expectation

Once a humorous context has been established, it can tolerate the violation of norms and taboos. Humorous interactions enable interlocutors to enjoy taboo violation without punishment (Freud, 1966). The element of surprise, caused by violation of expectations, is an important element in the humorous effect. Surprise can be achieved by violation of either interactional expectations or context expectations. Replacing an expected formula in the interactional exchange with an unexpected reply creates a violation of interactional expectation. Violation of context expectations is a result of repetition of phrases in an unexpected context. Using phrases with positive denotation in negative contexts produces irony.

Violation of Expectations—Interactions. In Example 41, the children are quarreling:

(41) Family 5: Niva (13 F), Yoav (11 M), Tama (4 F).

Tama:	*aba, tagid lo.*	*Daddy, tell him.*
Father:	*ani omer lo.*	*I'm telling him.*

In Example 42, with the same family, the observer is served strawberry mousse:

(42) Family 5: Niva (13 F), Yoav (11 M), Tama (4 F).

Observer:	*im mi ani mitxaleket?*	*Who am I sharing with?*

Father: *im acmex.*   *With yourself.*

In Example 43, it is Noga's unexpected answer that results in laughter:

(43) Family 10: Dafi (12 F), Riki (10 F), Mira (5 F).

Dafi: *hamora shel (shel noga)*   The teacher [Noga's teacher]
          xoshevet she'ani maxashefa.   thinks that I'm a witch. [with
                                           amusement]
Noga: *gam ani.*   Me too.

                                           [Everybody laughs]

In Example 44, a neighbor enters the house and the adults talk about a
children's book:

(44) Family 2: Shulamit (12 F), Riki (10 F), Mira (5 F).

Neighbor: *sefer shel pinya amitai.*   The book by Pinya Amitai.
                                           [author's name]
Mother: *Maksim.*   Beautiful.
Neighbor: *taxrixi et aba lehakri lax.* [to Riki] Make Daddy read
                                           it to you.
Father: *aba kara et ze. ze beseder.* Daddy read it already. It's
                                           OK.

Here the father means he read it to himself.

The responses in Examples 41–44 do not comply with the illocutionary
force of the stimuli that are presented as directives for action (as in Examples 41 and 44), as a plea for denial (Example 43), or as a request for directions (Example 42).

Violation of Context Expectations.   Here in Example 45, the mother
mentions her sister Hanna's surprising knowledge of football rules, following her son's intense interest in the game:

(45) Family 10: Dafi (12 F), Noga (8 F), Yaron (4 M).

Observer: *kesherami yihiye ben 11, at*   When Rami [the younger
            tir'i shegam at titmac'i.   son] is 11, you'll see that
                                            you'll learn too.
Mother: *ani betuxa.*   I'm sure.
Dafi: *axshav hi gam mitmacet.*   Now she also knows things.

Observer:	*axshav bame hi mitmacet?*	*Now, she knows what?*
Noga:	*hi mitmacet bexana.*	*She knows Hanna.*

In Example 46, the same family discusses Noga's refusal to go to school:

(46) Family 10: Dafi (12 F), Noga (8 F), Yaron (4 M).

Mother:	*ani xashavti she'hi lo roca lalexet lebeyt sefer ki ulay yesh la be'aya im eyzo xavera sham. Ken? ze yaxolihiyot?*	*I thought she doesn't want to go to school because maybe she has a problem with some friend there. Yes? Is it possible?*
Noga:	*lo.*	*No.*
Dafi:	*ve'im hamora?*	*And with the teacher?*
Noga:	*yaxol lihiyot sheyesh li be'aya im xaver she'kor'im lo beyt sefer. ani sonet oto.*	*It's possible I have a problem with a friend called school. I hate him.*

And regarding the same matter, the family discussion continues as follows:

(47) Family 10: Dafi (12 F), Noga (8 F), Yaron (4 M).

Father:	*rega, bo natxil axeret, eyze mikco'ot at ohevet bebeyt sefer?*	*Just a moment, let's begin the other way round, which subjects do you like in school?*
Noga:	*klum. et hamikco'a habayta.*	*None. The subject called going home.*

Violation of Expectations—Irony. In these cases, the speaker's intention is different or opposite to the meaning of the expression, as in the following exchange:

(48) Family 6: Lilach (6 F), Iris (6 F), Rami (1 M).

Observer:	*ma asitem baxofesh?*	*What did you do during your vacation?*
Lilach:	*tafru li kan. ze ma she'asinu.*	*They stitched something here [her chin]. That's what we did.*
Father:	*hi lo shakta al shmareyha.*	*She didn't sit idle [literally, she didn't sit on her yeast, an idiom in high register].*
Mother:	*yesh xavayot, at ro'a.*	*Great experience, you see.*

In this example, ironical effect is achieved by using expressions that usually carry positive meanings. The mixture of registers and use of a high register to comment on the girls' deeds also contribute to the irony.

In Example 49, the mother comments on her daughters' mutual teasing:

(49) Family 10: Dafi (12 F), Noga (8 F), Rami (4 M).

Mother: *im kcat mazal ha'aruxa hazo*   *With a little bit of luck this*
          yexola lehigamer bemakot   *meal could end in fatal blows.*
          recax.

As in the previous example, irony is achieved by the use of an expression carrying a positive connotations—"luck" in the context of grim expectations.

Sound and Word Games

In Example 50, the mother refers to the dog called Dubi:

(50) Family 6: Lilach (6 F), Iris (6 F), Rami (1 M).

Mother: *Hakelev shelanu nolad*   *Our dog (Dubi) was born on*
          betubishvat.   *Tubishvat.*
Lilach: *Dubishvat.*   *Dubishvat.*

Note that *tubishvat* is also the name of the holiday taking place on that day. Here, the similarity between the two sounds "Tu" and "Du" starts the game that ends in Lilach's creation of a new combination: that of the dog's name and its date of birth.

In the following exchange in the same family, the father creates a new word blend for pepper (*gamba*) and lettuce (*xasa*):

(51) Family 6: Lilach (6 F), Iris (6 F), Rami (1 M).

Father: *at yod'at ma ze xasa aduma?*   *Do you know what red lettuce*
          kmo gamba, xasamba.   *(xasa) is? It's like red pepper*
                                             (gamba), xassamba.

The combination word *xasamba* is the name of a very famous series of children's books.

In Example 52, Yoav inquires about dessert, which he knows was brought by the observer:

(52) Family 5: Niva (13 F), Yoav (11 M), Tama (4 F).

Yoav:	*et ze im <u>hakaseta</u>.*	*This with the <u>cassette</u>.*
Father:	*Tayprecorder.*	*Tape-recorder.*
Mother:	*ze bimkom <u>hakassata</u> hi hevi'a lanu <u>kaseta</u>.*	*Instead of ice cream she brought us a <u>cassette</u>.*

The play on words is based on the similarity between *kaseta* and *kasata* (which is a kind of ice cream). Yoav confuses the two words, and his parents continue playing out this confusion.

Original Combinations

Borrowing expressions from one domain and using them in another creates a refreshing effect. Like a metaphor the combined phrase projects reality in a new light.

For instance, in Example 53 the children are helping to set the table:

(53) Family 9: Sivan (8 M), Carmel (5.6 M).

Mother:	*Beseder? eyfo sivi. hu lo ozer? ma kara le'sivish?*	*OK? where's Sivi. He doesn't help? What happened to Sivish?*
Carmel:	*hu ayef.*	*He's tired.*
Mother:	*Eyfo hu?*	*Where is he?*
Sivan:	*hine ani.*	*(Sitting) Here I am.*
Mother:	*<u>ata ayef macuy</u>.*	*<u>You're a regular tired one.</u>*

In Hebrew the combination of *matzuy* (literally, "found") + NP denotes the native botanical species of plants and animals. For example, the accurate name for the common Israeli anemone is *kalanit metzuya*.

Humor With a Point

Sometimes humor is more complex: It makes a statement, though not always a pleasant one. The statement has to be decoded in the gap between the information given and that withheld, and listeners are required to fill in the gaps with their knowledge and logical inferences. This is a refined humor, and the more left unsaid, the greater the degree of sophistication required of the listener.

The following exchange is a good example:

(54) Family 9: Sivan (8 M), Carmel (5.6 M).

Observer:	*ma et ze kanita? ma ze?*	*What, you bought this? what is it?* (points at a book)
Father:	*kmo she'agnon haya omer "ishti koret ani lo".*	*As Agnon would say "my wife reads, I don't".*
Observer:	*lo pele, eyn lo zman.*	*It's no wonder, he doesn't have any time.*
Father:	*lo. Keshesha'alu im hu makir et kafka, az hu amar "ken, ani yode'a she'ishti koret et ze".*	*No, when he was asked if he knew Kafka he said "yes, I know that my wife is reading it".*

Agnon was a famous Israeli author considered a classic writer even in his own lifetime, and a Nobel Prize Laureate.

Here, in Example 55, the mother is telling about the special food at a Bar-Mitzvah party she attended:

(55) Family 2: Shlomit (12 F), Riki (10 F), Mira (5 F).

Mother:	*Vehaya sham ma'axalim ka'ele, axshav ani yexola lesaper laxem, axarey she'anaxnu kvar lo kol kax re'evim. eyze dvarim!*	*And there was such food there, now I can tell you, after we are not so hungry anymore. What things!*

The same family continues to discuss the lavish party as follows:

(56) Family 2: Shlomit (12 F), Riki (10 F), Mira (5 F).

Shlomit:	*le'ima yesh avoda shel xodashim axadim.*	*Mother has a job for several months.*
Mother:	*ma? Lehorid et ha +.. lehorid et hasentimetrim hamyutarim, ah?*	*What? to take off the +.. to take off the excess centimeters, ah?*

In Example 57, Dani and Hagit are recalling their father's past statements:

(57) Family 4: Rami (16 M), Xagit (12 F), Dani (8.5 M).

Dani:	*ani zoxer she'amarta shexatulim lo mafri'im lexa, rak sheyihiyu baxuc.*	*I remember you said that cats don't bother you, as long as they are outside.*
Xagit:	*velo yoxlu.*	*And they won't eat.*

Dani:	*aval klavim lo mafri'im lexa bitnay sheyihiyu shel mishehu axer.*	*But dogs don't bother you, as long as they belong to someone else.*

Social Criticism

In the following example, criticism is expressed openly. Humor is derived from the surprising generalized comparisons:

(58) Family 5: Niva (13 F), Yoav (11 M), Tama (4 F).

Father:	*kvar sikamnu sheyesh shney sugey uxlusia otistit bamedina shelanu shelo yod'im ma ne'esa basviva.*	*We have already concluded that there are two types of autistic populations in our country that don't know what's happening around them.*
Observer:		[laughs]
Father:	*ze hakibucnikim vehakneset. lo yod'im ma ze meci'ut bixlal.*	*It's the members of the kibbutz and the Knesset* (parliament). *They don't know what the reality is at all.*

Allegedly, the topic for the following conversation is the father's change of behavior; indirectly what is being discussed is the behavior of the state's higher officials:

(59) Family 4: Rami (16 M), Xagit (12 F), Dani (8.5 M).

Father:	*ani kvar mesugal leshaker bli lehasmik . . . lehistakel leben adam baeynayim, leshaker bli lehasmik.*	*I'm already able to lie without blushing . . . to look a man straight in the eye, and lie without blushing.*
Observer:	*tuxal lihiyot general keshetihiye gadol.*	*You'll be able to be a general when you grow up.*
Father:	*ani uxal lihiyot rosh memshala.*	*I'll be able to be Prime Minister.*

CONCLUSION

Cognitive expressions and humorous phrases function as distancing devices and extend the discourse, even when embedded in specific contexts. Both types of expressions enhance the involvement of speakers in the discourse. Sometimes cognitive expressions are used to regulate communication, to express awareness of the maxims of quality and relevance needed for continued cooperation. Other times they are utilized as phatic expressions, and serve to minimize surprise, caused by sudden shifts, and to mitigate the threat to face, where such a threat might disrupt interaction. When thinking management is the main reason for using a cognitive expression, involvement with other participants, involvement in the content, and ego involvement are combined in the critical dialogical procedures initiated by these expressions.

The mere fact that the very same expressions may indicate concerns for both communication maintenance and thinking management may point to the close ties existing, according to speakers, between thinking and communication. Cognitive expressions are utilized to detect gaps in communication and information and to minimize them. Thus they refer either to vertical thinking, by contributing to the analytical critical part of the discourse, or to its reflective metacognitive aspect. Cognitive expressions marking subjectivity may serve as openers for multiparty discussions, or be used, as in the case of mitigation, to avoid confrontation.

A humorous effect is created by controlling the manner and timing of expression and creating an intentional gap between what is mentioned and what is meant, what is mentioned and what is not, what is said and what is expected. The playful spirit allows unconventional combinations and takes pleasure in various poetic strategies, such as sound and word games, exaggerations, impersonation, and the violation of interactional expectations. Humorous phrases serve the emotive expressive and the poetic functions of discourse. They are based on lateral thinking and contribute to the aesthetic aspect.

As a cultural phenomenon, the multitude of the tested expressions analyzed can be viewed as a sign of a democratic discourse style, in which awareness exists of the individuality and uniqueness of the thinkers. This is a style that encourages reflective critical thinking tendencies on the one hand, and flexibility and originality on the other. Thus, this chapter supports previous evidence, brought to light by Snow (1991) and Ochs et al. (1992), that shows how consciousness is shaped by social means during discourse performed in the frame of the chief cultural agent—the family.

REFERENCES

Applegate, J. L., Burleson, B. R., & Delia, J. G. (1992). Parenting as an antecedent to children's social-cognitive and communicative development. In I. E. Sigel, A. McGillicuddy Delisi, & J. J. Goodnow (Eds.), *Parental belief systems: The psychological consequences for children* (pp. 5–25). Mahwah, NJ: Lawrence Erlbaum Associates.

Blum-Kulka, S. (1997). *Dinner talk: Cultural patterns of sociability and socialization in family discourse.* Mahwah, NJ: Lawrence Erlbaum Associates.

Bruner, J. S. (1983). *Child talk: Learning to use language.* Oxford, England: Oxford University Press.

Cazden, C. B. (1992). *Whole language plus.* New York: Teachers College Press.

Chafe, W. L. (1985). Linguistic differences produced by differences between speaking and writing. In D. Olson, N. Torrance, & A. Hildyard (Eds.), *Literacy, language and learning* (pp. 105–124). Cambridge, England: Cambridge University Press.

De Bono, E. (1977). *Lateral thinking/A textbook of creativity.* Middlesex, England: Penguin.

Ennis, R. H. (1987). A taxonomy of critical thinking dispositions and abilities. In J. B. Baron & R. S. Sternberg (Eds.), *Teaching thinking skills—Theory and practice* (pp. 9–26). New York: Freeman.

Feurstein, R., & Feurstein, R. (1996). *The process as a content guide for future teaching.* Hadassah Vizo Canada Research Institute, Jerusalem, Israel.

Flavell, J. H. (1978). Metacognition & cognitive monitoring: A new area of psychological inquiry. *American Psychologist, 34,* 906–911.

Freud, S. (1966). *Jokes and their relation to the unconscious.* London: Routledge & Kegan Paul.

Goffman, E. (1967). *Interactional rituals: Essays on face to face behavior.* New York: Doubleday Anchor.

Goodnow, J. J., & Collins, W. A. (1990). *Development according to parents.* Hove, England: Lawrence Erlbaum Associates.

Grice, H. P. (1975). Logic and conversation. In P. Cole & F. Morgan (Eds.), *Syntax and semantics: Vol. 3. Speech acts* (pp. 41–58). New York: Academic Press.

Jakobson, R. (1960). *Closing statement linguistics and poetics style in language* (T. A. Sebock, Ed.). Cambridge, MA: MIT Press.

McPeck, J. E. (1990). *Teaching critical thinking.* New York: Routledge.

Ochs, E., Taylor, C., Rudolph, D., & Smith, R. (1992). Storytelling as a theory building activity. *Discourse Processes, 15,* 37–72.

Perkins, D. (1993). Creating a culture of thinking. *Educational Leadership, 51*(3), 98–99.

Rogoff, B. (1990). *Apprenticeship in thinking.* New York: Oxford University Press.

Rogoff, B., & Lave, J. (Eds.). (1984). *Everyday cognition, its developmental and social context.* Cambridge, MA: Harvard University Press.

Rogoff, B., & Wertsch, J. (Eds.). (1984). *Children's learning in the zone of proximal development.* San Francisco: Jossey-Bass.

Sigel, I. E. (1979). On becoming a thinker, a psychoeducational model. *Educational Psychologist, 14,* 70–78.

Sigel, I. E. (1982). The relationship between parental distancing strategies and the child's cognitive behavior. In L. M. Laosa & I. E. Sigel (Eds.), *Families as learning environments for children* (pp. 47–86). New York: Plenum.

Sigel, I. E., & Saunders, R. (1979). An inquiry into inquiring. Question asking as an instructional model. In L. Katz (Ed.), *Current topics in early childhood education* (Vol. 2, pp. 169–193). Norwood, NJ: Ablex.

Sigel, I. E., Stinson, E. T., & Flaugher, J. (1991). Socialization of representational competence in the family: The distancing paradigm. In H. Okagaki & R. J. Sternberg (Eds.), *Directions of development/Influences on the development of children's thinking* (pp. 121–144). Hillsdale, NJ: Lawrence Erlbaum Associates.

Snow, C. (1991). Building memoirs: The ontogeny of autobiography. In D. Cichetti & M. Beeghly (Eds.), *The self-transition infancy to childhood* (pp. 213–242). Chicago: University of Chicago Press.

Swartz, R. J., & Perkins, D. N. (1990). *Teaching thinking: Issues and approaches.* Pacific Grove, CA: Midwest Publications.

Tannen, D. (1989). *Talking voices: Repetition, dialogue and imagery in everyday conversational discourse.* Cambridge, England: Cambridge University Press.

Vygotsky, L. S. (1962). *Thought and language.* Cambridge, MA: MIT Press.

Vygotsky, L. S. (1978). *Mind in society: The development of higher psychological processes.* Cambridge, MA: Harvard University Press.

Vygotsky, L. S. (1987). *Thinking and speech* (N. Minick, Ed. and Trans.). New York: Plenum.

Ziv, A. (1984). *Personality and sense of humor.* New York: Springer.

Ziv, A. (1989). Using humor to develop creative thinking. *Journal of Children in Contemporary Society, 20,* 99–116.

Ziv, A., & Gadish, A. (1988). *Relationships and influences on creativity: Personality, intelligence and parents' perception.* Tel Aviv, Israel: Tel Aviv University.

Chapter 8

Language Games in the Strict Sense of the Term: Children's Poetics and Conversation

Alessandra Fasulo
Vivian Liberati
Clotilde Pontecorvo
"La Sapienza," University of Rome

Excerpt 1 Terini family dn.1 Mother; Father; Federico, 8 years; Serena, 5 years
The parents are talking to each other

1	Federico	Mommy say what's your name Mommy say what's your name Mommy say—	Mamma dimmi come ti chiami Mamma dimmi come ti chiami Mamma dimmi—
2	Mom	Yeah *((turning to him))*	Eh. *((girandosi verso di lui))*
3	Federico	Say what's my name	Dimmi come mi chiamo
4	Mom	What's your <u>name</u>? *((understanding—check tone))*	<u>C</u>ome ti <u>chiami</u>? *((tono di verifica))*
5	Federico	Uh.	Eh.
6	Mom	Riccio *((the child's nick-name))*	Riccio *((nomignolo del bambino))*
7	Federico	No. <u>You</u> have to say "What's your name?"	No. <u>Te</u> devi dire "Come ti chiami?"
8	Mom	What's your name?	Come ti chiami?
9	Federico	I am eight *((laughs))*	Ho otto anni *((ride))*

In Excerpt 1, an 8-year-old boy summons his mother's attention in order to suggest a question that she should address to him. When she produces an answer instead of the desired question he clarifies the sense of his request, using a more suitable intonation (Line 7), and, finally, after the mother has followed his prompt, answers in a nonpertinent way, and laughs at it.

The last utterance turns out to be a punch line, which reframes the whole sequence as a language game based on the infraction of the rule of pertinence. The joke requires the participation of another person: To make it happen, the child assigns not only conversational roles (i.e., questioner and answerer) but also the words the other has to say. The sequence is thus organized in a presequence of instruction followed by the sequence of interest, namely the question and the "wrong" answer. Federico has to "sweep the floor" of the ongoing interaction between the parents in order to go through the whole activity, and he does so by repeated summoning, which eventually gets his mother's attention. After the exchange we have shown, the father continues asking the child questions in want of arbitrary answers, but the child has difficulties in playing his own game so the parents spell the rule out for him.

Playful exchanges are recurrent in our corpus of recordings of two-parent families with children in the preschool or primary school years. Our focus in this chapter is the conversational structure and interactional meaning of "poetic" talk.

METHODS

The recordings on which this study is based were collected in several phases of a research project on family dinner conversation developed since 1992. The families all have at least two children, with a specified age range for the younger one. At the beginning we selected families in which the younger child was between 5 and 6 years. More recently, we lowered the age of the target child so that it ranged between 3;5 and 4;5 years, with the rationale that this would be a more critical age for investigating language socialization in a multiparty context such as the dinner gathering (see later section Conversation at the Dinner Table).

All the families had been met by one or two researchers in a preliminary encounter where they were informed about the meaning of the research and the procedure of the recordings. In order to guarantee the least inconvenience for the people who participated, from the second run of the collection (from the fourth family on) we left them the camera for several weeks so that they could choose the evenings in which to record themselves autonomously. We asked for four recorded dinners in the first stage, and, when possible, we repeated the observation 6 months later.

Overall, we have data of 20 families for a total of 64 transcribed dinners (the first recording of each family was not considered). By reducing the age of the target child, and overall also of the elder sibling, there has been a substantial increase in the presence of "prepatterned" speech (Tannen, 1989) like poems, songs, various types of rhymes, and other instances of children's folklore.

PERSPECTIVES ON POETICS AND SPEECH PLAY

Work done in linguistics shows the difficulty of giving a definition of poetics. A possible reading of Jakobson's pages on this issue (Montani, 1990) views the essence of poetics not in the message or in the sender but in the receiver: Poetry is an *effect* rather than any substantial feature of a series of words. It would be accomplished when a piece of language manifests exemplarily the condition of language reflexivity.[1] Similar to this notion is that of foregrounding, a procedure that signals as relevant now "a particular conceptual framework for understanding what is said or done" (Basso, 1979, p. 12). Though obviously language can be shaped in a way oriented to the achievement of the effect, the poetic aspect can emerge without any intentionality on the part of the speaker or writer: One can be struck by the poetics of a shopping list or of a train timetable.

In the common sense, poetic language is defined by contrast with referential and instrumental communication, but in the literature it is rather a "continuum" model that is invoked to account for the difficulty of a clearcut distinction (Kirshenblatt-Gimblett, 1979). Spontaneous poetics is studied under the label of *speech play,* following the classical notion of play as specifically nonpurposeful (Huizinga, 1955; see also Schwartzmann, 1978). Kirschenblatt-Gimblett (1979) and Cazden (1976) also pointed out the difference between speech play and verbal games, games seen as more rigid, closer to *routines.* A similar opposition can be found in Bateson (1979), although it is not internal to the speech domain: He opposed play to *ritual,* with the first marked by the presence of creativity and unexpectedness in a sequence of actions. In play, relationships are created or explored, whereas rituals, Bateson said, make assertions about the relationship at stake. The difference between play and game is also a part of the Meadian theory on the development of social self: A game is an activity whereby children learn about roles as linked to particular positions in the structure of the activity, and it is successive to play, which is more imagina-

---

[1]"Exemplarity is like the unexpected and unexpectable emergence of a watershed, without any marker, any technical rule of production and recognition, which in a stroke offers language in its risk and in its liminal productivity" (Montani, 1990, p. 251, our translation).

tive and free (Mead, 1934). (For a discussion on role theory and children's play, see Aronsson & Thorell, chap. 10, this volume). We can now better focus our inquiry as the exploration of what happens when speech play is performed within an ordered system of activity such as conversation. Conversation is in fact a "game" in that there is sequential relevance, turn taking as a machinery of distribution of the speaking role, and the constitution, through different types of turns, of the relative kinds of speakership (e.g., questioner, answerer, teller, coteller) and recipienceship (e.g., addressee, knowing recipient, unknowing recipient, audience, etc.) (C. Goodwin, 1981; Sacks, Schegloff, & Jefferson, 1974). Within the conversational framework, we side with Basso (1979) in the argument that "as an instrument of metacommunication and a form of social interaction, play is intrinsically purposeful and inevitably consequential" (p. 100).

Operatively, in this study we looked at instances of talk in interaction in which the "design features" of talk (Schegloff, 1997), its formal properties, were particularly salient and seemed to contribute relevantly to the "point" of speech, or, in other words, to answer the fundamental conversational question "Why this now?" In the excerpt shown at the beginning, for example, it is the *violation of semantic relevance* that legitimates the establishment of a sequence of interrogation, justifying its emergence as something with interactional import and meaning.

The task set for us now is to show the functioning of verbal play in the detail of its occurrence and to describe the specific character it takes on when children and their parents are involved.

CHILDREN'S SPEECH PLAY

The social nature of language seems prior, and relatively independent, from referentiality. Studies of early interaction between caregivers and children in the first weeks of their relationship show that primary intersubjectivity is accomplished through reciprocal imitation of sound or motor patterns. Trevarthen (1988) reported that "by 5 months a baby can share in what seems like a kinematic and melodic narrative in the song game: its poetic form" (p. 21). Sensitivity to metrics and phonology is thus an early developed competence with adaptive value for the establishment of affective bounds and of primary forms of communication, besides that of exercising the phonetic apparatus and of fixing the improvements in language acquisition.

Children maintain in the following years a high propensity to be caught by the poetics of speech (Garvey, 1977; Weir, 1962), and this, following Sanches and Kirshenblatt-Gimblett (1976), seems to be due to a particular model of language, which they infer from the study of children's lore. In this model, which is different from the adult one, the phonological structure is more salient. A limited capacity of memory until at least the 7th or 8th year of life tends to favor the use of *concatenations* (reliance on fixed-order series of items already ensured in rote memory, such as numbers, the alphabet, days of the week, etc.), *gradatio* (repetition of the last words of a preceding utterance for the building of the next one), and stylistic devices acting on short spans (such as *rhyming couplets*). The frequency of *nonsense* in children's speech can also be accounted for by the construction of meaning through morphophonological patterning, that is, sound-based relations of similarity and other kinds of formal connection.

Children of different cultures, between 2 and 3 years, have been shown to engage with age-close peers in prolonged interactions largely based on sound or word repetition or on nonsense utterances rhythmically patterned (Ervin-Tripp, 1979; Iwamura, 1980; Ochs, 1983; Schieffelin, 1990). The ease in switching from content-based talk to sing-song or formulaic talk (*cantilena*) has also been observed in Italian children between 3 and 5 years (Corsaro, 1997).

The form assumed by speech play does not appear to be indifferent to its sociolinguistic habitat (Douglas, 1968; Powell & Paton, 1988; Radcliffe-Brown, 1952). Sensitivity to design features of talk provides children with tools for parodistic imitations of adult forms. This line of interpretation was advanced by Sutton Smith (1976) in his analysis of riddles. Riddles—that is, in a structural definition, questions followed by arbitrary answers—are more frequent in communities where interrogation is a central instrument of socialization. Because there is no right answer to a riddle (and however witty an answer is the questioner can always reject it), the riddle gives the questioner the chance to "exercise arbitrary power," and this is indeed an interesting representation of how the adults' practice of interrogation can appear to a child. Along the same lines proceeds Gossen's (1979) analysis of verbal dueling among male children and adolescents as a means to make fun of principles of ranking actually present in the Mexican community he studied. Parody of adults' talk addresses paradigms of social organization, but in so doing also plays with conversational conventions: In the case of riddles, for example, the target rule seems to be the conditional relevance between questions and answers (Sacks et al., 1974). An interesting possibility for the study of children's verbal play is thus to analyze it for the understanding it displays about the functioning of the language.

CONVERSATION AT THE DINNER TABLE

In the hours children spend with their caregivers and siblings in the family, they move through a variety of conversational settings, many of which are probably dyadic and not much different from early interactions in terms of reciprocal adjustment of the parties. Other types of exchanges are quite loose in conversational terms, centered on practical activities like playing games or watching TV, thus not requiring sustained verbal interactions. Dinner gatherings appear instead to demand a higher communicative involvement: True, there is the main activity concerning food, but allegedly eating together is not regarded as something to be accomplished in an utterly functional, literal fashion. Our families do not dine with their silverware, but do not supersede either to the ceremonial aspect of sharing food.

Children are not supposed to move around freely between one mouthful and another, although they frequently attempt to do so:

Excerpt 2 Soldano Family, dn.1
Mother, Father, Grandmother, Grandfather, Stefano 7 years, Gianluca, 4 years, Marina 3 months

Mom:	*((to Gianluca, who is eating yogurt and dripping it on the floor))* mouths stay over the table not all over the place	*((a Gianluca, che sta mangiando lo yogurt e versandolo per terra))* la bocca sta sul tavolo non sta in giro

Rules are often enunciated impersonally and by figurative speech: Gianluca's mother uses a synecdotic formulation to highlight the portion of the child's body over which restrain is exercised. Socialization to good manners implies a lot of formulaic and proverbial talk (Berko-Gleason, Perlmann, & Blank-Greif, 1984; Cahill, 1987); the dinner table is thus a place where such forms of language are particularly frequent.

Control over children appears to be a constant trait of dinners, which does not decrease in quantity when children grow but rather changes in content: Until they are 3 or 4 years old, children are required basically to eat what they have got, stay at the table properly seated, and use a fork instead of their hands; later on they can be told to not laugh, scream, sing, play, and talk with their mouth full, and maybe the next year they can be introduced to rules such as waiting for others to finish before passing to the next course, not eating with their face lowered over the plate, and so on. Briefly, rules get more and more detailed in terms of social coordination, respect for food as a valuable, and the assumption of thresholds of disgust (Elias, 1978).

In the forms of control required at different stages, one can also trace the extent of proximity between children and adults: At 3 or 4 years children may still have different food and be allowed toys for entertainment; later and increasingly, they eat the same things as adults and have to rely on talk for entertainment. This provokes an active request from children that parents talk about matters they can follow and participate in.

Excerpt 3, Fanaro family, dn.3. Mother, Father, Sergio, 7 years; Stefania, 5 years.

Mom and Dad are talking politics: Stefano stabs a piece of cheese with his fork but it slips off

Sergio:	Daddy when you talk about these things mozzarella unsticks itself and falls on the ground	Papà quando parli di queste cose la mozzarella si stacca e casca a terra

This time it is a member of the younger generation who, by a metaphoric interpretation of a casual event, remarks the undesired quality of the parent's behavior.

Dinner as a social setting is a "mundane" situation in which children find themselves under considerable normative restraints: One of the byproducts of this is children's attempts to shape the interaction so as to make it interesting, trading their compliance to the parents' will with a request for the parents' involvement in their own conversational agenda or to be let into the parents' one.

On the other hand, conversation as an activity in itself, that is, when talk is the primary focus of interaction, is quite a complicated business. Goffman (1967) argued that, in "focused interaction,"[2] "These obligations seem to be in opposition to each other, requiring a balance of conduct that is so delicate and precarious that alienation and uneasiness for someone in the interaction are the typical result" (p. 134). The obligations to which he referred concern following all the rules of conduct relevant in the situation, while introducing some degree of freedom in order to make the interaction interesting.

We believe that dinnertime plays a basic role in socialization to mundane conversation, in that it is a competitive environment where children are not only exposed to expert performance but also pushed to discover its strategies, because talk is the only available source of interest as long as the dinner lasts.[3]

POETICS AS TOPICAL TALK

In multiparty conversation among children and adults, poetry from children's folklore or other corpora, family repertoires included, are often used as a common platform for participation. Rhymes and song lines

---

[2]Goffman (1967) defined them as those in which there is "a single center of official cognitive and visual interest, that everyone participating in full right must collaborate to maintain" (p. 146).

[3]This may be one argument against watching TV at dinnertime, but of course TV talk is also a genre to which it could be useful to be socialized.

function as the common background on which to base variations and expansions. In this sense, the poetic character of talk performs topical work, the structure being a substitute for content in providing cohesion to a series of turns in a sequence.

Topic, that is, theme of conversation, is a controversial construct, in that it has a weak organizational power on talk and it is very hard to define, but as a members' category it may be exploited to display relevance of next contributions, it can be glossed (e.g., "what were we talking about?") and can arrange rounds of thematically related sequences (Button & Casey, 1984; Jefferson, 1996; Schegloff, 1990; Sterponi & Pontecorvo, 1996).

The structure of the poetry-based exchanges is not too different from adults' genres of talk in interaction such as joke-capping sessions (Chiaro, 1992); these are events whose coherence is based on the repeated production of the same type of structure (the joke), and typically in series or rounds generated by the content of the joke (pets, the jungle, etc.), the category (riddles), or the stylistic features (naive or "hard-core" ones). At the end of each performance there is an evaluation phase, with laughter and comments, until the beginning of the next one. For Sacks (1992), who found joke-capping sessions in the psychotherapeutic meetings of a group of adolescents, the utility of such talk lies, first, in the fact that rounds provide participation slots to everybody, and second that the impersonal[4] character of the jokes provides for low-risk, unaffiliated talk. As he said, "situations in which something holds for 'everybody' are far simpler than those which don't have that character" (p. 298, vol. 1). And, because joke telling is not easy for children (Fasulo & Pontecorvo, 1997), poems seems to offer a good way to facilitate participation of small children in a multiparty setting with adults and elder siblings.

In the following excerpt, a childish expression of complaint is the starting point of a long series of poemlike units recited by each of the three present (the father had left the table before this point). Some of these pieces have the same metric as the preceding ones; others are completely different, tied to the former only by dint of being "poetry."

Unfortunately, understanding these excerpts will be hard for nonreaders of Italian: They will have to look at both the columns, the left one for an English translation of the meaning of the words (when there is any) and the right one to appreciate the rhymes, alliteration, and the other sound-related features. (Numbers in parentheses within the comment section refer to lines of transcript.)

---

[4]"Notice about jokes, that when jokes are told they're are things that are just 'going around'; they are quotes" (Sacks, 1992, p. 101, vol. 1).

Excerpt 4.1, Minelli family, dn.2. Mother, Ugo, 11;8; Luisa, 3;5

1	Mom	Come on eat the pasta Luisa (1.0) when you are finished I give you some more maybe. ((of Coke)) [come on] ((M puts a mouthful on L's fork))	Dai be' mangiati la pasta Luisa (1.0) quando hai finito te la do un altro pochino magari. [dai] ((M prepara un boccone per L))
2	Luisa	[But] oof °with this ( )°	[Ma] uffa °con questo ( )°
3	Ugo	Oof the mould ((to L))	Uffa la mu:ffa:: ((a L))
4	Luisa	Look- listen- ((turns to U)) oof the mould come d- come down from the stars na na na: na [na: na ((keeping the rhythm))	Guarda- senti- ((si gira verso U)) uffa la muffa, scend- scendi le ste:lle, na na na: na [na: na ((tenendo il ritmo))
5	Mom	[Come a bit closer ((holding out to L a fork with the pasta))	[Avvicinati un po' ((porgendo a L una forchettata di pasta)).
6	Ugo	((shakes head, with reference to L's poem))	((fa cenni negativi col capo verso L))
7	Mom	Come a bit closer ((to L))	Avvicinati un po' ((a L))
8	Ugo	Uh:: (0.5) Luisa has lost her bib she looks for it in her drawer doesn't find it, uh:: kicks, (s)punches, stomps, and she sees it's on her head.	E:m: (0.5) Luisa ha perso il suo bavagli:no, lo cerca nel cassetti:no, non lo trova. e:m: calcia, spugna, spe:sta, e si accorge che l'ha in testa.
9	Luisa	((laughs))	((ride))
10	Mom	Come closer ((mouthing L))	Avvicinati ((a L, imboccandola))
11		(2.0)	(2.0)
12	Ugo	No:: I didn't li- I didn't like this one ((to Mom))	No:: non mi pia- non mi piaciuta questa qui ((a M))
13		((M prepares a mouthful on L's fork and puts it on her plate))	((M ha preparato un boccone per L e le lascia la forchetta pronta sul piatto))
14	Mom	No it was nice.	Invece era carina.

15 Ugo	((shakes head, mouth full))	((fa un cenno negativo con la testa))
	A poem let's see	Una poesia vediamo
	(° °) ((mumbling softly, lowers eyelids as in concentration))	( ) ((sussurra fra sè e sè, socchiude gli occhi come concentrandosi))

The starting point is the girl's expression of discontent ("uffa"), in itself an onomatopoeic lexicalization of the emission of breath typical of annoyance and boredom. Here it is part of a turn addressed to the mother, who has just urged the girl to eat up what is on her plate. The brother takes up the sound and creates a line with an internal rhyme: "uffa la muffa." In Line 4 Luisa rejoins immediately to her brother and starts a new poetic production, repeating Ugo's line and adding a new piece derived from the first verse of a very popular Christmas carol[5] for children. The third line is a one-syllable chant in the same tone and metric of the first two. The 3;5-year-old girl's readiness to respond at the level of verbal play shows that for her this speech activity is meaningful in itself.

The dialogue goes on with the brother evaluating negatively what Luisa has done and starting another poem. Luisa laughs at Ugo's poem in appreciation (Line 9), but he is not happy with his own poetry, as he says to his mother (Line 12). She counters that the poem was nice (Line 14). The dialogue was sustained by the exchange of modified verses taken from several items of a shared[6] poetic corpus. The "new" part of these contributions relies on assembly or variation of the original patterns, and this is what receives the assessments at the end of each performance (cf. Turns 6, 9, 12, 14).

Whereas in Excerpt 4.1 the two siblings produced a separate piece each, in the following the mother and the son alternate in shaping a new poem with the girl as protagonist:

Excerpt 4.2 [omitted five turns between M and U about how to eat spaghetti]

16 Mom	Eat Luisa and Ugo [will tell you the poem.]	Mangia Luisa che così Ugo [ti dice la poesia.]
17 Ugo	[Luisa looked for] her little bi:b,	[Luisa ha cercato] il suo bavagli:no,

---

[5]The first verse of the original song, "tu scendi dalle stelle," contains a pattern of alliteration with a double consonant similar to the one in "uffa la muffa." Though the child does not repeat the exact words, this similarity could have driven the association.

[6]Ugo's poem is in fact introduced during the previous video-recorded dinner, where we learn that the grandmother has taught it to the children in a version with the boy as protagonist.

		(.) looks for it in the little phone, (0.5) ((*these and the following verses' end rhymes are due in Italian to the masculine diminutive*))	(.) lo cerca nel telefonino (0.5)
18	Luisa	((*smiles to M, then turns to U*)) In the te:lephone? ((*in wonder*))	((*sorride a M, poi si gira verso U*)) Nel <u>tele</u>:fono? ((*con tono stupito*))
19	Ugo	<u>D</u>oesn't <u>f</u>ind it	<u>Non</u> lo <u>t</u>rova,
20	Mom	Takes a nap, in her little bed.	Si schiaccia un pisoli:no, ⁾ nel suo <u>lett</u>ino.
21	Ugo	And then— and she finds her little bib.	E dopo— e trova il suo bavaglino.
22		(3.5)	(3.5)
23	Mom	Together with her little dummy	Insieme al suo ciuccino.
24	Luisa	((*laughs*))	((*ride*))
25	Ugo	((*laughs*))	((*ride*))
26	Mom	And her (.) little dolly a little sick. ((*smiling voice*))	E al suo (.) bamboli::no (0.2) malati:no. ((*con voce sorridente*))
27	Luisa	((*nods, her mouth full of pasta*))	((*annuisce, a bocca piena*))
28	Mom	It's all in 'ino'.	Fa tutto in 'ino'.
29	Ugo	((*laughs*))	((*ride*))

After Ugo's announcement that he is searching for another poem, the mother encourages Luisa to eat as a condition for the reciting. Ugo starts the poem replaying the structure he had used before, but changing the places where the bib is looked for in the original poem. These create an open structure, which allows the mother to add her innovative contribution at a verse junction (Line 21), and they alternate for a couple of turns until the two children laugh. Then she provides a last verse (with concluding intonation) to which Luisa nods, and after that a metalinguistic comment on the rhyming device, to which only Ugo laughs.[7]

---

[7]The metalinguistic comment is actually shaped, for length and final rhyme, like a further verse.

In this sequence, the participation is distributed with Luisa in the audience position (as assigned in the Mom's initial turn at Line 16 and most convenient for Luisa's eating duty) and Ugo as performer. At the beginning the mother was just directing operations, and looking after the eating activity, but then she joins in as a coperformer. Mom's verses seem to have a special comic effect for both children, and the elder is also sensitive to her metalinguistic comment on the rhyming mechanism (Line 28).

We begin to see that poems in conversation can be performed either in individual rounds (i.e., one poem, one speaker) or in joint construction, where more than one participant collaborates in producing the same unit. Verses are demarcated with clear points of transitional relevance where smooth turn taking can occur (Garvey, 1974) and the similarity in shape between each verse helps recognition of the innovated parts (M. H. Goodwin & C. Goodwin, 1987; Tannen, 1987). As in storytelling and joke capping, the end of each unit is signaled by a concluding intonation and followed by an evaluation section (Chiaro, 1992; Labov & Waletzky, 1967). This sequencing of talk and order of participation is also visible in the continuation of the exchange.

After the mother and brother's duet in Excerpt 4.2, Luisa begins a new performance. She does not seem able to invent sensible verses at the necessary speed, so she just inserts nonsense words, which phonologically fit in with the pattern. Whereas Ugo, the boy, is ready to disregard this effort in a teasing comment addressed to his mother,[8] the latter addresses her daughter with a remark on the poetry, a comment that, though ironic, is not derogatory and stays within the frame of play.

Excerpt 4.3 (xxxxx are nonsense words)

30	Ugo	No I- Giuseppe tells me ((to M))	No io- a me Giuseppe mi dice: ((a M))
31	Luisa	Look listen	Guarda: senti
32	Ugo	[( )] ((looks at M, then at L))	[( )] ((guarda M e poi L))
33	Luisa	[Ugo] has lost his (xxxxx) and xxxxxxxxxx under the bed little mouse xxxxxxxx!	[Ugo] ha perso la sua (botta) e si allecche sotto il letto: topolino sottallet!
34	Ugo	((turns to M looking startled, then laughs)) [What's that!]	((si gira verso M perplesso, poi ride)) [Ma che è!]

[8]We discussed in a previous article a family participation framework based on speaking about the younger child in the third person, and treating her or him as a comic character (Fatigante, Fasulo, & Pontecorvo, 1998).

35 Mom	[It's even] in English this one? ((to L))	[E' anche in] inglese questa? ((a L))
36 Luisa	Yes ((laughing))	Si. ((ridendo))
37 Mom	Beautiful. (.) eat.	Be:lla. (.) mangia.
38 Ugo	((sings a nonsense song based on 'a' and 'o' vowels))	((canta una canzone nonsense sulle vocali 'a' e 'o'))
39 Mom	Now I tell one in Japanese. ↑ai ne nai e zica ao. e: ndi casc ai e o ao inghi nghi gao e ci cao e ao.	Ora ne dico una io in giapponese. ↑ai ne nai e zica ao. e: ndi casc ai e o ao. inghi nghi ngao e ci cao e ao.
40	((Ugo, Luisa and Mom laugh together))	((Ugo, Luisa e Mamma ridono insieme))
41 Ugo	Yes it's all ao this [poem] ((to M))	Si è tutta ao questa [poesia] ((a M))
42 Mom	[((laughs))]	[((ride))]
43 Ugo	And what does it mean?	E che vuol dire?
44 Mom	It's called ao.	S'intitola ao.
45 Ugo	((Ugo and Mom laugh))	((Ugo e Mamma ridono))

In Excerpt 4.3 the boy is starting a new topic, but the girl cuts in with another poem (Lines 30–31). Some of the words she puts in are invented (in italics on the right column), functioning as fillers similar in length and sound typology (a lot of double consonants) to the original poem and to its variation just heard. The result is quite nonsensical, though the original pattern is clearly recognizable (someone has lost something, and looks for it under the bed). In the evaluation section, her outcome is said to be a poem "in English." Then, acting again in two different capacities, the mother provides Luisa with a positive assessment and a reminder to eat. The round goes on with Ugo producing a new nonsense piece, to which the mother follows with the "Japanese" poem. Her contribution is linguistically more orderly than as those of her children: She announces what she is going to do and then produce a series of verses imitating what she presents as Japanese typical sounds.

The interest of this excerpt has to do with the conservation of *sense* when *signification* has almost disappeared. Poem-based talk allows for nonsense not to be extruded from the common discourse, as is often the case in different conversational moments (Fasulo & Antonelli, 1996), but to be absorbed in it and even to produce a new genre, "foreign language" poetry: Under a poetic definition of relevance there is a higher degree of tolerance for low degrees of signification. Sense is, however, interactionally built: The clumsy poem (in adults' standards) recited by Luisa is not left as it is but followed by a sense-giving remark. It is the elder child who picks up the possibility for a new series, to which the mother promptly adapts.

The sequence is "orchestrated" (Aronsson & Cederborg, 1994) by the mother in such a way as to be suited to the different linguistic competence of the two children: The younger one can be entertained by the manipulation of sounds and semantics within the poems; the elder one is interested in the metalinguistic rules accounting for coherent production and evolution from one poem to the next. In fact, Ugo participates in the talk between units with his own evaluation and metalinguistic comments, paralleling what is done by his mother. By entirely poetic means, this mother provides for an internal layering of audience,[9] gives meaning to a discourse that was going astray, and shows a way of parodying a foreign language that is also a mockery of her own children's nonsensical production.[10]

One last comment should be addressed to a possible reading of this exchange, namely its being at the service of a nurturing preoccupation, a means for distracting the child and making her eat. We saw at the beginning that the child had little will to finish her food, and that the mother tried to use Coke as a reward, but encountered another expression of discontent (Line 2). The poetry session proved more useful to this aim; indeed the child swallowed all the forkfuls prepared for her between one rhyme and the next. We would like to describe this as a mutual accommodation, in which the older members of the group have chosen a way of speaking that was of interest to the youngest one, who in turn responded by full participation in both streams of activity. Without diminishing the interest of the sequence, its immediate functionality only makes overt the participants' awareness that involvement in conversation can be an effective means of entertainment and reward.

Sacks (1992) noticed that in the adolescent group he had on tape, speaking slots were sometimes filled by "slogans, . . . a piece of an advertisement from the radio, or a jingle, or obvious quotations sarcastically said" (p. 101, vol. I). In former studies (Fasulo & Pontecorvo, 1999; Pontecorvo & Fasulo, 1999), we discussed "lists" as a talking facility for participation, and numbers (such as foot sizes) made into a topic and a way to control the floor. Sanches and Kirshenblatt-Gimblett (1976) also found that numbers can work as a built-in memory aid for children rhymes. In the following excerpt, we see that at the age of 5, simply counting can be

---

[9]The ability of mothers to address differentiated audiences through the same turn is discussed in Fatigante and Fasulo (1999).

[10]See Rossen-Knill and Richard (1997) for an analysis of parody and its potential for multiple targets.

an option for doing topical work. It is a case of almost zero degree of signification; nonetheless this is conversationally appropriate talk.

Excerpt 5 Sonetti family dn3. Mother, Father, Davide 5;3, Matteo, 2;5.

*Matteo has left the table. Mom is calling him back. After several calls Dad gets
up and goes to fetch him. Silence falls at the table where Davide and his mother
are left alone.*

1		(2.0)	(2.0)
2	Davide	*((looking at M, counts on his fingers))* One two three: four. (.) five=six, (.) seven eight nine ten eleven (.) eleven thirteen fourteen	*((guardando M, conta sulle dita))* Uno due tre: quattro (.) cinque=sei (.) sette otto nove dieci undici (.) undici tredici quattordici
3		(0.5)	(0.5)
4	Mom	How many mouthfuls left?	Quanti bocconi ti mancano?
5		(1.5)	(1.5)
6	Davide	O:ne, one two three four five. *((indicating in the plate with his fork))*	U:no, uno due tre quattro cinque. *((indicando con la forchetta))*
7		(2.0)	(2.0)
8	Davide	Five mouthfuls *((holding up a fully open hand))*	Cinque bocconi *((sollevando la mano aperta))*
9	Dad	*((talking loudly with Matteo still out of view of the camera))* And now come to the table	*((parlando forte con Matteo ancora fuori campo))* E adesso vieni a tavola.

After the long pause, which followed the father's leaving the table,
Davide, without looking up, starts counting. It is not clear whether there is
any specific referent: From the video it looks as if he's counting his own
chewing movements. This is treated by the mother as a rightful topic, and
she asks him about the pieces of meat Davide still has on his plate. The
child counts again and gives the result. The "topic" falls naturally when
the father reappears. The child seems to have taken responsibility of the
floor, and to have offered a suitable silence filler.

This example in its simplicity is a particularly neat illustration of what it
means to use language in interaction. It is common sense, but too easily

forgotten in scholarly writing about language acquisition, that talk in interaction is what children have to learn, not language per se. And this means, among other things, sensitivity to the locus where talk is appropriate, together and even primarily with respect to content or "information." This child displays exactly such understanding and, by his highly impersonal contribution, reveals also that it was specifically the problem of silence that he was orienting to. In this light, the mother's uptake appears as partially covering the nakedness of his conversational move, by making the counting a communication about a state of affairs in the world, a piece of information newly acquired. Acceptance and even welcome, of adults, for children's "baseline" language production, are often accompanied by a remodeling and an addition of meaning. These are occasions for learning a complicating rule, namely that turns addressed to fill silence must not appear to do so, or barely so, as any weather conversationalist would be ready to acknowledge.

Children solve the problem of having "provisions of topics," mentioned by Goffman (1967, p. 132), by picking from their provision of prepatterned speech. The problem with this kind of move, when they are "serious" and not in the frame of poetic talk as in the preceding example, is that they introduce the risk of "awareness of interaction" (Goffman, 1967, p. 132), that is, a too open preoccupation with the proceeding of interaction itself. Davide and his counting show that at the age of 5 children can be preoccupied with maintaining the state of talk, but that this preoccupation is not yet something that they feel the need to hide.

POETIC LISTENING

Poetics is not only a technique for production but also a mode of listening. During talk in interaction, analysis of the speech of others is done constantly: A good deal of conversational smoothness and coordination is due to bit-by-bit processing of others' turns in the course of production (Schegloff, 1987). If turn taking in talk draws on a competence in alternation that starts to develop since the time of breast feeding (Kaye, 1977), analysis of turns' shape probably develops out of children's sensitivity to morphology. On the other hand, as C. Goodwin (1981) hypothesized, the ungrammatical character of conversational language can provide children with empirical material to test their acquisitions.

Deconstructing Idioms

The following excerpt is an instance of a child's selective attention for departures from standard forms:

Excerpt 6 Terini family dn.1 Mother; Father; Federico, 8 years; Serena, 5 years

Dad and Mom are talking about the different prices of a food item in different shops

1	Dad	They make you pay seven–eight thousand lire	Se lo fanno pagare setteotto mila lire.
2	Mom	We:ll seven–eight thousand lire,	Si: setteotto mila lire,
3	Dad	All right ( ) otherwise	Va be:ne ( ) così se no po:i
4		(17.0)	(17.0)
		((M leaves and comes back with a baking dish, starts serving meat to D))	*((M si alza dalla tavola poi torna con una teglia con la carne e la serve a P))*
5	Federico	*((looking at D))* Mom isn't it true that thirty-seven and seventy-eight (.) eighty-seven and seventy-eight are equal?	*((guardando P))* Mamma vero che trentasette e settantotto (.) ottantasette e settantotto sono uguali?
6	Dad	*((shakes his head))*	*((fa cenno di no con il capo))*
7	Federico	Yes	Si
8	Dad	The <u>num</u>:bers are the same	I <u>nu</u>:meri so' uguali
9	Federico	That's it that's it	Infatti infatti

Federico, who was not a participant in the conversation, has heard twice in a row the pair of numbers "seven" and "eight" pronounced as a single word, as is common in Italian and particularly in Rome to indicate a gross estimation between the two quantities. Something in this use strikes him as remarkable and, after a very long pause (Line 4), he asks his parents (one by kin term and one by look) if the numbers "seventy-eight" and "eighty-seven" are equal. It is difficult to guess what the rationale of the question is exactly, but probably it has something to do with seven and eight being close quantities (in fact they have been used by the parents, in thousands of lire, as almost equivalent prices) and also with phonological reasons. The idiomatic use of the two numbers sounds similar to the number they compose together (setteotto/settantotto, seven-eight/seventy-eight), and both ciphers are phonologically marked by the double /t/. But of course the difference in quantity between seven and eight increases when they are associated in the arithmetical way, as in 78 and 87.

What seems to be at stake here is the relationship between arithmetical properties, sound similarities, and conventional ways of using numbers in conversation. And what we want to point out is that the child reveals a listening that is attentive to such facts, a readiness to detect formulaic talk, expressions that are exclusive to the oral domain and that for him are still noticeable, whereas in the eyes of adult mother tongue speakers they seem, and indeed are, absolutely "normal."

Interpreting Key

The practice of deconstructing idioms, or to intentionally exploit their multifaceted meaning, is not confined to infancy. On the contrary, it is often a technique for humor and irony in adult speech, as a vast literature can show, with Freud (1905, 1927) leading the parade (see Palmer, 1994). Jokes based on verbal play, as in switching from metaphoric to literal meaning or vice versa, stem from a readiness in both the joker and the listener to catch some internal possibility of words just said or about to be said. The creator of a joke is in fact often caught by a latent meaning of her or his own words and their potential humor, just as the listener will be a few seconds later. It is a sort of impersonal decision belonging to language itself that finds its way not through an act of intentionality of the speaker, but through a lapse of it (Ricci, 1997).

Verbal playfulness is a pervasive feature of mundane talk. Irony and puns can appear at any moment, even within an otherwise serious register, to remark on a passage or add a witty line to the unfolding discourse. Indeed, Goffman (1974) noted that on many occasions humor is so expected that it requires special bracketing—"no kidding"—to ensure the serious interpretation of what one is saying.

Being at the same time communication and metacommunication, humor based on verbal play implies a redefinition of the situation, a change of frame, or "rekeying," with a shift in the local rules of interpretation. Humor is only a species of "keyed" talk. *Key* is the term Goffman (1974) and Hymes (1974) used to refer to change in the basic (or primary) frame of a given situation. The effect of keying is that of creating a decoupled reality where truth value is suspended or altered, as happens, for example, in irony, sarcasm, innuendo, make-believe play, ceremonials, and technical redoings (i.e., practicing, demonstrating). Keying means hinting, often elliptically, to alternative possible readings of an utterance; besides nonverbal means, stylistic and poetic choices are crucial in this regard, keying often being achieved by rare words or figurative language, sound modification, morphological transformation of a previous utterance, and so on.

"Understanding key" then must be in the learning agenda of any young conversationalist, as Ochs (1988) clearly stated: "To be competent communicative partners, children must acquire knowledge of both contextual frames for interpreting action and metacommunicative markers indicating which frame should be supplied . . . we can see here that communication and survival rest on one's capacity to distinguish the metacommunicative markers of play from those associated with other activities" (p. 10). Ochs reported, from her observations in Western Samoa, that when adults are teasing children, they may change voice quality and facial expression in a more marked way than they would do with other adults, so that teasing children is also a way of socialization to keying.

In the dinner setting, keyed talk that is not directly addressed to the small children may not carry such indexes aimed to help interpretation. A child's "poetic ear" can help in the interpretation of meaning, although what it catches may not overlap perfectly with what the other participants think is going on.

The following example is a good case for sorting out possible differences among children of different ages: The father makes a pun that violates an idiom, in both aspects of a formulaic association of words and commonsense knowledge about cats and dogs. But whereas the elder son develops the joke at the semantic level, the younger one pursues a poetical transformation:

Excerpt 7 Gennari family dn. 2. Mother, Father, Silverio, 8 years, Gabriele, 3;4 years.

They are eating in the garden and discussing the visit of a new cat

1	Dad	*((looking first at S then at Mom))* Hey, maybe we got (0.2) a watch cat since the dog was good for nothing:	*((guardando prima S e poi M))* Aho hai visto mai che c'avemo (0.2) un gatto da guardia? visto che il cane nun valeva niente:
2	Silverio	A wild cat *((smiling))*	Un gatto feroce *((sorridendo))*
3	Gabriele	No: a speedy dog	No: un cane veloce.
4	Dad	Yeah a dog *((laughing))*	Si un cane *((ride))*.
5	Gabriele	With one eye only *((hand covers one eye))*	Con solo un occhio *((si copre un occhio con la mano))*
6		*((everybody laughs))*	*((tutti ridono))*
7	Mom	Sit down *((G. is kneeling on his chair))*	Mettiti seduto *((G è in ginocchio))*
8	Silverio	Perhaps	Quasi quasi
9		(1.0)	(1.0)

10	Mom	Will you sit down?	Ti metti sedu:to?
11	Gabriele	A: am:: ((takes a mouthful and sits down))	A: am:: ((mangia un boccone e si siede))
12	Silverio	A dog? ((to Gabriele))	Un cane?
13		(2.0)	(2.0)
14	Gabriele	It's a catlese!	E' un gattolese!
15	Mom	Pity there's no queen any longer otherwi:se I'd have sent you to be the Court Jester	Peccato che non c'è più la regina sennò: te mandavo a fà il buffon-cello de corte a te.
16	Silverio	The queen?	La regina?

After considering the large size and savage look of the foreign cat, the father comes up with a joke about the possibility that they have now got a "watch cat," recalling also that they had a dog that was not so good in that function. He has eye selected the wife and the elder son as primary audience, and it is Silverio who speaks next. He continues the joke, endowing the cat with the attribute of "wild," or "ferocious." What he seems to have picked out, then, as a mechanism of keying, is the semantic violation in the atypical descriptions of this cat compared to what is known, or ordinarily said, about "cats" as a category.

The younger child seems to follow a different track: In both his father's and brother's utterances he may also have detected a violation, or innovation, of sound patterns, as is inevitable when a word in an idiom is replaced with a different one (as in "watch cat" instead of "watchdog"). At least, this is the understanding he displays in his own elaboration of the joke. The first thing he does (Line 3) is to add a line that is clearly indifferent to the semantic pun (he talks about a dog), but attentive to the sound pattern, as revealed by the similarity between the adjective of the previous turn and his own. Wild is *feroce*, speedy is *veloce*: These words have the same length and the same alternation of vowel and consonants; second, fourth, fifth, and sixth letters are identical; and the remaining two consonants are very similar in phonetic terms (f/v are fricatives; l/r are alveolar). Gabriele has thus contributed to the developing joke with a typical technique for rhyme production, namely that of keeping the verse metric equal and replicating the terminal sound. The search for such a structure has given him a word that is phonologically almost identical to what was the "new" in his brother's turn, whereas the "given," the subject *gatto*, is carelessly substituted by another one of the same number of syllables, *cane*.

The semantic part of the exchange is not completely opaque to the child, as shown by his subsequent elaboration (Line 5) in which he visualizes, verbally and nonverbally, an animal with one eye only, one of the icons of savagery in cartoons' representations of pirates and the like. At this the family laughs, but because, in the swing of his performance, Gabriele has kneeled on the chair, his mother reminds him to sit down (Lines 7 and 10). The engagement in play at the dinner setting has specific limits, especially regarding body movement. The child then continues his joke by keying a table-appropriate action, eating, by an accompanying sound (Line 11: "a:am::"); the character he was impersonating a moment ago, by covering his own eye, lingers in this wild roar. As shown elsewhere (Fasulo & Antonelli, 1996), table constraints with regard to admitted activities push the structure of make-believe play (one of the frequently banned ones) to mesh with ordinary activities, thus encouraging the child to develop and use subtler framing devices, through which the same action can encompass a serious and a nonserious layer.

When Silverio, the elder brother, challenges his brother for his use of "dog" instead of cat (Line 12), Gabriele rebukes with a neologism based on the word *cat* (*gattolese*/catlese: Line 13). The point of the whole joke, which deals with an ill-classified item in the class of cats, finds here a further elaboration accomplished by poetic means. The anomaly of a "watchcat" is represented by a nonconventional transformation of the animal's correct name. To adult ears this is nonsense, and this yields Gabriele the label of Court Jester, and his talk that of buffoonery. To operate at the level of morphology *only*, without an adequate semantic contribution, can insulate children from the circulation of meaning, and determine a restructuring of participation in which children become *objects* of humor of a much higher degree of sophistication (so much higher, in fact, that the sarcastic comment of the mother is also hard for the elder brother to understand, as you can see in Line 16).

NEOLOGISMS

We want to conclude by briefly illustrating two more instances of neologism, in which diverse possibilities of exploiting poetics are illustrated. With the first one we are within the familiar realm of fairy tales: The mother and son that we have already met in the poem session are co-narrating Cinderella to the young girl.

Excerpt 8 Minelli family, dn.2. Mother, Ugo, 11;8; Luisa, 3;5

Mom is telling the story of Cinderella, with Ugo as conarrator. They are describing Cinderella's stepsisters.

1	Mom	. . . Who were very ugly. and jealous of Cinderella's beauty	. . . Che erano molto brutte. e invid<u>iose</u> della bellezza di Cenere:ntola.

		English	Italian
2	Luisa	[B:: but]	[M:: ma]
3	Ugo	[They were] ugly like	[Erano] brutte come::
4	Mom	Come on [like:,]	Dai [come:,]
5	Ugo	[Like a] [mouse].	[Come] [un topo].
6	Luisa	[A pa!ccio] ((to U, wringing her hands, a nasty expression on her face))	[Un pa!ccio]. ((a U, torcendo le mani, con espressione cattiva))
7	Mom	°But eat or I stop [telling°	°Pero' tu mangia se no io non racconto [niente°
8	Luisa	[A paccio is ugly? ((to M))	[Un paccio è brutto? ((a M))
9	Ugo	Huh?	Mhm?
10	Luisa	What 's a paccio?	Che cos'è un paccio?
11	Mom	A paccio? is nothing	Un paccio? è niente.
12		((Ugo and Luisa laugh))	((Ugo and Luisa ridono))
13	Mom	Something invented by Luisa Minelli	Una cosa inventata da Luisa Minelli.
14		((Ugo and Luisa laugh softly))	((Ugo and Luisa ridono piano))
15		(1.5)	(1.5)
16	Luisa	Mhm::::.! ((like a shriek but with mouth closed))	Mhm::::! ((a bocca piena e con tono acuto))
17	Mom	What? what did you re-member?	Che è? che ti sei ricordata?
18	Ugo	New entry in the Italian vocabulary, pa:ccio. (1.0) means? ((to M)) [boh::] ((Italian nonword for 'I don't know'))	Nuovo termine del vocabolario italiano, pa:ccio. (1.0) uguale? ((a M)) [boh::]
19	Luisa	[Po- the] the m- the thing of paccio means a little mouse ((animated)) all dressed in feathers= ((miming)) =can we- can we put it:: in- in the:: m:: [fairy-tales?] ((to M))	[Po- la-] paccio la m- la cosa del paccio vuol dire un topoli:no ((tono animato)) vestito tutto con le piume= ((mimando)) =possiamo- possiamo metterlo:: ne- nelle:: m: [favole?] ((a M))

20	Ugo	[In the vocabulary] ((*laughing*))	[Nel vocabolario] ((*ridendo*))
21	Mom	Mhm [okay]	Mhm [va bene].
22	Ugo	[Paccio] ((*laughing, to M*))	[Paccio] ((*ridendo, a M*))
23	Mom	Yes. (.) I think it's a good idea (1.0) we'll put it in the fairy tales.	Si. (.) mi pare una buona idea. (1.0) lo mettiamo nelle favole.

The passage in Cinderella's tale where the stepsisters are mentioned raises the interest of both children. Luisa starts to say something; her brother takes the turn and starts a comparison, but hesitates in the delivery of the second term. The mother encourages the search, and in overlap with the brother coming up with "mouse" Luisa proposes a "paccio." This is a neologism obtained by the semantization of a morpheme, "accio," which is the masculine form of a pejorative suffix (e.g., one could say "ragazz*accio*" to indicate a boy—"ragazzo"—who misbehaves). Pressed to find a suitable item to be compared in ugliness with the stepsisters, Luisa does not orient her search into some possible class of "disgusting animated beings" like her brother, but rather looks for an item that has the bad trait included in its morphology. She utters a word but shows uncertainty about its meaning, and asks about it. As usual, her brother comments sarcastically with his mother on Luisa's nonsense, but the girl, pretending she has suddenly "remembered" (the sound in Line 16 is in fact read by her mother as a "change of state token"[11]) contrasts the interpretation of her word as nonsense, provides a definition, and proposes to make the paccio a character in fairy tales (Line 19).

This example, besides showing again how children are keen to operate at the poetic level, is also an illustration of the strict connection between sign and signified that holds for children of this age. The generic negative attribute, which is the semantic value of the suffix "accio," is powerful enough for this child to generate a brand-new entity by simply putting a consonant before it. Of course, like in all the examples we have discussed, there is a certain degree of awareness on behalf of the child about the arbitrariness of what she is inventing. If it is difficult for small children to have adults laugh *with* them, to share a source of amusement that is linked to their level of language competence, they can nonetheless deploy their resources to have adults or elder siblings laugh *at* them (Glenn, 1995) and

---

[11]Interjections such as "oh" found in conversation manifest a change in the cognitive state of the speaker, for example, that some information is "new" (Heritage, 1984).

neologisms appear as a kind of verbal play in which everyone can get a share.

A last example serves to point out some formal devices involved in the creation of the special vocabulary whereby children and their parents can refer to the "objects" belonging to their common history. In Excerpt 9 there is reference to a mother–child bedside routine, the name of which, for its pattern of alliteration and repetition, is apt to preserve iconically some aspects of the activity (supposedly) hinted at.

Excerpt 9 Tempoli family dn3. Mother, Father, Lara 8;7 years, Mattia, 2;11 years

1	Dad	*((to Lara))* We'll let you sleep in the car all night and in the morning we'll wake you up	*((a Lara))* Ti facciamo dormire in macchina tutta la notte la mattina ti venimo a svegliare
2		(2.0)	(2.0)
3		*((to Lara))* (° °)	*((a Lara))* (° °)
4	Mom	( ) coccocococco? later we do coccocococo in bed uh?	( ) coccocococco? dopo si fa coccocococo a letto eh?
5		Now.	Ora.
6	Mom	N:ow?	O:ra?
7	Mattia	*((nods))*	*((annuisce))*
8	Dad	Now? hey! *((in mild reproach))*	Ora? oh! *((leggero rimprovero))*
9	Mattia	Eh!	Eh!
10	Dad	( ) cocco=cocco	( ) coccocococo
11	Mattia	Coccocococco *((clapping his hands))*	Cocco=cocco *((battendo le mani))*
12	Dad	So you are Mommy's cocco	Allora sei cocco di mamma tu.
13	Mattia	Mhm *((nods))*	Mhm *((annuisce))*

The mother makes the 3-year-old child a promise for "cuddling," later when he goes to sleep. This comes after a sequence in which another plan was illustrated by both parents to the elder daughter, concerning a trip to visit some friends and then the trip back to Florence, where the family lives. The daughter is told that she can sleep in the car all night and that the parents will wake her up in the morning. After that, the father adds something in a whisper. In the same low volume of voice, the mother speaks to the boy in the sequence that we are interested in. The topic selection seems to have been driven by the general idea of parental care about the children's sleep. The label for the sleeping routine mentioned by the mother has semantic relations with the Italian word for "cuddle," *coccole,* and is formed by a repetition of the root of this word, latched to sound like a single word. The reference to a verb referring to a "family of actions" ("cuddling" can comprehend hugging, caressing, etc.), plus the repetition of the same token (*coccococco*), creates a sense of iteration. Working as a synecdoche, repetition has in fact the capacity of conveying the idea of a longer series of the repeated token (Tannen, 1989). But repetition of the same sounds, that is, alliteration, was also a feature of the original word. So, in the idiolectal term that this family uses, there is in fact a syllable repeated four times, which iconically renders the idea of swinging like a cradle.

The named activity is mentioned as something to be done in a later moment: When the child proposes instead to do it "now," both parents react by teasing the child and treating the activity as inappropriate to the circumstances. Poetic means—word transformation, repetition, and alliteration—are devices by which family members can develop an internal vocabulary able to reproduce in the texture of its words some characters of idiosyncratic rituals, here the rhythmical movement and the affective mode of the mother–child night routine. But interestingly, this vocabulary appears highly contextual, and in the dinner setting it can be referred to but at the same time denied as a possible course of physical activity. The dinner setting thus confirms itself as a time of day when children are expected to behave differently, where types of exchange typical of the dyadic interaction are exiled, and children are encouraged to develop modalities of communication privileging the verbal channel.

CONCLUSIONS

Talking to adults, that is to say, in a multiparty situation in which adults can also speak among themselves, means in the first place developing a sense of the possible means to join in, sustain, or initiate talk. Competence on the formal aspects of language can help children between 3 and 5 years of age to understand adult speech, to extract underlying rules of production—keys—and also provide a way to "keep talking" before knowing much about the adults' world or being able to sustain long, entirely new contributions.

Prepatterned strings of language drawn by folklore or by the family corpus of poems, songs, and so on, can help children attain the speaker's position. Songs or poems do not behave in talk as closed frames with impermeable boundaries, but as open sequences in which ease of reproduction goes together with the possibility of variation and innovation. Culture, as instantiated in children's lore, provides the scaffolding that helps children perform at a higher level of competence; in interaction with their parents, children's long series of parallel verses evolve toward something similar to topical organization. Sensitivity to poetics can also be put at the service of extracting the "point" of others' words, manipulating frames, and iconically translating into verbal expression the features of activities involving affect and physical movement.

Overall, the difference between speech play and verbal games can be maintained for the sake of analytical taxonomies, but we have gathered some evidence that playing with language is not random and chaotic, and is not devoid of pragmatic functionality. When looking at children's poetic productions as enactments of their understanding of the conversational business, in the sequential environment in which they are uttered, lists, rhymes, and songs stop appearing nonsensical and gratuitous and reveal instead to be timed and shaped in conversationally appropriate ways.

If the essence of literary poetry is to be found in the capacity to bring to light the matter of language, "poetics" in conversation can open to view the matter of talk in interaction, its delicate balance between following rules and hiding them in the same move. Conversation with children is a good locus for this kind of study, because of the differential mastery children have in conversational rules of varying complexity.

In one of the best nonscientific treatises on conversation, *Zazie dans le metro*, Queneau chose a child to reveal the paradoxes of talk. In the introduction of the book, Barthes (1959) efficaciously pointed out the image of the adult language that Zazie kept challenging:

> Ce méta-langage est celui dont on parle, non pas le choses, mais *à propos* des choses (ou *à propos* du premier langage). C'est un langage parasite, immobile, de fond sentencieux, qui double l'acte comme la mouche accompagne la coche; face à l'imperatif et à l'optatif du langage-objet, son mode principiel est l'indicatif, sorte de degré zéro de l'acte destiné à représenter le réel, non à le modifier. Ce méta-langage dèveloppe autour de lettre du discours un sens complémentaire, éthique, ou plaintif, ou sentimental, ou magistral, etc.; bref, c'est un *chant:* on reconnaìt en lui l'ètre mème de la Littérature. (Barthes, 1959, p. 128, italics in original)

> [And it is from this language object that Zazie occasionally emerges in order to paralyze, with her murderous clausule, the metalanguage of the grownups. This metalanguage speaks not things but apropos of things (or apropos of the primary language). It is a parasitical, motionless, sententious language which doubles the act in the same way as the fly accompanies the coach; instead of the language object's imperative and optative, its principial mode is the indicative, a kind of zero degree of the act intended to represent

reality, not to change it. This metalanguage secretes, around the letter of utterance, complementary meaning—ethical, plaintive, sentimental, magisterial, etc.; in short, it is a song, an aria: in it we recognize the very being of literature. (Barthes, 1972, p. 120)]

It is this *chant* that children try to learn, as they innocently let us see by counting and rhyming through their turns at talk.

REFERENCES

Aronsson, K., & Cederborg, A. C. (1994). Conarration and voice in family therapy: Voicing, devoicing and orchestration. *Text, 14*(3), 345–370.

Barthes, R. (1959). Zazie et la littérature [Zazie and literature].

Barthes, R. (1972). Zazie and literature. In (Ed.), *Critical essays*. Evanston, IL: Northwestern University Press.

Basso, K. H. (1979). *Portraits of "the Whiteman." Linguistic play and cultural symbols among the Western Apache*. Cambridge, England: Cambridge University Press.

Bateson, G. (1979). *Mind and nature. A necessary unity*. New York: Bantam Books.

Berko-Gleason, J., Perlmann, R. Y., & Blank-Greif, E. (1984). What's the magic word: Learning language through politeness routines. *Discourse Processes, 7,* 493–502.

Button, G., & Casey, N. (1984). Generating topic: The use of topic initial elicitors. In J. M. Atkinson & H. Heritage (Eds.), *Structures of social action: Studies in conversation analysis* (pp. 167–190). Cambridge, England: Cambridge University Press.

Cahill, S. E. (1987). Children and civility: Ceremonial deviance and the acquisition of ritual competence. *Social Psychology Quarterly, 50*(4), 312–321.

Cazden, C. B. (1976). Play with language and meta-linguistic awareness: One dimension of language experience. In J. S. Bruner, A. Jolly, & K. Sylva (Eds.), *Play—Its role in development and evolution* (pp. 603–608). New York: Penguin.

Chiaro, D. (1992). *The language of jokes. Analysing verbal play*. London: Routledge.

Corsaro, W. (1997). *The sociology of childhood*. Thousand Oaks, CA: Pine Forge.

Douglas, M. (1968). The social control of cognition: Some factors in joke recognition. *Man, 3,* 361–376.

Elias, N. (1978). *The civilizing process*. Oxford, England: Blackwell.

Ervin-Tripp, S. (1979). Children's verbal turn-taking. In E. Ochs & B. B. Schieffelin (Eds.), *Developmental pragmatics* (pp. 391–414). New York: Academic Press.

Fasulo, A., & Antonelli, T. (1996). Buon senso o non senso? Aspetti normativi e ludici nel discorso familiare sul cibo [Common sense or nonsense? Normative and ludic aspects of family discourse on food]. *Età Evolutiva, 55,* 91–102.

Fasulo, A., & Pontecorvo, C. (1997). Il bisogno di raccontare. Analisi di narrazioni nel contesto familiare [The need for storytelling. Analysis of narratives in the family setting]. In A. Smorti (Ed.), *Il Sè come testo* (pp. 180–214). Firenze, Italy: Giunti.

Fasulo, A., & Pontecorvo, C. (1999). *Come si dice? Linguaggio e apprendimento in famiglia e a scuola* [How do you say? Language and learning in the family and school]. Rome, Italy: Carocci.

Fatigante, M., & Fasulo, A. (1999, April). *Simultaneous talk with different audiences*. Paper presented at the VII International Conference for Family Education, Abano Terme, Italy.

Fatigante, M., Fasulo, A., & Pontecorvo, C. (1998). Life with the alien: Role casting and face-saving techniques in family conversation with young children. *Issues in Applied Linguistics, 9*(2), 97–123.

Freud, S. (1975). *Il motto di spirito e la sua relazione con l'inconscio* [Wit and its relation to the unconscious]. Torino, Italy: Bollati Boringhieri. (Original work published 1905)

Freud, S. (1927). *L'umorismo* [the Humor]. In Opere Complete (pp. 503–508). Torino: Bollati Boringhieri.

Garvey, C. (1974). Some properties of social play. *Merrill–Palmer Quarterly, 20,* 163–180.

Garvey, C. (1977). Play with language and speech. In S. Ervin-Tripp & C. Mitchell-Kernan (Eds.), *Child discourse* (pp. 27–48). New York: Academic Press.

Glenn, P. H. (1995). Laughing at and laughing with: Negotiations of participant alignments through conversational laughter. In P. Ten Have & G. Psathas (Eds.), *Situated order: Studies in the social organization of talk and embodied activities.* Washington, DC: International Institute for Ethnomethodology and Conversation Analysis.

Goffman, E. (1971). *Il rituale dell'interazione* [Interaction ritual]. Bologna, Italy: Il Mulino.

Goffman, E. (1974). *Frame analysis.* New York: Harper & Row.

Goodwin, C. (1981). *Conversational organization. Interaction between speakers and hearers.* New York: Academic Press.

Goodwin, M. H., & Goodwin, C. (1987). Children's arguing. In S. U. Philips, S. Steele, & C. Tanz (Eds.), *Language, gender and sex in a comparative perspective* (pp. 200–298). Cambridge, England: Cambridge University Press.

Gossen, G. H. (1979). Verbal dueling in Chamula. In B. Kirshenblatt-Gimblett (Ed.), *Speech play* (pp. 121–146). Philadelphia: University of Pennsylvania Press.

Heritage, J. (1984). A change of state token and aspects of its sequential placement. In J. M. Atkinson & J. Heritage (Eds.), *Structures of social action. Studies in conversation analysis* (pp. 299–345). Cambridge, England: Cambridge University Press.

Huizinga, J. (1955). *Homo ludens.* Boston: Beacon.

Hymes, D. (1974). *Foundations of sociolinguistics: An ethnographic approach.* Philadelphia: University of Pennsylvania Press.

Iwamura, S. G. (1980). *The verbal games of pre-school children.* London: Billing & Sons.

Jefferson, G. (1996). On the poetics of ordinary talk. *Text and Performance Quarterly, 16*(1), 1–61.

Kaye, K. (1977). Towards the origin of dialogue. In H. R. Schaffer (Ed.), *Studies in mother–infant interaction.* London: Academic Press.

Kirshenblatt-Gimblett, B. (1979). Speech play and verbal art. In B. Sutton-Smith (Ed.), *Play and learning* (pp. 219–238). Philadelphia: University of Pennsylvania Press.

Labov, W., & Waletzky, J. (1967). Narrative analysis: Oral versions of personal experience. In J. Helm (Ed.), *Essays on the verbal and visual art* (pp. 12–44). Seattle: University of Washington Press.

Mead, G. H. (1934). *Mind, self and society.* Chicago: University of Chicago Press.

Montani, P. (1990). A che serve la poesia? [What is poetry for?]. In P. Montani & M. Prampolini (Eds.), *Roman Jakobson* (pp. 245–252). Rome, Italy: Editori Riuniti.

Ochs, E. (1983). Conversational competence in children. In E. Ochs & B. Schieffelin (Eds.), *Acquiring conversational competence* (pp. 3–25). London: Routledge & Kegan Paul.

Ochs, E. (1988). *Culture and language development: Language acquisition and language socialization in a Samoan village.* Cambridge, England: Cambridge University Press.

Palmer, J. (1994). *Taking humor seriously.* London: Routledge.

Pontecorvo, C., & Fasulo, A. (1999). Planning a typical Italian meal: A family reflection on culture. *Culture & Psychology, 5*(3), 313–335.

Powell, C., & Paton, G. E. (1988). *Humour in society: Resistance and control.* London: Macmillan.

Queneau, R. (1959). *Zazie dans le métro* [Zazie in the Metro]. Paris: Gallimard.

Radcliffe-Brown, A. R. (1952). *Structure and function in primitive society.* London: Cohen & West.

Ricci, G. (1997). Witz e soggettività nomade [Witz and nomadic subjectivity]. *Aut Aut, 282*, 131–143.

Rossen-Knill, D. F., & Richard, H. (1997). The pragmatics of verbal parody. *Journal of Pragmatics, 27*, 719–752.

Sacks, H. (1992). *Lectures on conversation* (G. Jefferson, Ed.). Cambridge, MA: Blackwell.

Sacks, H., Schegloff, E. A., & Jefferson, G. (1974). A simplest systematics for the organization of turn-taking for conversation. *Language, 50*(4), 696–735.

Sanches, M., & Kirshenblatt-Gimblett, B. (1976). Children's traditional speech play and child language. In B. Kirshenblatt-Gimblett (Ed.), *Speech play* (pp. 65–110). Philadelphia: University of Pennsylvania Press.

Schegloff, E. A. (1987). Recycled turn beginnings: A precise repair mechanism in conversation's turn-taking organisation. In G. Button & J. Lee (Eds.), *Talk and social organization* (pp. 152–205). Clevedon, England: Multilingual Matters.

Schegloff, E. A. (1990). On the organization of sequences as a source of "coherence" in talk-in-interaction. In R. Freedle (Ed.), *Advances in discourse processes: Conversational organization and its development* (Vol. 38, pp. 51–77). Norwood, NJ: Ablex.

Schegloff, E. A. (1997). Whose text? Whose context? *Discourse & Society, 8*(2), 165–187.

Schieffelin, B. (1990). *The give and take of everyday life: Language socialization of Kaluli children.* Cambridge, England: Cambridge University Press.

Schwartzmann, H. (1978). *Transformations. The anthropology of children's play.* New York: Plenum.

Sterponi, L., & Pontecorvo, C. (1996). Il farsi e il disfarsi dell'argomento di discorso nelle conversazioni familiari a tavola [The making and unmaking of discourse topic in family dinner conversations]. *Rassegna di Psicologia, 13*(3), 39–70.

Sutton Smith, B. (1976). A developmental structural account of riddles. In B. Kirshenblatt-Gimblett (Ed.), *Speech play* (pp. 111–119). Philadelphia: University of Pennsylvania Press.

Tannen, D. (1987). Repetition in conversation: Towards a poetics of talk. *Language, 63*(3), 574–605.

Tannen, D. (1989). *Talking voices. Repetition, dialogue and imagery in conversational discourse.* Cambridge, England: Cambridge University Press.

Trevarthen, C. (1988). Infants trying to talk: How a child invites communication from the human world. In R. Soderbergh (Ed.), *Children's creative communication* (pp. 9–31). Lund, Sweden: Lund University Press.

Weir, R. (1962). *Language in the crib.* The Haugue, Netherlands: Mouton.

Part III

ISSUES OF CONTEXT
AND CULTURE IN
PRAGMATIC DEVELOPMENT

Chapter 9

Everyone Has to Lie in Tzeltal

Penelope Brown
Max Planck Institute for Psycholinguistics,
Nijmegen, The Netherlands

"Lies" and "Truth" in Social Interaction

The subject of "lying"—not telling the "truth"—is one that tends to raise moral hackles whenever it is discussed. Lying is "bad," children are punished for it, it has even been claimed that children couldn't actually learn language if we do too much of it.[1] And yet lies are all around us, even, sometimes, emanating from ourselves.

Since in ordinary parlance there are many notions of lying, we need a working definition, which I take from Barnes' (1994) sociological study of lying (following Bok, 1978): "a lie, for our purposes, is a statement intended to deceive a dupe about the state of the world, including the intentions and attitudes of the liar"[2] (p. 11). A lie thus conceived must be stated, not just implied; not all "terminological inexactitudes" (in Churchill's phrase) are lies. We must also keep distinct the uttering of nontrue propo-

---

[1]See, for example, the philosophical theory of language expounded by David Lewis (1969, 1975), wherein the ability to learn and to use a language is based on conventions of truthfulness and trust in the language. In Lewis' theory, language as used by liars, jokers, and tall-tale tellers does not undermine the essential conventions of language, which are based on truth and trust; lies are exceptions, violations of the conventions of language (Lewis, 1975).

[2]Barnes (1994) went on to specify what "intending to deceive" entails: ". . . for our purposes I take it to mean intending to cause a dupe to adopt an understanding of the state of the world and/or of the mind of the liar that the liar believes to be false" (p. 11).

241

sitions (ones that deliberately mislead about states of affairs and events in the world) and the consequences or sanctions for doing this.[3] There are (at least) two relevant perspectives on lying in the linguistic and social interactional literature. The first, coming from linguistics and linguistic anthropology, was first articulated in an article by Coleman and Kay (1981) who considered the English word *lie* as a social construct, one whose meaning requires a prototype semantics analysis rather than a definition in terms of a checklist of semantic features. Lying, they argued, is a matter of degree, of more or less. Clear central cases fulfill the following conditions: (a) the speaker believes the statement is false; (b) the speaker intends to deceive the hearer by making the statement; and (c) the statement is in fact false. Sweetser (1987) extended the Coleman and Kay analysis in terms of "cultural models" (Quinn & Holland, 1987; Strauss & Quinn, 1997), pointing out that, in order to understand the word *lie*, "[i]t is necessary to examine folk understandings of knowledge, evidence, and proof; our cultural model of language (or at least of lying) cannot be analyzed independently of beliefs about information" (p. 44). She showed that if you spell out these cultural beliefs, you can have a simpler definition of lying than that of Coleman and Kay: Lies are simply false statements, assuming the statement occurs in a prototypical (informational) speech setting.[4] The complexity comes in the cultural models that surround the use and exchange of information.

A quite different perspective on lying comes from the conversation analytic tradition. In his classic paper, "Everyone Has to Lie," Harvey Sacks (1975) identified a general context (in our society) in which is it socially necessary to lie. Briefly, his argument goes as follows: In response to the greeting "How are you" from someone who is not the right person to receive the information that would explain the true answer (which may, after all, be "lousy," entailing further sequential diagnosis—"why? what's wrong?"), people are routinely forced to lie. In other words, everyone in that kind of situation (a situation that everyone might encounter) is forced

---

[3] The definition, as Barnes (1994) pointed out, ignores whether the attempted deceit actually succeeds or fails to deceive; it also allows that a statement may be incorrectly perceived to be a lie even if the speaker had no deceptive intention. Barnes also mentioned different motivations for lying (bad lies, motivated by self-interest, vs. "white lies" motivated by other-concern), which we will not draw upon here.

[4] Sweetser (1987) noted that this simple definition accords with spontaneous layperson definitions of *lie*; it also accords with a phenomenon observed by Piaget (1965), that children commonly pass through a stage in which the word *lie* is used to denote any false statement. Tzeltal children, as we see later, use their term for "lie" (*lot*) in the same way, to include unintended false statements.

to lie in anticipation that, unless you lie, you'll get into undesirable sequential binds. This is one kind of necessary social lie.

Intentional deception is the core of both these perspectives on lying, as well as of broader perspectives on deception that include misrepresentations other than lying—for example, Goffman (1975) provided a typology of "fabrications," which he characterized as "the intentional effort of one or more individuals to manage activity so that a party of one or more others will be induced to have a false belief about what is going on"[5] (p. 83). Restricting ourselves here to verbal misrepresentations, lying relates also to the thoroughly well established fact that very often people do not say exactly what they think. So lying relates to verbal indirectness in general, and to culturally based practices of indirectness.[6] These are a core part of what children learning language have to learn. The important question for our purposes here is this: *How do children learn the meaning of lie, in their society, and the culturally appropriate ways of lying?* This is actually a remarkably underresearched question (Barnes, 1994).

Plan for This Chapter

What I want to discuss here is a somewhat different "take" on Sacks' (1975) classic argument that "everyone has to lie," one that is adapted to a quite different cultural milieu. The people under consideration are Tzeltal-speaking Mayan corn farmers who live in the rural community of Tenejapa in southern Mexico. In this Mayan society, children are socialized from babyhood to "lie" in culturally appropriate ways; this practice I relate to the sociocultural context of a small, face-to-face society where privacy, the manipulation of information, and social control through gossip are major concerns. The themes of this chapter are thus lying threats to children as a form of control, children's acquisition of this practice, and its effect on their understanding and use of indirectness in language. I also briefly address more general questions, for example, that of the nature of "truth" in the context of nonverifiability in a nonliterate, small-scale society like Tenejapa.

---

[5]Relying on intentions for our definition raises a thorny question: How can we possibly know what others' intentions are? My answer, for present purposes, is this: We can often *presume* what others' intentions are, based on what they say and on what they say about what they say (e.g., "I meant to deceive here," "I meant to be sincere here"). Tzeltal speakers themselves make these sorts of assumptions.

[6]Of course, if the indirectness is culturally recognized in context as conveying particular implicatures and therefore everyone knows what the intended indirect message is, as in the Malagasy cases reported by Keenan (1976), lying is not at issue, because meeting others' communicational needs is not deceptive in contexts where you are clearly not expected to.

In this Tzeltal society, there is an apparent contradiction in the handling of small children. Babies are much wanted and loved, but they are considered to be very fragile, vulnerable, easily scared or shocked into losing their souls, and therefore at all costs to be protected and hidden from outsiders and other dangers. They are almost always being carried slung in a shawl on the caregiver's back. They are distracted whenever they are (or might be) upset; a baby's face is carefully turned away from feared things and covered when in public as protection from the evil eye. Crying puts small children at risk, so they are indulged, indeed given virtually everything they want prior to about age 2;6.[7] Nonetheless, the chief form of control (aside from physically removing a child from an undesirable activity) is to threaten. Some threats in Example 1 give the flavor of those routinely addressed to children between the ages of about 1;6 and 4;0:

(1) (naturally occuring examples, English glosses only)
"That woman will 'tzak' you." [grab you and take you away forever]
"The dog/bug/wasp will bite you."
"Don't go out on the trail, there are rabid dogs!"
"I'll take you to the clinic for an injection."
"I'll give you a bath."
"You want your hair washed?"
"I'll pour water on you if you don't pipe down."
"I'll give you medicine to drink."

Often, the threatened hazard is unspecified: "You'll 'get it' later," "Just you wait. . . ."

These overt scare threats are rarely actually carried out, and in fact they are often uttered in conjunction with contradictory bribes that are also not realized. This practice, I argue, leads Tzeltal children by the age of 2;6 to 3;0 to understand that speech does not necessarily convey true propositions, and thereby to a sensitivity to the underlying motivations for utterances distinct from their literal meaning. I relate this to four other aspects of communicative practices and social life in this community: (a) *"irony"* as a conventionalized mode of indirectness where utterances convey the opposite of what they literally mean, and children's adoption of this practice by the age of about 3, (b) *cultural models of "truth" and "lying"* captured in Tzeltal vocabulary, (c) the rich vocabulary of *evidentials* for denying or hedging self-knowledge about the truth of an utterance, and (d) *the social context,* including both childrearing practices in this society and adult practices of social lying and information protection.

---

[7]Further details about Tzeltal childrearing practices can be found in Brown (1996, 1998).

"LIES" TO TZELTAL CHILDREN

Lies to Children as Social Control

Let's look at some real examples of these threat lies in their sequential context, which makes clear their rhetorical force.[8] Lying threats to small children begin even before the child is talking at all, as in Example 2, and until the age of about 3;6 they are a routine, everyday occurrence:

(2) [bra27/1/96, p3] Mother to baby Antun (1;4):

Mo:	*ya xbaonix.*	"I'm going." [trying to scare him into following her]
[instead he goes off after the turkeys]		
Mo:	*jilan!*	"Remain behind!"
	[He ignores her.]	
Mo:	*yu' ya xjilat. ya me xban i' i.*	"Because you are staying behind. I'm going."
	ya me xbanix. la'. ya xban in ch'i. jilan.	"I'm going. Come on. I'm going then. Stay behind." [THREATS]
Aunt:	*kerem xa' mil me tuluk'e.*	"Boy, you'll kill the tur-
	ban me ix a. ban. ban.	keys. Go now. Go. Go."

[Here both aunt and mother know that she has no intention of leaving him behind.]

(3) [childtalk Mik 003, 5/12/95] Mik (2;0) and his brother Alux (4;7) are in the road, Alux has climbed onto a truck selling cooking gas that is parked in front of their house:

Alux [to Mik]:	*toj ya xmoat.*	"Climb straight on up."
Fa: [to both]:	*ma xa'toy!*	"Don't climb up!
	koanix a tey a.	Come down from there.
	ya me xtal nujkul.	'Leather' will come." [i.e., you'll get whipped if you don't get down] [THREAT]

---

[8]All examples are drawn from my database of videotaped natural interaction in five Tzeltal familes, collected every 4 to 6 weeks over 3½ years in the hamlet of Majosik', Tenejapa. The Tzeltal transcription is roughly phonemic; letters correspond approximately to their English equivalents except that x = sh, j = h, and ' indicates glottalization.

There are also many caregiver lies that are not exactly threats, but are still false statements or warnings meant to control the child's behavior:

(4) [cho26/9/94, p.14]: Xaw's mother to her (Xaw is 2;3):

Xaw:	*binti.*	"What?" [reaching for Mo's breast, wanting to nurse]
Xmi:	*ay me yichil.*	"There's chili (on it).
	och me tal yichil stukel ay yichil ye' i.	It's got chili on it." [FALSE WARNING]
Xaw:	*ijj.* [whining]	
Xmi:	*ay yichel. ban tajinan.*	"It's got chili on it. Go play.
	ban tzakla me a'wixta'be, ma stak' nuk'el.	Go take your toy, this [breast] can't be sucked.
	ay yichil.	It has chili on it.
	ban tzakla mene, tzaka tal mene.	Go take that (toy), bring that here.
	ya jtzaklatik.	We'll take it (to play with)."
// [later]		
Xmi:	*pasa me tz'i a'karoe.*	"Play with your car.
	ya me spojbet ya'tik me antune.	Antun [neighbor child] will steal it away from you soon." [FALSE WARNING]

Threat lies may be uttered with cajoling prosody and endearments, undercutting the scariness of the threat:

(5) [ant22ma6, p8]: Mother to daughter X'anton (3;4) who has walked away from playing with her brother, having quarreled with him:

Mo:	*tajinan. la'i kala me'.*	"Play. Come, my little mother.
	kala anton. ma me x'ilinat i.	My little X'anton. Don't be angry.
	ya me xtal sti'at bi sti'at (ya'tik) kala me'.	The thing that bites you will come and bite you (soon), my little mother."

But sometimes adults (and especially other child caregivers) intentionally try to scare little children, in an almost casual disregard for the fragility of their souls; or they may first threaten and then promptly reassure them, as in Example 6:

(6) [3chdia196.txt, cho29 jan96] Xaw is 3;7, Mat (her brother) is 6;0:

Mat: *ay la mach'a xmakliwan ek' i.*   "There's someone hiding in wait too."

[reference to toy wooden man; Xaw is afraid of it, thinking it's a skeleton of the sort that are said to hide in wait along the trails and jump out onto your back]

Mo: *eske ma xa' tejk'anbe ta spat.*   "Don't stand it (wooden man) up on her back."

Xaw: *iiiii* [crying]

Mo: *ya 'xi'. ju'uk, ma'ba ya sti'at.*   "You are afraid of it. No, it won't bite you.

   pere xa' tejk'an xan yan   But stand it up again,

   smakbex te ta ajk'ole.   it will lie in wait for you up there.

   ju'uk, ma xa'xi.' yu' ya sti'at.   No, don't be afraid of it. As if it would bite you."
   [THREAT + REASSURANCE]

Xaw: *ejnn*   [wingeing]

// [a bit later]

Mo: *la yich'ix k'ejel. tajinan me i.*   "It's been put away. Play.

   ya me xtal jukluk ta' pat ya'tik   It might come squat on your
   i me ma xtajinate.   back in a moment if you don't play.

   pasa me i' wixtabe, pasa me i.   Do your toys, do them. It is
   bajtix.   gone.

   yu' ay te a bi ya' k'abui. bajtix.   As if there were something you are watching. [i.e., there isn't]. It has gone.

   pasaik me i.   Do them (toys). Put them
   ak'aik ala bitik te a' ta'   onto your table."
   mesaike.   [THREAT + REASSURANCE]

When (as often happens) such threats are not at first reacted to by the child, they are often sequentially piled up one after another into a scenario of projected bad events constructed either by one caregiver (as in Example 7) or collaboratively by several participants (as in Example 8, where two adults and the child's brother gang up to pressure her to cooperate):

(7) [cho24/3/96] Xaw is 3;9:

Mo: *ba laj lika tal.*   "Go get it (a toy).

| *ja' ya katintestiki mach'a ma sk'an x'a'yani.* | We'll bathe the one who doesn't want to talk." [THREAT] |

[Xaw bursts into tears]
Soon afterwards:

| Mo: | *ya xtal jtomas ya'tik me x'ok'ate.* | "Tomas [the injection-giver] will come soon if you cry." [THREAT] |

A moment later:

| Mo: | *xa'mailiik wulwunel ya'tik . . .* | "Just wait for howling soon . . ." [i.e., you'll be really howling if you don't stop that whimpering] [THREAT] |

(8) [cho28se4.txt, p.18] Xaw is 2;3, her brother Mat is 4;8. Xxx is an unidentified adult:

Xaw:	*chikeee.*	"Candy"
Mo:	*ma'yuk.*	"There is none."
Xaw:	*eje'.*	"Eh."
Mo:	*ya xbatik ta eskwela ya'tik.*	"We'll go to the school (to buy some) later." [FAKE OFFER]
Xaw:	*jnn.*	"Hm."
Mo:	*sume ba i. tajinan me i.*	"Hurry up. Play."
	ya me xbatik ta eskwela.	"We'll go to the school."

// [a moment later]

Mo:	*ba pasaik i, ma me xbat te' a me ta xilaetike.*	"Go do it (play with toys), don't go over there to the chairs.
	la' me, ya me sjulat ya'tik ya me xjulawan.	Come, the shot-giver will inject you soon." [THREAT]
Mat:	*julawan.*	"The shot-giver."
Mo:	*la' me i. la' tajinan i antz. la' me.*	"Come. Come play here 'woman' [Xaw]. Come."
Xaw:	*jn'.*	"Hm."
Mo:	*ma xbat te' a mene. ay la me tza' te' a.*	"Don't go over there. There's shit over there."
Mat:	*ya ka'y chuxnel, ya ba ka'y chuxnel.*	"I'm going for a pee."

Mo: *julaik tal i antzi.*   "Bring the 'woman' [Xaw]
                                                back with you."

[Mat goes outside; Xxx is outside and speaks to Xaw who is still outside]

Xxx: *ban me antz.*   "Go 'woman'."

Mo: *julaik tal julaik tal.*   "Bring her in here, bring
                                                her in here."

Xxx: *ban me antz. ban me. ban me.*   "Go 'woman'. Go. Go. Go,
        ban me antz.   'woman'."

Mat: *la' me antz.*   "Come on, 'woman'."

Xaw: *ja.* [arriving]   "Huh."

Mat: *la' me tajinotik xan.*   "Come, let's play again."

// Later, after repeated urgings again for Xaw to come in:

Mat: *ya me yak' julel me jmamatike.*   "Mama will inject (you).
        ile' stzakoj ile' ch'i.   Look, she's taken up (the in-
                                                jection-hypodermic), look."
                                                [THREAT]

Mo: *ban me i. ya me julat ya'tik.*   "Go. I'll inject you soon. Go.
        ban i. ban. ba tajinan i.   Go. Go play. It will hurt."
        k'ux me.   [THREAT]

Mat: *la' me i antz.*   "Come, 'woman'."

Mo: *ban. tu tu tut i' karoik ine.*   "Go. Toot-toot-toot (goes)
                                                the (toy) car there."

Mat: *la' me antz.*   "Come, 'woman'."

Mo: *ban la me i'. ya julbe yakan*   "Go, it was said. I'll inject
        ya'tik.   her foot soon." [THREAT]

These threats are not jokes; they are not marked in any way as nonserious or playful, and the intention is to control the child's behavior by
making her believe that unless she cooperates the projected eventuality
will indeed come about. In this respect, they contrast with the oft-reported
language socialization practice of teasing small children (see, e.g., Miller,
1986; Schieffelin, 1986). However, in none of the previously cited Tzeltal
examples were the threats actually carried out or the things warned about
actually realized. Furthermore, these jointly produced sequentially piled-
up threats are often inconsistent, projecting a scenario that could not actually all come to pass. As Example 8 illustrates, threats are often combined
with fake promises, or bribes, of the sort: "You'll get such and such (a
treat) if you do what I want"; these are also piled up sequentially into often
inconsistent messages, as in Example 9:

(9) [cho29jan96 p23]: Xaw is 3;7, Mat is 6;0.

Mo: *ya la me xtal xan ta mal k'al*   " 'Mrs' (i.e., P. Brown) will
      ya'tik i jme'tike,   come again this afternoon,
      xi me 'wa'y. cha'ch'oj la me   she says. You'll get to play
      xtajinex ya'tik.   twice today." [FAKE OFFER]

// a little later:

Mo: *suj me 'ba i. tajinan me i.*   "Hurry up. Play.
      ya me 'jun be(l) jwixtik ta jejch.   You'll go visiting to your
      elder sister's house across
      the valley." [FAKE OFFER]

Mo: *ya me xbatik ya'tik.*   "We'll go (to see elder sister)
      soon."

. . .

Mo: *tajinan i. lajin a'wo'tan ta*   "Play. Finish up your play-
      tajimal i.   ing.
      me bajt jme'tik ek, jbatik ek' a.   When 'Mrs.' goes, then we'll
      go too (to ElSi's house)."

Mat: [playing] *ile' tak'in antz.*   "Here's money, 'woman'."
Xaw: *ya batik ta eskola.*   "We'll go to the school."
      [REQUEST]

Mo: *yak, ya juntik bel ta eskuela i*   "Yes. We'll go with 'Mrs.' to
      jme'tike.   the school." [FAKE OFFER,
      incompatible with going to
      ElSi's house]

Xaw: *jo.*   "Hm."
Mat: *ile' ni antz. ila ay.*   "Here, 'woman' (offering her
      a toy). Here it is."

Mo: *naklanik i.*   "Sit down.
      a jtabe jbaik me' tak'inike,   When we find the money,
      ya' jech pukbebaik i bi ya'   we'll take turns buying
      manbe jbaike.   things for each other."
      [FAKE OFFER]

// [children continue playing]

Mo: *ya me xbatik ta eskuela sok*   "We'll go to the school with
      jme'tik.   'Mrs.' " [FAKE OFFER]
Mat: *pakale, pakale.*   [nonsense sounds to self, ig-
      noring Mo]

Mo: *ya juntik bel ek.*   "We'll go with her." [FAKE
      OFFER]

Mat:	*pakali, pakali ji.* [to self]	
Mo:	*ya la me xta(l) jchon paleta ya'tik.*	"The ice-lolly seller will come soon.
	yu' ma'ba k'an paleta ya'tik i me ma x'a'tejate, ma pastik i 'wixtabike.	Because, if you don't work, you won't be wanting an ice-lolly later, if you don't do your toys." [FAKE OFFER + THREAT]

// [much later]

Mat:	[to pb] *ya to la wan xtalat ya'tiki i?*	"Are you really going to come again later today?" [re Mo's first fake promise]
PB:	*ju'uk. ja' to pajel.*	"No. Not till tomorrow."
Mat:	*jnn.*	"Hm."

Even 6-year-old children are not always certain when a caregiver's threats or bribes are lies and when they are true, as revealed by Mat's querying me in Example 9. But in general children develop an early skepticism toward this form of social control. This is partly because a number of culturally significant scare themes are repeatedly invoked until they become almost cliches: the *pukuj* "devil," *xutax* ("boogie-man"), *tzak*-ing (being stolen away by a stranger), being bitten, getting father to beat you. Other threats are fixed expressions: *xa'maili ya'tik* ("just you wait"), *ya 'wich'* ("you'll 'get it' "). Many threats, however, are opportunistic: Whatever recently the child has feared (for threats) or wanted (for bribes) may be invoked.

Are These Really "Lies"?

By our initial definition—statements intended to deceive a dupe about the state of the world, including the speaker's beliefs and intentions—these clearly are lies. They are also clearly not jokes, but uttered in a completely deadpan straightforward fashion and intended to be taken seriously. In this cultural context, these lies are nonsincere predictions, backed up by power: The caregiver *could* make them (at least some of them) be true, but experience soon teaches children that they usually are not backed up.[9] We may call them "control lies," fake scary predictions (threats) or offers (bribes) by a caregiver, intended to control the child's behavior. They diminish dramatically in frequency when the child becomes competent, between the ages of 3 and 4, when there is a seemingly magical shift in child

---

[9]Of course, if these threats were *never* carried out, these would not be lies; no one would expect them to convey true propositions. But being occasionally, albeit rarely, carried out, there is always a potential doubt.

behavior from ignoring such threats to complying with caretaker commands, without caregivers actually having had to carry out the threats or use explicit force. Given the rarity of enforcement this shift is remarkable; we return to its significance later.

It is important to note that, aside from the sanction of whipping with a belt (which is very rare[10]), Tzeltal caregivers have no power to enforce their will on children. This point has been made as well by Schieffelin (1986), discussing caregiving practices of the New Guinea Kaluli. But the Kaluli rely much more than Tzeltal caregivers on shaming.[11] Older Tzeltal children are also sometimes controlled with shaming, but it isn't always successful in modifying their behavior; they can brush it off, or ignore it, at least with caregivers who are not their parents.

Parental justification for the Tzeltal threat/bribe practice is usually phrased in terms of needing to protect the small child, control its behavior for its own good (e.g., danger) or for the parents' own well-being (e.g., quiet). In discussions of this, there is no sense expressed that this is a "bad" practice or that it sets a bad example. On the contrary, adults explicitly teach child caregivers to do it (see examples discussed later). As a result, children don't necessarily believe these threats, and they respond (in terms of compliance or not) to the emotional tone, not to the overt content of such caregiver utterances. There are at least three direct consequences of this practice for the children:

1. Passive resistance: Children often ignore threats and commands, sometimes even overtly say "No" to them, until age 4 or so, when there is a shift to remarkable compliance.

2. Early skepticism: By age 2;6 or earlier, Tzeltal children apparently know that many commands are not going to be enforced and that many threats are not going to be carried out. This knowledge amounts to awareness that there is often a difference between the state of the world and words used to describe or predict it.

---

[10]Despite the frequency of "getting leather" as a threat, I have seen a child hit with a "leather" belt only once in 30 years of participant observation in this community. I have twice seen the "belt" brought visibly out as an imminent threat. I have never witnessed a child being struck by the hand or any other form of physical punishment. Tzeltal parents say that without the threat of whipping, children would grow up undisciplined and spoiled.

[11]Kaluli threats to children are almost always third party, indirect. Schieffelin (1990) said:

> When adults intervene with small children, they make extensive use of third-party threats to create authority where none actually exists: "Someone will say something to you!"; "Your father (not present) will say something!" The threat is that one will be publicly and verbally confronted with the challenge "Is it yours?!" Mothers never threaten small children with what they themselves might do; rather, they refer to a third party who is not present as the agent who will act. (p. 155)

This is in strong contrast with the Tzeltal case.

3. Long-term fear of certain things: These include especially strangers, injections, and the scare monsters (*pukuj* "devil," or *xutax* "scarecrow") that are said to jump onto one's back if one walks alone in the dark.

I argue in the next section that there may also be an *indirect* consequence of this practice—an early appreciation of conventionalized irony. But first let us consider how children develop in their response to scare threats and their perception of lies.

Children's Developing Competence in Handling "Scare Threats" and Lies

Tzeltal children move from a stance of largely ignoring scare threats (and getting away with it), to recognizing and challenging falsehoods (at least some of the time) in what people say to them (see Examples 10 and 11), to producing lies themselves, both as self-protection and in efforts to control their younger siblings (Examples 12–14). This progression is monitored and aided by caregiving practices.

The ability to recognize the truth or falsity of statements is a prerequisite to recognizing intentionally deceptive ones. Recognizing that an utterance is false seems to be possible for children even by the age of about 2:

(10) [alv7/12/95] Mik is 2;0:

Mik:	*ej*	"eh." (playing with mother's breast)
Mo:	*ma'yukix.*	"There is none anymore." (milk in her breast)
Mik:	*ay!*	"There is!" (He examines her breast and shows her there is!)

But recognizing that a statement is intentionally deceptive is a more complex step. According to theory-of-mind theorists, it requires the child to have a conception that others' minds can hold different knowledge and beliefs than their own—a "theory of mind" that arguably develops between the ages of 4 and 6 (the exact timing is controversial).[12] By age 3;0 or 3;6, Tzeltal children react to parental control threats with a skepticism that often warrents explicit recognition:

---

[12]Very controversial, I might add. It seems likely that children's ability to handle certain indirect speech acts and implicatures between the ages of 2 and 3 indicates that at some level, they already operate with a theory of others' minds, and that experiments in the "theory of mind" paradigm are actually testing children for meta-awareness of others' minds (see, e.g., Barnes, 1994; Gopnik & Meltzoff, 1994).

(11) Wising up to parental control strategies:
[cho8de5], Mat (5;10) and Mother are looking at the "pear film," commenting on it, and trying to get Xaw (3;5) to come and look:

Mo:	jo'. ji k'ax ta tzakel.	"Hm. He went by, taking them (pears).
	jii busk'eix me perae.	Eh, the pears fell over!
	k'abu 'wil i antz. busk'eix.	Look, 'woman'. They fell over.
	ile' t'uxaj sok me sbisikletae.	Look, he fell with his bicycle."
Mat:	t'uxaj.	"He fell."
Mo:	antz.	" 'Woman.' " [addressing Xaw]
Xaw:	jo.	"Hm."
Mo:	k'abu 'wil. ile' ya stamix.	"Look. Look, he's picked them up."
Xaw:	ma'ba -	"He hasn't —"
Mo:	k'abu wil i. ma'ba kik'at bel ya'tik i ch'i.	"Look. I won't take you with me (when I go out) later." [THREAT]
Xaw:	ya jtalon li' ta ya'tik ek' i.	I'll come here in a moment too.
	ma me jun papatik ek mene ma.	I won't go with papa I guess."

[i.e., she's nonchalant about not going with them, when they go out later]

Mo:	yu' wan ma' xi'i ya xyakub i jpapatik ch'i.	"As if you weren't afraid (that) papa is getting drunk." [i.e., you are afraid!] [WARNING]
Mo:	lajuk a'wil ajk'ubee ya me xyakube'i.	"Remember you may have seen he was getting drunk last night."
Xaw:	ja.	"Huh."
Mo:	ya me xyakub ya' wil ja' i me la smajat a'tukel.	"He's getting drunk you see, it was the case that he hit you." [IMPLICIT WARNING]
Mat:	k'abu' wil a'tukel.	"Look at it [the pear film] yourself."

Mo:	k'abu wil. ile' ya skomon tamikix.	"Look at it. Look, they are communally picking them [pears] up.
Mo:	ile'i.	Look."
Xaw:	ya i talon li' ta ajk' ya'tik ek ini.	"I'll come in a minute here."
Mo:	mach'a 'jun tal i?	"Who will you come with?'
Xaw:	jun nax i ma.	"Just by myself I guess."
Mo:	a'tukel la xtalat i bi.	"You'll come you say by yourself?"
Xaw:	joo'.	"Yeah."
Mo:	ma'ba xiwat i bi.	"You aren't afraid, eh?"
Xaw:	jo'o.	"No."
Mo:	ja tz'i me ay ba' stzakat osil.	"What if Osil [a joke bad-guy] 'grabs' you?" [JOKE THREAT]
Xaw:	jo'.	"Huh."
Mo:	aye' ch'i ya xpiubaj. yakalatix ta piubtael.	"Golly, she is getting smart. You are in the process of getting smart." [RECOGNIZING THAT SHE DISTINGUISHES JOKE FROM SERIOUS THREAT]
Mo:	k'abu 'wil i. ji bajt yich' ak'el bel xpixol.	"Look. Eh, he went and got his hat given back to him [the guy in film]."
Xaw:	ya jtalon li' ta ajk' ya'tik ek' i ma.	"I'll come in a moment, I guess." [she still doesn't come watch the film]

Producing Threat Lies.   There is explicit socialization in lying, especially in telling older children how to lie to younger ones to get them to do what you want:

(12) (koj11apr4.txt, p.12); Petul (1;8), X'anton (4;3)

| Mo: | [to x'anton] ik'aix me tal a i alali. | "Bring the child back here." (re Petul, gone to the house just below) |
| Mo: | ik'a me tal ii. | "Bring him back." |

X'an:	*ji tz'ini*	"Eh, then."
Mo:	*aj ayane.*	"Speak (to him)."
X'an:	[calling] *kala papito.*	"My little 'father'."
Mo:	*bajtix me ta eskuela jmamatik uta.*	" 'Mama has gone to the school', say." [TEACHING LIE]
X'an:	[calling] *bajt me ta eskuela jmamatik.*	"Mama went to the school."

[Petul returns]

(13) [alv7jan6, p40]: Mik is 2;1, his sister Sil is 6;0. Mik is outside, Sil and her mother are indoors and want to get him inside.

Sil:	[calling] *la' me i kala miik!*	"Come here, my little Mik!"
Mo:	*wa'y lai. ba la albe bi xi ya' pase.*	"You hear?. Go tell him what you are doing." [TELLING SIL HOW TO GET MIK TO COME INSIDE]
Sil?:	*jay?*	"What?"
Mo:	*ay bi jpas uta.*	" 'There's something I am doing', say."
Sil:	[calling out to mik] *bi la' pasi ja'i jilat?*	"What're you doing, you are staying behind?"
Mik:	[calling back] *ja?*	"What?"
Sil:	*ja'i ban ta nopun jo'tik.*	"We are going to school."
Mo:	[to sil] . . . *jobel uta.*	" 'To San Cristóbal', tell him."
Mik:	*jo'.*	"Hm."
Sil:	*binti la?*	"What did you say?"
Mik:	*jo'.* [=jo'bel]	"San (Cris)tobal."
Sil:	*binti la? bajt ta yochib.*	"What did you say? Gone to Yochib."
Mik:	*jo'.*	"San (Cris)tobal."
Sil:	*bat ta bat ta lum.*	"Gone to town."
Mik:	*jo'.*	"San (Cris)tobal."
Sil:	*bat ta eskwela.*	"Gone to school."
Mo:	*ta na uta.*	"To a house, say."

[Sil gets the idea, and launches into her own inventive set of lies to entice Mik inside]:

Sil:	*la'i kala miik. ay lech lech la.*	"Come, my little Mik. There is milk, they say.
	lech lech la tal i . . .	Milk has come they say
	jii la la sti'on ek'i a'me'.	Ihh, your mother bit me.
	la la sti'on ek ta jnuk'. la sti'ben ta jch'ujt.	She bit me in the neck. She bit me in the belly.
	ta jch'ujt. ta kakan, ta kakan, ta kakan.	In the belly. In the foot, in the foot, in the foot.
	ti'ot la ta yutil kakan, lok' la xch'ich'el.	I've been bitten in the middle of the foot, its blood is coming out."
Mo:	. . . [whispers instructions to Sil]	
Sil:	*ja:*	"It's-"
Mo:	*xchu'non uta mike, lo'lo' tal.*	" 'I'm nursing', say to Mik. Lie to him to get him to come."
Sil:	*eso ya xchu'non i ch'i. eso xchu'non.*	"Thus, I am nursing [suckling mother's breast]! I'm nursing!
	ya la xchu'non mama.	I'm suckling on Mama.
	je ya xchu'non eso. ya xchu'non mik!	I'm nursing, thus. I'm nursing, Mik!
	mika. xxt mik. eso i ch'i! ya xchu'non.	Mik. Shsht Mik. Thus then! I'm nursing.
	ya xchu'non! mika. xchu'non.	I'm nursing! Mik. I'm nursing.
	ya xchu'non. chu'non. chu'non.	I'm nursing. I'm nursing. I'm nursing.
	ya xchu'non. xchu'non.	I'm nursing. I'm nursing."
[Mik comes in]		
Sil:	[to Mo] *i talix.*	"He's come in."
	[to mik] *eso lek a xchu'non.*	"Thus, I really suckled well.
	eso ya jlajesbet a'chu'. sale. yak.	Thus I've finished off your breast for you. Okay. Yes."

Sil's lies in Example 13 are adultlike in recognizing that credibility is not the only issue; emotional arousal is the desired outcome, so that the child will comply. These examples also illustrate the frequent Tzeltal practice of telling children explicitly what to say, using the quotative verb *uta* "say it" in a manner reminiscent of Kaluli *alema* (Schieffelin, 1986).[13]

In this kind of social environment, then, and in this context where children are expected to care for their younger siblings almost as soon as they *have* a younger sibling, we find Tzeltal child caregivers by the age of 5 or so producing this threat/lie form of control to younger children (and very young children to pets!).

(14) [ant22ma6, p18] X'anton (3;4) to her cat.

| X'anton: | *xa' maili ya'tik xawin.* | "Just you wait, cat." |

(15) [alv19mar6] Elder sister Sil (6;2) and brother Alu (4;9) to Mik (2;3):

| Sil: | *ch'enan i. ya me' wich' julel ya'tik me x'ok'at xane. me ya x'ok'at.* | "Pipe down. You'll get injected soon if you keep crying. If you cry." [THREAT] |

[a bit later, Mik is still crying]

GrMo:	*ch'enan i. tajinan i. ila' wala ixtab te ine.*	"Pipe down. Play. Here's your little toy."
Sil:	*ya' k'an julel. a yakuk i ch'i,*	"You want to be injected. Okay then, I'll go get the (shot-giver) girl,
	ya ba kik' tal ach'ix,	
	me ya x'ok'at, ya 'wich' julel.	if you cry, you'll get injected.
	ja'chuk puro ok'el.	After all, there's nothing but crying.
	ay a'kotz ile' kotzi. ya mes-	Here's your little (toy) turkey.
	ya me sluchat ya'tik i kotzi.	It will soon butt into you, your turkey." [THREATS]
Alu:	*ile' la ini - - - aj ay laj jo'wil tz'i'.*	"Look, here. They say there's a rabid dog." [THREAT]

---

[13]However, there is a difference between the two cases: The Kaluli examples are largely of small children being told what to say in order to stick up for themselves and learn to get what they want from older people. These Tzeltal examples involve teaching older children to control younger ones.

Young children will also pitch into a series of control lies in a familial ganging up in order to control the youngest—a conspiracy of child caregivers:

(16) [8/12/95, p41]: Mat (5;10) scolds and threatens Xaw (3;5) after Mo and ElBr Dan (18) have:

Xaw:	*ile' me'.*	"Look, mother." [at the video machine]
Mo:	*ja' ma' pik.*	"Don't touch."
Xaw:	*jnn.*	"Hm."
Dan:	*ma' pik.*	"Don't touch."
Mat:	*ma xa' pik. ya stzakat bel jme'tik.*	"Don't touch. 'Mrs.' will 'grab' you." [THREAT after two adult warnings]

Since children of 4 or 5 are often given responsibility for looking after younger ones, and since they have to get results (their caregiver performance being evaluated entirely on whether or not the baby is kept quiet and happy), whatever works is what is required to keep the younger one under control and quiet, even if it is lies.

But, let's think again: Maybe none of this is really—*by Tzeltal-speaker criteria*—"lying." Maybe, as argued by Rosaldo (1982) for the Ilongot of the Philippines, people here are not really concerned with "truth" or "sincerity"; these don't enter into their evaluations of utterances. Duranti (1993) argued along similar lines for Samoa, claiming that, in many contexts, words are viewed not as emanating from individuals but rather from a positional identity (for example, from a noble title), and words are evaluated according to their consequences, not as individual commitments: "For Samoans, *meaning is seen as the product of an interaction (words included) and not necessarily as something that is contained in someone's mind*" (p. 41; italics in original). Therefore Samoans hold speakers responsible for the social consequences of their speaking acts, not for their intentions.[14]

Actually Duranti (1993) conceded that in many everyday contexts Samoans do in fact hold one another accountable for personal commitments made through speech. In the Tzeltal case, there is also good counterevidence to the argument that "sincerity" or "intentions" are irrelevant in the interactional contexts under consideration here. In everyday transactions, people do hold one another to commitments, being surprised or even outraged if others do not stick to what they have said they intend to do. Furthermore, interactional uses of the terms *lot* ("lie") and *melel* ("true") in as-

---

[14]Susan Blum (1998) made a similar point with respect to Chinese society.

sessments of one another's (and indeed, one's own) utterances,[15] suggest that people *are* generally assumed to have communicative intentions that may be sincere or not, and that may or may not portray events and states of affairs that correspond to reality.

One way of assessing whether these actually are lies for Tzeltal people themselves is to look at their cultural concepts of "lie" and "truth" and at how these are interactionally invoked. The two core concepts to be explicated are expressed in the noun *lot* ("lie, nontruth, mistake") and the adverb *melel* ("genuinely true, sincerely"). These are implicated in Tzeltal cultural models of truth and lying, and of other practices involving nontrue utterances, including teasing and joking (expressed in the Tzeltal nouns *lo'lo'el* and *lo'il k'op*, "lies, or teasing and joking speech that is false"). People also assess the factuality of talk in terms of the verb *ya xlo'lo'wan* ("[s]he's telling lies, teasing, joking"). In contrast, the adverb *melel* ("truly") is used to emphasize the sincerity and factuality of one's utterance; it is used a great deal by speechmakers, and by adults in serious conversation, though not frequently by children. There is also prolific use of evidentials to hedge or emphasize the degree of one's own commitment to the truth of an utterance. Children learn to use a number of these remarkably early, suggesting an awareness of the interactional relevance of indicating degrees of commitment to the truth of an utterance.[16]

Furthermore, the young child does not at first *know* if a parent is sincere in these threats. The very occasional actual carrying-out of a threat leaves room for doubt. Adults also recognize that children are self-willed, goal-driven little creatures who frequently lie themselves, in order to get what they want, and some of them pile up lies sequentially in a transparent sequence of falsehoods. (For example, they routinely lie to me that the baby got their lolly, balloon, etc., in order to get another one.) Adults are routinely skeptical of what their children tell them in these contexts. Children also readily accuse one another of lying; they use "lie" as a routine response to others' talk (*a'lot*, "your-lie") and even as a comment on their own (*jlot*, "my-lie"). In my data, their uses of *lot* ("lie") do not distinguish falsehoods that are intentional from those that are not, nor jokes from mistakes.[17]

---

[15]For example, one child (Lus, age 4) says of herself: *yakalon ta pas lot* ("I'm in the process of lying") when she has been saying false things for a while.

[16]By about age 3;0 children use the quotative particle *laj*, which means, roughly, "I don't take responsibility for the truth of what I'm uttering, someone else said it." They, like adults, use *laj* especially when telling a story or reporting a dream. Other evidentials frequent in young children's speech by about 3;6 are *me* ("if, maybe"), *wan* ("maybe"), *ma* ("perhaps, I suppose" [implies speaker is inferring]). Tzeltal has some 20 of these evidential particles, most of which come in a nonsalient (second-position) syntactic slot (Brown & Levinson, 1987; see also J. B. Haviland, 1989, for evidentials in the closely related language Tzotzil).

[17]Western children of this age also fail to distinguish lies from mistakes, according to Piaget (1965). The meaning of *lie* in English has also been construed in the past as including "a mistake or error in relation" (in Dr. Johnson's dictionary, according to Barnes, 1994).

Instances of "lie" accusations are given in Examples 17–21:

(17) [lusa5p2', p.34] Lus 3;9 has told me earlier that there was a "scare-crow" (a kind of boogie-man) there.

Lus:	*in ma'yuk li' ay xutax i. jlot.*	"Look, there's no scarecrow here. My-lie." [LIE = NOT TRUE]
PB:	*lot. ma'yuk chikan.*	"Lie. There's nothing to be seen."
Lus:	*jo'.*	"Yeah."

(18) [bra17ap5, p.13]: Lus 3;9, in her sleeping house

PB:	*bit'il ya xwayat?*	"How do you sleep?"
Lus:	*jich mocholon bel ini.*	"Here lying down over here."
[shows me, on bed]		
PB:	*mochol.*	"Lying down."
Lus:	*jo'. la' ila'wil a.*	"Yeah. Come see."
PB:	*yakuk.*	"Okay."
Lus:	*jo'.*	"Hm."
PB:	*ju'uk to. ma to ba-*	"No, it's not yet- "
Lus:	*jo'.*	"Hm"
PB:	*ma to ba yorail.*	"Not yet time (for sleeping)"
Lus:	*jo'. jlot ek.*	"Hm. My-lie too." [LIE = JOKE]
PB:	*a'lot ek.*	"Your-lie too."

(19) [lusa5p1', p. 12]: Lus is 3;9, Nik is 4;3.

Lus:	*ay me yach'il k'ib jo'tik e'i.*	"We have a new water-pot."
PB:	*ay wan?*	"You do?"
Lus:	*jo'.*	"Yeah."
PB:	*lek bal?*	"Is it good?"
Lus:	*jo'.*	"Yeah."
PB:	*banti la' taj?*	"Where did you get it?"
Nik:	*ma mano tal tatik. mano tal tatik.*	"Didn't Grandfather buy it? Grandfather bought it."
PB:	*banti la sman tal?*	"Where did he buy it?"
Lus:	*mano tal tatik.*	"Grandfather bought it."
Nik:	*ta jo'bel. ta jo'bel.*	"In San Cristóbal. In San Cristóbal."
PB:	*ta jo'bel?*	"In San Cristóbal?"

Nik:	*jo'.*	"Yeah."
Lus:	*(s)lot.*	"His-lie." [LIE = ERROR]
PB:	*slot.*	"His-lie."
Lus:	*man-kajpe la sman tal a.*	"From a coffee-buyer here he bought it."

(20) [bra12ap5, p.24]: Lus (3;9)

Lus:	*ma me talatix a pajel me'tik.*	"Don't come again tomorrow, 'Mrs.' "
PB:	*jo' ma me talon. binti laj?*	"I won't come. Why not?"
Lus:	*jlot. yu' ya jlo'lo'at jichuk xanich. jejej.*	"My lie. I'm teasing you just like an ant." [LIE = TEASE]
PB:	*a jejej. ya 'lo'lo'on.*	"Oh, you're teasing me."

The following is an example of a genuine intentional lie:

(21) [lusa5p2',p.17], Cal (7;7) and Lus (3;9).

Cal:	*me'tika.*	"Mrs."
PB:	*binti la?*	"What?"
Cal:	*ma'yuk ku'un te'y karo ya' wale.*	"There isn't any car of mine like you said." [re: his own toy car]
PB:	*ma'yukix?*	"It doesn't exist anymore?"
Cal:	*ju'uk.*	"No."
PB:	*banti bajt?*	"Where did it go?"
Cal:	*ma xkil.*	"I don't know."
Lus:	*e lot. lum ay ta nae.*	"Eh, (your)-lie. It's there at (your) house." [LIE ACCU-SATION]
PB:	*jich kilo. te' ay ta sna.*	"So I've seen it, there at his house."
Cal:	*yu' wan ayi'i.*	"Because perhaps it is there." [i.e., it isn't!] [IRONY = DENIAL]
PB:	*yak. kilo woje cha'je.*	"Yes, I saw it yesterday."

The Tzeltal folk model of "truth/lying" includes a presumption that everyone lies for self-interest, when wanting to influence others or deflect unwanted consequences of one's actions. There is no sense that these lies are morally bad, and there are (as far as I've seen) no punishments of children for lying.[18] This moral neutrality toward lying suggests that no particular value is placed on truth and sincerity per se, in interaction, although the distinction between utterances that are true (*melel*) and non-true *(lot)* is clear. But it is also clear that, even in "information-exchange contexts," in many circumstances truth and sincerity are undesirable or inappropriate, indeed whenever motivations of politeness, or self-interest, or social manipulation, override what might be taken to be the natural urge to speak the truth in a context of information exchange.

LYING AND IRONY

There is another way in which this Tzeltal practice ties in with particular cultural habits. Part of what "lying" does, in this cultural context, is raise the issue of a different version of "how the world is"; it puts that version interactionally on the table, to be taken as one of the counters in the interactional game of who decides what happens next. This is parallel (it seems to me) to Sperber and Wilson's (1981) treatment of irony (and ironical utterance types) as echoic mention. In Brown (1995), I characterized their position as follows:

> All these sorts of "figures of speech" are seen as essentially "echoing" or more loosely evoking a proposition which is placed in the context to be laughed at, scorned, or whatever, in order for an attitude to be conveyed towards it. Ironic utterances are like things in quotes, so for example if someone says "Nice day, eh," in a context of a walk in the pouring rain and sleet, the false description evokes the image of the accurate description ("Rotten day, eh") as well as an image of who might have, or actually did, utter the hope/prediction/expectation that it would be a nice day, this person (or image) then being the imagined "victim" or target of the ironic utterance. (p. 156)

Therefore, tentatively, I want to relate Tzeltal lie/threats to another Tzeltal verbal practice: conventionalized irony. This form of manipulation of utterance of truth is conventionalized to a remarkable degree in this society. In formulating a Tzeltal ironic utterance, one states literally the opposite of what one intends to convey, preceded perhaps by hedging particles and accompanied by "skeptical" intonation, to emphatically convey the opposite. For example, one says the equivalent of "Perhaps maybe I really liked that event" to convey "Boy, I hated it." In Tzeltal adult speech,

---

[18] The same observation was reported for a Quechua society of Peru (Ackerman, 1990, as cited in Barnes, 1994).

there is pervasive use of conventionalized irony and other ironical forms to express attitudinal skepticism by putting forth different "voices," making propositions that are held up to affective comment or to ridicule. This is fundamentally a "positively polite" invitation to sharing of attitudes (Brown, 1995; Brown & Levinson, 1987).[19]

Tzeltal children learn very early to use this locution; they already are starting by age 3, and use conventionalized irony prolifically by 3;6–4;0.

(22) [24/1/96] X'an (3;3) showed me a cut on her finger, I looked at the wrong one and she said:

X'an:	*yu' wan ja'.*	"Because perhaps (I suppose) it's that one." [→ It isn't]

and she showed me the right one.

(23) [mikjul7s, p8] Mik is 3;7, trying to work a toy:

Mik:	*ee. ee. ma me pojbeni kala sil.*	"Eh, eh, don't steal it from me, my little Sil.
	ma jichuk ini me'tik.	Isn't it like this, Me'tik?" [asking PB how to make the toy work]
Sil:	*jo'o.*	"No."
Mik:	*jo'o. jo. yu' ya kalat.*	"No. Huh. Because (I suppose) I'm telling you. [→ No!]
	ja' ya kali kala me'tiki.	I'm telling my-little Me'tik."

(24) [lusapr5s, p.62] Can (5;2), Lus (3;9)

Can:	*tutut!*	"Toot toot!" [pretending cups are a car]
Lus:	*binti la sokat ini.*	"What are you doing with that?
	yu' wan jich ta pasel mene.	Because (I suppose) that's the way to do it." [→ it isn't!]

---

[19]See Clark and Gerrig (1984) and Isaacs and Clark (1990) for a somewhat different analysis of irony—and other forms of "nonserious" language use—as mutually recognized pretense. Their analysis works for Tzeltal irony, but not for what I am calling threat lies, because the pretense on the part of the threateners is not understood or shared by the intended recipient.

(25) 25/1/96 pet (3;5): [ironic response to my comment that the doll will die from the sun]

Pet: *yu' wan ay k'al.*   "Because perhaps there's sun." [→ Don't be silly, there isn't much sun!]

Lus by 3;9 uses irony so often it sometimes sounds like overuse of a conventionalized routine:

(26) lusapr5s, p8: (Lus is 3;9, Nik is 4;3)

Nik:	*la me niton chitam e'i lum ay snaik ta jejche.*	"A pig knocked me over at their house acrossways."
Lus:	*la nutz chitam e'i lum ta jejch.*	"A pig chased him over there acrossways."
PB:	*banti? mach'a yu'un?*	"Where? Whose?"
Lus:	*juju'—*	"Dunno"
Nik:	*yu'un li'i.*	"Their's here." [pointing to nearest neighbors]
PB:	*jo'.*	"Oh."
Lus:	*yu'un lumine.*	"Their's over there." [pointing to a different house]
PB:	*la sluchat.*	"It butted you?"
Lus:	*jo'o.*	"No."
PB:	*la' luch.*	"You butted it?"
Lus:	*la luchot i antuni.*	"Antun got butted by it."
PB:	*aj.*	"Ah"
Lus:	*yu' jo'on ek.*	"Because (I suppose it was) me." [→ It wasn't!"]

[a moment later]:

Nik:	*ja' me la nutzot e'i jich joy ek i lumine.*	"It is my companion from over there that got chased." [pointing towards a third house, that of cousin Antun]
PB:	*jo'.*	"Oh."
Nik:	*ma'ba jo'tik e'i.*	"It wasn't us."
PB:	*ju'uk.*	"No."
Nik:	*ma'ba ja' la nutzon jo'tik.*	"It didn't chase us."
PB:	*ju'uk.*	"No."

Lus:	k'an ok'on ek e 'i.	"I wanted to/almost cried too."
PB:	ya' xi'.	"You were afraid of it?"
Lus:	jo'oj.	"No."
PB:	bi yu'un?	"Why?"
Lus:	yu' wan ya jxi' (j)tukel i'i.	"Because perhaps I myself was afraid of it." [→No!]
PB:	ju'uk. bi yu'n ok'at?	"No. Why then did you cry?"
Lus:	yu' wan ya ok'on ek i'i.	"Because perhaps I cried." [I didn't]
PB:	ju'uk	"No (you didn't)."
Lus:	jo'. tantunon tukel e'i.	"Yes. I (my)self howled."
PB:	jo'.	"Yes."
Lus:	ok' tukel e'i antun.	"Antun (him)self cried."

By age 4;0 the children have the irony construction down pat: *yu'* ("because") or *yu'wan* ("because perhaps") combined with a proposition conveys emphatically that the proposition is *not* the case. To be able to use this construction appropriately, children must be able to distinguish the truth and falsity of propositions, and to recognize others' utterances as sometimes not corresponding to the state of affairs in the world. Arguably, they must also be able to attribute false beliefs to others, those false beliefs that they reject with an ironic retort. Children by age 3½ or 4 use this irony construction to convey an affective attitude of scorn or skeptical disagreement with a prior utterance; it is not used simply to correct a mistake, for the record. It is therefore not simply equivalent to negation, which well before this age Tzeltal children have acquired.[20] Although many theory of mind theorists would consider children of 4 too young to have such a model of others' minds, it is worth considering the possibility that Tzeltal childrearing practices actually promote the early development of an awareness of others' minds. In any case, it seems to me to be at least plausible that the earlyness with which Tzeltal children are able to do this kind of ironic, skeptical "backwards-talk" is related to the fact that from babyhood on they are routinely subjected to utterances that claim a certain state of affairs in the world (through threats, bribes) that in fact *does not* obtain, and *is not brought about* to happen. Tzeltal children of 3 or 4, though a long way from fully socialized adults, already have

---

[20]Tzeltal sentences are negated with the particles *ma* or *ma ba*; the grammatical contrast between positive and negative sentences appears by at least age 3 (e.g., *ma jk'an* ["I don't want it"] in contrast to *ya jk'an* ["I want it"]).

both the skeptical attitude, and the rhetorical flavor of indirectness—in the form of ironic skepticism—that is appropriate to this speech community. The cultural practice of lying threats to them has, I think, helped to inculcate it. In the process, they have been socialized through these uses of language to adopt the Tzeltal cultural ideas of "truth" and "lies." They have, in short, already learned something important about rhetorical modes, culture as "ways of putting things," ways of framing things.

ADULT LIES AND VERBAL SOCIAL CONTROL

Let us consider briefly the role of lying in the adult social world of Tenejapa. As in many societies, explicit lying is expected in many contexts. One must lie about private affairs, money, comings and goings, and not having things that people are asking to borrow. A preference for nonconfrontation interactionally means that people prefer overt lies (including bald-faced lies that are so obvious they are not expected to be believed) to a direct refusal of someone's request.[21] In addition to these contexts where there is no real deception, since everyone knows everyone lies, there are others where lying or nondirect dealing are chronically suspected: Two culturally recognized Tzeltal ones are (a) self-protective behavioral deceit (e.g., *mukin we'elil* ["secret eating"], a practice family members are often prone to suspect one another of), and (b) other-protective polite denial (e.g., as a visitor or guest you must routinely at least four or five times refuse food offers, before accepting; if you refuse you are not believed and the offer is reiterated until you accept; insistence on refusing is guaranteed to offend). There is a general cultural attitude of skepticism concerning news conveyed by outsiders, and extreme skepticism of others' motives, mixed with occasional gullibility.[22]

There are also some social lies analogous to those identified by Sacks, with the same motivation: attending to constraints on who should have access to what information, and when, and avoiding the sequential consequences of certain kinds of utterances. In Tenejapa these constraints come into play in the social greeting *banti ya xbaat?* ("Where are you going?"), a routine query when passing anyone on the trails. Because this question (analogously to the greeting "How are you?" in English) is askable by anyone, the answerer must monitor her response in relation to whether the

---

[21]For example, if someone wants to borrow your radio and you want to refuse, it is much better to say something like "I'm afraid it doesn't have any batteries" (whether or not this is true) than to refuse more directly.

[22]Gullibility tends to emerge in relation to modern contrivances to which exposure is very recent—for example, to television advertising.

asker has the right to know the true answer, and if not, has to offer a "lie" (the routine lies in response to "Where are you going?" being things like: "For a walk," "To work," or "Nowhere").[23] It strikes me as no accident that this cultural practice of routine lying exists in a small-scale, face-to-face society characterized by forms of social control and decision making that are almost exclusively oral. These include: (a) *gossip as social control* (with the concomitant fear of privacy breaches, fear of having one's reputation besmirched),[24] (b) *belief in witchcraft* (personal knowledge about people is potentially dangerous, and must be kept hidden), (c) *communal decision making* by acclamation, in community meetings where everyone must come to a consensus decision about the common policy to which all will adhere, despite individual cases of private dissension,[25] and (d) *justice by compromise* (local court cases reach a compromise solution to conflicts after both sides have presented their case in often nontrue testimony (see, e.g., Brown, 1995; Collier, 1973). This practice meshes uncomfortably with the practice of written testimony characterizing national Mexican court cases. The stakes may be large (for example in land claims), with a significant motivation to lie, and participants are often unaware of the standards of truth officially applicable in the national courts. These are all contexts providing strong motivation to lie, or conceal one's true opinions and beliefs. But equally, in everyday life, it is often appropriate and expected to lie; indeed Albert's (1972) comments on information control in Burundi apply equally to Tenejapa:

> In lesser matters than life and property and position, discretion still has its place. One may discuss with close friends and neighbors the problems created by a spouse who is a bit slow-witted, but not broadcast the fact far and wide. If one suspects that a neighbor is a witch, one refrains from mentioning it in his presence ... There are, then, some truths not to be spoken aloud to anyone; some to a faithful spouse or a blood brother but nobody else; some to close relatives or neighbors. Only rarely is any statement so innocent that it is not necessary to consider the possibility that it will bring trouble. (p. 91)

Therefore, in many ordinary social circumstances, it is necessary to lie. Informal observation suggests that Tzeltal children learn to manage these social lies with fair competence by the age of 5 or so, when they are called

---

[23] This "Where are you going?" question is a routine greeting in many societies, and raises the same Sacksian problems (see, e.g., Duranti, 1997, for Samoa).

[24] See L. K. Haviland and J. B. Haviland (1983) for an analysis of gossip and privacy in the nearby Mayan community of Zinacantán.

[25] For example, in a recent meeting, it was decided that everyone in the community would adhere to the same political party. A number of individuals wanting to belong to a rival party publicly acceded to the common policy, despite privately expressed misgivings and resentment.

upon to perform them as they are sent around to different households on errands.

CONCLUSIONS

I have argued that "everyone has to lie in Tzeltal," at least partly for Sacksian reasons, that is, by anticipation that, unless you lie, you may get into undesirable sequential binds. This is, indeed, one important source of conventional social lies—the kind of speech that is not expected by anyone to be true.[26] My point here is that conventional social lies are not only motivated in this way; in Tenejapa they are also motivated in contexts where rhetorical persuasion is called for. The Tzeltal control that have concerned us are not prompted by sequential concerns, nor by politeness or circumspectness about information distribution. They are uttered to children out of the blue, motivated by the child's (anticipated or actual) undesirable behavior, with the presumption that the child won't necessarily understand caregivers' inconsistent answers (whether threats or bribes) and won't hold caregivers accountable for the predicted events.

Is this Tzeltal practice simply a cultural idiosyncrasy, with no broader lessons? To conclude, we consider the Tzeltal phenomenon in relation to two general issues: (a) the notion and significance of "lying" cross-linguistically, and (b) the possible effects of such a practice of systematic lying on Tzeltal children's linguistic, cognitive, and social development, in the light of other research on children's lying and theory of mind.

Lies in Cross-Linguistic Perspective

Let us return to the criteria posed by Coleman and Kay (1981) for prototypical *lie* in English, and use them to assess the Tzeltal notion of *lot*: (a) the speaker believes the statement is false, (b) the speaker intends to deceive the hearer by making the statement, and (c) the statement is in fact false. It seems that, in the Tzeltal cultural model, the strongest criterion is (c)—to be a *lot*, the statement must indeed be false. But the weakest of these is (a), because the speaker may in fact mistakenly think the statement is true, and later realize it was false, or he or she may be agnostic or indifferent as to whether the threatened prediction will be carried out. And, in the control

---

[26]A similar argument made by Susan D. Blum (personal communication) in her book *Deception and Truth in China,* in which she argues "that in this society, language is believed to accomplish many things, just like other sorts of social action, but that it is not principally a vehicle for expression of the 'true feelings of the self.' Hence much behavior that appears to be 'lying' is not taken that way at all."

threats context, (b)—the intention to deceive the target child—is clearly there, or at least the intention exists to produce the desired affect that may motivate the child to cooperate. But there may well be no intention to deceive other participants including older children wise to this strategy, who often contribute to the collaborative effort to deceive the youngest.

The Tzeltal case is not entirely incompatible with Sweetser's (1987) conclusion about the universality of a notion of lying and its link to cultural understandings of information exchange:

> Very different cultures emerge from this discussion as possessing saliently similar understandings both of lying and of the general power and morality dimensions of informational exchange. This similarity presumably stems from universal aspects of human communication. Where cultures differ appears to be in *delimitation* of basic "informational exchange" settings and in *conventional use* of the relevant power parameters. Folk models of knowledge and informativeness (and the corresponding semantic domains) may universally involve strong shared elements. (p. 62)

But the negative moral associations of lying in English—the folk understanding that "deceit usually profits the deceiver, to the listener's detriment" (Sweetser, 1987, p. 55) and "lying as serious authority abuse" (Sweetser, 1987, p. 59)—are not always applicable in the Tzeltal community; hence the moral force against it is missing at least in the context of childrearing. Lies, then, are not everywhere considered to be bad, or antisocial. And non-anti-social lies are not everywhere just the "white lies" due to politeness, or to sensitivity to others' needs not to know the truth.

Thus, even across different cultural contexts that share a notion of "lie" as an intentionally nontrue statement, there may be different attitudes to individual responsibility for the truth of statements. The English notion of "lie" is, as argued by Sweetser (1987), tied to cultural views of information, to a culturally molded sense of "self," and of "individual," having one's own true opinions, intentions, and plans. It is also tied to a notion of "responsibility" which, for English speakers, as Hill and Irvine (1993) observed, relates to notions of "the continuity of a self with a relatively consistent scheme of interpretation of what it is reacting to . . . [and] continuity in the community of agents to which response is being made" (p. 1). This notion, as Hill and Irvine pointed out, is cross-culturally problematic, since "continuity of self" and "continuity in the community of agents" are cross-culturally variable notions; not everywhere is responsibility for the truth of an utterance assigned to the speaker. In assessing the Tzeltal case of lying threats to children, it is appropriate to follow Hill and Irvine's suggestion to shift away from assigning the locus of meaning to an individual caregiver toward a dialogic approach to meaning construction, since multiple participants often collaborate in the construction of control lies. But in these Tzeltal caregiver lies, there is no dialogue with the recipient of the lies—rather, there is a conspiracy of caregivers (including siblings) to control small children. Their collusion means that allocation of responsibility for authorship of the false message is diffuse. Meanings are constructed in interactional processes; in this Tzeltal case these are exercises of persuasion backed up by power. Responsibility and evidence in this context are not relevant. The meaning of sequentially piled up false threats/promises is "Do X, or bad things will ensue!" Agency (control) is central; knowledge and information are manipulated in pursuit of particular goals.

I would go further, and claim that, without cultural consensus on what constitutes proof of what the external reality is (e.g., writing, or religious dogma), there are bound to be different moral attitudes to lying and truth telling. Most Tenejapans have no relationship to the written word, except (for some) the Bible. The semantics of *lot* ("lie") and *melel* ("true") do indeed imply a cultural notion of truth analogous to the English one (there is a reality "out there"; true statements are ones that correspond to that reality, false ones don't). But in the absence of canons of provability, truth is slippery, often boiling down to what works, socially, including the practice of controlling small children by lying to them about the future consequences of their actions.[27]

Lying, Irony, and the "Theory of Mind" Theory

First let us be clear that the practice described here is not a bizarre one; similar routine practices of threatening, teasing, baiting, and lying to small children are found in many societies and subcultures.[28] Whereas the effect of such practices on children's socialization, and on the development of social abilities, has been stressed (e.g., by Heath, 1983; Miller, 1986; Schieffelin, 1986), no one, to my knowledge, has yet considered what effect such practices may have on children's developing cognitive abilities.

As Barnes (1994) pointed out, there has been relatively little research into how children develop an understanding of lies and an ability to convincingly lie.[29] Laboratory studies where contexts are constructed in which children will lie, in order to assess how adept they are at lying or at detecting lies at different ages, have shown that first and third graders cannot tell a convincing lie; they "leak" (DePaulo & Jordan, 1982). Nor are

---

[27]Concerning notions of "truth" in a related context of nonverifiability, see also Danziger (1998) on the Mopan Maya who implicitly believe stories; anything written down must be true.

[28]For example, in her study of rural Greece, Friedl (1962) reported that parents deliberately lie to their children in order to teach them that they shouldn't take others' words "at face value."

[29]In addition to Barnes' (1994) review, see DePaulo and Jordan (1982), DePaulo, Stone, and Lassiter (1985), Ekman (1989), Feldman and Custrini (1988), and Vasek (1985).

preadolescents very good at detecting lies and deceit. These researchers have suggested that English children are led into lying by the "training ground" of games that require deception (a context that, however, is virtually nonexistent for Tzeltal preadolescent children). Piaget (1965) also held that children do not achieve an adultlike definition of lie in terms of intent to deceive until the age of 10–11. It is also generally thought that irony will be a late acquisition for children, relying as it does on an understanding of multiple levels of communicative intent (see Winner, 1988; Ninio & Snow, 1996).

While recognizing the limitations of comparing laboratory results with natural situations, I do think that Tzeltal children seem to be remarkably adept at producing lies, and at producing and understanding ironic utterances, at a much younger age than these studies would lead one to expect. This suggests the hypothesis—which would need to be tested by structured cognitive tasks—that, through participation in the Tzeltal "language games" of lying threats, of ironic skepticism, of contradicting others, Tzeltal children by the age of 4 or even earlier are led to the mental awareness that others can hold false beliefs and can try to persuade others to hold them. Less speculatively, I would argue that the training in threat lies plays a role in leading Tzeltal children into taking on responsibility early. This comes about because this is an activity where the participation structure of multiple caregivers of widely differing ages motivates the child to shift from receiver to giver of these threats, and thereby to responsibility via collaboration with other caregivers. It is, then, not just skepticism that is being socialized by this practice; a child has to learn what to do to make such threats not happen—namely, take on responsibility for cooperating with the social unit, and for ensuring that even younger children also cooperate.[30] This accounts, perhaps, for the remarkable shift in child behavior around age 4, from ignoring control threats to complying with caretaker commands, without caregivers actually having had to carry out threats or use explicit force. This then may be the real significance of the multiparty, intergenerational talk that occurs in this context: Through these participation structures the young Tzeltal child doling out threat lies to an even younger sibling begins to acquire full membership in her household group. The result is that Tzeltal children, at a very early age (by at least age 5, and some by age 4), efficiently take on serious responsibility for child care of their younger siblings.

To participate in the threat-lie activity as a threatener, children do not at first actually need a theory of mind, or of others' intentions; nor do they

---

[30]Other things are being socialized as well, including specific cultural beliefs about what is frightening (being "grabbed" or stolen away, outsider dogs, medicine and injections, baths, etc.) and what is desirable (sweets, trips to school or shops, visiting, etc.), beliefs that are laid out, and reinforced, in the content of threats and bribes.

need one to participate in accusations that others are "lying," since for them, at first, Tzeltal *lot* do not rely on intentions but simply on a mismatch between a proposition uttered and reality. But it seems plausible that all this lying has effects on language learning and socialization, in a way perhaps not anticipated by the philosophers. Children exposed to language routinely used nonfactually readily learn to use it that way themselves—they are sensitive to the manipulability of people through manipulating truth. This leads to early acquisition of the culturally appropriate use of irony to convey skepticism about the stated position of one's interlocutor (or to some other target of the ironic utterance). The caregiver practice of lying to small children brings them quickly to culturally stabilized and pragmatically effective indirect uses of language—like irony—where the meaning of an utterance relies systematically on inverting notions of truth.

ACKNOWLEDGMENTS

This chapter is a revised version of talks presented at the CLIC conference at UCLA in May 1998 and at the American Anthropological Association meetings in November 1998. I am grateful to Susan Blum, Alessandro Duranti, Elinor Ochs, and Emanuel Schegloff for helpful critical comments.

REFERENCES

Ackerman, R. (1990). *Deception among the southcentral Quechua.* Unpublished manuscript.

Albert, E. (1972). Cultural patterning of speech behavior in Burundi. In J. J. Gumperz & D. Hymes (Eds.), *Directions in sociolinguistics* (pp. 72–105). New York: Holt, Rinehart & Winston.

Barnes, J. A. (1994). *A pack of lies: Towards a sociology of lying.* Cambridge, England: Cambridge University Press.

Blum, S. D. (1998, December). *Sincere words, clever words: Deception and truth in China.* Paper delivered at the 99th annual meeting of the American Anthropological Association, Philadelphia.

Bok, S. (1978). *Lying: Moral choice in public and private life.* New York: Pantheon.

Brown, P. (1995). Politeness strategies and the attribution of intention: The case of Tzeltal irony. In E. N. Goody (Ed.), *Social intelligence and interaction* (pp. 153–174). Cambridge, England: Cambridge University Press.

Brown, P. (1996, July). *The conversational context for language acquisition: A Tzeltal (Mayan) case study.* Plenary lecture, 5th International Pragmatics Association conference, Mexico City, Mexico.

Brown, P. (1998). Conversational structure and language acquisition: The role of repetition in Tzeltal adult and child speech. *Journal of Linguistic Anthropology, 8*(2), 197–221.

Brown, P., & Levinson, S. C. (1987). *Politeness: Some universals in language usage.* Cambridge, England: Cambridge University Press.

Clark, H. H., & Gerrig, R. J. (1984). On the pretense theory of irony. *Journal of Experimental Psychology: General, 113,* 121–126.

Coleman, L., & Kay, P. (1981). Prototype semantics: The English word "lie." *Language, 57*(1), 26–44.

Collier, J. F. (1973). *Law and social change in Zinacantán.* Stanford, CA: Stanford University Press.

Danziger, E. (1998). *To play a speaking part: Falsehood, fantasy, and fiction among the Mopan Maya.* Unpublished manuscript.

DePaulo, B. M., & Jordan, A. (1982). Age changes in deceiving and detecting deceit. In R. S. Feldman (Ed.), *Development of nonverbal behaviour in children* (pp. 151–180). New York: Springer-Verlag.

DePaulo, B. M., Stone, J. I., & Lassiter, G. D. (1985). Deceiving and detecting deceit. In B. R. Schlenker (Ed.), *The self and social life* (pp. 323–370). New York: McGraw-Hill.

Duranti, A. (1993). Intentions, self and responsibility: An essay in Samoan ethno-pragmatics. In J. H. Hill & J. T. Irvine (Eds.), *Responsibility and evidence in oral discourse* (pp. 24–47). Cambridge, England: Cambridge University Press.

Duranti, A. (1997). Universal and culture-specific properties of greetings. *Journal of Linguistic Anthropology, 7*(1), 63–97.

Ekman, P. (1989). *Why kids lie.* New York: Scribner's.

Feldman, R. S., & Custrini, R. J. (1988). Learning to lie and self-deceive. In J. S. Lockard & D. L. Paulhus (Eds.), *Self-deception: An adaptive mechanism?* (pp. 40–52). Englewood Cliffs, NJ: Prentice-Hall.

Friedl, E. (1962). *Vasilika: A village in modern Greece.* New York: Holt, Rinehart & Winston.

Goffman, E. (1975). *Frame analysis: An essay on the organization of experience.* Harmondsworth, England: Penguin.

Gopnik, A., & Meltzoff, A. N. (1994). Minds, bodies, and persons: Young children's under-standing of the self and others as reflected in imitation and theory of mind research. In S. T. Parker, R. W. Mitchell, & M. L. Boccia (Eds.), *Self-awareness in animals and humans* (pp. 166–186). Cambridge, England: Cambridge University Press.

Haviland, J. B. (1989). "Sure, sure": Evidence and affect. *Text, 9*(1), 27–68.

Haviland, L. K., & Haviland, J. B. (1983). Privacy in a Mexican village. In S. I. Benn & G. F. Gauss (Eds.), *Public and private in social life* (pp. 341–361). London: Croom Helm.

Heath, S. B. (1983). *Ways with words.* Cambridge, England: Cambridge University Press.

Hill, J. H., & Irvine, J. T. (1993). *Responsibility and evidence in oral discourse.* Cambridge, Eng-land: Cambridge University Press.

Isaacs, E. A., & Clark, H. H. (1990). Ostensible invitations. *Language in Society, 19,* 493–509.

Keenan, E. (1976). The universality of conversational implicatures. *Language in Society, 5,* 67–80.

Lewis, D. K. (1969). *Convention: A philosophical study.* Cambridge, MA: Harvard University Press.

Lewis, D. K. (1975). Languages and language. In K. Gunderson (Ed.), *Language, mind and knowledge* (pp. 3–35). Minneapolis: University of Minnesota Press.

Miller, P. (1986). Teasing as language socialization and verbal play in a White working class community. In B. B. Schieffelin & E. Ochs (Eds.), *Language socialization across cultures* (pp. 199–212). Cambridge, England: Cambridge University Press.

Ninio, A., & Snow, C. (Eds.). (1996). *Pragmatic development.* Boulder, CO: Westview Press.

Ochs, E. (1988). *Culture and language development.* Cambridge, England: Cambridge Univer-sity Press.

Piaget, J. (1965). *The moral judgment of the child.* New York: The Free Press.

Quinn, N., & Holland, D. (1987). Culture and cognition. In D. Holland & N. Quinn (Eds.), *Cultural models in language and thought* (pp. 3–42). Cambridge, England: Cambridge Uni-versity Press.

Rosaldo, M. (1982). The things we do with words: Ilongot speech acts and speech act theory in philosophy. *Language in Society, 11,* 203–237.

Sacks, H. (1975). Everyone has to lie. In M. Sanches & B. G. Blount (Eds.), *Sociocultural dimensions of language use* (pp. 57–80). New York: Academic Press.

Schieffelin, B. B. (1986). Teasing and shaming in Kaluli children's interactions. In B. B. Schieffelin & E. Ochs (Eds.), *Language socialization across cultures* (pp. 165–181). Cambridge, England: Cambridge University Press.

Schieffelin, B. B. (1990). *The give and take of everyday life: Language socialization of Kaluli children.* Cambridge, England: Cambridge University Press.

Sperber, D., & Wilson, D. (1981). Irony and the use–mention distinction. In P. Cole (Ed.), *Radical pragmatics* (pp. 295–318). New York: Academic Press.

Strauss, C., & Quinn, N. (1997). *A cognitive theory of cultural meaning.* Cambridge, England: Cambridge University Press.

Sweetser, E. (1987). The definition of "lie": An examination of the folk models underlying a semantic prototype. In D. Holland & N. Quinn (Eds.), *Cultural models in language and thought* (pp. 43–66). Cambridge, England: Cambridge University Press.

Vasek, M. E. (1985). Lying as a skill: The development of deception in children. In R. W. Mitchell & N. S. Thompson (Eds.), *Deception: Perspectives on human and nonhuman deceit* (pp. 271–292). Albany: State University of New York Press.

Winner, E. (1988). *The point of words: Children's understanding of metaphor and irony.* Cambridge, MA: Harvard University Press.

Chapter 10

Voice and Collusion in Adult–Child Talk: Toward an Architecture of Intersubjectivity

Karin Aronsson
Mia Thorell
Linköping University, Sweden

Drawing on Bakhtin (1984), this study explored multivoicedness in pre-schoolers' and young schoolchildren's play. Multivoicedness could be seen in preschoolers' and schoolchildren's differentiation between pretend and nonpretend voices: for example, in their regulation of tempo, loudness, and voice. These findings are in line with prior research in that several studies have demonstrated children's fine differentiation between pretend and nonpretend voices and between different pretend role voices. Similarly, this study corroborated earlier findings on a socialization dimension (Auwärter, 1986; Sawyer, 1996) in that schoolchildren were more likely than preschoolers to stay within the pretend frame, without talking out-of-frame in a nonpretend voice. Last, and most important, the play dialogues showed how children reproduced collusion in adult–child talk in enacting doctor–parent–child talk. Such collusion was seen in the children's subtle ways of employing collusive forms of production formats, such as the collaborative "we"-form when playing doctor (talking to a sick child). On the basis of these findings, it is argued that voice cannot merely be equated with "role" or roles. In employing a collusive production format, the children demonstrated a Bakhtinian awareness of subversion in adult–child talk. On a theoretical note, the present findings support voice models rather than frame models of children's play. Also, extending the work of Göncü (1993), it is proposed that children's collusive voices can be seen as an important type of tertiary intersubjectivity.

MULTIVOICEDNESS AND CHILDREN'S ROLE PLAY

Within a dramaturgic perspective, children's role play can be seen as a type of fictional genre (cf. Bakhtin, 1986; Goffman, 1959). A basic assumption of the present study is that such a fiction reflects societal hierarchies and the complexities of real-life discourse. In the following, we try to tease out different aspects of multivoicedness in children's play dialogues. Moreover, we discuss how children's role play can be seen to involve different types of coordinations of perspectives. The scope of the present study is broader than some previous work in that it focuses on the architecture of intersubjectivity on different levels. An overriding aim is to disclose some of these complexities through an analysis of *multivoicedness* in talk:

> For the word is not a material thing but rather the eternally mobile, eternally fickle medium of dialogic interaction. It never gravitates toward a single consciousness or a single voice. The life of the word is contained in its transfer from one mouth to another, from one context to another context, from one social collective to another, from one generation to another generation. In this process the word does not forget its own path and cannot completely free itself from the power of these concrete contexts into which it has entered. (Bakhtin, 1984, p. 202)

When speaking, we draw on different voices, which reflect past and prospective loyalties and alignments (Bakhtin, 1984, 1986). Language use, including role enactment, is always multivoiced in Bakhtin's dialogic epistemology.

Moreover, Bakhtin (1984) discussed how talk may be formulated with "a sideward glance," that is, subversively as in parodies or jokes. In such cases, the speaker deals not only with reference, but also with the "other's word"; that is, she or he exploits the talk of others for making a stylistic or parodical point. Bakhtin has shown us that language use always involves perspectives. What is said is always said by specific persons with specific perspectivity. Perspective taking can, for instance, be seen in parodic or ironic reports of others' talk. As discussed (Bakhtin, 1984), parody need not involve full-blown parodies. It may also surface in an exaggerated prosody, that is, in various ways of caricaturing the talk of others.

In Bakhtin's theorizing, "voice" thus cannot be equated with role. When speaking as a "role" member, a person will draw on many different, and at times conflicting voices. In professional life, a female doctor may, for instance, draw on the professional jargon of her discipline. Second, she may talk to child patients with endearment terms that echo words used by her parents when she herself was a child. Third, she may employ medical formulae to which she has herself been exposed as a patient. In one single professional role, a person may thus produce many different voices of the past. Moreover, she may align with ways of speaking typical for prestigious journals in her field.

Intersubjectivity and Children's Play

When young children know each other well, hardly any monitoring is needed in moving between different play roles (Example 1):

Example 1. Preschool boys playing "neighbors"

1 Nicke: Mow the lawn ((laughs)) mow the lawn, mow the lawn, mow the lawn. Well, now I've mown the lawn
2 John: ((enters)) Ra.-ta-ta-ta-ta-ta ((machine gun sound)) chucka chucka
3 Nicke: Ra-ta-ta Chucka chucka chucka ((aims his gun toward John's head. John throws himself down))

These two 6-year-olds know each other well, and they have probably enacted similar scenes many, many times. No monitoring is needed in order to regulate play as such. Their play is highly scripted on a local level and both boys know how to respond when one neighbor becomes unfriendly.

In other situations, children need to regulate what is pretend and what is nonpretend, producing metacomments on their playing (Example 2):

Example 2. Preschool boys playing mortals and immortals

1 Ola: I shot you, Isak. I shot you. ((to Isak, who still moves))
2 Isak: No, but I'm immortal
3 Ola: One can't do that. We're playing for real now. ((Linus grabs Isak's arm with a claw))
4 Linus: You are grabbing-mortal at least ((Isak runs away)
5 Ola: We're playing in reality

In Example 1, intersubjectivy was taken for granted. In contrast, intersubjectivity is foregrounded in Example 2 in that the children talk on play; that is, they explicitly make the playing a topic in its own right.

On a basic level, intersubjectivity can be seen in joint attention in early mother–infant coordination, that is, what Trevarthen and Hubley (1978) called *primary intersubjectivity*. On a somewhat higher level, intersubjectivity involves shared signs, such as the young child's first spoken words, that is, *secondary intersubjectivity*. Drawing on these notions of intersubjectivity, Göncü (1993) discussed a third type of intersubjectivity, metacommunication. The basic point he made about metacommunication is similar to that made in other constructivist models (Bateson, 1971; Mead, 1934; Piaget, 1951), that is, that more advanced forms of play involve perspective taking. In his discussion, metacommunication is achieved either explicitly (via comments on play) or implicitly through children's early differentiation between pretend language and nonpretend language. Göncü also discussed how role play involves a coordination of perspectives, implicitly discussing metacommunication in terms of a three-level hierarchy, including what we call a *tertiary intersubjectivity*.

Pretend Voices and Nonpretend Voices in Children's Play—Frame Models

Intersubjectivity has at times been discussed in terms of repertoires of voices in quite a literal sense. The type of voice repertoire that has been most thoroughly explored is the difference between nonpretend and pretend voices (cf. reviews by Garvey, 1993; Musatti & Orsolini, 1993). In most of these cases, the "unmarked" or real-life voice is differentiated from a pretend voice that is high-pitched or deep. Similarly, the nonpretend, real-life voice is characterized by a normal tempo, whereas the pretend voice is characterized by a marked tempo (slow or quick). Cook-Gumperz (1986) discussed how two young children playing house employed at least four different voices, two *in-character voices*—a "mum-to-mum" and a "mum-to-baby" voice—as well as an *everyday life voice* and a *narrative voice*. The voices were differentiated with respect to tempo, rhythm, and prosodic features. For instance, the real-life voice was characterized by greater urgency, whereas the narrative voice involved elongated vowels and a slower tempo. When employing two or more voices, players demonstrated that they were capable of perspective taking.

Auwärter (1986) discussed the pretend–nonpretend distinction in terms of three levels: an everyday level, a transitional level (of planning and negotiations), and a fictional level. In his analysis of fictionality, he differentiated between nine different modes, which are formed through various permutations of the three reality levels and three types of social identity: everyday personal identity/observer identity/role identity. In Auwärter's study, the fictional level was clearly differentiated from the everyday level both prosodically and syntactically, but there was less clear differentiation between the everyday and the transitional level. Several researchers have demonstrated the relation between syntactic form and type of *frame*: pretend frame and nonpretend frame. Modal constructions, such as "will" are associated with the playing, the so-called enactment, whereas amodal constructions, such as "gonna," are linked to the planning, the so-called emplotment (Gee & Savasir, 1985). Similarly, the imperfect tense is related to emplotment (Musatti & Orsolini, 1993). Such voice shifts mark the transition between everyday reality and completely staged fiction (Auwärter, 1986), and have been identified in a series of different typologies (Table 10.1). Several typologies discuss dramaturgy in terms of frames. In line with Bateson (1971) and Goffman (1974), stage directions and enactment versus "real" talk can be discussed in terms of different frames (cf. Table 10.1).

In line with social constructivist theorizing (e.g., Garvey, 1974, 1993; Schwartzman, 1982), Auwärter (1986) showed that play frames are co-created. In his own work on hand-puppet play among 3- to 10-year-old girls, Auwärter found that preschool children spent a great part of their time negotiating access to play, and discussing other aspects of emplotment whereas school-age children started to play almost without preparations ("jumping" into the fictional level). Similar trends were revealed in his longitudinal data. In the case of one 5-year-old girl, 33% of all utterances took place on the intermediate level in contrast to much less, 3%, about 3 years later. Saywer (1997) made similar observations among American preschoolers, in that younger children spent more time than older children in metacommunication. Friendship has an effect that is

TABLE 10.1
Levels of Reality—Frame Models and Voice Models

Frame Models			
Everyday Level	*Transitional Level*	*Fictional Level*	*Reference*
Everyday life frame	Preparatory phase	Game:play	Mead, 1934
		Play frame	Bateson, 1971
Nonpretend	Interpretative frame	Pretend frame	Garvey, 1993
Action	Emplotment	Enactment	Gee & Savasir, 1985
Voice Models			
Everyday Level	*Transitional Level*	*Fictional Level*	*Reference*
Everyday life	Narrative voice	In-character voice	Auwärter, 1986
			Cook-Gumperz, 1986
Real voice		Pretend voice	Garvey, 1993
Out-of-frame		In-frame-voice	Sawyer, 1997
Out-of-frame		Ventriloquation	Sheldon, 1996
		Indirect voicing	Sawyer, 1996
		Direct voicing	

similar to that of increased age, in that friends may go more directly into play. They need less time for metacommunication, less time for coordinating their actions. In the present study, we investigate whether this type of trend also shows up in Swedish children's play.

Subversion and Multivoicedness

Children's role play can be seen as a type of theatrical performance (Forbes, Katz, & Paul, 1986; Sawyer, 1993; Sheldon, 1996). Sawyer (1996) focused on what he called *direct voicing, indirect voicing,* and *collective voicing.* Direct voicing is when the child enacts a scene with her or his own body, whereas indirect voicing involves playing through a role figure (e.g., toy figure). Collective voicing is a chorus type play, in which several children stage a scene together. Yet, in his discussion of voicing and directness, Sawyer (1997) did not exclusively rely on Bakhtin—voice is used more or less synonymously with "voicing a character" (p. 86). Sawyer beautifully captured improvisations and recurrent themes in children's play, demonstrating the multivoicedness of role voices. His model, however, is not primarily formulated in terms of double meanings or collusion.

Sheldon (1996) focused on collusion in her focus on *double-voiced discourse,* discussing, for instance, when children speak angry words in a squeaky falsetto voice, that is, when there is a lack of congruence between form and content. She did not refer to Bakhtin, but in a Bakhtinian type of analysis this would correspond to collusion or to ways of saying one thing on one level, and something else on another (cf. *subversion* in the writing of Bakhtin, 1984; Sacks, 1992). For instance, a message may be aggressive on a verbal level and mitigated on a nonverbal level. Moreover, Sheldon discussed what Bakhtin called *ventriloquation,* that is, prompted talk or ways of saying something on behalf of someone else. In some of the early work, emplotment and enactment were described in terms of preparatory and play phases (Mead, 1934). Type of frame was thus primarily a matter of phase in a play sequence. Later on, Auwärter (1986) discussed how play frames must be discussed as a multilevel rather than multiphase phenomenon, in that children may move between the three levels at any stage in their play acting. In detailed analyses of children's voice modulations, he showed that children may mark change of role position at any stage of a play sequence, modifying their voices as they move in and out of different play roles or in and out of pretend and nonpretend roles.

In her work on children's so-called controlled improvisations, Andersen (1986, 1990) showed that even quite young children master a broad repertoire of role voices, changing their style of speaking, for example, degree of directness, to fit different position in societal power hierarchies, for example, gender or age hierarchies.

Some of the most ambitious recent formulations on play voices are those of Sawyer (1993, 1995, 1996). In his ethnographic study, younger children needed more regulatory talk than older children, but on the whole, his children effortlessly moved between different roles cocreating play motifs and play roles much in the way that instruments act in concert in a symphony. Drawing on Bakhtin, Sawyer (1995) primarily discussed voice in terms of different societal roles: "The term 'voice' then becomes 'ways of speaking' within the genred activity (usually, but not necessarily, associated with specific 'roles' of that genre). Thus each play activity, or genre or play, may contain several distinct voices, each typically associated with a distinct role in the interaction" (p. 140).

Bakhtin argued that individuals participate in a complex linguistic word, with many different ways of speaking, or "voices" that are each indexical of a recognizable social role and status (Sawyer, 1996). It can perhaps be argued that Sawyer partly reduced Bakhtin to a role theorist. In any case, he did not treat subversive discourse or genuine multi-voicedness, that is, many voices within one speaker at the same time. He has corroborated earlier work, in showing that children do differentiate between pretend and nonpretend voices, and in demonstrating that children easily move in and out of different pretend role voices. However, it still needs to be shown empirically that children's play involves "voices" in more complex ways, in ways that involve subversive voices.

One such study concerns children's enactment of family life. In a study of 6- and 8-year-old children's controlled improvisations of family life scenes, Aronsson and Thorell (1999) showed that children produced parodic scenes of family life, involving collusive alliances, and gleeful escalations of family life aggression.

The present investigation has applied Bakhtinian analyses to children's role play, mapping the architecture of intersubjectivity both in terms of role differentiation and "fictionality," and in terms of levels of coordination, exploring in what ways role play can be discussed with regard to subversion and multivoicedness.

Are young children aware of collusion in adult–child talk, for example, the "collusive we" in pediatric talk, and different forms of address, such as third-person directives?

METHOD

Subjects

The subjects in the present study were 96 preschoolers and schoolchildren. These two groups were chosen to represent preliterate and literate children. Moreover, the schoolchildren would have more experiences of interaction in formal institutional contexts. There were equal numbers of boys and girls, and equal numbers of 6-year-olds (preschool) and 8-year-olds (school). All were fluent speakers of Swedish, and no children were excluded due to language problems. They were all audiotaped in their normal preschool/school environment. Altogether, 48 children were invited to bring a peer to play with. It was important for us to study children who were familiar players, as friendship is an important parameter in children's play (Corsaro, 1985; Sawyer, 1997). Without exception, each subject chose a same-sex peer. All the 48 play dyads were encouraged to enact doctor–patient scenes, involving doctor + parent + sick child. In the present investigation, we have partly drawn on Andersen's (1990) method of *controlled improvisation*, but our focus is on children's social interaction (joint construction of play worlds), which is why we have studied child dyads (and not single children).

In a pilot study, it was found that the least preferred role was generally the sick child. In the main study, the research assistant therefore played the child. In each play session, the researcher presented the two children with a set of props, including clothing, such as a wig, glasses, a man's blazer, a lady's handbag, and the like for the parents, and a white coat and medical bag for the doctor. All boys chose to play fathers; all girls played mothers. The medical bag contained a real stethoscope, thermometer, bandages, sling, plasters, and a medicine bottle. The children were to decide among themselves who would play doctor first, and who would play the parent. The two children were allowed to play for a little while, and then a series of negotiations about hospitalization and medication were elicited by the researcher (*qua* child character) who claimed that she refused to take any medicine, to sleep in the hospital, or to take shots, protesting:

- "I don't want to take any medicine."
- "I don't want to stay here overnight."
- "I don't want to stay here alone."
- "I don't want any shots."

In some sessions, the parents spontaneously talked about keeping the child company, which means that the third refusal was superfluous. The scenarios were carefully selected after observations of everyday role play in day-care centers, and after a pilot study of child dyads enacting various doctor–patient scenarios. Among other things, it was found out that real objects (e.g., sling, bandages) increased the children's interest in doctor play as compared to trial sessions with toy objects. Both children got to play both roles (doctor/parent) because the roles were changed after all scenarios had been enacted. The children often improvised various activities such as physical examinations, operations, or payments.

Transcriptions

The analyses are based on 24 hours of audiotapes. The research assistant made notes of nonverbal interaction after each dyad had completed their playing. All play interactions were transcribed in extenso, including non-verbal information (e.g., about medication, shots, operations). The children at times employed the imperfect tense, whispers, or other linguistic markers in order to signal engagement in emplotment and not in enact-ment (cf. Garvey & Kramer, 1984). Comments made in such a play com-mentary voice have been transcribed in italics.

Transcription Notations

hehehe	Laughter.
:	Prolonged syllable.
-	An abrupt cut-off.
(.)	Audible pause.
(pause)	Marked pause.
bold	Indicates marked emphasis, that is, changes in pitch and/or increased amplitude.
x	Inaudible word.
(( ))	Encloses explanation or description of how talk is delivered.
[	Demarcates overlapping utterances.
italics	Play commentaries or planning (emplotment talk).
> <	Speeded-up delivery.

The translation of the examples from Swedish has been made by a native English speaker. The translator was asked to be as literal as possible with minor modifications in order to preserve child speech and style.

PRETEND AND NONPRETEND VOICES— CHILDREN AS ANIMATORS OR PRINCIPALS IN PLAY ACTIVITIES

When inspecting the children's employment of pretend and nonpretend voices, it could be seen that the schoolchildren mainly played within an in-frame voice in the terminology of Sawyer (1997). They stayed within the play mode significantly more often than did the preschooolers, who recur-rently moved out of the play frame, negotiating how to play (Table 10.2). As can be seen, schoolchildren also negotiate about how to play. Meta-communication is an important aspect of the schoolchildren's play dia-

TABLE 10.2
Pretend Voices and Nonpretend Voices in Doctor–Patient Episodes

	Preschool	School
Nonpretend voices	24	13
Pretend voices only	0	11

Note. The number of dyads were: $\chi^2 = 9.48$, $df = 1$, $p < .01$.

logues. Intersubjectivity is thus not achieved effortlessly. It has to be negotiated in more than half of the dyads at some point.

In Goffman's (1974, 1981) discussion of *production formats*, children can be seen as *animators* when employing pretend voices, and as *principals* when speaking in their everyday voices. Moreover, a person may speak on behalf of someone else, as when mothers ventriloquated for their children in authentic pediatric interviews, or as when mother-players acted as *say-for* persons (cf. Goffman's discussion of production formats). As can be seen, the "I" in children's role play may be quite ambiguous. The epistemic responsibility for what is said is total (principal) or partial (animator). Moreover, the present play sessions showed that "code switching" between different production formats may be a discursive resource in itself.

Example 3. Doctor–father (Preschool boys 20:7)

1   Dr: Mhm huh, let's see here. Let's see.
2   C: Is it bad daddy?
3   F: Well not so bad. It's not so bad but it's gonna hurt a little.
4   C: Oh.
5   Dr: Tying- we- ((authoritative voice; tying a bandage))
6   F: ((clears throat)) That one, doctor! >*Are you playing?*<
7   Dr: But hehehe I decide.
8   F: Mhm ((to peer)) °*You may listen.*°
9   Dr: (to MT) °*Is this for listening to the leg, or?*°
10 MT: °*Well, yes one listens to the heart and one listens to the lungs.*°
11 Dr: °*Yeah, okay*°
12 F: Now you take the bandage.
13 Dr: °*First a bandaid.*°
14 F: >*No I mean a shot.*<
15 Dr: °*No where is my bandaid?*° Nope ((authoritative voice))
16 F: ((sighs))

17	Dr:	°*It takes a little while, takes a little while, it takes a little while*° Would you like a bandaid or a Bamse bandaid? ((commanding voice))
18	C:	I want a Bamse bandaid.
19 →	Dr:	Cos now we will have a shot.
		[
20	F:	Shot.
21	C:	But I don't want to have any shot.
22	Dr:	Well, you've got to.
23 →	F:	And you were so brave that last time.
24	C:	Yes, but I don't want another one. It hurts.
25	F:	Well you take (x) but-
26	Dr:	You will have some plaster later.
27	F:	>*No, then we said like this* < er this is the type of shot that won't be felt and (C:mhm mhm) it was such a good shot. It cannot be felt then cos it was a putting-to-sleep shot, cos we- we should operate your leg.
28	Dr:	It is a- °*Now, what did dad say it was?*°
29	F:	°*A putting to sleep shot*°
30	Dr:	Yes, so you'll fall asleep. You have to-
31	C:	Ouch
32	F:	You're falling asleep now.
33	Dr:	Now you can-
34	F:	Then we opoperate.
35	Dr:	Opanate with this.
36	F:	Yeah right.
37	Dr:	Hey you!
38	F:	I'm gonna listen oh dji:ng brr.
39	Dr:	Ouch ouch hehe now it's done ((solo laughter))

In this example, as in many other play sessions, the children drew on a broad range of discursive resources for signaling a change of play frame: (a) *nonpretend voice*: lowered voice (Turns 8–11, 13, 15, 17, 28, 29), and altered tempo (nonpretend or emplotment voice: greater speed; Turns 14, 27); (b) *pretend voice*: register variation (e.g., technical vocabulary; Turns 23, 34, 35), sound effects (Turn 38), and authoritative voice or other dramatic voice (Turns 5, 15, 17). The role voice was often indicated by a high pitch (mother/female doctor) and/or husky or authoritative voice (father/male doctor). As can be seen, the children at times changed play frame within one turn, "code switching" between a pretend frame and an emplotment frame or between emplotment and an everyday frame (e.g., Turns 6, 17, 27–28). In addition to the aforementioned cues, emplotment was sometimes marked by address terms, in that the players at times addressed their coplayers by their Christian names.

As can be seen, this example involves what Goffman (1981) called *crossplay*, that is, the players' consulting an unratified participant, the research assistant, about how the medical equipment may be used (Turn 9), and *byplay*, that is, communication between ratified speakers—here, the two child players (Turns 6, 8, 11, 13–17, 27–29). Phrased somewhat differently, byplay and crossplay both take place on a meta-level, in that they involve metacomments, that is, communication about communication.

MULTIVOICEDNESS AND COLLUSION

Collusive "We"-Form

As discussed by R. Brown and Gilman (1960), ways of speaking signal social distances between persons of different status ranks (power dimension), and between persons of different affective alignments (solidarity dimension). In real-life medical encounters, social distance is quite complex, in that doctors try to convey some type of intimacy, whereas patients try to convey appropriate respect distance. This means that first naming is generally asymmetric (West, 1984). In a Swedish context (Aronsson & Sätterlund-Larsson, 1987), the doctors in authentic medical interviews often employed the informal *du*, whereas the patients avoided personal pronouns when addressing the doctor (*Ni*, the Swedish V-form, was apparently overly formal, and *du*, the Swedish T-form, being seen as overly intimate).

Moreover, the doctors employed the "inclusive we," or what has also been called "collaborative we" of medical discourse, implicitly signaling that they were not speaking as individuals but on behalf of the medical team or the medical system, or on behalf of the doctor–patient alliance (Aronsson & Sätterlund-Larsson, 1987). The collaborative we (positive politeness #12 in the terminology of Brown & Levinson, 1987) is inherently collusive in that collaboration can be seen as indirectly taken for granted. Are children aware of such collusive language? The present role-play data suggest that they are.

As in real-life pediatric encounters, the doctor players employed the collusive we to quite a great extent, in more than three fourths of all consultations—67% among the preschooolers and 88% among the school-age children, which probably signals an increasing awareness of collusive talk

TABLE 10.3
Collusive "We" in the Preschoolers'
and Schoolchildren's Play Dialogues

Role	Preschoolers (N = 24 Dyads)	Schoolchildren (N = 24 Dyads)
Parent role	6	3
Doctor role	16	21

Binomial test: $p < .011$. $p < .001$.

among older children (there were no gender differences). When comparing the children's enactment of the parent role and the doctor role, it could be seen that the same child would employ the collusive we-form more often in the doctor role than in the parent role (Table 10.3). As can be seen, the collusive we-form was many times more common in the doctor role than in the parent role There was a significant difference between the way that the children played doctor and the way that they played parent, regardless of whether they played mothers (girls) or fathers (boys) or whether they belong to the preschool or school-age group. All children thus differentiated between the two roles. To most children, subversive communication can thus be seen as an intrinsic part of the doctor's voice.

In employing the collaborative we-form, the doctor can be seen to create a collusive type of solidarity, implying that the doctor and child are in fact part of a team or an alliance, which may, of course, not be the case (Example 4).

Example 4. Doctor–mother (Schoolgirls 32:4)

1 → Dr: If you'll be back in a week then we can take X rays as well.

2 C: Mhm (pause) ((Dr puts on a bandage around child's foot))

3 → Dr: So. Mhm, now we will see then (.) you may take it a little easy as well (C:mm) you can sit and rest your foot.

4 M: Should she have sticks or something like that?

5 → Dr: Well, that's what she may get after that we have made the X rays (xx) there might be fractures.

6 M: Yes (.) but- but you-

Other interpretations are, of course, possible. In Turn 1, the doctor may invoke the medical collective in her collaborative we-form (signaling that her actions are backed up by the medical collective). In Turn 3, her inclusive we may allude to doctor–patient collaboration or, again, to the backing of the medical team. The doctor is the one who *"will see,"* but as she is

authorized by the medical system, she may talk about how *"we will see."*
Similarly, she may invoke the medical team backing her up, when she talks
about what will happen after *"we have made the X rays"* (Turn 5).

Both girl and boy dyads employed what P. Brown and Levinson (1987)
called the positive politeness strategy of inclusive we (Table 10.4). Moreover, several dyads softened the face-threatening action by using "a little"
or "a minute" and other euphemisms or belittling expressions that soften
the impact of a face threat (Items c, f, h, i, and j), minimizing the imposi-
tion (negative politeness, Item d) in the terminology of P. Brown and
Levinson (1987). As is done in real-life pediatric encounters (Aronsson &
Rundström, 1989), these play dyads combined negative and positive politeness moves within single utterances.

As can be seen, the child doctors at times had somewhat hazy ideas
about what the medical examinations were all about; for example, they
checked whether the heart was beating (b) and whether the patient had
any blood pressure (e). Also, they did not behave as "normal" doctors. For
instance, they upgraded (rather than downgraded) the threat of the physical examination, talking about how the situation "doesn't seem too good"
(e) or that "This is really bad" (3). Such upgradings were quite typical for
what we have called boys' escalations (cf. Aronsson & Thorell, 1999).

CONCLUDING DISCUSSION

Both preschoolers and schoolchildren differentiated between pretend
voices and "real" voices. In their negotiations about play, they employed
"real" voices, and in their enactment, they employed a distinctly slower

TABLE 10.4
Collaborative "We" in Doctor Player's Turns

a.	Dr.	Now we're going to use this. ((puts on bandage)) (PG 1)
b.	Dr.	Let's start by checking that your heart is beating. (PG 4)
c.	Dr.	Mm: (xx) Right, first we will give you a little shot. (PG 5)
d.	Dr.	Aha ((sighs)) now let's have a look at your arm. Well, this looks bad, pretty bad. (PG 7)
e.	Dr.	Let's see that thermometer. Nope, no temperature. It says zero. Let's listen to your heartbeat ((pause, listening)) Hm, it doesn't seem too good. Aha.
	Dr.	You seem - you've got blood pressure. (PB 21)
f.	Dr.	It also looks like- like you have a little (x). I'll look. I think we will give you a shot. (SG 30)
g.	Dr.	Let's see now. Yes, that sounds good anyway ((listening with the stetho-scope)) Now we'll have to give you a shot ((firm voice)). (SG 34)
h.	Dr.	Let's listen to that little heartbeat of yours. Take a little shot! (SG 36)
i.	Dr.	I think we need a little (.) of this. (SB 40)
j.	Dr.	Now we're going to listen to your heartbeat for a minute. (SB 47)

P = preschool; S = school; G = girls; B = boys.

tempo and distinct (bass and falsetto) voice qualities. In line with the reasoning of Bateson (1971) and Mead (1934), and as in Sawyer (1996), we have shown how children's pretend voices can be related to metapragmatics.

In some work, emplotment and enactment have been described in terms of preparatory and play phases (Mead, 1934). However, our data show that the children sometimes changed frames within a single turn (e.g., Example 1). At times, naturalistic play involved constant "code switching" in which the children moved in and out of the pretend frame. Our data thus support the notion of what has here been called voice-type models (cf. Auwärter, 1986; Sawyer, 1997) rather than phase-type models of role play.

Most of the children in both age groups employed subversive ways of indexing speaker roles, and more specifically the collusive we of medical authority. Thus the children seemed to be aware of the subversive quality of adult–child talk—how adult talk is often talk "with a sideward glance" or subversive talk in a Bakhtinian sense. These different ways of employing distinct voices can be discussed in terms of a third level of intersubjectivity, a level of subversive intersubjectivity in children's role play (Table 10.5). The present play dialogues show that voice cannot be equated with role voice alone. As in Bakhtin's treatment of multivoicedness, voices are undermined with innuendos and sideward glances. The boy dyads produced more jokes than the girl dyads. However, girls as well as boys

TABLE 10.5
Intersubjectivity and Social Coordination in Children's Play

Level	Joint Coordination	Reference
I		
Primary intersubjectivity	*Shared attention*	Trevarthen & Hubley, 1978
II		
Secondary intersubjectivity	*Shared meaning*	Trevarthen & Hubley, 1978
III		
Tertiary intersubjectivity	*Pretend and nonpretend*	Mead, 1934
Explicit level	Metacommunication	Bateson, 1971
		Garvey, 1974
		Auwärter, 1986
Implicit level	*Repertoires of pretend voices*	Andersen, 1986, 1990
	Play role taking	Cook-Gumperz, 1986
		Aronsson & Thorell, 1998
Collusive level	*Collusive voice*	
	Pretend voices in joking mode	Aronsson & Thorell, 1999
	Pretend voices and ambiguous production formats	Schwartzmann, 1982; Sheldon, 1996; Aronsson & Thorell, 1999 (present study)

employed parodic formulations in their playing. By enacting adults in collusive ways—parody or jokes, collusive we-forms, and collusive types of address—the children demonstrated their insights about children's subordination in society. Yet, in their gleeful parodizing of such patterns, they simultaneously displayed their role detachment and agency.

REFERENCES

Andersen, E. (1986). The acquisition of register by Anglo-American children. In B. B. Schieffelin & E. Ochs (Eds.), *Language socialization across cultures* (pp. 153–161). Cambridge, England: Cambridge University Press.

Andersen, E. (1990). *Speaking with style. The sociolinguistic skills of children.* London: Routledge & Kegan Paul.

Aronsson, K., & Thorell, M. (1999). Family politics in children's play directives. *Journal of Pragmatics, 31,* 25–47.

Aronsson, K., & Rundström, B. (1989). Cats, dogs and sweets in the clinical negotiation of reality. On politeness and coherence in pediatric discourse. *Language in Society, 18,* 483–504.

Aronsson, K., & Sätterlund-Larsson, U. (1987). Politeness strategies and doctor–patient communication. On the social choreography of collaborative thinking. *Journal of Language and Social Psychology, 6,* 1–27.

Auwärter, M. (1986). Development of communicative skills. The construction of fictional reality in children's play. In J. Cook-Gumperz, W. A. Corsaro, & J. Streeck (Eds.), *Children's worlds and children's language* (pp. 205–230). New York: Mouton.

Bakhtin, M. (1984). *Problems of Dostoevsky's poetics.* Manchester, England: Manchester University Press.

Bakhtin, M. (1986). *Speech genres and other late essays.* Austin: University of Texas Press.

Bateson, G. (1956/1971). The message "This is play." In R. E. Herron & B. Sutton-Smith (Eds.), *Child's play* (pp. 261–266). New York: Wiley.

Brown, P., & Levinson, S. (1987). *Politeness. Some universals in language usage.* Cambridge, England: Cambridge University Press.

Brown, R., & Gilman, A. (1960). The pronouns of power and solidarity. In T. A. Sebeok (Ed.), *Style in language* (pp. 253–276). Cambridge, MA: MIT Press.

Cook-Gumperz, J. (1986). Keeping it together. Text and context in children's language socialization. In D. Tannen & J. E. Alatis (Eds.), *Georgetown University Roundtable on language and linguistics 1985. Language and linguistics. The interdependence of theory, data, and application* (pp. 337–356). Washington, DC: Georgetown University Press.

Corsaro, W. (1985). *Friendship and peer culture in the early years.* Norwood, NJ: Ablex.

Forbes, D., Katz, M. M., & Paul, B. (1986). "Frame talk." A dramatistic analysis of children's pretend play. In E. C. Mueller & C. R. Cooper (Eds.), *Process and outcome in peer relationships* (pp. 249–265). Orlando, FL: Academic Press.

Garvey, C. (1974). Some properties of social play. *Merrill–Palmer Quarterly, 20,* 163–180.

Garvey, C. (1993). Diversity in the conversational repertoire. The case of conflicts and social pretending. *Cognition and Instruction, 11,* 251–264.

Garvey, C., & Kramer, T. (1984). The language of social pretend play. *Developmental Review, 9,* 364–382.

Gee, J., & Savasir, I. (1985). On the use of will and gonna. Toward a description of activity-types for child language. *Discourse Processes, 8,* 143–175.

Goffman, E. (1959). *The presentation of self in everyday life.* New York: Anchor.

Goffman, E. (1972). *Encounters.* London: Allen Lane.

Goffman, E. (1981). *Forms of talk.* Oxford, England: Basil Blackwell.

Göncü, A. (1993). Development of intersubjectivity in social pretend play. *Human Development, 36,* 185–198.

Mead, G. H. (1934). *Mind, self, and society. From the standpoint of a social behaviorist.* Chicago: University of Chicago Press.

Musatti, T., & Orsolini, M. (1993). Uses of past forms in the social pretend play of Italian children. *Journal of Child Language, 20,* 619–639.

Piaget, J. (1951). *Play, dreams and imitation in childhood.* London: Routledge & Kegan Paul.

Sacks, H. (1992). *Lectures on conversation. Volumes I and II* (G. Jefferson, Ed.). Oxford, England: Basil Blackwell.

Sawyer, R. K. (1993). The pragmatics of play. Interactional strategies during children's pretend play. *Pragmatics, 3,* 259–282.

Sawyer, R. K. (1995). A developmental model of heteroglossic improvisation in children's fantasy play. *Sociological Studies of Children, 7,* 127–153.

Sawyer, R. K. (1996). Role voicing, gender, and age in preschool play discourse. *Discourse Processes, 22,* 289–307.

Sawyer, R. K. (1997). *Pretend play as improvisation. Conversation in the preschool classroom.* Mahwah, NJ: Lawrence Erlbaum Associates.

Schwartzman, H. (1982). *Transformations. The anthropology of children's play.* New York: Plenum.

Sheldon, A. (1996). You can be the baby brother, but you aren't born yet. Preschool girls' negotiations for power and access in pretend play. *Research on Language and Social Interaction, 29,* 57–80.

Trevarthen, C., & Hubley, P. (1978). Secondary intersubjectivity. Confidence, confiding and acts of meaning in the first year. In A. Lock (Ed.), *Action, gesture and symbol. The emergence of language* (pp. 183–229). London: Academic Press.

West, C. (1984). *Troubles with talk between doctors and patients.* Bloomington: Indiana University Press.

Chapter **11**

Bilingual Context
for Language Development

Hiroko Kasuya
Bunkyo Women's University, Saitama, Japan

LANGUAGE SOCIALIZATION

The term *language socialization* is used to reflect the underlying assumption that the development of language in young children depends on the language environment, regardless of how many languages or what kinds of languages are involved. In other words, language is learned in the context of the environment, where the learner learns the local rules for communication in general as well as the specifics of the language system(s) in use. Opportunities for socialization arise in the context of routine daily activities, in the context of family mealtimes, or in the context of fighting with a friend over a Pokemon card. What it is that motivates a child to learn language in order to operate within those contexts is clear: The child wants to communicate. Communication stands in a reflexive relationship with the self, the other, and the self–other relationship (Schiffrin, 1994). Therefore, language not only functions in context, but also provides a context, as Lanza (1997) put it.

Most studies of language socialization have focused on children growing up in monolingual family environments. In such environments, much of what children need to learn about language can come from any of a variety of interlocutors. The facilitative effects of parents' and others' input on the child's speech are compounded, making it hard to assess exactly where or from whom children have acquired their language skills. Thus, crucial determinants of success may be masked. If the results from studies of the quality of child-directed speech do not reveal clear-cut patterns, one of the reasons may be that influence from the mother and from the father, let alone from all the other interlocutors within the environment, cannot be easily distinguished in an individual child.

In a bilingual family environment, particularly one in which access to one of the two languages is largely limited to input from a single parent (as is the case in the present study), we have a better possibility of tracing influences on language learning. For instance, the parent whose native language is the minority language (the language not used in the wider community as the societal language) may be entirely responsible for teaching this language to the child. Much evidence suggests that, when one parent is the sole or primary transmitter of a language, chances for long-term successful bilingualism are reduced. The number of interlocutors is one of the factors that helps determine whether young children will grow up speaking two languages rather than just one (De Houwer, 1999). Need to use the language with particular (monolingual) interlocutors and acceptability of the minority language in the larger language community are other such factors. In other words, there are some socialization circumstances, which almost always produce bilingual children and other socialization circumstances, that produce monolingual children with a fairly high probability.

Furthermore, when we examine more closely the process of language socialization, we may have to come to grips with the relation of language to sociocultural context. Ochs (1992) pointed out that language indexes or signals social identity; for example, code switching may index or signal a bilingual identity. Different sociocultural groups will have different norms for mixing languages, or code switching, as will different families (Lanza, 1997). These norms and beliefs about language mixing are an important aspect of the child's acquisition of two languages and socialization into the rules for their use.

Minority Language Maintenance

In many social settings, successful language socialization means producing bilingual children. However, what are the circumstances that are favorable to creating active bilinguals? Looking at studies of language choice and language maintenance by individual speakers in immigrant families can help us identify factors affecting minority children's mother tongue maintenance. In Li Wei's (1993) study of British-born children in Chinese families, parental language ability as well as social network structure were related to the children's language learning. Li Wei found that parents with greater ability to use English had children with better Chinese. This sounds paradoxical, as Li Wei also admitted, but he further explained:

[T]he more speakers have in common, socially and linguistically, the closer they are and the more they learn from each other. Some children have commented quite explicitly that their parents cannot speak English and do not understand the local culture, and as a result there is little that they feel they can talk about with their parents. They, therefore, turn to their English-speaking peers, moving themselves gradually away from the family and the community. (p. 210)

These comments suggest strongly that interaction with adults that is based on large funds of shared knowledge is a crucial context for children's language development. For bilingual children of linguistically mixed families, a minority language parent often forces his or her children to speak the language by pretending not to understand the children when they speak another language (Saunders, 1982; Taeschner, 1983). This is done in order to improve the children's skill in speaking the weaker language. This approach appears to cause a conversation breakdown because of lack of shared knowledge in the child's weaker language. Thus, many parents adopt a more laissez-faire approach (Arnberg, 1987; Clyne, 1982), choosing to avoid the affective conflicts caused by temporarily rejecting the children's communicative attempts. This strategy of insisting/pretending to be monolingual, however, can be effective when children are very young because the children would naturally learn that they can get what they want only when they use a particular language when speaking with each parent. Therefore, this pattern or arrangement can become a habitual mode of communication in a family. Conversely, the findings in Li Wei's (1993) study may be relevant to school-age children who need to be able to discuss concepts more easily expressed in the majority language and express them clearly with their parents if they are to carry on useful conversations. Among the questions that arise are under what circumstances these various language socialization strategies work.

Children's maintenance of their weaker/ethnic language, as Li Wei (1993) suggested, is influenced by the immediate social environment of which the parent is an important part. Yoshimitsu (1999), who has studied language maintenance of Japanese schoolchildren in Australia, confirmed this view as well as that it is crucial for parents who initiate the maintenance strategies or efforts to be aware of their goal in maintenance and why they set such a goal for their children. In a large-scale study of the maintenance of non-English immigrant languages and the shift to English in Australia, Clyne (1985) reported that one of the factors influential in determining the rate of language maintenance and shift was cultural core values. For instance, in nuclear families based on interethnic marriages, the Italian language appears to be maintained more than other languages, which may reflect family structure; Italians are depicted as having a culture centered on family cohesion, so the larger, extended Italian-speaking family may function to transmit Italian to children even if one parent does not speak Italian.

The Japanese are also said to have a closely knit family structure that requires a great deal of empathy from other members in the family and promotes dependency as well (Clancy, 1986; Doi, 1973; Lebra, 1976). This cultural value (family cohesion), however, does not seem to affect the maintenance of children's Japanese in Japanese/English bilingual families in the United States (Kasuya, 1997; Mishina, 1997) where there is usually no community support for their language maintenance. In addition, these children are usually isolated from other children with whom they could speak the minority language (Döpke, 1992). In Okita's (1999) recent ethnographic study of Japanese/British intermarried families in the UK, she revealed that language maintenance was a complex and dynamic process. Her interviews generated rich insights into the ways language choices were shaped by the complex interactions of a multitude of factors. Some of these factors included parents' childrearing aspirations, which were largely associated with husband–wife relations, mothers' minority status and their necessity of dealing with internal conflicts between the desire for warm communication and the need to constantly remind themselves and their children to use Japanese, and parents' sources of support and information (e.g., the husband, the family in Japan and in the UK, the Japanese community network).

Immigrant parents as well as intermarried parents who speak a minority language react to their children learning the societal language with a sense of pride mingled with a sense of loss (Ochs, 1993). Their sense of loss concerns children's shifting cultural values and ethnic identities, including shifts in their relationship to their parents. These shifts come to affect children's linguistic development in each language received from their parents, as seen in the earlier excerpt from Li Wei (1993). In other words, family values may change in the process of children's adoption of another language. In the cases reported, including the study presented in this chapter, parents of bilingual families differed considerably with respect to their language choice when addressing their children. More important, children who do not actively choose a language will fail to fully acquire it. To understand how children who will become bilingual develop a comfortable degree of proficiency in the minority language in a situation where input in this language comes primarily from only one adult in the children's environment, we need to consider how the linguistically mixed families' actual bilingual discourse promotes bilingualism as a goal of language socialization (Blum-Kulka, 1997).

This chapter thus addresses two parallel issues in childhood bilingualism: Under what social circumstances is it likely that a child will learn two languages and how does our understanding of bilingualism change when we view it as a product of language socialization from birth? In other words, we need to consider not just socialization, but proficiency and competence in the two languages. Questions that might illuminate these issues include: How do children's languages differ? Does the young children's code switching/mixing model itself on the code switching/mixing of the adults? How does language performance differ when children are alone with one parent compared with the times when both parents are present? Are there rules for being bilingual that can only be learned from interaction in groups larger than the dyad? How is bilingual competence promoted in dyadic versus larger-group interactions?

Multiparty Conversations Among Bilingual Adults

To discuss the aforementioned issues more specifically, I start with a consideration of multiparty conversations among bilingual adults, as these illustrate how the language choice mechanism functions. The patterns of language use are so complex that it is difficult to determine at first how bilinguals choose the appropriate language with a particular person in a specific situation. Nevertheless, if a bilingual initiates a conversation in a particular language, other bilinguals are most likely to answer in that language. Observation in bilingual speech communities suggests that the underlying choice is made rapidly and automatically (Zentella, 1990). The following example, however, does not follow this pattern. Haru brings her American friend, Mike, to lunch at Mari and Bob's house in Tokyo. Haru and Mari, both Japanese, are teachers of English in Japan. Bob, who is American and Mari's husband, has been in Japan for more than 20 years and is also teaching English. Mike, an American, is a college student who is studying engineering and Japanese and has been in Japan for a year and a half. Mari and Bob are meeting Mike for the first time. They are all English-Japanese bilinguals with different degrees of fluency and motivation in using the two languages.

Example 1: Bob, Mari, and Haru (all bilingual); Mike (less bilingual than others)

[Everybody sits down at the table]
1 Mari: Hai, itadakimasu.
          (hai = OK, right, well in this case, itadakimasu = no translation in English, a routine expression before eating meals)
2 Bob: Itadakimasu.
3 Haru: Itadakimasu.
4 Mike: Hai, itadakimasu.

[Everybody says at the same time]
5   Mari: (looking at Mike) Nice to meet you.
6   Mike: Hajimemashite.
            (Nice to meet you/how do you do?)
[Everybody laughs]

Because there is no English equivalent for *itadakimasu* (Lines 1–4), although *bon appetit* could be close to it, everybody seemed to agree to follow
the Japanese custom and thus indirectly give the participants the hint to
use Japanese language from this point on. Mari, however, greeted Mike in
English in the next (Line 5). This choice was determined by her estimate
of his language proficiency. She knew Mike had been studying Japanese
since he came to Japan but expected his Japanese would be the weakest of
all the languages spoken by the party. Mike's choice of language then was
not reciprocal: He responded to her English with Japanese (Line 6). This
turned out to be an important choice that seemed to confirm that the
agreed-on language would be Japanese. All the participants tried to use
Japanese thereafter, to give Mike practice in Japanese.

According to Fantini (1987) and McClure (1977), when children notice
that an interlocutor is speaking in his or her weaker language, they will re-
liably choose to respond in the interlocutor's stronger language. Children
are much less prepared to "play games" with the person–language bond
than bilingual adults like those in Example 1. Later, in fact, Bob confessed
that he never spoke Japanese to American friends in Japan, even if they
were fluent in Japanese. Some other factors such as group dynamics, the
degrees of intimacy, the adults' comfort with the role of teacher, and age
and social differences may have played a role informing decision making
in this discourse.

Although the base language in the interaction from which Example 1
was taken was established as Japanese, this did not imply that no English
was used or that the participants never code switched at sentence boundaries. Examples 2 and 3, which follows, show some of the language choices
and communicative strategies used.

Example 2:

[Talking about engineering classes at college]
1   Haru: Demo, totta kurasu wa anmari yokunakatta wake?
            (Well, then it means the class you took was not very good?)
2   Mike: So, nanka gakusei mo konaishi . . .
            (Right, like not many students showed up in class and . . .)
3   Haru: That's very typical at a Japanese college nanda yo.

(nanda yo=[it is so], you know).

4 Mike: So, shitteru. Gakusei wa san-bun-no-ichi shika konaishi, san-bun-no-ichi no nakade hanbun wa okiteru, sono hanbun no nakade habun wa naishoku o shiteru.

(Yeah, I know. Only 1/3 of the students come to class and half of the students in the classroom are awake, and half of the other half are doing something besides studying in class [lit.: Doing a side job]).

5 Mari: (laughs) Yoku miteru ne.

(You observe it very well)

6 Bob: Sore wa soo desu ne.

(That is right, isn't it?)

Example 3:

[Talking about growing rice]

1 Mari: Okome wa jooryuushakai no hito shika ne . . .

(Rice was only for people of the upper classes and . . .)

2 Bob: Soo desu ne, samurai toka ue no hito shika ano tabenakatta.

(That's right, and so only Samurai and the upper people ate [rice])

3 Mike: Umm.

4 Bob: Ippan no hito wa daimyoo no kome wa tsukuttan dakedo jibun de taberarenakatta.

(Ordinary people grew rice for their lord but were not able to eat it for themselves.)

5 Mike: Nani o tabeta?

(What did they eat?—[awkward Japanese])

6 Bob: Awa to mugi toka soo . . . mullet to barley to rye to ano ironna . . . jisho miru to maa various grasses.

(Something like millet and barley, so . . . millet and barley and rye and others . . . looking at the dictionary, it says various grasses.)

7 Mike: Soo ka, grasses wa betsuni taishita mono ja nakatta.

(I see, grasses were things which mean nothing special.)

In Example 2, Haru switched to English with an attachment of a Japanese tag to emphasize or highlight the information (Line 3). Because this topic was very familiar to all of the participants, the conversation could have continued in English, triggered by Haru's initial switching to English

(Line 3). This, however, did not occur. Besides the fact that Japanese had now been established as the base language, Mike's now demonstrated level of fluency in Japanese may have undermined any reason for a switch to English: Furthermore, his firm consistency of language choice became a norm in this interaction.

In Example 3, however, the topic seemed to make it difficult for Mike to say much in Japanese, which resulted in him producing shorter utterances and somewhat awkward expressions (Lines 3 and 5). Bob also seemed to help him understand rare words in Japanese such as *awa* (millet) and *mugi* (barley) by inserting English words in a Japanese sentence. Lexical mixing has been reported often when bilinguals cannot find an appropriate word or expression in one language. Bob's mixing obviously was different from this type. It was rather like one teaching method that is often used in interactions between mother and child in bilingual families; that is, translating a word into the other language and saying the two words back to back (Döpke, 1992). The underlying motivation for this type of intrasentential mixing is that the bilingual person simply has not learned or is not equally familiar with the terms in both languages.

As seen in the previous three examples, in everyday life the adult bilingual will go through his or her daily activities quite unaware of the many psychological and sociolinguistic factors that interact in what are probably complex weighted formulas to help choose one language over another (Grosjean, 1982). How then do young children come to be able to function using these verbal strategies? How they know what is allowed and what is not allowed in family discourse? What are the factors that lead a child to be bilingual? How do they develop both proficiency and pragmatic language skills to be able to deal with various contexts? What is essential in the maintenance of the "weaker" (often the minority) language and hence in the development of bilingualism seems to be that the child feels the need to use two languages in everyday life. Popular views about the development of bilingualism are quite conflicted. Should a child be socialized to bilingualism through exposure to language mixing during the early years, or should the child be exposed to a good rich monolingual input first? Strong arguments can be given for both approaches, but no data that could help us decide which is a surer route to bilingualism.

Early Childhood Bilingualism

In individual bilingualism within the family in which two languages are spoken, the patterns of language use are central in the examination of the bilingual child's language socialization (Lanza, 1997). The child responds to socialization that directs an appropriate language choice within the family at preschool ages. This process occurs within interactional contexts such as dinner table conversations with both parents, as socialization is an interactive process (Scheiffelin & Ochs, 1986). Moreover, dinner talk allows for pragmatic socialization that Blum-Kulka (1997) described as "the ways in which children are socialized to use language in context in socially and culturally appropriate ways" (p. 3). A characteristic activity of family dinners, for example, is collaborative or jointly produced storytelling and reporting of the day's events (Ochs, Taylor, Rudolph, & Smith, 1992). People participating in the dinner talk constitute themselves as a family not only through the activity of eating together but also through the activity of conarration. In the bilingual family dinner talk, this can be done in two languages that often have different communicative styles.

Minami and McCabe's (1995) study has shown the different communicative styles of Japanese mothers and English-speaking mothers. Japanese mothers pay considerable attention to their children's narratives and contribute to the tendency for their children to avoid "taking the floor" for more than three utterances, whereas English-speaking mothers allow their children to continue speaking for greater lengths of time. From early childhood on, children of both cultures are exposed to culturally valued narrative discourse skills through interactions with their mothers. Minami (1995) also argued that "the fewer evaluative comments of Japanese mothers reflect Japanese socialization practices, which de-emphasize verbal praise in favor of a more implicit evaluation" (p. 226). Japanese mothers in interethnic marriages who are living in the United States are also very likely to display this communicative style, which is reflective of their native culture and which may differ markedly from the style preferred by their English-speaking husbands. While they are learning the two languages used in their families, the children of these parents are also learning from socialization strategies influenced by both parents' cultural beliefs about how to care for and educate young children.

Most children exposed simultaneously to two languages from birth demonstrate the ability to switch codes, that is, to shift from one language to another (Fantini, 1987). Those children are required to make language choices depending on the person, time, and place. Our choices about language often change in our daily interactions with others. For example, we frequently shift from colloquial to formal speech styles. In addition to stylistic variation, bilingual speakers also have the option of switching from one language to another. Bilinguals must assess social factors such as participant, situation, context, and function of discourse in deciding which language to use, as partly seen in the earlier examples among adult bilinguals. Very little is written in the literature about how children acquire such sociolinguistic competence (Fantini, 1976; McClure, 1977). A rich language environment, which features plenty of minority language input, seems to be one of the most important factors determining success or failure in raising children to be active bilinguals. Researchers are, however, still not in agreement on the extent to which the linguistic pattern in the home should emphasize the minority language.

An unstated assumption is that the role of the home is central until children reach school age. De Houwer (1999) further explained that parental "beliefs and attitudes can be seen to lie at the basis of parents' language behavior towards their children, which in turn is a powerful contributive factor in children's patterns of language use" (p. 75). Parental reports collected to obtain such information as parental linguistic practices, however, may not always accurately represent their interactions with their children. For example, Goodz (1994) found that parents who reported they followed the "one parent/one language" principle in fact often were observed to violate that rule. Nevertheless, parents' open attitudes toward their children's bilingualism and willingness to candidly describe their children's linguistic practices are crucial in understanding children's language environments. More important, because parents are models for their children, their beliefs and behaviors are often imitated by their children. Thus, if parents indicate that it is a useful and a positive thing to know two languages and to belong to two cultural groups, this will help their children to develop similarly positive attitudes.

ENGLISH/JAPANESE BILINGUAL FAMILIES: CASE STUDIES

When exploring some possible parental factors concerning children's bilingual language development, it is essential to take a look at actual cases. I have chosen to examine family mealtime conversation as my source of data. The data from two bilingual families used here is drawn from longitudinal case studies of four children growing up in English/Japanese-speaking families living in the United States (Kasuya, 1997). Speech samples analyzed here were collected during dinner-table conversations with both parents at two points in time when the children were 3;6 and 4;1. The bilingual observer, the author, was present at all times at the table. All transcripts were formatted according to the CHILDES (Child Language Data Exchange System) (MacWhinney, 1995; MacWhinney & Snow, 1990). For the Japanese utterances, the JCHAT format was used (Oshima-Takane, MacWhinney, Sirai, Miyata, & Naka, 1998). Approximately 30 minutes of dinner talk at each point in time for both families is reported here.

First, I briefly present parental reports on the children's language environment, their own attitudes toward their children's bilingualism, and each parent's conscious language strategy at home. Then I discuss bilingual contexts in which these children have grown up, focusing particularly on parents' language input. Looking at the parental input confirms the traditional notion that the quantity of input matters and highlights how hard it is to practice the one parent/one language principle in everyday conversations. I provide some descriptive data on the distribution of languages used by two bilingual families during family mealtimes to illustrate several points. I also examine how the actual bilingual discourse of the families promotes bilingualism as a goal of language socialization. In particular, I focus on the choice of language in addressing each parent and children's switching and mixing behavior, which I consider not only from the perspective of the single speaker but also in terms of the dynamics of all members of the families. Finally, in the discussion and conclusion I relate my discussion of two bilingual families to broader issues, considering children's language development from the perspective of how they are being socialized to adopt familial ways of talking. I also touch on how this socialization process and the skills necessary to the child end up differing in monolingual and bilingual families.

Parental Reports on Their Children's Bilingualism

Prior to data collection, the parents were interviewed regarding their children's bilingualism. Also questionnaires were sent to each family at the beginning of the data collection; each parent was asked to answer questions separately about the child's language environment from birth on, questions about the parents' own attitudes toward their children's bilingualism, and each parent's language strategy at home. Reported next is a brief summary of the results of the lengthy interviews and questionnaires with two of the families in the study.

Ray's Case.   Ray was born in the United States and his sister was born 3 years later. Ray had been taken care of only by his mother and had never been in any school situation during the study, mostly because the family had lived in different places in the United States. Ray's family had hardly any Japanese-speaking friends or acquaintances. The parents initially reported that Ray was spoken to in Japanese by his mother who is a native speaker of Japanese and in English by his father who is a native speaker of English. English was used between the parents. The mother is bilingual and the father fundamentally monolingual with some limited production capacity in Japanese. Ray's mother reported that she used "mostly Japanese" when she spoke to her son, whereas the father answered that he used "only English." Ray's mother and father, however, described their own code switching:

> Mother: "I do code switch. Sometimes it is easier to say things in English or in Japanese, and I am so used to using English

that I can't find proper Japanese words/phrases spontaneously as I speak. And I choose English when bilinguals are
present."

Father: "I sometimes switch [the language at sentence boundaries]
because Ray only understands some things in English and
some things in Japanese. Also I often mixed [two languages
within a single sentence] but I really don't know why."

As seen in the preceding answers, both the parents admitted that they
used both languages to their son under some conditions despite the initial
answers, "mostly Japanese" and "only English," to the question about their
language choice with their son. Unlike the immigrant families in which
both parents speak in the minority language at home, Ray's parents were
not worried about Ray's acquisition of English because he has had enough
input in English from his environments including his English-speaking father. Rather, both parents reported strong motivation for Ray's maintenance of Japanese because the language is part of his cultural heritage and
a valued skill. In particular, the mother wanted Ray to keep contact with
his grandfather in Japan who occasionally called him. However, they also
expressed their fear that Ray would fail to become bilingual due to a lack
of contact with Japanese.

Sho's Case.   Sho was born in Japan to a Japanese mother and an American father, and came to the United States when he was 6 months old. He
is an only child. He had been in a playgroup and nursery school where he
was exposed to only English every weekday morning although his primary
caregiver in the afternoon was his mother. Sho's family had some Japanese friends around and visitors from Japan about once a year during the
period of the study. Like Ray, the parents reported that Sho was spoken to
in Japanese by his mother and in English by his father. Sho's mother is bilingual and his father a passive bilingual with a limited production capacity in Japanese. English was used between the parents. The mother further
reported that she used "Japanese with some English for specific occasions
such as scolding," whereas the father said that he used "90% English and
10% Japanese." As for their own mixing and code-switching behaviors,
each said:

Mother: "I sometimes mix words [in a single sentence] often because
Sho did so. I usually speak Japanese when bilinguals are
present."

Father: "[Code switching and mixing are] a habit from living in Japan. For instance, we mixed languages among Japanese bilingual friends. I choose English when I speak to Sho in the

situation where English monolinguals are present and mixed languages when Japanese monolinguals and bilinguals are present."

These reports from Sho's parents also suggest that a strict one parent/one language practice was not executed. Sho's mother expressed the desire to communicate with Sho in Japanese when he grew up as part of his identity formation, whereas the father focused more on academic and social advantages related to bilingual upbringing. The mother in particular was concerned about the affective consequences of being a minority language speaker and the consequences for her further relationship with the child, by claiming that she would be heartbroken if Sho "rejected her Japanese identity" (and therefore his own identity) in the future.

She also mentioned that there would be peer pressure that may lead him to reject her being Japanese when he was at school where children do not want to appear to be different from their friends, as this phenomenon has been reported anecdotally by researchers (Grosjean, 1982; Romaine, 1995; Saunders, 1982). For instance, the mother of a Japanese boy who was born in the United States of Japanese parents reported that her child rejected eating the Japanese lunch his mother made (i.e., rice ball wrapped with seaweed) and ate only sandwiches at school (Kasuya, 1994). She did not expect this to happen in the first grade so she seemed shocked to see his uneaten lunch the first time this happened. As children grow older, their identity development can be a serious issue for bilingual families.

As both mothers of minority language speakers worried, affective factors seem to play an important role in their children's bilingualism as do ethnic identity issues for children growing up in bilingual households. Identity is one aspect of development that is derived from the psychobehavioral system we have internalized as a guiding pattern for behavior in the process of socialization (Minoura, 1995). In families with culturally different parents, another aspect of identity is derived from the individual's conscious choice of a cultural group in which the child aspires to membership, even early in his or her life. Ray's younger sister at 3, for instance, wanted to have long black hair just like her mother does because she claims that she is Japanese, whereas in her worldview her brother, Ray, is just as American as her father.

Murphy-Shigematsu (1997) explored the ethnic identity development that occurs during adolescence and early adulthood for persons of Japanese and American ancestry by interviewing 47 individuals with Japanese mothers and American fathers in Japan and the United States (termed as American-Japanese by Murphy-Shigematsu, which is different from Japanese-American in the United States). He emphasized that one unique aspect of ethnic identity for multiethnic individuals is that, in contrast with persons of monoethnic ancestry such as those from immigrant families, multiethnic persons often find that their achievement of an ethnic identity does not meet with acceptance or validation by others. Multiethnic individuals are therefore faced with the challenge of repeatedly confronting the personal meaning of ethnicity. Under these circumstances language, as Murphy-Shigematsu argued, is the most basic cultural skill that enables a person to say with confidence that she or he belongs to a group. This type of identity is apparently not static and should be viewed in a developmental context in which a young child's feeling and behavior evolves as she or he moves through interactions with the parents who can be the first and most influential representatives of two cultures.

Bilingual Context

Similar to Goodz's (1994) findings, in the parental reports, the parents in bilingual families explained that they used the non-native language because of extralinguistic variables such as the number of other people who were present while the parent was addressing the child, the languages they spoke, the linguistic context in which a given conversational topic occurred, and the parent's degree of fluency in each language. For instance, a Japanese-speaking mother, alone with her child, typically spoke entirely in Japanese (monolingual context), switching to English only if English speakers were present. This was particularly the case if the mother's fluency in English was superior to the Japanese competence of the others present, which is most likely in the United States. In this context when the mother is alone with the child, the child seems to be more encouraged to use only the addressee's (mother's) preferred language than in the interactions with more than one parent as long as the addressee keeps using that language.

In contrast, family dinnertime is one of the few regular time frames for a bilingual and intergenerational gathering in which children can both listen to adult talk and participate in collaboratively produced discourse. As Blum-Kulka (1997) discussed, bilingual practices also are one component in the building of an intercultural (or bicultural) identity through language interactions in the bilingual families. This identity-building process, which relies on language interactions, involves switching languages depending on who is being addressed. It can be speculated through referring to other studies (Fantini, 1987; Lindholm & Padilla, 1978; McClure, 1977; Saunders, 1988; Taeschner, 1983) that the addressee could be one of the major factors in a child's language choice. Kwan-Terry (1992) also examined the code-switching and code-mixing behavior of a child learning English and Chinese simultaneously and concluded that the child's choice of code was dependent on socialization and on one very important communicative strategy for the child with significant psychological and affective implications. The child not only code switched to accommodate monolingual speakers, but he associated certain languages with certain persons, the result of socialization. Furthermore, when he was emotionally excited, he was more prone to use the language norm he had identified with each speaker.

However, in their study of Dutch-Turkish children's language-mixing behavior, using typologically different languages, Boeschoten and Verhoeven (1987) claimed that no single parameter seems to be capable of predicting language choice consistently. English and Japanese are also typologically different, particularly morphosyntactically different. Hayashi (1994), who studied two pairings of Danish/Japanese and Danish/English (exemplifying a combination of two remote and two close languages respectively), suggested that the structural differences between the two languages might play a role in bilingual development. However, to my knowledge there has been no empirical research revealing that differences of word order and grammaticalization strategies influence ease of code switching and mixing in bilingual children.

It seemed likely that the children I studied would address their fathers in English and switch to Japanese when addressing their mothers (just as the mothers addressed their children in Japanese and switched to English when they spoke to their husbands, switching back to Japanese in addressing the children again). Alternatively, the children might use only English with both parents, choosing for most purposes the language everybody in the family knows and reserving Japanese, their mothers' preferred language, for moments of high demand or for times when they were alone with the mothers.

Two scenarios can also be considered in this bilingual context regarding parental attitudes and their impact on a child's development in the two languages. One is that each parent may be promoting the maintenance of his or her native language by sticking to the one parent/one language principle. This would create an environment where the child is expected to choose an appropriate language for each parent. Alternately, both parents may adopt a more laissez-faire approach in order to privilege communicative participation regardless of the language being used. As a result of this approach, the absolute frequency of input in the minority language would decrease and eventually the child risks never fully acquiring that language. This is also the common pattern described by Harding and Riley (1986), who found that as the children of immigrant parents grew older and the content of talk became more complex, they refused more and more to speak their parents' native language.

Quantity of Input. The question that arises is what consequences these two scenarios have for children's access to competence in either or both languages. To answer this question, we need to examine actual parental speech in bilingual families to determine the extent to which parents use only their own native language in a bilingual context. The quantity of input in each of two languages and the relative frequency or the balance in the input of two languages have been investigated in a few studies (Kasuya, 1998; Pearson, Fernández, Lewedeg, & Oller, 1997). These investigations reveal rather different patterns of language use in different families; the patterns in Ray's and Sho's families are presented in Table 11.1. I coded all child and parent utterances for language type—an utterance containing only Japanese (J), only English (E), and at least one morpheme (bound or free) from each of the two languages (Mixed), or an utterance attributable to either or neither language (Non-language-specific). Non-language-specific utterances (e.g., onomatopoeia, proper nouns, or unintelligible speech) were excluded from the analyses in the present study.

In Ray's family, Ray's proportional use of English (88.4%) was much higher than that of Japanese (7.9%) similar to his father's pattern (87.7% for English and 10.5% for Japanese). Ray's mother's relative frequency of use of the two languages was more balanced than that of the other two members of the family (40.0% for English and 57.8% for Japanese). Moreover, the mother's use of Japanese seemed to be relatively low considering her role as a Japanese speaker although she used a little more Japanese than English.

In Sho's family, however, the parents seemed to practice the one parent/one language linguistic input pattern fairly consistently, as shown by the parents' inverse patterns of relative frequency of use of the two languages (mother, 9.5% for English and 87.8% for Japanese; father, 86.0% for English and 7.4% for Japanese). Sho's proportional use of Japanese (40.4%) was a little lower than that of English (52.6%) but much higher than Ray's. To summarize these patterns, the members of the two families

TABLE 11.1
Languages Used by the Children and Parents During Mealtimes

	ENG (%)	*JPN* (%)	*MIX* (%)	*Total Number of Utterances*
Ray	88.4	7.9	3.7	190
Mother	40.0	57.8	2.2	134
Father	87.7	10.5	1.8	171
Sho	52.6	40.4	7.0	286
Mother	9.5	87.8	2.7	262
Father	86.0	7.4	6.6	136

Note. ENG = English. JPN = Japanese. MIX = Mixed utterances.

could be categorized as follows in terms of relative frequency of the two languages at mealtimes:

Ray—an English speaker   Sho—a bilingual speaker
Ray's mother—a bilingual speaker   Sho's mother—a Japanese
                                    speaker
Ray's father—an English speaker   Sho's father—an English speaker

As for mixed utterances, there were few for all the members of Ray's family but slightly more for Sho (7.0%) and his father (6.6%). This may imply that Ray's family has switched to using one language entirely rather than mixing words from another language in a single sentence. On the other hand, Sho mixed words whose forms appeared to act as a "bridge" between the two languages, as seen in some excerpts in the next section. Sho's father also mixed words more than other parents just as he claimed in the parental reports.

Considering absolute frequency of language input, children talked more than the parents (190 utterances for Ray and 286 utterances for Sho). Ray's mother talked the least (134 utterances) and Sho's mother the most (262 utterances) among the parents. On top of this, the relative frequency of Sho's mother's Japanese was higher than Ray's mother's. It would be quite reasonable to suspect that these input factors are associated with the children's choice of language.

Finally, although neither father seemed to have much choice about language use because of their limited fluency in Japanese, they in fact used Japanese, almost always in one-word clauses or fixed phrases such as routine expressions related to table manners and disciplining the child. Their contributions to an increased amount of input in Japanese, however, might be another factor to be considered when looking at children's maintenance of the minority language in order to balance the dominating influence of the majority language from the outside environment.

Child Initiations.   As shown in the previous section, I found that both parents and children in the families studied spoke two languages, with English being dominant in Ray's family and approximately an equal balance of the two languages in Sho's family. This, however, does not indicate which language the child chose when he addressed each parent and these choices were categorized as child initiations. The language of child initiations tends to be less constrained by the language of the immediately preceding adult utterance and more constrained by the addressee, whereas for child responses, a category that is not addressed here, the opposite should be true. For example, a child would tend to address a person who is a native Japanese speaker in Japanese even when that speaker had been speaking another language immediately preceding the child's initiation.

Conversely, a child would tend to respond in the language in which he was addressed regardless of whether or not it was the addresser's native tongue. In other words, the choice of a language when addressing each parent should show a child's language preference, which in turn may be shaped by parental expectations and attitudes related to language socialization.

Moreover, direct socialization through language occurs in response to children's initiations, through questions about or challenges to rules and standards of conduct (Ely & Gleason, 1995). In many cases, children's initiations were used to initiate or interrupt an ongoing conversation (e.g., attention getter such as "Mommy, look" and "See?") and to ask questions, such as requests for information or confirmation. These initiations seem to trigger parental involvement in the child's directed speech, which may lead to a form of "guided participation" (Rogoff, 1990) or problem solving during family mealtimes. Parents dutifully replied to children's initiations and occasionally the conversation lasted for a few turns when the stronger language, English, was used, but it was much shorter in Japanese, as seen in Table 11.2.

The child's initiations shown in Table 11.2 were the utterances in English or Japanese clearly addressing either the father or the mother, which were immediately followed by the parents' responses (for details, see Kasuya, 1997). The total number of English and Japanese utterances in initiations addressing two parents was 96 for Ray and 90 for Sho; these accounted for a half of all Ray's utterances (190 in total from Table 11.1) and a little more than one third of all Sho's utterances (286 in total from Table 11.1). Considering that Sho talked more than Ray, it could be speculated that Ray's turns were shorter because they were produced in the context of a dialogue, that is, of alternate utterances from the child and parent, whereas Sho's were longer, resembling a monologue without parental interruption. Of course there were some other factors to explain this such as frequency of responses to each parent.

Ray produced many more English initiations (91 utterances) than Japanese ones (5 utterances) regardless of the addressee. Sho, on the other

TABLE 11.2
Child Language Choice in Initiations

		Father	Mother
Ray	Initiation in ENG	42	49
	Initiation in JPN	1	4
Sho	Initiation in ENG	22	31
	Initiation in JPN	2	35

Note. Unit = utterance. ENG = English. JPN = Japanese.

hand, acted differently depending on the addressee: He initiated more utterances in English (22 utterances) than in Japanese (2 utterances) when addressing his father, whereas there were a few more initiations in Japanese (35 utterances) than in English (31 utterances) when addressing his mother. In other words, Ray's preferred language was English regardless of the addressee and Sho's preferred language was determined by whom he talked to although he still used quite a lot of English with his Japanese-speaking mother.

Both Ray and Sho produced more initiations in English than in Japanese when addressing their English-speaking fathers, which is quite reasonable because the children considered their fathers to be monolinguals rather than bilinguals. As for addressing bilingual mothers, however, we see a different picture; Ray continued to use English with his mother, whereas Sho seemed to prefer Japanese when addressing his mother. It seems to be difficult to pinpoint a single factor to explain how these children chose the language, particularly the minority language, when speaking with bilingual parents. I would emphasize, however, that Sho, whose mother used more Japanese, showed a higher relative use of Japanese when addressing his mother when compared to Ray. This finding could be interpreted as showing that the Japanese parent's consistency in using Japanese with the child was related to the child's choice of Japanese when addressing the parent. It should be noted, however, that these interpretations assume a bidirectionality between mother and child: that is, it may be that the mother of the child who used less Japanese had been discouraged from using Japanese by the child's language choice rather than the other way around where the child had been discouraged from using Japanese by the mother's use of English.

Other aspects of input, for example, mothers' discourse strategies in response to child's utterances in English, were found to be one of the factors that promote children's Japanese maintenance. Explicit strategies such as explicitly asking or telling the child to speak Japanese had a higher success rate in influencing the child to immediately choose Japanese than did implicit or code-switching strategies in most cases (Kasuya, 1998). The study also revealed that the likelihood of parents' using English increases immediately following a child utterance containing English. This result was compatible with Pan's (1995) study on English-Chinese bilingual children.

Lastly, I could suggest that differences between Ray's and Sho's language choices indicate how one language became more salient or prominent for the child at the time of selection. For instance, Sho may see Japanese as being strongly associated with his Japanese-speaking mother who often speaks to him in Japanese and thus choose Japanese when addressing the mother. On the other hand, Ray might not see Japanese as being directly associated with his mother because the mother used both languages. Thus, he may feel it is unnecessary to choose Japanese when addressing the mother. We can see some discourse features related to children's choice of languages in the observed interaction that follows.

Code Switching. Gumperz (1982) suggested that linguists look at code switching as a discourse mode, or a communicative option that is available to a bilingual member of a speech community on much the same basis as switching between styles or dialects is an option for the monolingual speaker. Like adults, children occasionally switch their own utterances in English, Japanese, or mixed to different language choices at sentence boundaries. Language dominance may play an important role in switching language. The prerequisite for mutual comprehensibility in bilingual conversations is high proficiency of all family members in both languages. Sho, who spoke both languages fairly equally, code switched often, whereas Ray stuck more to English and code switched rarely. Sho was able to hold a long conversation in Japanese with Japanese-speaking adults, as seen in Lines 1 to 8 in Example 4. However, he sometimes switched from Japanese to English, perhaps to emphasize his intention or get attention (Line 9).

Example 4: Sho (3;6), Mother (bilingual), Observer (bilingual)

[At a dinner table]
1 Sho: Boku noodle suki damon.
(I like noodles.)
2 Mother: Hai soo ne.
(Yeah, right.)
3 Sho: Chotto boku mo . . .
(Well, I also . . .)
[He reaches for some food]
4 Observer: Totte ageru.
(I'll get it for you.)
5 Sho: Iyaa boku no . . .
(No, I'll . . .)
6 Observer: Jaa, jibun de ne.
(Well, then you do it yourself.)
7 Sho: Boku yaritain da mon.
(I want to do it.)
8 Mother: Sho-kun sa ohirune shitenai kara sa . . .
(You know you didn't take a nap today so . . .)
9 Sho: I want I want I want.
10 Mother: Sho, stop, Sho yame nasai.
(Sho, stop it.)

11 Sho: Yada.
               (No.)

Sho's switching to English in Line 9 could be a protest against his mother's comment in Line 8, where the mother tried to stop Sho's whining, which she assumed was caused by lack of a nap. He could have felt that he needed to say something that sounded stronger and different so he protested by repeating the same thing three times. Thus, his strategy of changing to English might have been a use of switching as a discourse mode or a communicative option. McClure (1977) found as well that children as young as 3 years old can code switch for expressive or stylistic effects.

In Line 8 in this example, Sho's mother uses typically Japanese indirect speech—an utterance that may sound ambiguous or even enigmatic (Clancy, 1986; Doi, 1974). The mother used this context-dependent and incomplete expression, literally a statement about Sho's day but in fact, of course, a reproach about his behavior. Sho nonetheless seemed to understand her real meaning. In Japanese communicative styles, the main responsibility lies with the listener, who must know what the speaker means regardless of the words that are used (Clancy, 1986). A mother's communicative style is an important factor in the socialization of children to culture-specific values. Sho's last negative reply (Line 10), however, would not be accepted from a "good Japanese child," who should respond to his mother according to the traditional belief that the overt expression of conflicting opinions should be avoided.

In Example 5 from Ray's family mealtime, however, code switching occurred only in the mother's utterances (Lines 5, 7, 11, 13).

Example 5: Ray (3;6), Father (monolingual), Mother (bilingual)

1 Father: What did your grandpa say, Ray?
2 Ray: He's fine.
3 Mother: Hoka niwa nante itteta?
             (What else did he say?)
4 Ray: He's gone.
5 Mother: He's gone?
6 Ray: He's gone xxx to pick up the mail.
7 Mother: Did he say that?
8 Ray: (Looking at the plate) # I want grapes.
9 Mother: Moo ii wa, Ray.
             (That's enough, Ray.)
10 Ray: Want grapes.

11 Mother: Ray, mama said no.
12 Ray: 0 (making noise).
13 Father: Ray, man, stop it.
14 Mother: Honey, no more, no more.
15 Mother: (Looking closely at Ray) Takusan tabeta ja nai moo.
                 (You had enough already, didn't you?)
(xxx = Unintelligible speech, # = Pause, 0 = Actions without speech)

The dominance of English in Ray's speech seems to have had a significant impact on the mother or the mother's English use has influenced
Ray. The mother often switched over to English, especially when she
needed to discipline him for bad behavior. She does this, for example, in
Line 11 after her initial caution in Japanese was ineffective (Line 9), presumably because she wanted to make sure that the child clearly understood what she said. It seems that when the demand for successful communication is high, the parent who speaks the child's weaker language tends
to switch to the other language when a communication difficulty is experienced, whereas the parent who speaks the child's stronger language may
change his expression without switching languages (Hayashi, 1994). Ray's
mother demonstrated this discourse style: Ray's response in Line 4 was
not appropriate to the mother's question in Line 3. He might have mis-
taken Line 4, "Hoka ni wa nante itteta?" (What else did he say?), for "Doko
ni itteta?" (Where has he gone?). Therefore the mother switched to English (Line 7) to make sure that he understood what she said. As for the father's interaction in this excerpt, there were only two turns (Lines 1 and
13), both in English. However, they sounded powerful and authoritative to
the child, particularly Line 13, and this may be a widespread feature of paternal speech. Malone and Guy (1982) found that fathers were more controlling in conversation as evidenced by their more frequent use of imper-
atives and directives. On the other hand, the mother's speech is more
empathetically attuned to the young child than is the father's speech
(Mannle & Tomasello, 1987). The mother's last sentence (Line 15) not
only switched the linguistic code but also changed the commanding and
aggressive tone adopted in Lines 9, 11 and 13 to a more sympathetic and
soothing tone in order to try to comfort the child. This may be an example
of a Japanese mother's typical style of fostering empathy, as Clancy (1986)
claimed.

Language Mixing. The majority of empirical investigations of bilingual development have found that mixing of elements from two languages
within a single sentence occurs with considerable frequency. Phonological,
lexical, morphological, syntactic, and pragmatic mixing have all been re-

ported. By far the most frequent type of mixing reported involves whole lexical items. Example 6 shows lexical mixing, namely a Japanese insertion (adjective) in an English utterance.

Example 6: Ray (3;6), Mother (bilingual)

1 Mother:	Moo ii no.
	(Have you had enough?)
2 Ray:	Full.
3 Mother:	Ara, mada nokotteru ja nai.
	(There is still some left on your plate.)
4 Ray:	This is ookii fish.
	(This is a big fish.)
5 Mother:	Right, finish your meal, honey.

Adjective insertions are not as common as noun insertions, but in Line 4 *ookii* might have been used because this was Ray's favorite word in Japanese, according to his mother. Also the mother just moved on without noticing this mixing by switching her own utterance to English, which might have been triggered by the child's language choice (Line 4 = English-based mixed utterance). The mother's desire to promote Japanese (Lines 1 and 3) at a certain point in the interaction clashes with her wish to maintain a more content-centered family interaction during a routine activity like mealtime talk (Line 5). Example 7 displays Sho's way of inserting English into a Japanese utterance.

Example 7: Sho (4;1), Mother (bilingual), Observer (bilingual)

1 Mother:	Sho-kun, sore shita ni oite.
	(Put that down on the floor, Sho.)
2 Sho:	Kore protection da yo bicycle no.
	(This is protection for riding a bike.)
3 Observer:	Ee, honto.
	(Oh, really.)
4 Sho:	boku dekiru yo.
	(I can do it.)

Some insertions may be the result of the child's not knowing a particular lexical item's translated equivalent in the other language. This seems to be the case with *protection* in Line 2 of Example 4. However, the use of *bicycle* is different because he used the Japanese equivalent (*jitensha*) of bicycle in a different context around this time. Perhaps Sho was simply highlighting content words such as *protection* and *bicycle* by using English to impress the observer who was a guest for dinner. This was followed by the last utterance (Line 4), which clearly expressed his boasting. This type of mixing, when inserting some words without violating the syntactic rules of both languages, also requires more morphosyntax skills than simply switching language entirely.

Alternately, perhaps bilingual children mix words from two languages within a single sentence because their mixed utterances are modeled on mixed utterances provided in the input (Goodz, 1989). Example 8 demonstrates this phenomenon.

Example 8: Sho (4;1), Father (a passive bilingual)

1   Father: You want a fork or ohashi or both?
              (ohashi = chopsticks)
2   Sho: I want ohashi.
3   Father: Is this the way you ate ebi before?
              (ebi = shrimp)
4   Sho: I don't like ebi.

In Example 8, Sho's father typically used Japanese words inserted in English utterances and then Sho modeled his own utterances on them. This type of mixing by the father might be effective in showing the child the father's positive attitude toward Japanese use although he is not a primary transmitter of the minority language. Ray's father used mixed utterances very infrequently although he reported that he often employed mixing. He appeared to prefer being a role model for Ray's English. On the whole, however, all of the parents produced very few mixed utterances, as seen in the results of the previous section. Switching languages and mixing words involve many complex factors, but even young children can choose to do so purposefully in interaction with parents who speak different languages. As in monolingual families, language learning is one of the ways children assert themselves in becoming members of the family group. The choice of which language to use at a certain time and with a particular person determines exactly how the child will situate him or herself in the family in regard to the other family members.

DISCUSSION

It has been shown that young immigrant children are very likely to lose or fail to develop native language skills fully even when parents continue to speak the native language at home (Milroy & Li Wei, 1995). In contrast to these families in which both parents speak the same minority language, children's language environments in mixed-language families are more complex. Thus, promoting active bilingualism in mixed-language families appears to be even more difficult than in the immigrant families. The findings from the two bilingual families reported here have shown how difficult it is for the child to use the minority language frequently when the input in this language comes from only one adult in the child's environment. In this situation, the child is often not consistent in choosing the minority language when addressing his minority-language-speaking parent because he seems to know that he can also communicate with the parent in another language. Yet, as in Sho's case, a high frequency of minority language use at home may be helpful in maintaining that language. The issue of what minimum amount of input is required in order for young children to be able to learn to speak a language, however, is far from settled (De Houwer, 1999). The input situation is also constantly changing as the children grow up. Wakabayashi (1995) investigated the goals and strategies of Japanese mothers in promoting their children's bilingualism in the United States. Although she studied parents of older children, she found that all the mothers she interviewed stressed that their strategies had changed as the children's linguistic capacities had shifted; thus, as a result of external pressures, they "emphasized English initially, yet shifted back to Japanese as the children became well assimilated into the American environment" (p. 52). A similar phenomenon was also observed in my study of much younger children: The balance of home language input changed according to children's language skills.

We have become aware of the huge effect of the societal language or the majority language on children's active bilingualism. A study of bilingual children from English-Japanese mixed families living in Japan where the minority language is English would provide an interesting contrast as a further study. This is a situation similar to Blum-Kulka's (1997) study of American Israeli families in Israel who succeeded in providing support for dual-language development, despite the pressures of the Hebrew environment, because of the high prestige of English and the cultural and practical benefits associated with high English proficiency. English has a very high status in Japan as well, and this factor may facilitate the success of socialization toward bilingualism. Though in Japan there is an increasing number of linguistically mixed families, immigrant families and returning families whose children learned a second language while they stayed abroad, only a few studies in the context of the Japanese environment have been concerned with the issues investigated in the present study (Noguchi, 1996; Yamamoto, 1992). These studies found that many parents of bilingual families in Japan seemed to struggle with maintaining their children's English when they went to local Japanese schools despite the high prestige of English. It may be difficult to single out influential factors in the process of language maintenance. We need to point to the interrelatedness of several factors that often determine language maintenance or language change in the individuals involved. Moreover, bilingualism should be treated as an issue of socialization in a variety of social environments, such as learning how to talk in various situations in which the whole family is together, because each of these situations presents some unique communicative challenges.

Bilingual practices have important implications for how the different members of the family negotiate their social identities within the family unit (Blum-Kulka, 1997). Each parent in this study has an advantage in his or her native language and the children have already had an advantage in English. The Japanese-speaking mothers' knowledge of Japanese serves to reinforce their social identities as language teachers. The children at this stage were still language learners. They, however, would challenge this role in the future when they might correct the mother's grammatical mistakes or accent. For instance, Sho corrected the mother's sentence "we excuse you" when he was about to leave the dinner table, by simply providing "you are excused" right after the mother's original sentence. In fact, Sho's mother expressed her fear of Sho rejecting her Japanese identity in regard to situations like this.

For the child growing up bilingually, learning when and when not to code switch is an important aspect of language socialization: The child learns to differentiate his or her ways of speaking according to the needs of the social situation (Lanza, 1997). The two case studies reported here help identify circumstances that can produce an active bilingual and those that produce a more limited or passive bilingual; both outcomes can be related to the language socialization practice of both parents. I believe that these examples show that language socialization from early on equips the bilingual children with the capacity to use language in a contextually sensitive way while they are well exposed to linguistic interactions in the two languages. Quay (1995) found that a degree of contextual sensitivity even started occurring around age 1;8. She also suggested that contextually appropriate linguistic behavior should be seen to be built up over time and with experience and not be expected to occur overnight.

This is exactly comparable to the case where monolinguals at the beginning of speech development do not have a language system identical to an adult one. For example, different members of a monolingual family always speak somewhat different variations on the same language. In a bilingual family, the same thing can be said, but such variations, in this situation, constitute two different languages. In this context, bilingualism might become an option for the child through dyadic interactions with each parent separately. In multiparty interactions with both parents, however, the child needs to learn code switching and code mixing, which are special challenges for a young language learner. The bilingual child's language socialization can illuminate aspects of language development in general and illustrates the parallels that can be drawn between monolingual and bilingual development.

CONCLUSION

We know that children follow rather divergent paths to language mastery. Every learning pattern is the product of a learner–environment interaction (Sokolov & Snow, 1994), and language learning is an ongoing process. Schieffelin and Ochs (1986) pointed out that children are both socialized through language and are socialized to use language in culturally preferred ways. In other words, children acquire social knowledge as they acquire knowledge of language structure and use. As the interactions during family mealtimes discussed in this chapter have shown, the investigation into the relationship between the form and function of the child's code switching and language mixing provides us with a picture of the child's socialization into bilingualism.

The contribution of multiple party talk such as that which occurs at dinner to children's language skills must be understood within a theoretical perspective that emphasizes pragmatic socialization rather than language training. It has been suggested that there may be positive effects of participating in multispeaker interactive contexts, for example, interactions with mother, father, and siblings (Strapp, 1999; Tomasello & Mannle, 1985). The posited benefits in all cases involved pragmatic skills rather than the more strictly linguistic skills (Barton & Tomasello, 1991). Moreover, individual participants in multiple party talk are provided with greater opportunities and some practice at joining ongoing conversational interactions between other persons, which is simply not possible in dyadic interactions of any type. In the case of bilingual context, conversing with two or more other people really matters because the children need to monitor how each language is used.

In my own research and in many previous studies, it is fairly obvious that if a child is to acquire a given language including pragmatic skills, he or she must have ample opportunity to hear that language. What seems more important, however, is that parents engage their children in conversations, that they provide the opportunity for children to take their turns as active participants in conversational exchanges in a variety of contexts, and that they respond to and encourage their children's linguistic efforts (Goodz, 1994). It appears that parents from different cultures who thus have different language socialization experiences can have an impact on their children's bilingualism by providing such a rich linguistic environment.

The challenge of learning one communicative system is great, and that of learning two communicative systems even greater. Thus, it is perhaps not surprising that many children in environments that are bilingual end up monolingual. However, it is crucial to study those cases where children end up bilingual by defeating the odds against that happening, in order to be able to answer a number of questions. Some of these questions include how much input is needed in each language, how minimally bilingual parents help promote children's bilingualism, how the parental role changes as children get older and topics of conversation expand, and what parental discourse strategies promote effective participation in three discourse communities—that of the majority language, that of the minority language, and that of bilingual speakers of both of those languages.

REFERENCES

Arnberg, L. (1987). *Raising children bilingually: The pre-school years*. Clevedon, England: Multilingual Matters.

Barton, M. E., & Tomasello, M. (1991). Joint attention and conversation in mother–infant–sibling triads. *Child Development, 62*, 517–529.

Blum-Kulka, S. (1997). *Dinner talk: Cultural patterns of sociability and socialization in family discourse*. Mahwah, NJ: Lawrence Erlbaum Associates.

Boeschoten, H. E., & Verhoeven, L. T. (1987). Language-mixing in children's speech: Dutch language use in Turkish discourse. *Language Learning, 37*, 191–215.

Clancy, P. (1986). The acquisition of communicative style in Japanese. In B. B. Schieffelin & E. Ochs (Eds.), *Language socialization across cultures* (pp. 213–250). Cambridge, England: Cambridge University Press.

Clyne, M. (1982). *Multilingual Australia*. Melbourne, Australia: River Seine Publications.

Clyne, M. (1985). Language maintenance and language shift: Some data from Australia. In N. Wolfson & J. Mane (Eds.), *Language of inequality* (pp. 195–206). The Hague, Netherlands: Mouton.

De Houwer, A. (1999). Environmental factors in early bilingual development: The role of parental beliefs and attitudes. In G. Extra & L. Verhoeven (Eds.), *Bilingualism and migration* (pp. 75–95). Berlin: Mouton de Gruyter.

Doi, T. (1973). *The anatomy of dependence* (J. Bester, Trans.). New York: Harper & Row.

Doi, T. (1974). Some psychological themes in Japanese human relationships. In J. C. Condon & M. Satito (Eds.), *Intercultural encounters with Japan: Communication—contact and conflict* (pp. 17–26). Tokyo: Simul.

Döpke, S. (1992). *One parent-one language: An interactional approach*. Amsterdam/Philadelphia: John Benjamins.

Ely, R., & Gleason, J. B. (1995). Socialization across contexts. In P. Fletcher & B. MacWhinney (Eds.), *The handbook of child language* (pp. 251–270). Oxford, England: Blackwell.

Fantini, A. V. (1976). *Language acquisition of a bilingual child: A sociolinguistic perspective*. Brattleboro, VA: The Experiment Press.

Fantini, A. V. (1987). Developing bilingual behavior: Language choice and social context. (ERIC Document Reproduction Service No. ED 281 389).

Goodz, N. S. (1989). Parental language mixing to children in bilingual families. *Infant Mental Health Journal, 10,* 22–25.

Goodz, N. S. (1994). Interactions between parents and children in bilingual families. In F. Genesee (Ed.), *Educating second language children: The whole child, the whole curriculum, the whole community* (pp. 61–81). New York: Cambridge University Press.

Grosjean, F. (1982). *Life with two languages: An introduction to bilingualism.* Cambridge, MA: Harvard University Press.

Gumperz, J. J. (1982). *Discourse strategies.* Cambridge, England: Cambridge Univesity Press.

Harding, E., & Riley, P. (1986). *The bilingual family: A handbook for parents.* Cambridge, England: Cambridge University Press.

Hayashi, M. (1994). *A longitudinal investigation of language development in bilingual children.* Unpublished doctoral dissertation, University of Aarhus, Institute of Psychology, Aarhus, Denmark.

Kasuya, H. (1994). *Language choice and code-switching in a young Japanese child's early acquisition of English: A pilot case study.* Qualifying paper, Harvard University Graduate School of Education, Cambridge, MA.

Kasuya, H. (1997). *Sociolinguistic aspects of language choice in English/Japanese bilingual children.* Unpublished doctoral dissertation, Harvard University, Cambridge, MA.

Kasuya, H. (1998). Determinants of language choice in bilingual children: The role of input. *International Journal of Bilingualism, 2,* 327–346.

Kwan-Terry, A. (1992). Code-switching and code-mixing: The case of a child learning English and Chinese simultaneously. *Journal of Multilingual and Multicultural Development, 13,* 242–259.

Lanza, E. (1997). *Language mixing in infant bilingualism: A sociloinguistic perspective.* Oxford, England: Oxford University Press.

Lebra, T. S. (1976). *Japanese patterns of behavior.* Honolulu: University of Hawaii Press.

Li Wei. (1993). Mother tongue maintenance in a Chinese community school in Newcastle upon Tyne: Developing a social network perspective. *Language and Education, 7,* 199–215.

Lindholm, K., & Padilla, A. M. (1978). Language mixing in bilingual children. *Journal of Child Language, 5,* 327–335.

MacWhinney, B. (1995). *The CHILDES project: Tools for analyzing talk.* Hillsdale, NJ: Lawrence Erlbaum Associates.

MacWhinney, B., & Snow, C. E. (1990). The child language data exchange system: An update. *Journal of Child Language, 17,* 457–472.

Malone, M. J., & Guy, R. F. (1982). A comparison of mothers' and fathers' speech to their 3-year-old sons. *Journal of Psycholinguistics Research, 11,* 599–608.

Mannle, S., & Tomasello, M. (1987). Fathers, siblings, and the bridge hypothesis. In K. E. Nelson & A. van Kleeck (Eds.), *Children's language* (Vol. 6, pp. 23–41). Hillsdale, NJ: Lawrence Erlbaum Associates.

McClure, E. (1977). Aspects of code-switching in the discourse of bilingual Mexican children. In M. Savile-Troike (Ed.), *Linguistics and anthropology* (Georgetown University Round Table on Language and Linguistics). Washington, DC: Georgetown University Press.

Milroy, L., & Li Wei. (1995). A social network approach to code-switching: The example of a bilingual community in Britain. In L. Milroy & P. Muysken (Eds.), *One speaker, two languages: Cross-disciplinary perspectives on code-switching* (pp. 136–157). Cambridge, England: Cambridge University Press.

Minami, M. (1995). Long conversational turns or frequent turn exchanges: Cross-cultural comparison of parental narrative elicitation. *Journal of Asian Pacific Communication, 6,* 213–230.

Minami, M., & McCabe, A. (1995). Rice balls and bear hunts: Japanese and North American family narrative patterns. *Journal of Child Language, 22,* 423–445.

Minoura, Y. (1995). Culture and self-concept among adolescents with bicultural parentage: A social constructionist approach. In J. Valsiner (Ed.), *Child development within culturally structured environments: Vol. 3. Comparative cultural perspectives* (pp. 189–209). Norwood, NJ: Ablex.

Mishina, S. (1997). *Language separation in early bilingual development: A longitudinal study of Japanese/English bilingual children.* Unpublished doctoral dissertation, University of California, Los Angeles.

Murphy-Shigematsu, S. (1997). American-Japanese ethnic identities: Individual assertions and social reflections. *Japan Journal of Multilingualism and Multiculturalism, 3,* 23–37.

Noguchi, M. G. (1996). The bilingual parent as model for the bilingual child. *Policy Science, 3.* Kyoto, Japan: The Policy Science Association of Ritsumeikan University.

Ochs, E. (1992). Indexing gender. In A. Duranti & C. Goodwin (Eds.), *Rethinking context: Language as an interactive phenomenon* (pp. 335–358). Cambridge, England: Cambridge University Press.

Ochs, E. (1993). Constructing social identity: A language socialization perspective. *Research on Language and Social Interaction, 26,* 287–306.

Ochs, E., Taylor, C., Rudolph, D., & Smith, R. (1992). Story-telling as a theory-building activity. *Discourse Processes, 15,* 37–72.

Okita, T. (1999). *Childrearing, language choice and bilingualism in Japanese-British intermarried families.* Unpublished doctoral dissertation, University of Cambridge, Cambridge, England.

Oshima-Takane, Y., MacWhinney, B., Sirai, H., Miyata, S., & Naka, N. (Eds.). (1998). *Nihongo no tame no CHILDES manyuaru [CHILDES manual for Japanese]* (2nd ed.). Nagoya, Japan: The JCHAT Project.

Pan, B. A. (1995). Code negotiation in bilingual families: "My body starts speaking English." *Journal of Multilingual and Multicultural Development, 16,* 315–327.

Pearson, B. Z., Fernández, S. C., Lewedeg, V., & Oller, D. K. (1997). The relation of input factors to lexical learning by bilingual infants. *Journal of Applied Psycholinguistics, 18,* 41–58.

Quay, S. (1995). The bilingual lexicon: Implications for studies of language choice. *Journal of Child Language, 22,* 369–387.

Rogoff, B. (1990). *Apprenticeship in thinking: Cognitive development in social context.* New York: Oxford University Press.

Romaine, S. (1995). *Bilingualism* (2nd ed.). Oxford, England: Basil Blackwell.

Saunders, G. (1982). *Bilingual children: Guidance for the family.* Clevedon, England: Multilingual Matters.

Saunders, G. (1988). *Bilingual children: From birth to teens.* Clevedon, England: Multilingual Matters.

Scheiffelin, B., & Ochs, E. (1986). *Language socialization across cultures.* Cambridge, England: Cambridge University Press.

Schiffrin, D. (1994). *Approaches to discourse.* Oxford, England: Basil Blackwell.

Sokolov, J. L., & Snow, C. E. (1994). The changing role of negative evidence in theories of language development. In C. Gallaway & B. Richards (Eds.), *Input and interaction in language acquisition* (pp. 38–55). Cambridge, England: Cambridge University Press.

Strapp, C. M. (1999). Mothers', fathers', and siblings' responses to children's language errors: Comparing sources of negative evidence. *Journal of Child Language, 26,* 373–391.

Taeschner, T. (1983). *The sun is feminine: A study of language acquisition in bilingual children.* Berlin: Springer.

Tomasello, M., & Mannle, S. (1985). Pragmatics of sibling speech to one-year-olds. *Child Development, 56,* 911–917.

Wakabayashi, T. (1995). *Becoming bilingual in the United States: The goals and strategies of Japanese mothers in promoting children's bilingualism.* Qualifying paper, Harvard University Graduate School of Education, Cambridge, MA.

Yamamoto, M. (1992). Linguistic environments of bilingual families in Japan. *The Language Teacher, 16,* 13–15.

Yoshimitsu, K. (1999). *Population of Japanese school children in Melbourne and their language maintenance efforts.* Paper presented at the 2nd International Symposium on Bilingualsim, University of Newcastle, England.

Zentella, A. C. (1990). Integrating qualitative and quantitative methods in the study of bilingual code-switching. In E. Bendix (Ed.), *The uses of linguistics: Annals of the New York Academy of Sciences* (Vol. 53, pp. 75–92). New York: New York Academy of Sciences.

Chapter 12

From Home to School: School-Age Children Talking With Adults

Catherine E. Snow
Harvard University

Shoshana Blum-Kulka
Hebrew University, Jerusalem

We have focused in this book on children's learning about communication from participation in various constellations of conversational settings. Most of the chapters have dealt with familial interactions, though a few (e.g., chaps. 5 and 10) have also displayed the value of analyzing peer interactions, both in revealing novel aspects of children's competence in using language, and in creating contexts for children's development of novel pragmatic skills. The range of phenomena dealt with has been broad, but it would be a mistake to think of the skills focused on in the previous chapters as the only ones that children need to learn in becoming competent members of their language communities. In this chapter, we introduce two new themes:

- A consideration of domains in which development continues after the preschool years, and outside the relatively informal contexts of family conversations and preschool peer groups.
- A consideration of how the language skills developed in multiparty discourse during the preschool years relate to those required for success in school, both in classroom participation and in literacy.

One message of the previous chapters has been the wide variety of interactive and discourse skills that fall within the domain of what children need to learn about language. Children learn to request and participate in providing narratives and explanations. They learn to provide culturally appropriate forms of and occasions for humor, poetics, fantasy, and irony. They learn the difference between serious threats and teasing, between literal and rhetorical questions, between performed narratives and strictly factual reports. They also learn who can be considered an expert in various domains of knowledge, what events can be promoted to tellability in group contexts, whether physical or psychological explanations are more likely to be valued, and how much knowledge about which topics to presuppose from various listeners.

A second message has been the contribution of multiparty discourse to children's opportunities to learn to function as members of their families or their peer groups. Within families and preschool classrooms, telling stories, giving explanations, and participating in nonliteral discourse exchanges is crucial, as is knowing the rules for conversational management and one's own rights and responsibilities as a participant.

As we turn, in this final chapter, to a brief discussion of the role of the knowledge and skills acquired in these multiparty conversations in promoting children's success in school, we again note that the task children face in the formal learning settings of the elementary school has two dimensions—knowing what to say, and knowing the rules of interaction that allow one to say it. At school, children will need to learn the new rules for participating—for example, how to volunteer to be called on, when spontaneous contributions to whole-class discussions are permitted, and when and how one may talk to peers. In addition to the new interactive rules though, children will also need to learn new language skills—metalinguistic skills prerequisite to literacy, the new vocabulary needed for content areas, and the forms of discourse specific to the many new tasks they face (composing short answers to test questions, e.g., or answering teacher questions "with a complete sentence"). We have little data on how children exploit the linguistic knowledge already acquired from family and preschool conversations in meeting these new challenges, though of course the widespread social class differences in school performance suggest that some children arrive at school with more skills to exploit than do others.

In the following sections, we briefly discuss first the interactive skills children need at school, then the cognitive/linguistic skills, for effective participation in learning interactions. We provide some examples of how classroom discourse research has addressed these issues. However, just as dyadic discourse dominated research on young children's language development for many years, studies of older children's language learning are rarely located in the full complexities of the classroom context. Studies of classroom discourse are fairly numerous, but many focus on issues that have to do with the overall structure and dynamics of classroom talk, often as related to the quality of teaching (e.g., Cazden, 2001; Edwards & Westgate, 1994; Lemke, 1989; Mehan, 1979), rather than on the language acquisition of the children.

INTERACTIVE CHALLENGES: WHAT CHILDREN HAVE LEARNED AND STILL NEED TO LEARN ABOUT USING LANGUAGE

Multiparty familial discourse gives children exposure to rules governing who has the right to speak when, practice with mechanisms for capturing the floor and completing one's turn, and in some families induction into the rules governing which language is to be used with each addressee or in different situations. The social sensitivities and flexibilities thus developed are likely to be of considerable value in classroom settings, where the rules for language use both reflect aspects of the larger culture, and instantiate local, often classroom-specific decisions.

Participation in IRE Sequences. Many researchers have described the ubiquitous Initiation-response-evaluation (IRE) sequence in classroom discourse. Indeed, as a prototypically dyadic encounter (at least, the RE part of the sequence), it might even be suggested that the wealth of data on IREs proves our point that classroom discourse research has been dominated by the presumption of dyads in interaction.

Though IRE sequences are very common, they do not of course constitute the only form of teacher-initiated talk in classrooms. Thus, the IRE sequence poses two problems to the child. First, children need to have a strategy for deciding which teacher utterances constitute initiations of an IRE sequence, as opposed, for example, to a genuine question, or a simple conversational topic initiator.

Assuming that hurdle is successfully negotiated and an initiation has been responded to, children need to determine how the teacher evaluation should be interpreted. One might assume that evaluation is straightforward, for example, "Good" or "No, who has the right answer?" Indeed, such evaluations do occur. In some classrooms, though, no response in the next turn (silence, or shifting topic) on the part of the teacher might signal success. In others, such a response would signal an inadequate response and the need to try again. How can children know? An interesting case in point is the use of repetitions. Answers repeated with no further expansion can serve to validate a correct answer, to reject it or to prompt an elaboration. The intonational countours used to differentiate between the functions of repetitions might vary with teacher and classroom, and are in any event unique to the subtleties of "teacher talk" register children need to come to terms with.

Furthermore, for many children the rules governing the feedback element of the teacher's response are quite different from those encountered at home (e.g., Au, 1980). In native American homes, for example, correct answers are simply accepted without response, whereas non-native teachers are more likely to respond explicitly to success and to respond to incorrect answers with silence. Thus, learning to function in the classroom requires learning quite new rules of discourse management for the native American child—but the advantage of the classroom setting is that it offers considerable opportunity for observational as well as participatory learning.

Further analyses of IRE sequences in classroom discourse reveal that providing the correct answer is a necessary, but not sufficient, condition for receiving teacher approbation. Very often in whole-class settings several children offer correct answers, but not atypically the teacher elects to validate only a subset, by acknowledging the respondent or repeating the answer. A further hurdle for children is learning how to deal with teacher inconsistency in relation to discourse managment norms. In Israeli classrooms, teachers have been observed deliberately ignoring correct answers provided out of turn on some occasions though accepting them happily on others. The inconsistency can be explained by implicit teacher goals. The children's difficulty lies in distinguishing the cues that the teacher's implicit goal is to promote the norms for an egalitarian but also orderly discussion, where all children are encouraged to speak but only in turn, in contrast to instances where promoting the liveliness and interest of the discussion, or just the focus on topic, override considerations of orderliness (Peled & Blum-Kulka, 1997). We present here two examples, in the first of which the teacher cues her interest in protecting speaking rights, whereas in the second she is focusing on topic development:

Example 1. Focus on speaking rights:

Teacher: Look how beautiful it is: Yael has already understood perfectly well, Itzik?
Itzik (while Yael tries to continue speaking):   And there's also a cycle of
. . .
Teacher: Just a moment, now we are still with Yael . . .

Example 2. Focus on topic:

Teacher: So is there a cycle here?
Children (several children together):   Yes.
Teacher: It's always repeating itself, isn't it?
Child (calling out):   Day.

Teacher: Right. The cycle of the day.

Here again, learning to function well as a participant in classroom discourse requires being alert to the dynamic governing interactions in the whole group; the child who tries to function only as a member of a teacher–child dyad will violate many rules and function ineffectively in this complex setting.

Rules About Social Relations With Teachers, in Particular, Rules for Address Forms Signaling Degree of Intimacy Versus Formality. Moving from preschool classrooms into elementary classrooms in English-speaking North America, it is typical for students to shift from use of first name with teachers to more formal address, using title and last name. In some schools, this shift happens at kindergarten, in others only at first grade. It is associated with a shift to deference politeness on the part of the teacher, and a construction of a relatively impersonal relationship between teacher and student (Cazden, 1986, 1988). In classrooms with Latino teachers, however, this shift happens much later; first and second graders are addressed by teachers using pet names and terms of affection, and the teacher–student relationship is much more similar to a familial relationship, involving physical affection and intimacy.

Politeness is also linked to directness and indirectness. In Israeli classrooms, teachers use solidarity politeness in all types of student-directed utterances, but also use a relatively high level of indirectness—sometimes rather opaque, and occasionally ironically keyed, forms of indirectness (Vardi, 1999):

Example 3.

Teacher: Do you want to bring chewing gum for the whole class?
Child (alarmed):   No!
Teacher: Then why are you chewing?

At home, children of course encounter and use indirect forms. However, parental use of indirectness is relatively conventional—using either the conventions of the larger linguistic community (*do you mind . . . ?*) or relying on historically embedded family scripts (*we don't usually sing at the table, what's the magic word?*). Schoolteachers, on the other hand, often attempt to control children or to signal shifts in activity using hints or signals that are highly ambiguous and thus potentially misinterpretable. Such hints may be embedded in genre-specific norms that the children are not familiar with:

Example 4.
Teacher: Have you done your homework?
Child: Yes.
Teacher: Could you read it from your notebook?
Child: I don't have my notebook with me. .
Teacher: Then you haven't done the homework!

Thus the types of indirectness used in school are very different from those at home, and in coming to school children need to acquire a whole new repertoire for indirectness, having to learn how to interpret its use by teachers and (differently) in textbooks, and how and to what extent use is allowable for them in school.

Rules About Which Language to Choose in Bilingual Classrooms and in Classrooms With Linguistically Diverse Students. We have seen from Kasuya's chapter (chap. 11, this volume) that children growing up in bilingual households can learn to use different languages with different addressees, acquiring rules that parents may enforce about language choice (e.g., Japanese with mother and English with father). Kasuya also demonstrated, though, that children often violate language choice guidelines selected by parents in making decisions that help ease their burden as bilinguals. Thus, even very young children often choose to be monolingual if there is a language they can use with both parents, and if the home language is not injected into their environment with great vigor.

Classrooms serving bilingual children similarly get configured with varying degrees of proficiency among the participants in the languages represented, and with varying types of formal organization for use of the two codes. The differential institutional and social statuses of the languages involved become even more powerful influences in schools, which are after all typically institutions designed to ratify societal values around language learning and language use. Thus, in the United States studies of transitional bilingual programs—programs that by design offer environments that are meant to shift from using the home language predominantly in kindergarten to using English predominantly in third grade—consistently show failure to abide by these guidelines. Such programs typically deviate in the direction of overusing English (particularly in high-accountability environments, when tests that have consequences are all administered in English). However, deviations toward the use of the other language a very high proportion of the time also occur. Violations emerge from many sources. One is teachers insufficiently skilled in the children's home language to use it for content teaching; in such cases, teaching occurs in English and classroom organizational talk in the home language.

Conversely, though, teachers with insufficient skill in English may tend to overuse the children's home language, particularly when discussing difficult content area material. Furthermore, as children get older and more focused on the societal context outside the bilingual classroom, they may initiate the switch away from the home language.

The two-way bilingual classroom is of particular interest in this regard, because it operates under the same constraints as the family trying to produce proficiently bilingual children. Two-way programs deliver half their instruction in each of the two languages involved, and compose classrooms so that half the children are native speakers of each of those languages. Thus, such programs are designed not just to serve the immigrant, language-minority child by providing access to English, but also to serve the otherwise monolingual English speaker by providing access to a second language. Furthermore, two-way programs are designed explicitly to exploit the value of multiparty discourse in each language—to avoid the situation typical of the transitional bilingual classroom, in which children often have access to only a sole speaker of the societal language, the teacher.

Studies of language use in two-way programs, though, have consistently shown that English speakers end up less proficient in their second language than other-language speakers in English (Carrigo, 2000; Lindholm, 1990). Furthermore, careful language use studies in two-way classrooms demonstrate that English is the default language, even during times of the schedule designated for the other language. In fact, the two major goals of the program design—promoting continuing development of the minority language among its native speakers, and encouraging bilingualism among English speakers—seem to be somewhat in conflict. Carrigo, studying fourth and fifth grades in a Spanish-English two-way program, found that Spanish was most likely to be used (during "Spanish time") with groups of students who were all native Spanish speakers and least likely to be used in language-heterogeneous groups. If groups of students included both native Spanish and native English speakers, peer talk tended to switch to English, and teachers showed a greater tendency to use English as well. It is difficult to determine if the power of English in this setting reflects its social status in the United States, its recognized importance to academic achievement for all the children, or the simple fact that overall proficiency levels were much higher in English than in Spanish, so communication tended to occur in the easier, common language.

Immigrant children in Israel meet with little tolerance for bilingualism and are faced with strong pressures to shift completely to Hebrew. Though many Israeli classrooms are highly linguistically diverse, there is no formal bilingual education. Only three groups maintain their language and culture institutionally: Russian immigrants who create their own political parties and schools, Israeli Arabs who maintain Arabic in their educational system, and the ultraorthodox groups with Yiddish schools (Spolsky & Shohamy, 1999). Newcomers are taught Hebrew in special classes during the first year, and immersed in regular classes afterwards. The official institutional message to immigrant children is quite mixed: On the one hand, it stresses the importance for them of mastering Hebrew quickly, whereas on the other hand it allows children who arrive in the country as teenagers to take their final high school tests in their first language. Historically attitudes have shifted away from the strict melting-pot assimilative ideology of the 1950s to a more tolerant recognition of the value of multiculturalism: No more are immigrant children required to change their names on arrival. But in actual practice the teaching of Hebrew as a second language to immigrant children is still deeply immersed in collectivist ideological discourse (Blum-Kulka & Peled-Elhanan, 2000). Parental attitudes to home language maintenance are also highly diverse: We have evidence for the promotion of English (Blum-Kulka, 1997) and Russian (through schools set up by parents), but know little about what happens in the homes of immigrant children from other communities. The lack of clear institutional language policy toward home language maintenance is reflected in school practices; some schools even forbid children to speak their home language among themselves in school, whereas other schools embrace a multicultural policy and encourage recognition of home languages, though not active bilingualism in classes. Thus it is not surprising that recent studies show that bilingualism is declining in the second generation of immigrants even for strongly identified communities like the Russian Jews (Spolsky & Shohamy, 1999).

COGNITIVE CHALLENGES: WHAT CHILDREN
HAVE LEARNED ABOUT LANGUAGE
AND HOW IT HELPS IN SCHOOL

Multiparty conversations such as those analyzed in this volume provide children with sources of skill that may well become enormously important in school, as they encounter the new demands of understanding the content of formal classroom discourse and of literacy. We attempt here to relate some of the issues raised in the various data-based chapters in the volume to descriptions of the demands of schooling, recognizing that in most cases we are speculating in ways that go well beyond the data currently available.

In many schools, children are expected to be able to engage in verbal performances—sharing time turns, book reports, or contributions to science discussions. The challenge of being a verbal performer is multifaceted—having the right amount to say, having the self-confidence to say it in front of an audience, holding the floor until one's message is completed, and so forth. Practice in producing such verbal performances in the familial context might be presumed to promote children's abilities to perform in other contexts. The impact of verbal performance ability on teacher judgments of student school readiness has been documented (e.g, Michaels & Cazden, cited in Cazden, 1988). In the United States, standards for student oral language skills are being proposed, to complement standards for reading and writing (New Standards, 2001). In Israel, the new genre-based curriculum for language skills in the elementary school calls for balanced oral and written practice in each genre taught (*Language Education in the Elementary School,* in press). One of the New Standards oral language standards is "talk a lot," and another is precisely "produce verbal performances when appropriate." Such demands are responsive to the call for more attention in schools to the preparation of a workforce that will be heavily dependent on communication skills for employability (Murnane & Levy, 1996). Thus it is reassuring to note that the working-class families whose conversations are analyzed by Beals and Snow and by Blum-Kulka (chaps. 1 and 4, this volume) provide many opportunities for their children to acquire performance skills. It is sobering, though, that social class comparisons show the amount of time engaged in talk with preschool-age children within the family is typically considerably greater in middle-class families.

Several of the chapters in this volume have emphasized the special contributions to learning made by participating in interactions within groups that demand distinguishing more than just two points of view. Whereas a traditional Piagetian notion represents the decentering of the child from his or her own perspective as a major cognitive achievement of the preschool years, the chapters gathered in this volume suggest that children learn very young, and often in the context of multiparty interactions, to consider a perspectival complexity much greater than just *ego* versus *alter*. Children learn to deal with the perspectives of mother and father and siblings simultaneously, but also with the possibility that each of those interlocutors might shift from a literal to a nonliteral stance, use a variety of languages and voices, violate rules enforced for others, and hold simultaneously incompatible beliefs. Familiarity with the need to juggle multiple perspectives is a key capacity in understanding written texts, and it seems very likely that the kinds of experiences described here will provide a basis of knowledge that is directly available for use when engaging in classroom discussions (see O'Connor & Michaels, 1996; Wilkinson & Silliman, 2000, for a review) and when reading both narrative and persuasive texts.

The specific linguistic forms that children are exposed to in the context of multiparty conversations, often forms designed to signal perspective or perspectival shift, will also come in handy in acquiring literacy. Words such as *whereas, nonetheless,* and *actually,* structures such as conditional and counterfactual, and markers of sarcasm, irony, and other nonliteral voices represent resources children can call upon in their own writing as well as in understanding written texts. These language forms are characteristic of the "decontextualized language" used in academic contexts, language that is well designed to represent certain kinds of realities but that also serves as a shibboleth in distributing scarce academic resources.

Finally, the relevance of sophistication with extended discourse to literacy success is well documented (see Goldman & Rakestraw, 2000, for a review). We have seen in the various analyses presented here the opportunities that multiparty discourse offers to learn about the details of genre macrostructure and about the organizational features that distinguish genres from one another.

Answering Questions: Recognizing the Different Demand of Different Question Types.   Within a Gricean model, responses to questions can be seen as being judged on criteria of quantity, relevance, quality (truth value), and manner. Classroom discourse sets its own criteria for judging adherence to the maxims, and these criteria are seldom negotiable.

Observations in classrooms yield a rich array of examples in which teachers engage in critical comments or questions that hint at the lack of adherence to any one of the maxims.

Example 5. Quantity:

Teacher: How can you explain the fall of Rome?
Student: The barbarians
Teacher: What about the barbarians?

Example 6. Quality:

Student: The Greeks
Teacher: No, the Greeks were not responsible. Anyone else?

Example 7. Relevance:

Teacher: What other things do we know about the hero?
Student: The writer was born. .
Teacher: No, we are talking about the hero, not the writer.

Example 8. Manner:

Teacher: Why did Rome fall?

Student: Because he. .

Teacher: Because? Do we start an answer with "because"?

One of the difficulties children may encounter in trying to adhere to the teacher's discursive norms is that at times these norms might be defined highly narrowly, as when an answer is "relevant" only if it is on target with what the teacher has in mind:

Example 9 (Peled & Blum-Kulka, 1997).

Teacher: What other things do we have that repeat themselves exactly?

Child: The heart

Teacher: I'll give you a clue. I get up in the morning, right? I brush my teeth, I go to work . . . I come back . . . I do my house chores . . . I go to sleep again, and what do we have again when night ends?

Child: Morning.

Teacher: Right.

We presume that these Gricean dimensions are familiar to members of the speech community, though children might be confused about which is the one that applies in a particular case. In addition, though, efforts to improve the quality of classroom interaction have pushed teachers to ask questions and initiate discussions that go beyond these four dimensions to a fifth, which Resnick referred to as "accountability." By "accountable talk" Resnick meant talk that speakers can justify, on grounds of (a) previous talk in the classroom, (b) a recognized knowledge source, and/or (c) the thinking behind the talk. The criterion Resnick would impose for accountable talk is that the speaker can respond to the query "*why do you say that?*" It is perhaps not surprising that children who have been well socialized into expecting their responses to questions to be judged based on quantity and quality can be baffled by teacher responses that demand accountability.

The Notion of Dialogue in Classrooms. In ideal dialogic conversations, the status of all contribution is theoretically equal (Goffman, 1981). The emergence of such conversational dialogues at school is obviously a priori constrained by inequalities of age and knowledge. One of the tasks children face in schools is to differentiate between pseudodialogues, in which they are required to echo the teacher or the textbook ("remind me, what did we say about . . ."), and Socratic dialogues, which leave room for individual thinking. In Socratic dialogues, the teacher withholds her or his knowledge and encourages children through guided discussion to reach the topically valid conclusions on their own. In Israeli classroom practice, where both practices prevail, true dialogic breakthroughs occur mainly in case of nonschool topics, or during group work between children (Peled & Blum-Kulka, 1997):

> Example 10. *First graders were given the task of drawing a picture and telling a story about it:*

> Dan (explaining his drawing):   This is the laser from his eyes.
> Gil: Flying dinosaurs don't have lasers.
> Dan: This is my story and in my story flying dinosaurs have lasers.

New Genres That Emerge in Classrooms.   A characteristic of parental interaction with very young children in many cultures is repetition formats for display of child knowledge. For example, mothers reread picture books with 2-year-olds repeatedly, providing opportunities for the child to display knowledge of the names of the pictures (DeTemple & Snow, in press). This sort of knowledge display, though, declines radically in frequency in these families as children become more competent conversationalists, and capable of contributing novel content to conversations. In dinner table conversations among both Israeli and Jewish-American middle-class (Blum-Kulka, 1997) and working-class American (Beals & Snow, 1994) families, though, the occurrence of such display talk is scarce. Children are given opportunities to display competence in recounting or entertaining much more than they are allowed to display factual knowledge.

In many classrooms, on the other hand, requests for display of factual knowledge dominate, and teachers often define the relevant factual knowledge to be displayed quite rigidly. Thus, correct answers may be rejected if not provided in the right mode or with reference to the right topic, as in Example 9 cited earlier. Furthermore, the persistent demands for display of knowledge often include demands to provide information that is to the child self-evident.

Talk for Talk's Sake.   Another challenge facing children in classrooms is that of coming to understand the role of performances, with attendant attention to the performer's relationship with the audience and the responsibility of the audience to the performer. Though children may produce miniperformances in familial contexts, while recounting "what happened today" at the dinner table, for example, some classrooms impose demands for more formal verbal performances, such as the familiar "sharing time" routine (Michaels, 1981). What distinguishes classroom performances from the performer's point of view is the expectation that the performance be prepared, and that it be adapted both to student audience and to teacher expectations, somehow negotiating these when they are in conflict.

Furthermore, classroom performances create demands on listeners, to attend and respond within the specific norms of the performance type. This might involve giving explicit evaluations (the norm in process-writing classrooms after a student has read his or her work aloud), asking questions, or simply displaying listenership. An additional challenge in producing adequate "talk for talk's sake" is that teachers may be operating with a well-articulated set of norms that are never made explicit. These norms may be displayed by teacher reactions, but not necessarily in ways that children understand, whereas the explicit norms are likely to be understood. Explicit norms identified by Michaels (1981) for sharing time, for example, included "talk about just one thing." However, the implicit norm that children should say just one thing about the single topic selected emerged only in teacher responses to child sharing turns.

It is likely that the implicit norms for "good sharing turns" in any given classroom are somewhat obscure to all the children the first few times they are asked to perform. However, these implicit norms may be particularly difficult to understand and threatening to comply with for children from certain backgrounds whose norms for good storytelling are radically different. For example, Michaels (1981) documented the case of Gloria, whose notion of a good story differed radically from that of her teacher. McCabe (1995) presented a story told by a Latina 6-year-old in which the background information the child supplied focused much more on the nature of the personal relationships among the characters and the full variety of family members who were somehow involved in the event reported, in accordance with quite a different set of norms about what listeners need to know than those familiar to Anglo narrators. We have many examples from the chapters in this volume of how family rules for storytelling vary as a function of culture. But how those family norms impact school performance, particularly in culturally heterogeneous societies with large immigrant populations, such as the United States and Israel, constitutes an area that needs a great deal more research.

CONCLUSION

In this final chapter, we have attempted at least slightly to restore the balance between focusing on familial and extrafamilial contexts for learning from multiparty talk. Most of the data presented in the volume reflect family interactions or interactions in informal, nonacademic settings modeled on families. We have presented in this chapter some ways of thinking about extrafamilial sources of learning about communicative rules, by fo-

cusing on the ways in which social organization of the academic enterprise
in preschools and in elementary and secondary classrooms create new demands and provide new opportunities for learning about communication
and for mastering the skills to participate. Some of the new demands encountered in classroom settings are explicit, whereas many are implicit for
most or all children. For example, most teachers think of the challenge of
teaching reading as having to do with decoding print, and focus on that
explicitly in their teaching, leaving as implicit the challenges of understanding the differences between written and spoken language and of cop-
ing with different genres. Beyond the focus on the specific vocabulary
used, teachers may be unaware of the differences in discourse demands associated with different subject matters. Thus they may well judge children's contributions on the basis of criteria that are implicit and opaque to
the child.

We have contented ourselves with presenting and discussing briefly an
array of examples of the kinds of learning about communication that are
displayed and supported in classroom settings. Some of these are familiar
from a long history of studies of classroom discourse, though the view we
take of them focuses more on them as opportunities to learn about alternative modes of discourse than as classroom-specific models for interaction. We hope that our attention to this topic at least in this brief and cur-
sory form serves to stimulate much more extensive attention to it.

REFERENCES

Au, K. (1980). Participation structures in a reading lesson with Hawaiian children: Analysis of
    a culturally appropriate instructional event. *Anthropology and Education Quarterly, 11,*
    91–115.
Beals, D., & Snow, C. (1994). "Thunder is when the angels are upstairs bowling": Narratives
    and explanations at the dinner table. *Journal of Narrative and Life History, 4,* 331–352.
Blum-Kulka, S. (1997). *Dinner talk: Cultural patterns of sociability and socialization in family dis-
    course.* Mahwah, NJ: Lawrence Erlbaum Associates.
Blum-Kulka, S., & Peled-Elhanan, N. (2000). Child-directed Ulpanit: Language and ideol-
    ogy in Israeli second language classrooms for children. In C. Riemer (Ed.), *Cognitive as-
    pects for language learning and teaching* (pp. 70–84). Tubingen, Germany: Gunter Narr.
Carrigo, D. (2000). *Just how much English are they using? Teacher and student language distribu-
    tion patterns, between Spanish and English, in upper-grade, two-way immersion Spanish classes.*
    Unpublished doctoral dissertation, Harvard University, Cambridge, MA.
Cazden, C. (1986). Classroom discourse. In M. E. Wittrock (Ed.), *Handbook of research on
    teaching* (3rd ed., pp. 121–136). New York: Macmillan.
Cazden, C. (2001). *Classroom discourse: The language of teaching and learning* (2nd ed.).
    Portsmouth, NH: Heineman.
DeTemple, J., & Snow, C. (in press). Learning words from books. In A. van Kleeck, S. A.
    Stahl, & E. B. Bauer, *On reading books to children: Teachers and parents.* Mahwah, NJ: Law-
    rence Erlbaum Associates.

Edwards, A. D., & Westgate, D. P. (1994). *Investigating classroom discourse*. London: Palmer Press.

Goffman, E. (1981). *Forms of talk*. Philadelphia: University of Pennsylvania Press.

Goldman, S., & Rakestraw, J., Jr. (2000). Structural aspects of constructing meaning from text. In M. Kamil, P. B. Mosenthal, P. D. Pearson, & R. Barr (Eds.), *Handbook of reading research* (Vol. 3, pp. 311–335). Mahwah, NJ: Lawrence Erlbaum Associates.

Language Education in the Elementary School. (in press). Jerusalem: Ministry of Education.

Lemke, J. L. (1989). *Using language in the classroom*. Oxford, England: Oxford University Press.

Lindholm, K. (1990). Bilingual immersion education: Criteria for program development. In A. Padilla, H. Fairchild, & C. Valadez (Eds.), *Bilingual education: Issues and strategies* (Vol. 112, pp. 91–105). Newbury Park, CA: Sage.

McCabe, A. (1995). *Chameleon readers: Teaching children to appreciate all kinds of stories*. New York: McGraw-Hill College Division.

Mehan, H. (1979). *Learning lessons*. Cambridge, MA: Harvard University Press.

Michaels, S. (1981). "Sharing time": Children's narrative styles and differential access to literacy. *Language in Society, 10*, 423–442.

Murnane, R., & Levy, F. (1996). *Teaching the new basic skills: Principles for educating children to thrive in a changing economy*. New York: The Free Press.

New Standards Project. (2001). *Speaking and listening: Oral language standards for preschool through third grade*. Pittsburgh, PA: Author.

O'Connor, M., & Michaels, S. (1996). Shifting participant frameworks: Orchestrating thinking practices in group discussion. In D. Hicks (Ed.), *Discourse, learning and schooling* (pp. 63–103). Cambridge, England: Cambridge University Press.

Peled, N., & Blum-Kulka, S. (1997). Dialogigut be-siax kita [Dialogicity in classroom discourse]. *Helkat Lashon, 24*, 29–60.

Spolsky, B., & Shohamy, E. (1999). *The languages of Israel: Policy, ideology and practice*. Clevedon, England: Multilingual Matters.

Vardi, E. (1999, July). *The role of discourse in the construction of social realities in the classroom: Control and politeness in teacher talk*. Paper delivered at the annual SCRIPT conference, Jerusalem.

Wilkinson, L., & Silliman, E. (2000). Classroom language and literacy learning. M. Kamil, P. B. Mosenthal, P. D. Pearson, & R. Barr (Eds.), *Handbook of reading research* (Vol. 3, pp. 351–360). Mahwah, NJ: Lawrence Erlbaum Associates.

Author Index

Subject Index